MASS CALENDAR FOR 2006-2007

Using this Book in Prayer

You can use this book to help your prayer, alone or with your family and friends:

- Read the gospel or other readings for last Sunday, and pray about them.

- Read the gospel or other readings for next Sunday, and begin to pray about them.

- Think about God's word: what is the Holy Spirit telling you?

- Pray the responsorial psalm from any of the Masses in the book.

- Reflect on the opening prayer from last Sunday's Mass, and pray it slowly.

- Use some of the prayers in the treasury.

- Say the Lord's Prayer slowly (page 71).

This Missal belongs to

....

New *Saint Joseph*

SUNDAY MISSAL

PRAYERBOOK AND HYMNAL

CANADIAN MISSAL

For 2006-2007

Cycle C

ORDER OF MASS (Ordinary) pp. 10-76

MASS TEXT for each Sunday pp. 111-585

How easy it is to use this Missal

- Refer to the Calendar inside the front cover for the page of the Sunday Mass (the "Proper").

- This arrow (↓) means continue to read. This arrow (→) indicates a reference back to the Order of Mass ("Ordinary") or to another part of the "Proper."

- Boldface type always indicates the people's parts that are to be recited aloud.

POPULAR HYMNS pp. 586-627

TREASURY OF PRAYERS pp. 628-670

The People of God together with Christ worship the heavenly Father

CANADIAN EDITION

New . . . St. Joseph

SUNDAY MISSAL

PRAYERBOOK AND HYMNAL

For 2006-2007

THE COMPLETE MASSES FOR
SUNDAYS, HOLYDAYS, and the
EASTER TRIDUUM

**With the People's Parts Printed in Boldface Type
and Arranged for Parish Participation**

**The liturgical texts are approved by
the Catholic Bishops of Canada.**

**With the
"NEW REVISED STANDARD VERSION" Text**

Dedicated to St. Joseph
Patron of the Universal Church

CATHOLIC BOOK PUBLISHING CORP.
New Jersey

The *St. Joseph Sunday Missal* for 2006-2007 is approved for use in Canada by the National Liturgy Office, Canadian Conference of Catholic Bishops.

Acknowledgements:

The St. Joseph Missals have been diligently prepared with the invaluable assistance of a special Board of Editors, including specialists in Liturgy and Sacred Scripture, Catechetics, Sacred Music and Art.

English translation of the Roman Missal, Rites for Holy Week, original texts of Invitatories and the Penitential Rites; The Rite of Christian Initiation of Adults; The Rite of Penance; titles, responsorial psalms and alleluia verses of the Lectionary for Mass. Copyright © 1969, 1970, 1973, 1975, International Committee on English in the Liturgy, Inc. All rights reserved.

English translations of the Gloria, Creeds, and Sanctus by the International Consultation on English Texts.

The Scripture quotations contained herein are adapted from the New Revised Standard Version of the Bible, copyrighted 1989 by the Division of Christian Education of the National Council of the Churches of Christ in the United States of America, and are used with permission. All rights reserved.

The lectionary texts contained herein are taken from the Lectionary of the Canadian Conference of Catholic Bishops, copyright © Concacan Inc. 1992 and are used with permission. All rights reserved.

Grail texts of the responsorial psalms, published by William Collins Sons & Company Ltd., and canticles © copyright, The Grail (England) 1963. Used by permission. All rights reserved.

The Sequences for Easter and Pentecost are translated and copyrighted 1992 by Peter J. Scagnelli. The Sequence for the Body and Blood of Christ is translated by John C. Hibbard and copyrighted 1992 by Concacan. Used with permission. All rights reserved.

Texts on pages 628-641 in the "Treasury of Prayers"—copyright © Concacan Inc., 1983. Used by permission.

All other texts and illustrations © Copyright by Catholic Book Publishing Corp., N.J.

(T-2107)

PREFACE

IN the words of the Second Vatican Council in the *Constitution on the Sacred Liturgy*, the Mass "is an action of Christ the priest and of his body which is the Church; it is a sacred action surpassing all others; no other action of the Church can equal its efficacy by the same title and to the same degree" (art. 7). Hence the Mass is a sacred sign, something visible which brings the invisible reality of Christ to us in the worship of the Father.

The Mass was first instituted as a meal at the Last Supper and became a living memorial of Christ's sacrifice on the cross:

"At the Last Supper, on the night when he was betrayed, our Saviour instituted the Eucharistic sacrifice of his body and blood. He did this in order to perpetuate the sacrifice of the Cross throughout the centuries until he should come again, and so to entrust to his beloved spouse, the Church, a memorial of his death and resurrection: a sacrament of love, a sign of unity, a bond of charity, a Paschal banquet in which Christ is eaten, the mind is filled with grace, and a pledge of future glory is given to us.

"The Church, therefore, earnestly desires that Christ's faithful, when present at this mystery of faith, should not be there as strangers or silent spectators; on the contrary, through a good understanding of the rites and prayers they should take part in the sacred action conscious of what they are doing, with devotion and full collaboration. They should be instructed by God's word and be nourished at the

7

table of the Lord's body; they should give thanks to God; by offering the immaculate Victim, not only through the hands of the priest, but also with him, they should learn also to offer themselves; through Christ the Mediator, they should be drawn day by day into ever more perfect union with God and with each other, so that . . . God may be all in all" (art. 47-48).

Accordingly, this Sunday Missal has been edited, in conformity with the latest findings of modern liturgists, to enable the people to attain the most active participation.

To insure that "each . . . lay person who has an office to perform [will] do all of, but only, those parts which pertain to his office" (art. 28), a simple method of identification of the various parts of the Mass, has been designed, using different type faces:

(1) **boldface type** — clearly identifies all people's parts

(2) lightface type—indicates the priest's or lector's parts.

In order to enable the faithful to prepare for each Mass at home and so participate more actively at Mass, the editors have added short helpful explanations of the scripture readings, geared to the spiritual needs of daily life. A large selection of hymns for congregational singing has been included as well as a treasury of personal prayers.

We trust that all these special features will help Catholics who use this new St. Joseph Missal to be led—in keeping with the desire of the Church—"to that full, conscious, and active participation in liturgical celebrations which is demanded by the very nature of the liturgy. Such participation by the Christian people as a chosen race, a royal priesthood, a holy nation, a redeemed people (1 Pt 2, 9; cf. 2, 4-5), is their right and duty by reason of their baptism" (art. 14).

PLAN OF THE MASS

INTRODUCTORY RITES
1. Entrance Antiphon (**Proper**)
2. Greeting
3. Blessing and Sprinkling Water
4. Penitential Rite
5. Kyrie
6. Gloria
7. Opening Prayer (**Proper**)

LITURGY OF THE WORD
8. First Reading (**Proper**)
9. Responsorial Psalm (**Proper**)
10. Second Reading (**Proper**)
11. Gospel Acclamation (**Proper**)
12. Gospel (**Proper**)
13. Homily
14. Profession of Faith (**Creed**)
15. General Intercessions

(Preparation of the Gifts)
16. Song
17. Preparation of the Bread
18. Preparation of the Wine
19. Invitation to Prayer
20. Prayer over the Gifts (**Proper**)

(Eucharistic Prayer)
LITURGY OF THE EUCHARIST
21. Introductory Dialogue
22. Preface
23. Acclamation
    Eucharistic Prayer
    1, 2, 3, 4
    Reconciliation 1, 2
    Children 1, 2, 3

(Communion Rite)
24. Lord's Prayer
25. Sign of Peace
26. Breaking of the Bread
27. Prayers before Communion
28. Reception of Communion
29. Communion Antiphon (**Proper**)
30. Silence after Communion
31. Prayer after Communion (**Proper**)

CONCLUDING RITE
32. Greeting
33. Blessing
34. Dismissal

THE ORDER OF MASS

Options are indicated by A, B, C, D in the margin.

INTRODUCTORY RITES

Acts of prayer and penitence prepare us to meet Christ as he comes in Word and Sacrament. We gather as a worshipping community to celebrate our unity with him and with one another in faith.

1 ENTRANCE ANTIPHON `STAND`

Joined together as Christ's people, we open the celebration by raising our voices in praise of God who is present among us. This song should deepen our unity as it introduces the Mass we celebrate today. (If there is no singing, the entrance antiphon is read.)

→ `Turn to Today's Mass`

2 GREETING (3 forms)

When the priest comes to the altar, he makes the customary reverence with the ministers and kisses the altar. Then he goes to his seat. After the entrance song, all make the sign of the cross:

Priest: In the name of the Father, ✠ and of the Son, and of the Holy Spirit.

PEOPLE: **Amen.**

The priest welcomes us in the name of the Lord. We show our union with God, our neighbour, and the priest by a united response to his greeting.

A ────────────────────────────────────

Priest: The grace of our Lord Jesus Christ and the love of God and the fellowship of the Holy Spirit be with you all.

PEOPLE: And also with you.

B ─────────── OR ───────────

Priest: The grace and peace of God our Father and the Lord Jesus Christ be with you.

PEOPLE: And also with you.

or:

Blessed be God, the Father of our Lord Jesus Christ.

C ─────────── OR ───────────

Priest: The Lord be with you.

PEOPLE: And also with you.

[Bishop: Peace be with you.

People: **And also with you.**]

3 RITE OF BLESSING and SPRINKLING HOLY WATER

The rite of blessing and sprinkling holy water may be celebrated at all Sunday Masses celebrated on Sunday or on Saturday evening. See pp. 77-79.

4 PENITENTIAL RITE

(Omitted when the rite of blessing and sprinkling holy water has taken place or some part of the liturgy of the hours has preceded.)

Before we hear God's word, we acknowledge our sins humbly, ask for mercy, and accept his pardon.

Invitation to repent:

In these or similar words, the priest invites the people to recall their sins and to repent of them in silence:

A As we prepare to celebrate the mystery of Christ's love,
  let us acknowledge our failures
  and ask the Lord for pardon and strength.

B Coming together as God's family,
  with confidence let us ask the Father's forgiveness,
  for he is full of mercy and compassion.

C My brothers and sisters,
  to prepare ourselves to celebrate the sacred mysteries,
  let us call to mind our sins.

Then, after a brief silence, one of the following forms is used.

A Priest and **People:**
  **I confess to almighty God,
  and to you, my brothers and sisters,
  that I have sinned through my own fault**

They strike their breast:

  **in my thoughts and in my words,
  in what I have done,
  and in what I have failed to do;
  and I ask blessed Mary, ever virgin,**

all the angels and saints,
and you, my brothers and sisters,
to pray for me to the Lord our God.

Priest: May almighty God have mercy on us,
forgive us our sins,
and bring us to everlasting life.

PEOPLE: Amen.

5 KYRIE

The Kyrie is sung by all with alternating parts for the choir or cantor and for the people:

All ask the Lord Jesus for his mercy.

℣. Lord, have mercy.   ℟. **Lord, have mercy.**

℣. Christ, have mercy.   ℟. **Christ, have mercy.**

℣. Lord, have mercy.   ℟. **Lord, have mercy.**

B ———————— **OR** ————————

Priest: Lord, we have sinned against you:
Lord, have mercy.

PEOPLE: Lord, have mercy.

Priest: Lord, show us your mercy and love.

PEOPLE: And grant us your salvation.

Priest: May almighty God have mercy on us,
forgive us our sins,
and bring us to everlasting life.

PEOPLE: Amen.

C ———————— **OR** ————————

Priest or other minister:

You were sent to heal the contrite:
Lord, have mercy.

PEOPLE: Lord, have mercy.

Priest or other minister:

> You came to call sinners:
> Christ, have mercy.

PEOPLE: Christ, have mercy.

Priest or other minister:

> You plead for us at the right hand of the
> Father:
> Lord, have mercy.

PEOPLE: Lord, have mercy.

(Other invocations may be used as on pp. 80-81.)

Priest: May almighty God have mercy on us,
forgive us our sins,
and bring us to everlasting life.

PEOPLE: Amen.

6 GLORY TO GOD (GLORIA)

As the Church assembled in the Spirit, we praise and pray to
the Father and the Lamb.

*When the Gloria is sung or said, the priest or the can-
tors or everyone together may begin it:*

Glory to God in the highest,
and peace to his people on earth.

Lord God, heavenly King,
almighty God and Father,
we worship you, we give you thanks,
we praise you for your glory.

Lord Jesus Christ, only Son of the Father,
Lord God, Lamb of God,
you take away the sin of the world:
    have mercy on us;
you are seated at the right hand of the Father:
    receive our prayer.

For you alone are the Holy One,
you alone are the Lord,
you alone are the Most High,
    Jesus Christ,
    with the Holy Spirit,
    in the glory of God the Father. Amen.

7 OPENING PRAYER

The priest invites us to pray silently for a moment and then, in our name, petitions God the Father through the mediation of Christ in the Holy Spirit.

Priest: Let us pray.

→   **Turn to Today's Mass**

Priest and people pray silently for a while. Then the priest says the opening prayer and concludes:

Priest: For ever and ever.

PEOPLE: Amen.

LITURGY OF THE WORD

The proclamation of God's Word is always centered on Christ, present through his Word. Old Testament writings prepare for him; New Testament books speak of him directly. All scripture calls us to believe once more and to follow. After the reading we reflect upon God's words and respond to them.

As in Today's Mass   **SIT**

8   FIRST READING

At end of reading: Reader: The word of the Lord.

PEOPLE: **Thanks be to God.**

9   RESPONSORIAL PSALM

The people repeat the response sung by the cantor the first time and then after each verse.

10   SECOND READING

At end of reading: Reader: The word of the Lord.

PEOPLE: **Thanks be to God.**

11   GOSPEL ACCLAMATION (Alleluia)   **STAND**

Jesus will speak to us in the gospel. We rise now out of respect and prepare for his message with the alleluia.

The people repeat the alleluia after the cantor's alleluia and then after the verse.

During Lent one of the following invocations is used as a response instead of the alleluia:

(a) **Praise to you, Lord Jesus Christ, king of endless glory!**
(b) **Praise and honour to you, Lord Jesus Christ!**
(c) **Glory and praise to you, Lord Jesus Christ!**
(d) **Glory to you, Word of God, Lord Jesus Christ!**

16

12 GOSPEL

Before proclaiming the gospel, the deacon asks the priest: Father, give me your blessing. *The priest says:*

The Lord be in your heart and on your lips
that you may worthily proclaim his gospel.
In the name of the Father, and of the Son, ✚ and of the Holy Spirit. *The deacon answers:* Amen.

If there is no deacon, the priest says quietly:

Almighty God, cleanse my heart and my lips
that I may worthily proclaim your gospel.

Deacon (or Priest):

> The Lord be with you.

PEOPLE: **And also with you.**

Deacon (or Priest):

✚ A reading from the holy gospel according to N.

PEOPLE: **Glory to you, Lord.**

At the end:

Deacon (or priest):

> The gospel of the Lord.

PEOPLE: **Praise to you, Lord Jesus Christ.**

Then the deacon (or priest) kisses the book, saying quietly: May the words of the gospel wipe away our sins.

13 HOMILY   `SIT`

God's word is spoken again in the homily. The Holy Spirit speaking through the lips of the preacher explains and applies today's biblical readings to the needs of this particular congregation. He calls us to respond to Christ through the life we lead.

14 PROFESSION OF FAITH (CREED) `STAND`

As a people we express our acceptance of God's message in the scriptures and homily. We summarize our faith by proclaiming a creed handed down from the early Church.

All say the profession of faith on Sundays.

──────────── **APOSTLES' CREED** ────────────

I believe in God, the Father almighty,
   creator of heaven and earth.
I believe in Jesus Christ, his only Son, our
     Lord.
  He was conceived by the power of the Holy
     Spirit
    and born of the Virgin Mary.
  He suffered under Pontius Pilate,
    was crucified, died, and was buried.
  He descended to the dead.
  On the third day he rose again.
  He ascended into heaven,
    and is seated at the right hand of the
     Father.
  He will come again to judge the living and the
     dead.
I believe in the Holy Spirit,
   the holy catholic Church,
   the communion of saints,
   the forgiveness of sins,
   the resurrection of the body,
   and the life everlasting. Amen.

OR

THE NICENE CREED

We believe in one God,
  the Father, the Almighty,
  maker of heaven and earth,
  of all that is seen and unseen.

We believe in one Lord, Jesus Christ,
  the only Son of God,
  eternally begotten of the Father,
  God from God, Light from Light,
  true God from true God,
  begotten, not made, one in Being with the
    Father.
  Through him all things were made.
  For us men and for our salvation
    he came down from heaven:
  by the power of the Holy Spirit
    he was born of the Virgin Mary, ⎫ *bow*
      and became man. ⎭
  For our sake he was crucified under Pontius
      Pilate;
    he suffered, died, and was buried.
    On the third day he rose again
      in fulfillment of the Scriptures;
    he ascended into heaven
        and is seated at the right hand of the
        Father.
  He will come again in glory to judge the living
        and the dead,
      and his kingdom will have no end.

We believe in the Holy Spirit, the Lord, the giver
   of life,
  who proceeds from the Father and the Son.
  With the Father and the Son he is worshipped
     and glorified.
  He has spoken through the Prophets.
  We believe in one holy catholic and apostolic
     Church.
  We acknowledge one baptism for the forgive-
     ness of sins.
  We look for the resurrection of the dead,
     and the life of the world to come. Amen.

15 GENERAL INTERCESSIONS

Prayer of the Faithful

As a priestly people we unite with one another to pray for today's needs in the Church and the world.

After the priest gives the introduction the deacon or other minister sings or says the invocations.

PEOPLE: Lord, hear our prayer.

(or other response, according to local custom)

At the end the priest says the concluding prayer:

PEOPLE: Amen.

LITURGY OF THE EUCHARIST

Made ready by reflection on God's Word, we enter now into the eucharistic sacrifice itself, the Supper of the Lord. We celebrate the memorial which the Lord instituted at his Last Supper. We are God's new people, the redeemed brothers and sisters of Christ, gathered by him around his table. We are here to bless God and to receive the gift of Jesus' body and blood so that our faith and life may be transformed.

PREPARATION OF THE GIFTS

16 SONG `SIT`

The bread and wine for the Eucharist, with our gifts for the Church and the poor, are gathered and brought to the altar. We prepare our hearts by song or in silence as the Lord's table is being set.

17 PREPARATION OF THE BREAD

Before placing the bread on the altar, the priest says quietly:

Blessed are you, Lord, God of all creation.
Through your goodness we have this bread to
offer,
which earth has given and human hands have
made.
It will become for us the bread of life.

If there is no singing, the priest may say this prayer aloud, and the people may respond:

PEOPLE: Blessed be God for ever.

18 PREPARATION OF THE WINE

When he pours wine and a little water into the chalice, the deacon (or the priest) says quietly:

By the mystery of this water and wine
may we come to share in the divinity of
Christ,
who humbled himself to share in our humanity.

Before placing the chalice on the altar, he says:

Blessed are you, Lord, God of all creation.
Through your goodness we have this wine to
offer,
fruit of the vine and work of human hands.
It will become our spiritual drink.

If there is no singing, the priest may say this prayer aloud, and the people may respond:

PEOPLE: Blessed be God for ever.

The priest says quietly:

Lord God, we ask you to receive us
and be pleased with the sacrifice we offer you
with humble and contrite hearts.

Then he washes his hands, quietly saying:

Lord, wash away my iniquity;
cleanse me from my sin.

19 INVITATION TO PRAYER   `STAND`

Priest: Pray, my brothers and sisters, that our sacrifice may be acceptable to God, the
almighty Father.

PEOPLE:

**May the Lord accept the sacrifice at your
hands
for the praise and glory of his name,
for our good, and the good of all his Church.**

20 PRAYER OVER THE GIFTS

The priest, speaking in our name, asks the Father to bless
and accept these gifts.

→   `Turn to Today's Mass`

At the end, **PEOPLE:** **Amen.**

EUCHARISTIC PRAYER

We begin the eucharistic service of praise and thanksgiving, the center of the entire celebration, the central prayer of worship. We lift our hearts to God, and offer praise and thanks as the priest addresses this prayer to the Father through Jesus. Together we join Christ in his sacrifice, celebrating his memorial in the holy meal and acknowledging with him the wonderful works of God in our lives.

21 INTRODUCTORY DIALOGUE

Priest: The Lord be with you.

PEOPLE: And also with you.

Priest: Lift up your hearts.

PEOPLE: We lift them up to the Lord.

Priest: Let us give thanks to the Lord our God.

PEOPLE: It is right to give him thanks and praise.

22 PREFACE

As indicated throughout this Missal, the priest may say one of the following Prefaces (listed in numerical order).

23 ACCLAMATION

Priest and **People:**

Holy, holy, holy Lord, God of power and might, heaven and earth are full of your glory.

Hosanna in the highest.

Blessed is he who comes in the name of the Lord.

Hosanna in the highest.   `KNEEL`

Then the priest continues with one of the following Eucharistic Prayers.

EUCHARISTIC PRAYER   **Choice of nine**

1	*We come to you, Father*	*p. 26*
2	*Lord, you are holy indeed*	*p. 32*
3	*Father, you are holy indeed*	*p. 35*
4	*Father, we acknowledge your*	*p. 41*
R1	*Father, from the beginning*	*p. 47*
R2	*God of power and might*	*p. 52*
C1	*Father, you are always thinking*	*p. 56*
C2	*Blessed be Jesus*	*p. 62*
C3	*Yes, Lord, you are holy*	*p. 67*

EUCHARISTIC PRAYER No. 1

The Roman Canon

(This eucharistic prayer is especially suitable for Sundays and Masses with proper "Communicantes" and "Hanc igitur.")

[The words within brackets may be omitted.]

[Praise to the Father]

We come to you, Father,
with praise and thanksgiving,
through Jesus Christ your Son.
Through him we ask you to accept and bless
these gifts we offer you in sacrifice.

[Intercessions: For the Church]

We offer them for your holy catholic Church,
watch over it, Lord, and guide it;
grant it peace and unity throughout the world.
We offer them for N. our Pope,
for N. our bishop,
and for all who hold and teach the catholic faith
that comes to us from the apostles.

Remember, Lord, your people,
especially those for whom we now pray, N. and
  N.

Remember all of us gathered here before you.
You know how firmly we believe in you
and dedicate ourselves to you.
We offer you this sacrifice of praise
for ourselves and those who are dear to us.
We pray to you, our living and true God,
for our well-being and redemption.

[In Communion with the Saints]   **1**

In union with the whole Church*
we honour Mary,
the ever-virgin mother of Jesus Christ our Lord
    and God.
We honour Joseph, her husband,
the apostles and martyrs
Peter and Paul, Andrew,

> [James, John, Thomas,
> James, Philip,
> Bartholomew, Matthew, Simon and Jude;
> we honour Linus, Cletus, Clement, Sixtus,
> Cornelius, Cyprian, Lawrence, Chrysogonus,
> John and Paul, Cosmas and Damian]

and all the saints.
May their merits and prayers
gain us your constant help and protection.

Father, accept this offering*
from your whole family.
Grant us your peace in this life,
save us from final damnation,
and count us among those you have chosen.

Bless and approve our offering;
make it acceptable to you,
an offering in spirit and in truth.
Let it become for us
the body and blood of Jesus Christ,
your only Son, our Lord.

*See page 95 for special Communicantes and Hanc
Igitur.

1 *[The Lord's Supper]*

The day before he suffered
he took bread in his sacred hands
and looking up to heaven,
to you, his almighty Father,
he gave you thanks and praise.
He broke the bread,
gave it to his disciples, and said:

Take this, all of you, and eat it:
this is my body which will be given up for you.

When supper was ended,
he took the cup.
Again he gave you thanks and praise,
gave the cup to his disciples, and said:

Take this, all of you, and drink from it:
this is the cup of my blood,
the blood of the new and everlasting covenant.
It will be shed for you and for all
so that sins may be forgiven.
Do this in memory of me.

[Memorial Acclamation]

Priest: Let us proclaim the mystery of faith:

PEOPLE:

A **Christ has died,**
Christ is risen,
Christ will come again.

Priest: Praise to you, Lord Jesus,
firstborn from the dead!*

B **Dying you destroyed our death,**
rising you restored our life.
Lord Jesus, come in glory.

*Optional Invitation.

Priest: We are faithful, Lord, to your command:*

**C When we eat this bread and drink this cup,
we proclaim your death, Lord Jesus,
until you come in glory.**

Priest: Christ is Lord of all ages!*

**D Lord, by your cross and resurrection
you have set us free.
You are the Saviour of the world.**

Father,   *[The Memorial Prayer]*
we celebrate the memory of Christ, your Son.
We, your people and your ministers,
recall his passion,
his resurrection from the dead,
and his ascension into glory;
and from the many gifts you have given us
we offer to you, God of glory and majesty,
this holy and perfect sacrifice:
the bread of life
and the cup of eternal salvation.

Look with favour on these offerings
and accept them as once you accepted
the gifts of your servant Abel,
the sacrifice of Abraham, our father in faith,
and the bread and wine offered by your priest
    Melchisedech.
Almighty God,
we pray that your angel may take this sacrifice
to your altar in heaven.
Then, as we receive from this altar
the sacred body and blood of your Son,
let us be filled with every grace and blessing.

*Optional Invitation.

1

[For the Dead]

Remember, Lord, those who have died
and have gone before us marked with the sign
   of faith,
especially those for whom we now pray, N. and
   N.
May these, and all who sleep in Christ,
find in your presence
light, happiness, and peace.

For ourselves, too, we ask
some share in the fellowship of your apostles
   and martyrs,
with John the Baptist, Stephen, Matthias,
   Barnabas,
   [Ignatius, Alexander, Marcellinus, Peter, Felicity,
   Perpetua, Agatha, Lucy, Agnes, Cecilia, Anastasia]
and all the saints.

Though we are sinners,
we trust in your mercy and love.
Do not consider what we truly deserve,
but grant us your forgiveness.

Through Christ our Lord
you give us all these gifts.
You fill them with life and goodness,
you bless them and make them holy.

Through him,   *[Concluding Doxology]*
with him,
in him,
in the unity of the Holy Spirit,
all glory and honour is yours,
almighty Father,
for ever and ever.

All reply: **Amen.** *Continue with the Mass, as on p. 71.*

(This eucharistic prayer is particularly suitable on weekdays or for special circumstances.)

℣. The Lord be with you.
℟. **And also with you.**
℣. Lift up your hearts.
℟. **We lift them up to the Lord.**
℣. Let us give thanks to the Lord our God.
℟. **It is right to give him thanks and praise.**

PREFACE   *[Praise to the Lord]*
(Another form may be used)

Father, it is our duty and our salvation,
always and everywhere
to give you thanks
through your beloved Son, Jesus Christ.

He is the Word through whom you made the universe,
the Saviour you sent to redeem us.
By the power of the Holy Spirit
he took flesh and was born of the Virgin Mary.

For our sake he opened his arms on the cross;
he put an end to death
and revealed the resurrection.

In this he fulfilled your will
and won for you a holy people.

And so we join the angels and the saints
in proclaiming your glory
as we say:

2 SANCTUS   *[First Acclamation of the People]*

**Holy, holy, holy Lord, God of power and
    might,
heaven and earth are full of your glory.
    Hosanna in the highest.
Blessed is he who comes in the name of the
    Lord.
    Hosanna in the highest.**

[Invocation of the Holy Spirit]

Lord, you are holy indeed,
the fountain of all holiness.
Let your Spirit come upon these gifts to make
    them holy,
so that they may become for us
the body and blood of our Lord, Jesus Christ.

[The Lord's Supper]

Before he was given up to death,
a death he freely accepted,
he took bread and gave you thanks.
He broke the bread,
gave it to his disciples, and said:

Take this, all of you, and eat it:
this is my body which will be given up for you.

When supper was ended, he took the cup.
Again he gave you thanks and praise,
gave the cup to his disciples, and said:

Take this, all of you, and drink from it:
this is the cup of my blood,
the blood of the new and everlasting covenant.
It will be shed for you and for all
so that sins may be forgiven.
Do this in memory of me.

2

[*Memorial Acclamation*]

Priest: Let us proclaim the mystery of faith:

PEOPLE:

A **Christ has died,**
Christ is risen,
Christ will come again.

Priest: Praise to you, Lord Jesus,
    firstborn from the dead!*

B **Dying you destroyed our death,**
rising you restored our life.
Lord Jesus, come in glory.

Priest: We are faithful, Lord, to your command:*

C **When we eat this bread and drink this cup,**
we proclaim your death, Lord Jesus,
until you come in glory.

Priest: Christ is Lord of all ages!*

D **Lord, by your cross and resurrection**
you have set us free.
You are the Saviour of the world.

[*The Memorial Prayer*]

In memory of his death and resurrection,
we offer you, Father, this life-giving bread,
this saving cup.
We thank you for counting us worthy
to stand in your presence and serve you.

[*Invocation of the Holy Spirit*]

May all of us who share in the body and blood
    of Christ
be brought together in unity by the Holy Spirit.
*Optional Invitation.

2 *[Intercessions: For the Church]*

Lord, remember your Church throughout the
   world;
make us grow in love,
together with N. our Pope,
N. our bishop, and all the clergy.*

[For the Dead]

Remember our brothers and sisters
who have gone to their rest
in the hope of rising again;
bring them and all the departed
into the light of your presence.

[In Communion with the Saints]

Have mercy on us all;
make us worthy to share eternal life
with Mary, the virgin Mother of God,
with the apostles,
and with all the saints who have done your will
   throughout the ages.
May we praise you in union with them,
and give you glory
through your Son, Jesus Christ.

Through him,   *[Concluding Doxology]*
with him,
in him,
in the unity of the Holy Spirit,
all glory and honour is yours,
almighty Father,
for ever and ever.

All reply: **Amen.** *Continue with the Mass, as on p. 71.*

* *In Masses for the Dead the following may be added:*
Remember N., whom you have called from this life.
In baptism he (she) died with Christ:
may he (she) also share his resurrection.

(This eucharistic prayer may be used with any preface and preferably on Sundays and feast days.)

[Praise to the Father]

Father, you are holy indeed,
and all creation rightly gives you praise.
All life, all holiness comes from you
through your Son, Jesus Christ our Lord,
by the working of the Holy Spirit.
From age to age you gather a people to your-
    self,
so that from east to west
a perfect offering may be made
to the glory of your name.

[Invocation of the Holy Spirit]

And so, Father, we bring you these gifts.
We ask you to make them holy by the power
    of your Spirit,
that they may become the body and blood
of your Son, our Lord Jesus Christ,
at whose command we celebrate this eucharist.

[The Lord's Supper]

On the night he was betrayed,
he took bread and gave you thanks and
    praise.
He broke the bread, gave it to his disciples,
    and said:

Take this, all of you, and eat it:
this is my body which will be given up for
    you.

3 When supper was ended, he took the cup.
Again he gave you thanks and praise,
gave the cup to his disciples, and said:

Take this, all of you, and drink from it:
this is the cup of my blood,
the blood of the new and everlasting covenant.
It will be shed for you and for all
so that sins may be forgiven.
Do this in memory of me.

[Memorial Acclamation]

Priest: Let us proclaim the mystery of faith:

PEOPLE:

A **Christ has died,**
Christ is risen,
Christ will come again.

Priest: Praise to you, Lord Jesus,
firstborn from the dead!*

B **Dying you destroyed our death,**
rising you restored our life.
Lord Jesus, come in glory.

Priest: We are faithful, Lord, to your command:*

C **When we eat this bread and drink this cup,**
we proclaim your death, Lord Jesus,
until you come in glory.

Priest: Christ is Lord of all ages!*

D **Lord, by your cross and resurrection**
you have set us free.
You are the Saviour of the world.

Optional Invitation.

[The Memorial Prayer]

Father, calling to mind the death your Son
    endured for our salvation,
his glorious resurrection and ascension into
    heaven,
and ready to greet him when he comes again,
we offer you in thanksgiving this holy and living
    sacrifice.
Look with favour on your Church's offering,
and see the Victim whose death has reconciled
    us to yourself.

[Invocation of the Holy Spirit]

Grant that we, who are nourished by his body
    and blood,
may be filled with his Holy Spirit,
and become one body, one spirit in Christ.

[Intercessions: In Communion with the Saints]

May he make us an everlasting gift to you
and enable us to share in the inheritance of your
    saints,
with Mary, the virgin Mother of God;
with the apostles, the martyrs,
(Saint *N.*) and all your saints,
on whose constant intercession we rely for
    help.

Lord, may this sacrifice,   *[For the Church]*
which has made our peace with you,
advance the peace and salvation of all the
    world.
Strengthen in faith and love your pilgrim
    Church on earth;
your servant, Pope *N.*, our bishop *N.*,
and all the bishops,

3 with the clergy and the entire people your Son
has gained for you.
Father, hear the prayers of the family you have
gathered here before you.
In mercy and love unite all your children
wherever they may be.*

[For the Dead]

Welcome into your kingdom our departed
brothers and sisters,
and all who have left this world in your friendship.
We hope to enjoy for ever the vision of your glory,
through Christ our Lord, from whom all good
things come.

[Concluding Doxology]

Through him,
with him,
in him,
in the unity of the Holy Spirit,
all glory and honour is yours,
almighty Father,
for ever and ever.

All reply: **Amen.** *Continue with the Mass, as on p. 71.*

In the Masses for the Dead the following is said:

Remember N.
In baptism he (she) died with Christ:
may he (she) also share his resurrection,
when Christ will raise our mortal bodies
and make them like his own in glory.

3

Welcome into your kingdom our departed
   brothers and sisters,
and all who have left this world in your friendship.
There we hope to share in your glory
when every tear will be wiped away.
On that day we shall see you, our God, as you are.
We shall become like you
and praise you for ever through Christ our Lord,
from whom all good things come.

Through him,   *[Concluding Doxology]*
with him,
in him,
in the unity of the Holy Spirit,
all glory and honour is yours,
almighty Father,
for ever and ever.

All reply: **Amen.**   *Continue with the Mass, as on p. 71.*

℣. The Lord be with you.
℟. **And also with you.**
℣. Lift up your hearts.
℟. **We lift them up to the Lord.**
℣. Let us give thanks to the Lord our God.
℟. **It is right to give him thanks and praise.**

PREFACE

Father in heaven,
it is right that we should give you thanks and
 glory:
you are the one God, living and true.

Through all eternity you live in unapproachable
 light.
Source of life and goodness, you have created
 all things,
to fill your creatures with every blessing
and lead all men to the joyful vision of your
 light.

Countless hosts of angels stand before you to
 do your will;
they look upon your splendour
and praise you, night and day.
United with them,
and in the name of every creature under heav-
 en,
we too praise your glory as we say:

SANCTUS *[First Acclamation of the People]*
**Holy, holy, holy Lord, God of power and might,
heaven and earth are full of your glory.**

4

Hosanna in the highest.
Blessed is he who comes in the name of the
Lord.
Hosanna in the highest.

[Praise to the Father]

Father, we acknowledge your greatness:
all your actions show your wisdom and love.
You formed man in your own likeness
and set him over the whole world
to serve you, his creator,
and to rule over all creatures.

Even when he disobeyed you and lost your
friendship
you did not abandon him to the power of death,
but helped all men to seek and find you.
Again and again you offered a covenant to
man,
and through the prophets taught him to hope
for salvation.

Father, you so loved the world
that in the fullness of time you sent your only
Son to be our Saviour.
He was conceived through the power of the
Holy Spirit,
and born of the Virgin Mary,
a man like us in all things but sin.

To the poor he proclaimed the good news of salvation,
to prisoners, freedom,
and to those in sorrow, joy.

4 In fulfilment of your will
he gave himself up to death;
but by rising from the dead,
he destroyed death and restored life.

And that we might live no longer for ourselves
     but for him,
he sent the Holy Spirit from you, Father,
as his first gift to those who believe,
to complete his work on earth
and bring us the fullness of grace.

[Invocation of the Holy Spirit]

Father, may this Holy Spirit sanctify these
     offerings.
Let them become the body and blood of Jesus
     Christ our Lord
as we celebrate the great mystery
which he left us as an everlasting covenant.

[The Lord's Supper]

He always loved those who were his own in the
     world.
When the time came for him to be glorified by
     you, his heavenly Father,
he showed the depth of his love.

While they were at supper,
he took bread, said the blessing, broke the
     bread,
and gave it to his disciples, saying:

Take this, all of you, and eat it:
this is my body which will be given up for
     you.

4

In the same way, he took the cup, filled with
   wine,
He gave you thanks, and giving the cup to his
   disciples, said:

Take this, all of you, and drink from it:
this is the cup of my blood,
the blood of the new and everlasting covenant.
It will be shed for you and for all
so that sins may be forgiven.
Do this in memory of me.

[Memorial Acclamation]

Priest: Let us proclaim the mystery of faith:
PEOPLE:

A **Christ has died,**
   Christ is risen,
   Christ will come again.

Priest: Praise to you, Lord Jesus,
   firstborn from the dead!*

B **Dying you destroyed our death,**
   rising you restored our life.
   Lord Jesus, come in glory.

Priest: We are faithful, Lord, to your command:*

C **When we eat this bread and drink this cup,**
   we proclaim your death, Lord Jesus,
   until you come in glory.

Priest: Christ is Lord of all ages!*

D **Lord, by your cross and resurrection**
   you have set us free.
   You are the Saviour of the world.

*Optional Invitation.

4

[The Memorial Prayer]

Father, we now celebrate this memorial of our
   redemption.
We recall Christ's death, his descent among the
   dead,
his resurrection, and his ascension to your right
   hand;
and, looking forward to his coming in glory,
we offer you his body and blood,
the acceptable sacrifice
which brings salvation to the whole world.

Lord, look upon this sacrifice which you have
   given to your Church;
and by your Holy Spirit, gather all who share
   this one bread and one cup
into the one body of Christ, a living sacrifice of
   praise.

[Intercessions: For the Church]

Lord, remember those for whom we offer this
   sacrifice,
especially N., our Pope,
N., our bishop, and bishops and clergy everywhere.
Remember those who take part in this offering,
those here present and all your people,
and all who seek you with a sincere heart.

[For the Dead]

Remember those who have died in the peace of Christ

and all the dead whose faith is known to you alone.

[In Communion with the Saints]

Father, in your mercy grant also to us, your children,

to enter into our heavenly inheritance

in the company of the Virgin Mary, the Mother of God,

and your apostles and saints.

Then, in your kingdom, freed from the corruption of sin and death,

we shall sing your glory with every creature through Christ our Lord,

through whom you give us everything that is good.

[Concluding Doxology]

Through him,

with him,

in him,

in the unity of the Holy Spirit,

all glory and honour is yours,

almighty Father,

for ever and ever.

All reply: **Amen.**

Continue with the Mass, as on p. 71.

℣. The Lord be with you.
℟. **And also with you.**
℣. Lift up your hearts.
℟. **We lift them up to the Lord.**
℣. Let us give thanks to the Lord our God.
℟. **It is right to give him thanks and praise.**

Father, all-powerful and ever-living God,
we do well always and everywhere to give you
    thanks and praise.
You never cease to call us
to a new and more abundant life.

God of love and mercy,
you are always ready to forgive;
we are sinners,
and you invite us
to trust in your mercy.

Time and time again
we broke your covenant,
but you did not abandon us.
Instead, through your Son, Jesus our Lord,
you bound yourself even more closely to the
    human family
by a bond that can never be broken.

Now is the time
for your people to turn back to you
and to be renewed in Christ your Son,
a time of grace and reconciliation.

**R
1**

You invite us
to serve the family of mankind
by opening our hearts
to the fullness of your Holy Spirit.

In wonder and gratitude,
we join our voices with the choirs of heaven
to proclaim the power of your love
and to sing of our salvation in Christ:

All:

**Holy, holy, holy Lord, God of power and
    might,
heaven and earth are full of your glory.
    Hosanna in the highest.
Blessed is he who comes in the name of the
    Lord.
    Hosanna in the highest.**

Father,
from the beginning of time
you have always done what is good for man
so that we may be holy as you are holy.

Look with kindness on your people
gathered here before you:
send forth the power of your Spirit
so that these gifts may become for us
the body and blood of your beloved Son, Jesus
    the Christ,
in whom we have become your sons and daugh-
    ters.

When we were lost
and could not find the way to you,
you loved us more than ever:

R 1

Jesus, your Son, innocent and without sin,
gave himself into our hands
and was nailed to a cross.
Yet before he stretched out his arms between
    heaven and earth
in the everlasting sign of your covenant,
he desired to celebrate the Paschal feast
in the company of his disciples.

While they were at supper,
he took bread and gave you thanks and
    praise.
He broke the bread, gave it to his disciples, and
    said:

Take this, all of you, and eat it:
this is my body which will be given up for you.

At the end of the meal,
knowing that he was to reconcile all things in
    himself
by the blood of his cross,
he took the cup, filled with wine.
Again he gave you thanks,
handed the cup to his friends, and said:

Take this, all of you, and drink from it:
this is the cup of my blood,
the blood of the new and everlasting covenant.
It will be shed for you and for all
so that sins may be forgiven.
Do this in memory of me.

R 1

Priest: Let us proclaim the mystery of faith:

PEOPLE:

A **Christ has died,
Christ is risen,
Christ will come again.**

Priest: Praise to you, Lord Jesus,
  firstborn from the dead!*

B **Dying you destroyed our death,
rising you restored our life.
Lord Jesus, come in glory.**

Priest: We are faithful, Lord, to your command:*

C **When we eat this bread and drink this cup,
we proclaim your death, Lord Jesus,
until you come in glory.**

Priest: Christ is Lord of all ages!*

D **Lord, by your cross and resurrection
you have set us free.
You are the Saviour of the world.**

We do this in memory of Jesus Christ,
our Passover and our lasting peace.
We celebrate his death and resurrection
and look for the coming of that day
when he will return to give us the fullness of
   joy.
Therefore we offer you, God ever faithful and
   true,
the sacrifice which restores man to your friendship.

*Optional Invitation.

R 1 **F**ather,
look with love
on those you have called
to share in the one sacrifice of Christ.
By the power of your Holy Spirit
make them one body,
healed of all division.

Keep us all
in communion of mind and heart
with N., our pope, and N., our bishop.
Help us to work together
for the coming of your kingdom,
until at last we stand in your presence
to share the life of the saints,
in the company of the Virgin Mary and the
    apostles,
and of our departed brothers and sisters
whom we commend to your mercy.

Then, freed from every shadow of death,
we shall take our place in the new creation
and give you thanks
with Christ, our risen Lord.

Through him,
with him,
in him,
in the unity of the Holy Spirit,
all glory and honour is yours,
almighty Father,
for ever and ever.

All reply: **Amen.**

Continue with the Mass, as on p. 71.

EUCHARISTIC PRAYER FOR
MASSES OF RECONCILIATION II

℣. The Lord be with you.
℟. **And also with you.**
℣. Lift up your hearts.
℟. **We lift them up to the Lord.**
℣. Let us give thanks to the Lord our God.
℟. **It is right to give him thanks and praise.**

Father, all-powerful and ever-living God,
we praise and thank you through Jesus Christ
    our Lord
for your presence and action in the world.

In the midst of conflict and division,
we know it is you
who turn our minds to thoughts of peace.
Your Spirit changes our hearts:
enemies begin to speak to one another,
those who were estranged join hands in friend-
    ship,
and nations seek the way of peace together.

Your Spirit is at work
when understanding puts an end to strife,
when hatred is quenched by mercy,
and vengeance gives way to forgiveness.

For this we should never cease
to thank and praise you.
We join with all the choirs of heaven
as they sing for ever to your glory!

51

R 2

All:

Holy, holy, holy Lord, God of power and might.

Heaven and earth are full of your glory.
    Hosanna in the highest.

Blessed is he who comes in the name of the Lord.
    Hosanna in the highest.

God of power and might,
we praise you through your Son, Jesus Christ,
who comes in your name.
He is the Word that brings salvation.
He is the hand you stretch out to sinners.
He is the way that leads to your peace.

God our Father,
we had wandered far from you,
but through your Son you have brought us back.
You gave him up to death
so that we might turn again to you
and find our way to one another.

Therefore we celebrate the reconciliation
Christ has gained for us.

We ask you to sanctify these gifts
by the power of your Spirit,
as we now fulfil your Son's ✠ command.

R 2

While he was at supper
on the night before he died for us,
he took bread in his hands,
and gave you thanks and praise.
He broke the bread,
gave it to his disciples, and said:

Take this, all of you, and eat it:
this is my body which will be given up for
    you.

At the end of the meal he took the cup.
Again he praised you for your goodness,
gave the cup to his disciples, and said:

Take this, all of you, and drink from it:
this is the cup of my blood,
the blood of the new and everlasting covenant.
It will be shed for you and for all
so that sins may be forgiven.
Do this in memory of me.

Priest: Let us proclaim the mystery of faith:

PEOPLE:

A **Christ has died,**
   Christ is risen,
   Christ will come again.

Priest: Praise to you, Lord Jesus,
    firstborn from the dead!*

B **Dying you destroyed our death,**
   rising you restored our life.
   Lord Jesus, come in glory.

Optional Invitation.

R
2

Priest: We are faithful, Lord, to your command:*

C **When we eat this bread and drink this cup,**
we proclaim your death, Lord Jesus,
until you come in glory.

Priest: Christ is Lord of all ages!*

D **Lord, by your cross and resurrection**
you have set us free.
You are the Saviour of the world.

Lord our God,
your Son has entrusted to us
this pledge of his love.
We celebrate the memory of his death and
    resurrection
and bring you the gift you have given us,
the sacrifice of reconciliation.
Therefore, we ask you, Father,
to accept us, together with your Son.

Fill us with his Spirit
through our sharing in this meal.
May he take away all that divides us.

May this Spirit keep us always in communion
with N., our pope, N., our bishop,
with all the bishops and all your people.
Father, make your Church throughout the
    world
a sign of unity and an instrument of your
    peace.

Optional Invitation.

You have gathered us here
around the table of your Son,
in fellowship with the Virgin Mary, Mother of
God, and all the saints.

In that new world where the fullness of your
peace will be revealed,
gather people of every race, language, and way of
life
to share in the one eternal banquet
with Jesus Christ the Lord.

Through him,
with him,
in him,
in the unity of the Holy Spirit,
all glory and honour is yours,
almighty Father,
for ever and ever.

The people respond: **Amen.**

Continue with the Mass, as on p. 71.

℣. The Lord be with you.
℟. **And also with you.**
℣. Lift up your hearts.
℟. **We lift them up to the Lord.**
℣. Let us give thanks to the Lord our God.
℟. **It is right to give him thanks and praise.**

God our Father,
you have brought us here together
so that we can give you thanks and praise
for all the wonderful things you have done.

We thank you for all that is beautiful in the world
and for the happiness you have given us.
We praise you for daylight
and for your word which lights up our minds.
We praise you for the earth,
and all the people who live on it,
and for our life which comes from you.

We know that you are good.
You love us and do great things for us.
So we all sing together:

Holy, holy, holy Lord, God of power and might, heaven and earth are full of your glory.
    Hosanna in the highest.

Father,
you are always thinking about your people;
you never forget us.

**C
1**

You sent us your Son Jesus,
who gave his life for us
and who came to save us.
He cured sick people;
he cared for those who were poor
and wept with those who were sad.
He forgave sinners
and taught us to forgive each other.
He loved everyone
and showed us how to be kind.
He took children in his arms and blessed
   them.
So we all sing together:

**Blessed is he who comes in the name of the
   Lord.
   Hosanna in the highest.**

God our Father,
all over the world your people praise you.
So now we pray with the whole Church:
with N., our pope and N., our bishop.
In heaven the blessed Virgin Mary,
the apostles and all the saints
always sing your praise.
Now we join with them and with the angels
to adore you as we sing:

All:

**Holy, holy, holy Lord, God of power and
   might,
heaven and earth are full of your glory.
   Hosanna in the highest.**

C
1

Blessed is he who comes in the name of the Lord.
Hosanna in the highest.

God our Father,
you are most holy
and we want to show you that we are grateful.

We bring you bread and wine
and ask you to send your Holy Spirit to make these gifts
the body and blood of Jesus your Son.
Then we can offer to you
what you have given to us.

On the night before he died,
Jesus was having supper with his apostles.
He took bread from the table.
He gave you thanks and praise.
Then he broke the bread, gave it to his friends, and said:

Take this, all of you, and eat it:
this is my body which will be given up for you.

When supper was ended,
Jesus took the cup that was filled with wine.
He thanked you, gave it to his friends, and said:

Take this, all of you, and drink from it:
this is the cup of my blood,
the blood of the new and everlasting covenant.
It will be shed for you and for all
so that sins may be forgiven.

C 1

Then he said to them:
Do this in memory of me.

We do now what Jesus told us to do.
We remember his death and his resurrection
and we offer you, Father, the bread that gives us
   life,
and the cup that saves us.
Jesus brings us to you;
welcome us as you welcome him.

Priest: Let us proclaim the mystery of faith:

PEOPLE:

A   **Christ has died,**
     Christ is risen,
     Christ will come again.

Priest: Praise to you, Lord Jesus,
   firstborn from the dead!*

B   **Dying you destroyed our death,**
     rising you restored our life.
     Lord Jesus, come in glory.

Priest: We are faithful, Lord, to your command:*

C   **When we eat this bread and drink this cup,**
     we proclaim your death, Lord Jesus,
     until you come in glory.

Priest: Christ is Lord of all ages!*

D   **Lord, by your cross and resurrection**
     you have set us free.
     You are the Saviour of the world.

Optional Invitation.

C 1

Father,
because you love us,
you invite us to come to your table.
Fill us with the joy of the Holy Spirit
as we receive the body and blood of your Son.

Lord,
you never forget any of your children.
We ask you to take care of those we love,
especially of N. and N.;
and we pray for those who have died.

Remember everyone who is suffering from pain
    or sorrow.
Remember Christians everywhere
and all other people in the world.

We are filled with wonder and praise
when we see what you do for us
through Jesus your Son,
and so we sing:

Through him,
with him,
in him,
in the unity of the Holy Spirit,
all glory and honour is yours,
almighty Father,
for ever and ever.

The people respond: **Amen.**

Continue with the Mass, as on p. 71.

EUCHARISTIC PRAYER FOR
MASSES WITH CHILDREN II

℣. The Lord be with you.
℟. **And also with you.**
℣. Lift up your hearts.
℟. **We lift them up to the Lord.**
℣. Let us give thanks to the Lord our God.
℟. **It is right to give him thanks and praise.**

God our loving Father,
we are glad to give you thanks and praise
because you love us.
With Jesus we sing your praise:

All:
Glory to God in the highest.

> *or:*

Hosanna in the highest.

Because you love us,
you gave us this great and beautiful world.
With Jesus we sing your praise:

All:
Glory to God in the highest.

> *or:*

Hosanna in the highest.

Because you love us,
you sent Jesus your Son
to bring us to you
and to gather us around him

C 2

as the children of one family.
With Jesus we sing your praise:

All:

Glory to God in the highest.

> *or:*

Hosanna in the highest.

For such great love
we thank you with the angels and saints
as they praise you and sing:

All:

**Holy, holy, holy Lord, God of power and
    might,**
heaven and earth are full of your glory.
> **Hosanna in the highest.**
**Blessed is he who comes in the name of the
    Lord.**
> **Hosanna in the highest.**

Blessed be Jesus, whom you sent
to be the friend of children and of the poor.

He came to show us
how we can love you, Father,
by loving one another.
He came to take away sin,
which keeps us from being friends,
and hate, which makes us all unhappy.

He promised to send the Holy Spirit,
to be with us always
so that we can live as your children.

**C
2**

All:

Blessed is he who comes in the name of the Lord.

　Hosanna in the highest.

God our Father,
we now ask you
to send your Holy Spirit
to change these gifts of bread and wine
into the body and blood
of Jesus Christ, our Lord.

The night before he died,
Jesus your Son showed us how much you love us.
When he was at supper with his disciples,
he took bread,
and gave you thanks and praise.
Then he broke the bread,
gave it to his friends, and said:

Take this, all of you, and eat it:
This is my body which will be given up for you.

All:

Jesus has given his life for us.

When supper was ended,
Jesus took the cup that was filled with wine.
He thanked you, gave it to his friends, and said:

C 2

Take this, all of you, and drink from it:
this is the cup of my blood,
the blood of the new and everlasting covenant.
It will be shed for you and for all
so that sins may be forgiven.

All:

Jesus has given his life for us.

Then he said to them:
Do this in memory of me.

And so, loving Father,
we remember that Jesus died and rose again
to save the world.
He put himself into our hands
to be the sacrifice we offer you.

All:

We praise you. We bless you. We thank you.

Lord our God,
listen to our prayer.
Send the Holy Spirit
to all of us who share in this meal.
May this Spirit bring us closer together
in the family of the Church,
with N., our pope,
N., our bishop,
all other bishops,
and all who serve your people.

All:

We praise you. We bless you. We thank you.

Remember, Father, our families and friends
(. . .),
and all those we do not love as we should.
Remember those who have died (. . .).
Bring them home to you
to be with you for ever.

All:

We praise you. We bless you. We thank you.

Gather us all together into your kingdom.
There we shall be happy for ever
with the Virgin Mary, Mother of God and our
mother.
There all the friends
of Jesus the Lord
will sing a song of joy.

All:

We praise you. We bless you. We thank you.

Through him,
with him,
in him,
in the unity of the Holy Spirit,
all glory and honour is yours,
almighty Father,
for ever and ever.

The people respond: **Amen.**

Continue with the Mass, as on p. 71.

EUCHARISTIC PRAYER FOR MASSES WITH CHILDREN III

℣. The Lord be with you.
℟. **And also with you.**
℣. Lift up your hearts.
℟. **We lift them up to the Lord.**
℣. Let us give thanks to the Lord our God.
℟. **It is right to give him thanks and praise.**

Outside Easter season:

We thank you,
God our Father.
You made us to live for you and for each other.
We can see and speak to one another,
and become friends,
and share our joys and sorrows.

During Easter Season:

We thank you,
God our Father.
You are the living God;
you have called us to share in your life,
and to be happy with you for ever.
You raised up Jesus, your Son,
the first among us to rise from the dead,
and gave him new life.
You have promised to give us new life also,
a life that will never end,
a life with no more anxiety and suffering.

And so, Father, we gladly thank you
with everyone who believes in you;
with the saints and the angels,
we rejoice and praise you, singing:

**Holy, holy, holy Lord, God of power and
    might,**
heaven and earth are full of your glory.
    Hosanna in the highest.
**Blessed is he who comes in the name of the
    Lord.**
    Hosanna in the highest.

Yes, Lord, you are holy;
you are kind to us and to all.
For this we thank you.
We thank you above all for your Son, Jesus
    Christ.

Outside Easter season:

You sent him into this world
because people had turned away from you
and no longer loved each other.
He opened our eyes and our hearts
to understand that we are brothers and sisters
and that you are Father of us all.

During Easter season:

He brought us the Good News
of life to be lived with you for ever in heaven.
He showed us the way to that life,
the way of love.
He himself has gone that way before us.

C 3

He now brings us together to one table
and asks us to do what he did.

Father,
we ask you to bless these gifts of bread and
    wine
and make them holy.
Change them for us into the body and blood of
    Jesus Christ, your Son.

On the night before he died for us,
he had supper for the last time with his disci-
    ples.
He took bread
and gave you thanks.
He broke the bread
and gave it to his friends, saying:

Take this, all of you, and eat it:
this is my body which will be given up for you.

In the same way he took a cup of wine.
He gave you thanks
and handed the cup to his disciples, saying:

Take this, all of you, and drink from it:
this is the cup of my blood,
the blood of the new and everlasting covenant.
It will be shed for you and for all
so that sins may be forgiven.
Then he said to them:
Do this in memory of me.

**C
3**

God our Father,
we remember with joy
all that Jesus did to save us.
In this holy sacrifice,
which he gave as a gift to his Church,
we remember his death and resurrection.

Father in heaven,
accept us together with your beloved Son.
He willingly died for us,
but you raised him to life again.
We thank you and say:

All:
Glory to God in the highest.

(Or some other suitable acclamation of praise.)

Jesus now lives with you in glory,
but he is also here on earth, among us.
We thank you and say:

All:
Glory to God in the highest.

One day he will come in glory
and in his kingdom
there will be no more suffering,
no more tears, no more sadness.
We thank you and say:

All:
Glory to God in the highest.

Father in heaven,
you have called us
to receive the body and blood of Christ at this
    table

C 3

and to be filled with the joy of the Holy Spirit.
Through this sacred meal
give us strength to please you more and more.

Lord, our God,
remember N., our pope,
N., our bishop, and all other bishops.

Outside Easter season:

Help all who follow Jesus
to work for peace
and to bring happiness to others.

During Easter season:

Fill all Christians with the gladness of Easter.
Help us to bring this joy
to all who are sorrowful.

Bring us all at last
together with Mary, the Mother of God,
and all the saints,
to live with you
and to be one with Christ in heaven.

Through him,
with him,
in him,
in the unity of the Holy Spirit,
all glory and honour is yours,
almighty Father,
for ever and ever.

The people respond: **Amen.**

COMMUNION RITE

To prepare for the paschal meal, to welcome the Lord, we pray for forgiveness and exchange a sign of peace. Before eating Christ's body and drinking his blood, we must be one with him and with all our brothers and sisters in the Church.

24 LORD'S PRAYER `STAND`

Priest:

A Let us pray with confidence to the Father in the words our Saviour gave us:

B Jesus taught us to call God our Father, and so we have the courage to say:

C Let us ask our Father to forgive our sins and to bring us to forgive those who sin against us.

D Let us pray for the coming of the kingdom as Jesus taught us.

Priest and **PEOPLE**:

> **Our Father, who art in heaven,**
> **hallowed be thy name;**
> **thy kingdom come;**
> **thy will be done on earth as it is in heaven.**
> **Give us this day our daily bread;**
> **and forgive us our trespasses**
> **as we forgive those who trespass against us;**
> **and lead us not into temptation,**
> **but deliver us from evil.**

71

Priest: Deliver us, Lord, from every evil,
and grant us peace in our day.
In your mercy keep us free from sin
and protect us from all anxiety
as we wait in joyful hope
for the coming of our Saviour, Jesus Christ.

PEOPLE: **For the kingdom, the power, and the glory are yours, now and for ever.**

25 SIGN OF PEACE

The Church is a community of people joined by the Spirit in love. It needs to express, deepen, and restore its peaceful unity before eating the one body of the Lord and drinking from the one cup of salvation. We do this by a sign of peace.

The priest says the prayer for peace:

Lord Jesus Christ, you said to your apostles:
I leave you peace, my peace I give you.
Look not on our sins, but on the faith of your
    Church,
and grant us the peace and unity of your
    kingdom
where you live for ever and ever.

PEOPLE: **Amen.**

Priest: The peace of the Lord be with you
    always.

PEOPLE: **And also with you.**

Deacon (or priest):
  Let us offer each other the sign of peace.

The people exchange a sign of peace and love, according to local custom.

26 BREAKING OF THE BREAD

Christians are gathered for the "breaking of the bread," another name for the Mass. In communion, though many we are made one body in the one bread, which is Christ.

Then the following is sung or said:

PEOPLE:

Lamb of God, you take away the sins of the world:

 have mercy on us.

Lamb of God, you take away the sins of the world:

 have mercy on us.

Lamb of God, you take away the sins of the world:

 grant us peace.

The hymn may be repeated until the breaking of the bread is finished, but the last phrase is always: "Grant us peace."

Meanwhile the priest breaks the host over the paten and places a small piece in the chalice, saying quietly:

May this mingling of the body and blood of our Lord Jesus Christ
bring eternal life to us who receive it.

27 PRAYERS BEFORE COMMUNION

We pray in silence and then voice words of humility and hope as our final preparation before meeting Christ in the eucharist.

Before communion, the priest says quietly one of the following prayers:

Lord Jesus Christ, Son of the living God, by the will of the Father and the work of the Holy Spirit your death brought life to the world. By your holy body and blood free me from all my sins and from every evil. Keep me faithful to your teaching, and never let me be parted from you.

OR

Lord Jesus Christ, with faith in your love and mercy I eat your body and drink your blood. Let it not bring me condemnation, but health in mind and body.

28 RECEPTION OF COMMUNION

The priest genuflects. Holding the host elevated slightly over the paten, the priest says:

Priest: This is the Lamb of God
who takes away the sins of the world.
Happy are those who are called to his supper.

Priest and **People** (once only):
**Lord, I am not worthy to receive you,
but only say the word and I shall be healed.**

Before receiving communion, the priest says quietly:

May the body of Christ bring me to everlasting life.
May the blood of Christ bring me to everlasting life.

He then gives communion to the people.

Priest: The body of Christ. Communicant: **Amen.**
Priest: The blood of Christ. Communicant: **Amen.**

29 COMMUNION SONG or ANTIPHON

The communion psalm or other appropriate song or hymn is sung while communion is given to the faithful. If there is no singing, the communion antiphon is said:

→ **Turn to Today's Mass**

The vessels are cleansed by the priest or deacon or acolyte, now or after Mass. Meanwhile he says quietly:

Lord, may I receive these gifts in purity of heart
May they bring me healing and strength, now
and for ever.

30 PERIOD OF SILENCE or Song of Praise

*After communion there may be a period of silence. Then
a song of praise may be sung.*

31 PRAYER AFTER COMMUNION `STAND`

The priest prays in our name that we may live the life of faith
since we have been strengthened by Christ himself. Our
Amen makes this prayer our own.

Priest: Let us pray.

*Priest and people may pray silently for a while. Then
the priest says the prayer after communion.*

→ `Turn to Today's Mass`

At the end, **PEOPLE:** **Amen.**

CONCLUDING RITE

We have heard God's Word and eaten the body of Christ.
Now it is time for us to leave, to do good works, to praise and
bless the Lord in our daily lives.

32 GREETING

*After any brief announcements, the blessing and dis-
missal follow:*

Priest: The Lord be with you.

PEOPLE: And also with you.

33 BLESSING

A Simple form

Priest: May almighty God bless you,
the Father, and the Son, ✠ and the Holy
Spirit.

PEOPLE: Amen.

On certain days or occasions another more solemn form of blessing or prayer over the people may be used.

B Solemn blessing

Texts of all the solemn blessings are given on pp. 96-104.

Deacon: **Bow your heads and pray for God's blessing.**

After each invocation, the people answer: **Amen.**

The priest always concludes the solemn blessing by adding:

**May almighty God bless you,
the Father, and the Son, ✠ and the Holy Spirit.**

PEOPLE: Amen.

C Prayer over the people

Texts of all prayers over the people are given on pp. 104-108.

After the prayer over the people, the priest always adds:

**May almighty God bless you,
the Father, and the Son, ✠ and the Holy Spirit.**

PEOPLE: Amen.

34 DISMISSAL

Deacon (or priest):

A **Go in the peace of Christ.**

B **The Mass is ended, go in peace.**

C **Go in peace to love and serve the Lord.**

PEOPLE: Thanks be to God.

If any liturgical service follows immediately, the rite of dismissal is omitted.

RITE OF BLESSING AND
SPRINKLING HOLY WATER

When this rite is celebrated it takes the place of the penitential rite at the beginning of Mass. The Kyrie is also omitted.

After greeting the people the priest remains standing at his chair. A vessel containing the water to be blessed is placed before him. Facing the people, he invites them to pray, using these or similar words:

Dear friends,
this water will be used
to remind us of our baptism.
Let us ask God to bless it,
and to keep us faithful
to the Spirit he has given us.

After a brief silence, he joins his hands and continues:

A.
God our Father,
your gift of water
brings life and freshness to the earth;
it washes away our sins
and brings us eternal life.

We ask you now
to bless ✠ this water,
and to give us your protection on this day
which you have made your own.
Renew the living spring of your life within us
and protect us in spirit and body,
that we may be free from sin
and come into your presence
to receive your gift of salvation.
We ask this through Christ our Lord. ℟. **Amen.**

B. Or:

Lord God almighty,
creator of all life,
of body and soul,
we ask you to bless ✠ this water:
as we use it in faith
forgive our sins
and save us from all illness
and the power of evil.

Lord,
in your mercy
give us living water,
always springing up as a fountain of salvation:
free us, body and soul, from every danger,
and admit us to your presence
in purity of heart.
Grant this through Christ our Lord.

C. Or (during the Easter season):

Lord God almighty,
hear the prayers of your people:
we celebrate our creation and redemption.
Hear our prayers and bless ✠ this water
which gives fruitfulness to the fields,
and refreshment and cleansing to man.
You chose water to show your goodness
when you led your people to freedom
through the Red Sea
and satisfied their thirst in the desert
with water from the rock.
Water was the symbol used by the prophets
to foretell your new covenant with man.
You made the water of baptism holy
by Christ's baptism in the Jordan:

by it you give us a new birth
and renew us in holiness.
May this water remind us of our baptism,
and let us share the joy
of all who have been baptized at Easter.
We ask this through Christ our Lord.

*Where it is customary, salt may be mixed with the
holy water. The priest blesses the salt, saying:*

Almighty God,
we ask you to bless ✝ this salt
as once you blessed the salt scattered over the
    water
by the prophet Elisha.
Wherever this salt and water are sprinkled,
drive away the power of evil,
and protect us always
by the presence of your Holy Spirit.
Grant this through Christ our Lord.

Then he pours the salt into the water in silence.

*Taking the sprinkler, the priest sprinkles himself and
his ministers, then the rest of the clergy and people.
He may move through the church for the sprinkling
of the people. Meanwhile, an antiphon or another
appropriate song is sung.*

*When he returns to his place and the song is finished,
the priest faces the people and, with joined hands,
says:*

May almighty God cleanse us of our sins,
and through the eucharist we celebrate
make us worthy to sit at his table
in his heavenly kingdom.

The people answer: **Amen.**

When it is prescribed, the Gloria is then sung or said.

PENITENTIAL RITE

ALTERNATIVE FORMS FOR C (p. 13)

ii

Priest or other minister:

Lord Jesus, you came to reconcile us
to one another and to the Father:
Lord, have mercy.

People: **Lord, have mercy.**

Priest or other minister:

Lord Jesus, you heal the wounds of sin and division:
Christ, have mercy.

People: **Christ, have mercy.**

Priest or other minister:

Lord Jesus, you intercede for us with your Father:
Lord, have mercy.

People: **Lord, have mercy.** (→ p. 14)

iii

Priest or other minister:

You raised the dead to life in the Spirit:
Lord, have mercy.

People: **Lord, have mercy.**

Priest or other minister:

You bring pardon and peace to the sinner:
Christ, have mercy.

People: **Christ, have mercy.**

Priest or other minister:

You bring light to those in darkness:
Lord, have mercy.

People: **Lord, have mercy.** (→ p. 14)

iv

Priest or other minister:

Lord Jesus, you raise us to new life:
Lord, have mercy.

People: **Lord, have mercy.**

Priest or other minister:

Lord Jesus, you you forgive us our sins:
Christ, have mercy.

People: **Christ, have mercy.**

Priest or other minister:

Lord Jesus, you feed us with your body and
   blood:
Lord, have mercy.

People: **Lord, have mercy.** (→ p. 14)

v

Priest or other minister:

Lord Jesus, you healed the sick:
Lord, have mercy.

People: **Lord, have mercy.**

Priest or other minister:

Lord Jesus, you forgave sinners:
Christ, have mercy.

People: **Christ, have mercy.**

Priest or other minister:

Lord Jesus, you give us yourself to heal us and
   bring us strength:
Lord, have mercy.

People: **Lord, have mercy.** (→ p. 14)

PREFACES

ADVENT I (1)

The Two Comings of Christ

(From the First Sunday of Advent to December 16)

Father, all-powerful and ever-living God,
we do well always and everywhere to give you thanks
through Jesus Christ our Lord.

When he humbled himself to come among us as a man,
he fulfilled the plan you formed long ago
and opened for us the way to salvation.

Now we watch for the day,
hoping that the salvation promised us will be ours
when Christ our Lord will come again in his glory.

And so, with all the choirs of angels in heaven
we proclaim your glory
and join in their unending hymn of praise:

➜ No. 23, p. 25

ADVENT II (2)

Waiting for the Two Comings of Christ

(From December 17 to December 24)

Father, all-powerful and ever-living God,
we do well always and everywhere to give you thanks
through Jesus Christ our Lord.

His future coming was proclaimed by all the prophets.
The virgin mother bore him in her womb
with love beyond all telling.
John the Baptist was his herald
and made him known when at last he came.

In his love Christ has filled us with joy
as we prepare to celebrate his birth,
so that when he comes he may find us watching in
    prayer,
our hearts filled with wonder and praise.

And so, with all the choirs of angels in heaven
we proclaim your glory
and join in their unending hymn of praise:

→ No. 23, p. 25

CHRISTMAS I (3)

Christ the Light

(From Christmas to Saturday before Epiphany)

Father, all-powerful and ever-living God,
we do well always and everywhere to give you thanks
through Jesus Christ our Lord.

In the wonder of the incarnation
your eternal Word has brought to the eyes of faith
a new and radiant vision of your glory.
In him we see our God made visible
and so are caught up in love of the God we cannot see.

And so, with all the choirs of angels in heaven
we proclaim your glory
and join in their unending hymn of praise:

→ No. 23, p. 25

CHRISTMAS II (4)

Christ Restores Unity to All Creation

(From Christmas to Saturday before Epiphany)

Father, all-powerful and ever-living God,
we do well always and everywhere to give you thanks
through Jesus Christ our Lord.

Today you fill our hearts with joy
as we recognize in Christ the revelation of your love.
No eye can see his glory as our God,
yet now he is seen as one like us.

Christ is your Son before all ages,
yet now he is born in time.
He has come to lift up all things to himself,
to restore unity to creation,
and to lead mankind from exile into your heavenly kingdom.
With all the angels of heaven
we sing our joyful hymn of praise:

→ No. 23, p. 25

CHRISTMAS III (5)

Divine and Human Exchange in the
Incarnation of the Word
(From Christmas to Saturday before Epiphany)

Father, all-powerful and ever-living God,
we do well always and everywhere to give you thanks
through Jesus Christ our Lord.

Today in him a new light has dawned upon the world:
God has become one with man,
and man has become one again with God.

Your eternal Word has taken upon himself our human
    weakness,
giving our mortal nature immortal value.
So marvellous is this oneness between God and man
that in Christ man restores to man the gift of everlast-
    ing life.

In our joy we sing to your glory
with all the choirs of angels: → No. 23, p. 25

LENT I (8)

The Spiritual Meaning of Lent

Father, all-powerful and ever-living God,
we do well always and everywhere to give you thanks
through Jesus Christ our Lord.

Each year you give us this joyful season
when we prepare to celebrate the paschal mystery
with mind and heart renewed.
You give us a spirit of loving reverence for you, our
    Father,
and of willing service to our neighbour.

As we recall the great events that gave us new life in
    Christ,
you bring the image of your Son to perfection within
    us.

Now, with angels and archangels,
and the whole company of heaven,

we sing the unending hymn of your praise:

→ No. 23, p. 25

LENT II (9)
The Spirit of Penance

Father, all-powerful and ever-living God,
we do well always and everywhere to give you thanks.

This great season of grace is your gift to your family
to renew us in spirit.
You give us strength to purify our hearts,
to control our desires,
and so to serve you in freedom.
You teach us how to live in this passing world
with our heart set on the world that will never end.

Now, with all the saints and angels,
we praise you for ever:

→ No. 23, p. 25

EASTER I (21)
The Paschal Mystery
(Easter Vigil, Easter Sunday, and during the octave)

Father, all-powerful and ever-living God,
we do well always and everywhere to give you thanks
through Jesus Christ our Lord.

We praise you with greater joy than ever
on this Easter night (day),
when Christ became our paschal sacrifice.

He is the true Lamb who took away the sins of the world.
By dying he destroyed our death;
by rising he restored our life.

And so, with all the choirs of angels in heaven
we proclaim your glory
and join in their unending hymn of praise:

→ No. 23, p. 25

EASTER II (22)
New Life in Christ

Father, all-powerful and ever-living God,
we do well always and everywhere to give you thanks
through Jesus Christ our Lord.

We praise you with greater joy than ever in this Easter
   season,
when Christ became our paschal sacrifice.

He has made us children of the light,
rising to new and everlasting life.
He has opened the gates of heaven
to receive his faithful people.
His death is our ransom from death;
his resurrection is our rising to life.

The joy of the resurrection renews the whole world,
while the choirs of heaven sing for ever to your glory:
➡ No. 23, p. 25

EASTER III (23)

Christ Lives and Intercedes for Us for ever

Father, all-powerful and ever-living God,
we do well always and everywhere to give you thanks
through Jesus Christ our Lord.

We praise you with greater joy than ever in this Easter
   season,
when Christ became our paschal sacrifice.

He is still our priest,
our advocate who always pleads our cause.
Christ is the victim who dies no more,
the Lamb, once slain, who lives for ever.

The joy of the resurrection renews the whole world,
while the choirs of heaven sing for ever to your glory:
➡ No. 23, p. 25

EASTER IV (24)

*The Restoration of the Universe through the
Paschal Mystery*

Father, all-powerful and ever-living God,
we do well always and everywhere to give you thanks
through Jesus Christ our Lord.

We praise you with greater joy than ever in this Easter
   season,
when Christ became our paschal sacrifice.

In him a new age has dawned,
the long reign of sin is ended,
a broken world has been renewed,
and man is once again made whole.

The joy of the resurrection renews the whole world,
while the choirs of heaven sing for ever to your glory:

➞ No. 23, p. 25

EASTER V (25)

Christ Is Priest and Victim

Father, all-powerful and ever-living God,
we do well always and everywhere to give you thanks
through Jesus Christ our Lord.

We praise you with greater joy than ever in this Easter
season,
when Christ became our paschal sacrifice.

As he offered his body on the cross,
his perfect sacrifice fulfilled all others.
As he gave himself into your hands for our salvation,
he showed himself to be the priest, the altar, and the
lamb of sacrifice.

The joy of the resurrection renews the whole world,
while the choirs of heaven sing for ever to your glory:

➞ No. 23, p. 25

ASCENSION I (26)

The Mystery of the Ascension
(Ascension to the Saturday before Pentecost inclusive)

Father, all-powerful and ever-living God,
we do well always and everywhere to give you thanks.

[Today] the Lord Jesus, the king of glory,
the conqueror of sin and death,
ascended to heaven while the angels sang his praises.

Christ, the mediator between God and man,
judge of the world and Lord of all,
has passed beyond our sight,
not to abandon us but to be our hope.

Christ is the beginning, the head of the Church;
where he has gone, we hope to follow.

The joy of the resurrection and ascension renews the
    whole world,
while the choirs of heaven sing for ever to your glory:
→ No. 23, p. 25

ASCENSION II (27)

The Mystery of the Ascension
(Ascension to the Saturday before Pentecost inclusive)

Father, all-powerful and ever-living God,
we do well always and everywhere to give you thanks
through Jesus Christ our Lord.

In his risen body he plainly showed himself to his dis-
    ciples
and was taken up to heaven in their sight
to claim for us a share in his divine life.

And so, with all the choirs of angels in heaven
we proclaim your glory
and join in their unending hymn of praise:
→ No. 23, p. 25

SUNDAYS IN ORDINARY TIME I (29)

The Paschal Mystery and the People of God

Father, all-powerful and ever-living God,
we do well always and everywhere to give you thanks
through Jesus Christ our Lord.

Through his cross and resurrection
he freed us from sin and death
and called us to the glory that has made us
a chosen race, a royal priesthood,
a holy nation, a people set apart.

Everywhere we proclaim your mighty works
for you have called us out of darkness
into your own wonderful light.

And so, with all the choirs of angels in heaven
we proclaim your glory
and join in their unending hymn of praise:
→ No. 23, p. 25

SUNDAYS IN ORDINARY TIME II (30)

The Mystery of Salvation

Father, all-powerful and ever-living God,
we do well always and everywhere to give you thanks
through Jesus Christ our Lord.

Out of love for sinful man,
he humbled himself to be born of the Virgin.

By suffering on the cross
he freed us from unending death,
and by rising from the dead
he gave us eternal life.

And so, with all the choirs of angels in heaven
we proclaim your glory
and join in their unending hymn of praise:

➥ No. 23, p. 25

SUNDAYS IN ORDINARY TIME III (31)

The Salvation of Man by a Man

Father, all-powerful and ever-living God,
we do well always and everywhere to give you thanks.

We see your infinite power
in your loving plan of salvation.
You came to our rescue by your power as God,
but you wanted us to be saved by one like us.
Man refused your friendship,
but man himself was to restore it
through Jesus Christ our Lord.

Through him the angels of heaven offer their prayer of
        adoration
as they rejoice in your presence for ever.
May our voices be one with theirs
in their triumphant hymn of praise: ➥ No. 23, p. 25

SUNDAYS IN ORDINARY TIME IV (32)

The History of Salvation

Father, all-powerful and ever-living God,
we do well always and everywhere to give you thanks
through Jesus Christ our Lord.

By his birth we are reborn.
In his suffering we are freed from sin.
By his rising from the dead we rise to everlasting life.
In his return to you in glory
we enter into your heavenly kingdom.

And so, we join the angels and the saints
as they sing their unending hymn of praise:

➡ No. 23, p. 25

SUNDAYS IN ORDINARY TIME V (33)

Creation

Father, all-powerful and ever-living God,
we do well always and everywhere to give you thanks.

All things are of your making,
all times and seasons obey your laws,
but you chose to create man in your own image,
setting him over the whole world in all its wonder.
You made man the steward of creation,
to praise you day by day
for the marvels of your wisdom and power,
through Jesus Christ our Lord.

Glory and honour are his
as heaven and earth, angels and archangels,
cry out in unending praise:

➡ No. 23, p. 25

SUNDAYS IN ORDINARY TIME VI (34)

The Pledge of an Eternal Easter

Father, all-powerful and ever-living God,
we do well always and everywhere to give you thanks.

In you we live and move and have our being.
Each day you show us a Father's love;
your Holy Spirit, dwelling within us,
gives us on earth the hope of unending joy.

Your gift of the Spirit,
who raised Jesus from the dead,
is the foretaste and promise
of the paschal feast of heaven.

With thankful praise,
in company with the angels,
we glorify the wonders of your power: → No. 23, p. 25

SUNDAYS IN ORDINARY TIME VII (35)

Salvation through the Obedience of Christ

Father, all-powerful and ever-living God,
we do well always and everywhere to give you thanks.

So great was your love
that you gave us your Son as our redeemer.
You sent him as one like ourselves,
though free from sin,
that you might see and love in us
what you see and love in Christ.
Your gifts of grace, lost by disobedience,
are now restored by the obedience of your Son.

We praise you, Lord, with all the angels and saints
in their song of joy: → No. 23, p. 25

SUNDAYS IN ORDINARY TIME VIII (36)

The Church United in the Mystery of the Trinity

Father, all-powerful and ever-living God,
we do well always and everywhere to give you thanks.

When your children sinned
and wandered far from your friendship,
you reunited them with yourself
through the blood of your Son
and the power of the Holy Spirit.

You gather them into your Church,
to be one as you, Father, are one
with your Son and the Holy Spirit.
You call them to be your people,
to praise your wisdom in all your works.
You make them the body of Christ
and the dwelling-place of the Holy Spirit.

In our joy we sing to your glory
with all the choirs of angels: → No. 23, p. 25

HOLY EUCHARIST I (47)

The Sacrifice and Sacrament of Christ

Father, all-powerful and ever-living God,
we do well always and everywhere to give you thanks
through Jesus Christ our Lord.

He is the true and eternal priest
who established this unending sacrifice.
He offered himself as a victim for our deliverance
and taught us to make this offering in his memory.
As we eat his body which he gave for us,
we grow in strength.
As we drink his blood which he poured out for us,
we are washed clean.

Now, with angels and archangels,
and the whole company of heaven,
we sing the unending hymn of your praise:

➡ No. 23, p. 25

HOLY EUCHARIST II (48)

The Effects of the Holy Eucharist

Father, all-powerful and ever-living God,
we do well always and everywhere to give you thanks
through Jesus Christ our Lord.

At the last supper,
as he sat at table with his apostles,
he offered himself to you as the spotless lamb,
the acceptable gift that gives you perfect praise.
Christ has given us this memorial of his passion
to bring us its saving power until the end of time.

In this great sacrament you feed your people
and strengthen them in holiness,
so that the family of mankind
may come to walk in the light of one faith,
in one communion of love.
We come then to this wonderful sacrament
to be fed at your table
and grow into the likeness of the risen Christ.

Earth unites with heaven
to sing the new song of creation
as we adore and praise you for ever: ➤ No. 23, p. 25

CHRISTIAN DEATH I (77)

The Hope of Rising in Christ

Father, all-powerful and ever-living God,
we do well always and everywhere to give you thanks
through Jesus Christ our Lord.

In him, who rose from the dead,
our hope of resurrection dawned.
The sadness of death gives way
to the bright promise of immortality.

Lord, for your faithful people life is changed, not ended.
When the body of our earthly dwelling lies in death
we gain an everlasting dwelling place in heaven.

And so, with all the choirs of angels in heaven
we proclaim your glory
and join in their unending hymn of praise:
➤ No. 23, p. 25

CHRISTIAN DEATH II (78)

Christ's Death, Our Life

Father, all-powerful and ever-living God,
we do well always and everywhere to give you thanks
through Jesus Christ our Lord.

He chose to die
that he might free all men from dying.
He gave his life
that we might live to you alone for ever.

In our joy we sing to your glory
with all the choirs of angels: ➤ No. 23, p. 25

CHRISTIAN DEATH III (79)

Christ, Salvation and Life

Father, all-powerful and ever-living God,
we do well always and everywhere to give you thanks
through Jesus Christ our Lord.

In him the world is saved,
man is reborn,
and the dead rise again to life.

Through Christ the angels of heaven
offer their prayer of adoration
as they rejoice in your presence for ever.
May our voices be one with theirs
in their triumphant hymn of praise: → No. 23, p. 25

CHRISTIAN DEATH IV (80)

From Earthly Life to Heaven's Glory

Father, all-powerful and ever-living God,
we do well always and everywhere to give you thanks.

By your power you bring us to birth.
By your providence you rule our lives.
By your command you free us at last from sin
as we return to the dust from which we came.
Through the saving death of your Son
we rise at your word to the glory of the resurrection.

Now we join the angels and the saints
as they sing their unending hymn of praise:
→ No. 23, p. 25

CHRISTIAN DEATH V (81)

Our Resurrection through Christ's Glory

Father, all-powerful and ever-living God,
we do well always and everywhere to give you thanks
through Jesus Christ our Lord.

Death is the just reward for our sins,
yet, when at last we die,
your loving kindness calls us back to life
in company with Christ,
whose victory is our redemption.

Our hearts are joyful,
for we have seen your salvation,
and now with the angels and saints
we praise you for ever: → No. 23, p. 25

PROPER COMMUNICANTES
AND HANC IGITUR
FOR EUCHARISTIC PRAYER I

Communicantes for Christmas

In union with the whole Church
we celebrate that day (night)
when Mary without loss of her virginity
gave the world its Saviour.
We honour Mary,
the ever-virgin mother of Jesus Christ, our Lord and
    God, etc., p. 27.

Communicantes for the Epiphany

In union with the whole Church
we celebrate that day
when your only Son,
sharing your eternal glory,
showed himself in a human body.
We honour Mary, etc., p. 27.

Communicantes for Easter

In union with the whole Church
we celebrate that day (night)
when Jesus Christ, our Lord,
rose from the dead in his human body.
We honour Mary, etc., p. 27.

Hanc Igitur for Easter

Father, accept this offering
from your whole family
and from those born into the new life
of water and the Holy Spirit,
with all their sins forgiven.
Grant us your peace in this life,
save us from final damnation,
and count us among those you have chosen.
[Through Christ our Lord. Amen.]

→ Canon, p. 27: Bless, etc.

Communicantes for Ascension

In union with the whole Church
we celebrate that day
when your only Son, our Lord,
took his place with you
and raised our frail human nature to glory.
We honour Mary, etc., p. 27.

Communicantes for Pentecost

In union with the whole Church
we celebrate the day of Pentecost
when the Holy Spirit appeared to the apostles
in the form of countless tongues.
We honour Mary, etc., p. 27.

SOLEMN BLESSINGS

The following blessings may be used, at the discretion of the priest, at the end of Mass, or after the liturgy of the word, the office, and the celebration of the sacraments.

The deacon gives the invitation, or in his absence the priest himself may also give it: Bow your heads and pray for God's blessing. *Another form of invitation may be used. Then the priest extends his hands over the people while he says or sings the blessings. All respond:* Amen.

I. Celebrations During the Proper of Seasons

1. ADVENT

You believe that the Son of God once came to us;
you look for him to come again.
May his coming bring you the light of his holiness
and free you with his blessing. ℞. **Amen.**

May God make you steadfast in faith,
joyful in hope, and untiring in love
all the days of your life. ℞. **Amen.**

You rejoice that our Redeemer came to live with us as
    man.
When he comes again in glory,
may he reward you with endless life. ℟. **Amen.**

May almighty God bless you,
the Father, and the Son, ✠ and the Holy Spirit. ℟. **Amen.**

2. CHRISTMAS

When he came to us as man,
the Son of God scattered the darkness of this world,
and filled this holy night (day) with his glory.
May the God of infinite goodness
scatter the darkness of sin
and brighten your hearts with holiness. ℟. **Amen.**

God sent his angels to shepherds
to herald the great joy of our Saviour's birth.
May he fill you with joy
and make you heralds of his gospel. ℟. **Amen.**

When the Word became man,
earth was joined to heaven.
May he give you his peace and good will,
and fellowship with all the heavenly host. ℟. **Amen.**

May almighty God bless you,
the Father, and the Son, ✠ and the Holy Spirit. ℟. **Amen.**

3. BEGINNING OF THE NEW YEAR

Every good gift comes from the Father of light.
May he grant you his grace and every blessing,
and keep you safe throughout the coming year. ℟.
    Amen.

May he grant you unwavering faith,
constant hope, and love that endures to the end. ℟.
    Amen.

May he order your days and work in his peace,
hear your every prayer,
and lead you to everlasting life and joy. ℟. **Amen.**

May almighty God bless you,
the Father, and the Son, ✠ and the Holy Spirit. ℟. **Amen.**

4. EPIPHANY

God has called you out of darkness
into his wonderful light.
May you experience his kindness and blessings,
and be strong in faith, in hope, and in love. ℟. **Amen.**

Because you are followers of Christ,
who appeared on this day as a light shining in dark-
　　ness,
may he make you a light to all your sisters and brothers.
　　℟. **Amen.**

The wise men followed the star,
and found Christ who is light from light.
May you too find the Lord
when your pilgrimage is ended. ℟. **Amen.**

May almighty God bless you,
the Father, and the Son, ✠ and the Holy Spirit. ℟. **Amen.**

5. PASSION OF THE LORD

The Father of mercies has given us
an example of unselfish love
in the sufferings of his only Son.
Through your service of God and neighbour
may you receive his countless blessings. ℟. **Amen.**

You believe that by his dying
Christ destroyed death for ever.
May he give you everlasting life. ℟. **Amen.**

He humbled himself for our sakes.
May you follow his example
and share in his resurrection. ℟. **Amen.**

May almighty God bless you,
the Father, and the Son, ✠ and the Holy Spirit. ℟. **Amen.**

6. EASTER VIGIL AND EASTER SUNDAY

May almighty God bless you on this solemn feast of
Easter,
and may he protect you against all sin. ℟. **Amen.**

Through the resurrection of his Son
God has granted us healing.
May he fulfil his promises,
and bless you with eternal life. ℟. **Amen.**

You have mourned for Christ's sufferings;
now you celebrate the joy of his resurrection.
May you come with joy to the feast which lasts for ever.
℟. **Amen.**

May almighty God bless you,
the Father, and the Son, ✠ and the Holy Spirit. ℟. **Amen.**

7. EASTER SEASON

Through the resurrection of his Son
God has redeemed you and made you his children.
May he bless you with joy. ℟. **Amen.**

The Redeemer has given you lasting freedom.
May you inherit his everlasting life. ℟. **Amen.**

By faith you rose with him in baptism.
May your lives be holy,
so that you will be united with him for ever. ℟. **Amen.**

May almighty God bless you,
the Father, and the Son, ✠ and the Holy Spirit. ℟. **Amen.**

8. ASCENSION

May almighty God bless you on this day
when his only Son ascended into heaven
to prepare a place for you. ℟. **Amen.**

After his resurrection, Christ was seen by his disciples.
When he appears as judge
may you be pleasing for ever in his sight. ℟. **Amen.**

You believe that Jesus has taken his seat in majesty
at the right hand of the Father.

May you have the joy of experiencing
that he is also with you to the end of time,
according to his promise. ℞. **Amen.**

May almighty God bless you,
the Father, and the Son, ✠ and the Holy Spirit. ℞. **Amen.**

9. HOLY SPIRIT

(This day) the Father of light
has enlightened the minds of the disciples
by the outpouring of the Holy Spirit.
May he bless you
and give you the gifts of the Spirit for ever. ℞. **Amen.**

May that fire which hovered over the disciples
as tongues of flame
burn out all evil from your hearts
and make them glow with pure light. ℞. **Amen.**

God inspired speech in different tongues
to proclaim one faith.
May he strengthen your faith
and fulfil your hope of seeing him face to face. ℞. **Amen.**

May almighty God bless you,
the Father, and the Son, ✠ and the Holy Spirit. ℞. **Amen.**

10. ORDINARY TIME I

Blessing of Aaron (Num 6:24-26)

May the Lord bless you and keep you. ℞. **Amen.**

May his face shine upon you,
and be gracious to you. ℞. **Amen.**

May he look upon you with kindness,
and give you his peace. ℞. **Amen.**

May almighty God bless you,
the Father, and the Son, ✠ and the Holy Spirit. ℞. **Amen.**

11. ORDINARY TIME II *(Phil 4:7)*

May the peace of God
which is beyond all understanding
keep your hearts and minds

in the knowledge and love of God
and of his Son, our Lord Jesus Christ. ℟. **Amen.**

May almighty God bless you,
the Father, and the Son, ✠ and the Holy Spirit. ℟. **Amen.**

12. ORDINARY TIME III

May almighty God bless you in his mercy,
and make you always aware of his saving wisdom. ℟.
    Amen.

May he strengthen your faith with proofs of his love,
so that you will persevere in good works. ℟. **Amen.**

May he direct your steps to himself,
and show you how to walk in charity and peace. ℟.
    Amen.

May almighty God bless you,
the Father, and the Son, ✠ and the Holy Spirit. ℟. **Amen.**

13. ORDINARY TIME IV

May the God of all consolation
bless you in every way
and grant you peace all the days of your life. ℟. **Amen.**

May he free you from all anxiety
and strengthen your hearts in his love. ℟. **Amen.**

May he enrich you with his gifts of faith, hope, and love,
so that what you do in this life
will bring you to the happiness of everlasting life. ℟.
    Amen.

May almighty God bless you,
the Father, and the Son, ✠ and the Holy Spirit. ℟. **Amen.**

14. ORDINARY TIME V

May almighty God keep you from all harm
and bless you with every good gift. ℟. **Amen.**

May he set his Word in your heart
and fill you with lasting joy. ℟. **Amen.**

May you walk in his ways,
always knowing what is right and good,
until you enter your heavenly inheritance. ℟. **Amen.**

May almighty God bless you,
the Father, and the Son, ✠ and the Holy Spirit. ℟. **Amen.**

II. Celebrations of the Saints

15. BLESSED VIRGIN MARY

Born of the Blessed Virgin Mary,
the Son of God redeemed mankind.
May he enrich you with his blessings. ℟. **Amen.**

You received the author of life through Mary.
May you always rejoice in her loving care. ℟. **Amen.**

You have come to rejoice at Mary's feast.
May you be filled with the joys of the Spirit
and the gifts of your eternal home. ℟. **Amen.**

May almighty God bless you,
the Father, and the Son, ✠ and the Holy Spirit. ℟. **Amen.**

16. PETER AND PAUL

The Lord has set you firm within his Church,
which he built upon the rock of Peter's faith.
May he bless you with a faith that never falters. ℟.
   Amen.

The Lord has given you knowledge of the faith
through the labours and preaching of St. Paul.
May his example inspire you to lead others to Christ
by the manner of your life. ℟. **Amen.**

May the keys of Peter, and the words of Paul,
their undying witness and their prayers,
lead you to the joy of that eternal home
which Peter gained by his cross, and Paul by the sword.
   ℟. **Amen.**

May almighty God bless you,
the Father, and the Son, ✠ and the Holy Spirit. ℟. **Amen.**

17. APOSTLES

May God who founded his Church upon the apostles
bless you through the prayers of St. N. (and St. N.). ℟.
   Amen.

May God inspire you to follow the example of the apostles,
and give witness to the truth before all men. ℟. **Amen.**

The teaching of the apostles has strengthened your faith.
May their prayers lead you
to your true and eternal home. ℟. **Amen.**

May almighty God bless you,
the Father, and the Son, ✝ and the Holy Spirit. ℟. **Amen.**

18. ALL SAINTS

God is the glory and joy of all his saints,
whose memory we celebrate today.
May his blessing be with you always. ℟. **Amen.**

May the prayers of the saints deliver you from the present evil.
May their example of holy living
turn your thoughts to service of God and neighbour. ℟.
   Amen.

God's holy Church rejoices that her saints
have reached their heavenly goal,
and are in lasting peace.
May you come to share all the joys of our Father's house.
   ℟. **Amen.**

May almighty God bless you,
the Father, and the Son, ✝ and the Holy Spirit. ℟. **Amen.**

III. Other Blessings

19. DEDICATION OF A CHURCH

The Lord of earth and heaven
has assembled you before him this day
(to dedicate this house of prayer)

(to recall the dedication of this church).
May he fill you with the blessings of heaven. ℟. **Amen.**

God the Father wills that all his children
scattered throughout the world
become one family in his Son.
May he make you his temple,
the dwelling-place of his Holy Spirit. ℟. **Amen.**

May God free you from every bond of sin,
dwell within you and give you joy.
May you live with him for ever
in the company of all his saints. ℟. **Amen.**

May almighty God bless you,
the Father, and the Son, ✠ and the Holy Spirit. ℟. **Amen.**

20. THE DEAD

In his great love,
the God of all consolation gave man the gift of life.
May he bless you with faith
in the resurrection of his Son,
and with the hope of rising to new life. ℟. **Amen.**

To us who are alive
may he grant forgiveness,
and to all who have died
a place of light and peace. ℟. **Amen.**

As you believe that Jesus rose from the dead,
so may you live with him for ever in joy. ℟. **Amen.**

May almighty God bless you,
the Father, and the Son, ✠ and the Holy Spirit. ℟. **Amen.**

PRAYERS OVER THE PEOPLE

*The following prayers may be used, at the discretion
of the priest, at the end of the Mass, or after the
liturgy of the word, the office, and the celebration of
the sacraments.*

*The deacon gives the invitation, or in his absence the
priest himself may also give it:* Bow your heads and
pray for God's blessing. *Another form of invitation*

may be used. Then the priest extends his hands over the people while he says or sings the prayer. All respond: Amen.

After the prayer, the priest always adds:

May almighty God bless you,
the Father, and the Son, ✠ and the Holy Spirit. ℟. **Amen.**

1. Lord,
   have mercy on your people.
   Grant us in this life the good things
   that lead to the everlasting life you prepare for us.
   We ask this through Christ our Lord.

2. Lord,
   grant your people your protection and grace.
   Give them health of mind and body,
   perfect love for one another,
   and make them always faithful to you.
   Grant this through Christ our Lord.

3. Lord,
   may all Christian people both know and cherish
   the heavenly gifts they have received.
   We ask this in the name of Jesus the Lord.

4. Lord,
   bless your people and make them holy
   so that, avoiding evil,
   they may find in you the fulfillment of their longing.
   We ask this through Christ our Lord.

5. Lord,
   bless and strengthen your people.
   May they remain faithful to you
   and always rejoice in your mercy.
   We ask this in the name of Jesus the Lord.

6. Lord,
   you care for your people even when they stray.
   Grant us a complete change of heart,
   so that we may follow you with greater fidelity.
   We ask this through Christ our Lord.

7. Lord,
   send your light upon your family.
   May they continue to enjoy your favour
   and devote themselves to doing good.
   Grant this in the name of Jesus the Lord.

8. Lord,
   we rejoice that you are our creator and ruler.
   As we call upon your generosity,
   renew and keep us in your love.
   Grant this through Christ our Lord.

9. Lord,
   we pray for your people who believe in you.
   May they enjoy the gift of your love,
   share it with others,
   and spread it everywhere.
   We ask this in the name of Jesus the Lord.

10. Lord,
    bless your people who hope for your mercy.
    Grant that they may receive
    the things they ask for at your prompting.
    Grant this through Christ our Lord.

11. Lord,
    bless us with your heavenly gifts,
    and in your mercy make us ready to do your will.
    We ask this through Christ our Lord.

12. Lord,
    protect your people always,
    that they may be free from every evil
    and serve you with all their hearts.
    We ask this through Christ our Lord.

13. Lord,
    help your people to seek you with all their hearts
    and to deserve what you promise.
    Grant this through Christ our Lord.

14. Father,
    help your people to rejoice in the mystery of re-
    demption

and to win its reward.
We ask this in the name of Jesus the Lord.

15. Lord,
    have pity on your people;
    help them each day to avoid what displeases you
    and grant that they may serve you with joy.
    We ask this through Christ our Lord.

16. Lord,
    care for your people and purify them.
    Console them in this life
    and bring them to the life to come.
    We ask this in the name of Jesus the Lord.

17. Father,
    look with love upon your people,
    the love which our Lord Jesus Christ showed us
    when he delivered himself to evil men
    and suffered the agony of the cross,
    for he is Lord for ever.

18. Lord,
    grant that your faithful people
    may continually desire to relive the mystery of the
        eucharist
    and so be reborn to lead a new life.
    We ask this through Christ our Lord.

19. Lord God,
    in your great mercy,
    enrich your people with your grace
    and strengthen them by your blessing
    so that they may praise you always.
    Grant this through Christ our Lord.

20. May God bless you with every good gift from on
        high.
    May he keep you pure and holy in his sight at all
        times.
    May he bestow the riches of his grace upon you,
    bring you the good news of salvation,
    and always fill you with love for all men.
    We ask this through Christ our Lord.

21. Lord,
    make us pure in mind and body,
    that we will avoid all evil pleasures
    and always delight in you.
    We ask this in the name of Jesus the Lord.

22. Lord,
    bless your people and fill them with zeal.
    Strengthen them by your love to do your will.
    We ask this through Christ our Lord.

23. Lord,
    come, live in your people
    and strengthen them by your grace.
    Help them to remain close to you in prayer
    and give them a true love for one another.
    Grant this through Christ our Lord.

24. Father,
    look kindly on your children who put their trust in
        you;
    bless them and keep them from all harm,
    strengthen them against the attacks of the devil.
    May they never offend you
    but seek to love you in all they do.
    We ask this through Christ our Lord.

Feasts of the Saints

25. God our Father,
    may all Christian people rejoice in the glory of
        your saints.
    Give us fellowship with them
    and unending joy in your kingdom.
    We ask this in the name of Jesus the Lord.

26. Lord,
    you have given us many friends in heaven.
    Through their prayers we are confident
    that you will watch over us always
    and fill our hearts with your love.
    Grant this through Christ our Lord.

PROPER OF SEASONS

OUR CHURCH'S YEAR OF PRAYER

Advent
> We prepare for the coming of Jesus,
> who is here and yet to come

Christmas season
> We celebrate the gift of our Father's love:
> Jesus is our brother and our Lord

Ordinary time
> With Jesus
> we enter into the work of his body, the Church

Lent
> In our daily life and prayer
> we die with Christ to sin,
> and live with him for God

Easter triduum
> We celebrate Jesus' dying and rising
> and our sharing with him through baptism

Easter season
> Sharing in the new life of Christ
> we are filled with his Spirit

Ordinary time
> Guided by the Spirit of Jesus
> we build the kingdom of God by our lives

"Be alert at all times, praying . . . to escape
all these things . . . and to stand before the Son of Man."

YEAR C
DECEMBER 3, 2006
1st SUNDAY OF ADVENT

ENTRANCE ANTIPHON Ps. 24 (25).1-3   [Hope]
To you, my God, I lift my soul, I trust in you;
let me never come to shame. Do not let my
enemies laugh at me. No one who waits for
you is ever put to shame.

➜ No. 2, p. 10 (Omit Gloria)

OPENING PRAYER   [Welcome for Christ]
All-powerful God,
increase our strength of will for doing good
that Christ may find an eager welcome at his
     coming
and call us to his side in the kingdom of
     heaven,
where he lives and reigns with you and the
     Holy Spirit,
one God, for ever and ever. ℟. **Amen.** ↓

FIRST READING Jer. 33.14-16   [The Lord's Messiah]

> Jeremiah reveals the promise of the Lord made to the house of Israel. A Branch from David shall do what is right and just. Judah and Jerusalem shall be saved.

A reading from the book of the prophet Jeremiah

THE days are surely coming, says the Lord, when I will fulfil the promise I made to the house of Israel and the house of Judah.

In those days and at that time I will cause a righteous Branch to spring up for David; and he shall execute justice and righteousness in the land.

In those days Judah will be saved and Jerusalem will live in safety. And this is the name by which it will be called: "The Lord is our righteousness."—The word of the Lord. ℟. **Thanks be to God.** ↓

RESPONSORIAL PSALM Ps.24 (25)   [Eye on God]

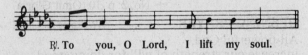

℟. To you, O Lord, I lift my soul.

(NRSV Text)	(GRAIL Text)
Make me to know your ways, O Lord,	Lord, make me know your ways.
teach me your paths.	Lord, teach me your paths.
Lead me in your truth and teach me,	Make me walk in your truth, and teach me,
for you are the God of my salvation.—℟.	for you are God my saviour.—℟.

Good and upright is the Lord,
therefore he instructs sinners in the way.
He leads the humble in what is right,
and teaches the humble his way.—
R̸.

All the paths of the Lord are steadfast love and faithfulness,
for those who keep his covenant and his decrees.
The friendship of the Lord is for those who fear him,
and he makes his covenant known to them.—R̸. ↓

The Lord is good and upright.
He shows the path to those who stray,
he guides the humble in the right path,
he teaches his way to the poor.—R̸.

His ways are faithfulness and love
for those who keep his covenant and will.
The Lord's friendship is for those who revere him;
to them he reveals his covenant.—
R̸. ↓

SECOND READING 1 Thess. 3.12—4.2 [Pleasing to God]

Paul prays that the Lord will increase love among the Thessalonians. In turn they must live a life pleasing to God so that they may progress in the way of perfection.

A reading from the first letter of Paul
to the Thessalonians

BELOVED: May the Lord make you increase and abound in love for one another and for all, just as we abound in love for you. And may he so strengthen your hearts in holiness that you may be blameless before our God and Father at the coming of our Lord Jesus with all his saints.

Finally, brothers and sisters, we ask and urge you in the Lord Jesus that, as you learned from us how you ought to live and to please God, as, in fact, you are doing, you should do so more and more. For you know what instructions we gave you through the Lord Jesus.—The word of the Lord. R̸. **Thanks be to God.** ↓

GOSPEL ACCLAMATION Ps. 84 (85).7

[God's Salvation]

(If the Alleluia is not sung, the acclamation is omitted.)

℣. Alleluia. ℟. **Alleluia.**
℣. Lord, show us your mercy and love,
and grant us your salvation.
℟. **Alleluia.** ↓

GOSPEL Lk. 21. 25-28, 34-36   [Prayerful Vigilance]

Jesus tells his disciples that there will be signs before his second coming. The sun, moon, stars, anguish among people, fright—these will warn of his coming. They should watch and pray to be able to stand with confidence before the Son of Man.

℣. The Lord be with you. ℟. **And also with you.**
✠ A reading from the holy gospel according to Luke. ℟. **Glory to you, Lord.**

JESUS spoke to his disciples about his return in glory. "There will be signs in the sun, the moon, and the stars and on the earth distress among nations confused by the roaring of the sea and the waves. People will faint from fear and foreboding of what is coming upon the world, for the powers of the heavens will be shaken.

"Then they will see 'the Son of Man coming in a cloud' with power and great glory. Now when these things begin to take place, stand up and raise your heads, because your redemption is drawing near.

"Be on guard so that your hearts are not weighed down with dissipation and drunkenness and the worries of this life, and that day catch you unexpectedly, like a trap. For it will come upon all who live on the face of the whole earth. Be alert at all times, praying that you may have the strength to escape all these things that will take place, and to stand before the Son of Man."—The gospel of the Lord. R̸. **Praise to you, Lord Jesus Christ.** ➜ No. 14, p. 18

PRAYER OVER THE GIFTS   [Promise of Eternal Life]

Father,
from all you give us
we present this bread and wine.
As we serve you now,
accept our offering
and sustain us with your promise of eternal life.
Grant this through Christ our Lord.
R̸. **Amen.**   ➜ No. 21, p. 24 (Pref. 1)

COMMUNION ANTIPHON Ps.84 (85).13

[A New World]

The Lord will shower his gifts, and our land will yield its fruit. ↓

PRAYER AFTER COMMUNION   [Love for Heaven]

Father,
may our communion
teach us to love heaven.
May its promise and hope
guide our way on earth.
We ask this through Christ our Lord.
R̸. **Amen.**   ➜ No. 32, p. 75

Optional Solemn Blessings, p. 96, and Prayers Over the People, p. 104

"He went into all the region around the Jordan, proclaiming a baptism of repentance."

DECEMBER 10

2nd SUNDAY OF ADVENT

ENTRANCE ANTIPHON See Isa. 30.19, 30

[Saving Lord]

People of Zion, the Lord will come to save all nations, and your hearts will exult to hear his majestic voice.   ➙ No. 2, p. 10 (Omit Gloria)

OPENING PRAYER   [Receiving Christ]

God of power and mercy,
open our hearts in welcome.
Remove the things that hinder us
from receiving Christ with joy,
so that we may share his wisdom
and become one with him
when he comes in glory,
for he lives and reigns with you and the Holy
   Spirit,
one God, for ever and ever. ℞. **Amen.** ↓

116

FIRST READING Bar. 5.1-9   [God's Favour on Jerusalem]

Baruch tells Jerusalem of God's favour. God will gather
the people together that Israel may grow secure in the
glory of God. God leads Israel in joy, mercy, and righteousness.

A reading from the book of the prophet Baruch

TAKE off the garment of your sorrow and affliction, O Jerusalem,
and put on forever the beauty of the glory from
God.
Put on the robe of the righteousness that
comes from God;
put on your head the diadem of the glory of the
Everlasting;
for God will show your splendour everywhere
under heaven.
For God will give you evermore the name,
"Righteous Peace, Godly Glory."

Arise, O Jerusalem, stand upon the height;
look toward the east,
and see your children gathered from west and
east
at the word of the Holy One,
rejoicing that God has remembered them.
For they went out from you on foot,
led away by their enemies;
but God will bring them back to you,
carried in glory, as on a royal throne.

For God has ordered that every high mountain
and the everlasting hills be made low
and the valleys filled up, to make level ground,
so that Israel may walk safely in the glory of
God.

The woods and every fragrant tree
have shaded Israel at God's command.
For God will lead Israel with joy,
in the light of his glory,
with the mercy and righteousness that come
    from him.
The word of the Lord. ℟. **Thanks be to God.** ↓

RESPONSORIAL PSALM Ps. 125 (126)

[God's Wonders]

℟. **The Lord has done great things for us; we are filled with joy.**

(NRSV Text)	(GRAIL Text)
When the Lord restored the fortunes of Zion, we were like those who dream. Then our mouth was filled with laughter, and our tongue with shouts of joy.— ℟.	When the Lord delivered Zion from bondage, it seemed like a dream. Then was our mouth filled with laughter, on our lips there were songs.— ℟.
Then it was said among the nations, "The Lord has done great things for them." The Lord has done great things for us, and we rejoiced.— ℟.	The heathens themselves said: "What marvels the Lord worked for them!" What marvels the Lord worked for us! Indeed we were glad.— ℟.
Restore our fortunes, O Lord, like the watercourses in the desert of the Negev. May those who sow in tears reap with shouts of joy.— ℟.	Deliver us, O Lord, from our bondage as streams in dry land. Those who were sowing in tears will sing when they reap.— ℟.
Those who go out weeping, bearing the seed for sowing, shall come home with shouts of joy, carrying their sheaves.-- ℟. ↓	They go out, they go out, full of tears, carrying seed for the sowing; they come back, they come back, full of song, carrying their sheaves.— ℟. ↓

SECOND READING Phil. 1. 3-6, 8-11   [Prayers in Faith]

Paul rejoices in the progress of faith among the Philippians. He is sure that God who began this good work
will help it grow. Paul prays that their love may continue to grow so that they may be rich in harvest.

A reading from the letter of Paul
to the Philippians

MY brothers and sisters, I thank my God
every time I remember you, constantly
praying with joy in every one of my prayers for
all of you, because of your sharing in the
gospel from the first day until now.

I am confident of this, that the one who
began a good work among you will bring it to
completion by the day of Jesus Christ.

For God is my witness, how I long for all of
you with the compassion of Christ Jesus. And
this is my prayer, that your love may overflow
more and more with knowledge and full in-
sight to help you to determine what is best so
that in the day of Christ you may be pure and
blameless, having produced the harvest of
righteousness that comes through Jesus Christ
for the glory and praise of God.—The word of
the Lord. ℟. **Thanks be to God.** ↓

GOSPEL ACCLAMATION Lk. 3.4, 6   [All Shall See]

(If the Alleluia is not sung, the acclamation is omitted.)

℣. Alleluia. ℟. **Alleluia.**
℣. Prepare the way of the Lord, make straight
his paths:
all people shall see the salvation of God.
℟. **Alleluia.** ↓

GOSPEL Lk. 3.1-6   [Prepare for the Lord]

Luke outlines some historical facts at the time of John the Baptist's preaching. It is the fulfilment of the prophecy of Isaiah. John prepares the way for the Lord.

℣. The Lord be with you. ℟. **And also with you.**
✛ A reading from the holy gospel according to Luke. ℟. **Glory to you, Lord.**

IN the fifteenth year of the reign of Emperor Tiberius, when Pontius Pilate was governor of Judea, and Herod was ruler of Galilee, and his brother Philip ruler of the region of Ituraea and Trachonitis, and Lysanias ruler of Abilene, during the high priesthood of Annas and Caiaphas, the word of God came to John son of Zechariah in the wilderness.

He went into all the region around the Jordan, proclaiming a baptism of repentance for the forgiveness of sins, as it is written in the book of the words of the prophet Isaiah,

"The voice of one crying out in the wilderness:
'Prepare the way of the Lord,
    make his paths straight.
Every valley shall be filled,
    and every mountain and hill shall be made
        low,
and the crooked shall be made straight,
    and the rough ways made smooth;
    and all flesh shall see the salvation of God.' "

The gospel of the Lord. ℟. **Praise to you, Lord Jesus Christ.**   ➜ No. 14, p. 18

PRAYER OVER THE GIFTS   [Our Offering]

Lord,
we are nothing without you.
As you sustain us with your mercy,
receive our prayers and offerings.
We ask this through Christ our Lord.
℟. **Amen.**   ➜ No. 21, p. 24 (Pref. 1)

COMMUNION ANTIPHON Bar. 5.5; 4.36 [Coming Joy]

**Rise up, Jerusalem, stand on the heights, and
see the joy that is coming to you from God.** ↓

PRAYER AFTER COMMUNION   [Wise Judgment]

Father,
you give us food from heaven.
By our sharing in this mystery,
teach us to judge wisely the things of earth
and to love the things of heaven.
Grant this through Christ our Lord.
℟. **Amen.**   ➜ No. 32, p. 75

Optional Solemn Blessings, p. 96, and Prayers Over the People, p. 104

"John proclaimed the good news to the people."

DECEMBER 17

3rd SUNDAY OF ADVENT

ENTRANCE ANTIPHON Phil. 4.4, 5   [Mounting Joy]
**Rejoice in the Lord always; again I say, rejoice!
The Lord is near.**   → No. 2, p. 10 (Omit Gloria)

OPENING PRAYER   [Joy of Salvation]
Lord God,
may we, your people,
who look forward to the birthday of Christ
experience the joy of salvation
and celebrate that feast with love and thanks-
     giving.
We ask this through our Lord Jesus Christ,
     your Son,
who lives and reigns with you and the Holy
     Spirit,
one God, for ever and ever. ℟. **Amen.** ↓

FIRST READING Zeph. 3.14-18a   [Joy Over the Saviour]

Zephaniah writes that Israel should shout for joy. Her king, the Lord, is in her midst. The Lord is a mighty saviour. Israel should not be discouraged.

A reading from the book of the
prophet Zephaniah

SING aloud, O daughter Zion; shout, O Israel!
Rejoice and exult with all your heart,
O daughter of Jerusalem!
The Lord has taken away the judgments
    against you,
 he has turned away your enemies.
The king of Israel, the Lord, is in your midst;
you shall fear disaster no more.

On that day it shall be said to Jerusalem:
Do not fear, O Zion;
do not let your hands grow weak.
The Lord, your God, is in your midst,
a warrior who gives victory;
he will rejoice over you with gladness,
he will renew you in his love.
The Lord, your God, will exult over you with
    loud singing
as on a day of festival.
The word of the Lord. ℟. **Thanks be to God.** ↓

RESPONSORIAL CANTICLE Isa. 12
[Joy Over the Holy One]

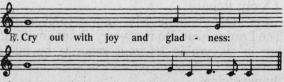

℟. Cry out with joy and glad - ness:

for among you is the great and Holy One of Is - ra - el.

(℟. Sing and shout for joy for great in your midst is the Holy One of Israel.)

(NRSV Text)	(GRAIL Text)
Surely God is my salvation; I will trust, and will not be afraid, for the Lord God is my strength and my might; he has become my salvation. With joy you will draw water from the wells of salvation.—℟.	Truly, God is my salvation, I trust, I shall not fear. For the Lord is my strength, my song, he became my saviour. With joy you will draw water from the wells of salvation.—℟.
Give thanks to the Lord, call on his name; make known his deeds among the nations; proclaim that his name is exalted.—℟.	Give thanks to the Lord, give praise to his name! Make his mighty deeds known to the peoples! Declare the greatness of his name.—℟.
Sing praises to the Lord, for he has done gloriously; let this be known in all the earth. Shout aloud and sing for joy, O royal Zion, for great in your midst is the Holy One of Israel.—℟. ↓	Sing a psalm to the Lord for he has done glorious deeds, make them known to all the earth! People of Zion, sing and shout for joy for great in your midst is the Holy One of Israel.—℟. ↓

SECOND READING Phil. 4.4-7   [Rejoice in the Lord]

Christians should rejoice in the Lord. We should take our prayers and petitions to God, who watches over us as beloved children.

A reading from the letter of Paul
to the Philippians

REJOICE in the Lord always; again I will say, Rejoice.

Let your gentleness be known to everyone. The Lord is near. Do not worry about anything, but in everything let your requests be made known to God by prayer and supplication with thanksgiving.

And the peace of God, which surpasses all understanding, will guard your hearts and your minds in Christ Jesus.—The word of the Lord. ℟. **Thanks be to God.** ↓

GOSPEL ACCLAMATION Lk. 4.18 (Isa. 61.1)

[Good News]

(If the Alleluia is not sung, the acclamation is omitted.)

℣. Alleluia. ℟. **Alleluia.**
℣. The Spirit of the Lord now upon me
has sent me to bring good news to the poor.
℟. **Alleluia.** ↓

GOSPEL Lk. 3.10-18   [Majesty of the Messiah]

John preached a law of sharing. He baptized and admonished all to be just and loving and to pray. John tells the people about the majesty of the Messiah.

℣. The Lord be with you. ℟. **And also with you.**
✣ A reading from the holy gospel according to Luke. ℟. **Glory to you, Lord.**

THE crowds, who were gathering to be baptized by John, asked him, "What should we do?" In reply John said to them, "Whoever has two coats must share with anyone who has none; and whoever has food must do likewise."

Even tax collectors came to be baptized, and they asked him, "Teacher, what should we do?" He said to them, "Collect no more than the amount prescribed for you." Soldiers also asked him, "And we, what should we do?" He said to them, "Do not extort money from anyone by threats or false accusation, and be satisfied with your wages."

As the people were filled with expectation, and all were questioning in their hearts concerning John, whether he might be the Messiah, John answered all of them by saying, "I baptize you with water; but one who is more powerful than I is coming; I am not worthy to untie the thong of his sandals. He will baptize you with the Holy Spirit and fire. His winnowing-fork is in his hand, to clear his threshing floor and to gather the wheat into his granary; but the chaff he will burn with unquenchable fire."

So, with many other exhortations, John proclaimed the good news to the people.—The gospel of the Lord. ℟. **Praise to you, Lord Jesus Christ.**   → No. 14, p. 18

PRAYER OVER THE GIFTS   [Continual Sacrifice]

Lord,
may the gift we offer in faith and love
be a continual sacrifice in your honour
and truly become our eucharist and our salvation.
We ask this in the name of Jesus the Lord.
℟. **Amen.**   → No. 21, p. 24 (Pref. 1)

COMMUNION ANTIPHON See Isa. 35.4 [Trust in God]

Say to the anxious: be strong and fear not, our God will come to save us. ↓

PRAYER AFTER COMMUNION   [Preparation]

God of mercy,
may this eucharist bring us your divine help,
free us from our sins,
and prepare us for the birthday of our Saviour,

who is Lord for ever and ever.
R̸. **Amen.**   ➜ No. 32, p. 75

Optional Solemn Blessings, p. 96, and Prayers Over the People, p. 104

"Blessed are you among women, and blessed
is the fruit of your womb."

DECEMBER 24

4th SUNDAY OF ADVENT

ENTRANCE ANTIPHON Isa. 45.8   [The Advent Plea]
**Let the clouds rain down the Just One, and the
earth bring forth a Saviour.**

➜ No. 2, p. 10 (Omit Gloria)

OPENING PRAYER   [From Suffering to Glory]
Lord,
fill our hearts with your love,
and as you revealed to us by an angel
the coming of your Son as man,
so lead us through his suffering and death
to the glory of his resurrection,

for he lives and reigns with you and the Holy
   Spirit,
one God, for ever and ever. ℟. **Amen.** ↓

FIRST READING Mic. 5.2-5a [The Messiah from Bethlehem]

**Micah speaks of the glory of Bethlehem, a little town of
Judah. From Bethlehem will come forth the promised
one who will stand firm and strong in the Lord.**

A reading from the book of the prophet Micah

THE Lord says to his people:
   "You, O Bethlehem of Ephrathah,
who are one of the little clans of Judea,
from you shall come forth for me
one who is to rule in Israel,
whose origin is from of old, from ancient days."

Therefore he shall give them up until the time
when she who is in labour has brought forth;
then the rest of his kindred
shall return to the people of Israel.
And he shall stand and feed his flock
in the strength of the Lord,
in the majesty of the name of the Lord his God.

And they shall live secure,
for now he shall be great to the ends of the earth;
and he shall be the one of peace.
The word of the Lord. ℟. **Thanks be to God.** ↓

RESPONSORIAL PSALM Ps. 79 (80) [Turn to the Lord]

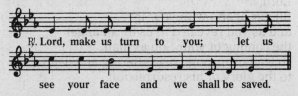

℟. Lord, make us turn to you; let us
see your face and we shall be saved.

(℟. **God of hosts, bring us back; let your face shine on us and we shall be saved.**)

(NRSV Text)	**(GRAIL Text)**
Give ear, O Shepherd of Israel, you who are enthroned upon the cherubim, shine forth. Stir up your might, and come to save us.—℟.	O Shepherd of Israel, hear us, shine forth from your cherubim throne. O Lord, rouse up your might, O Lord, come to our help.—℟.
Turn again, O God of hosts, look down from heaven and see; have regard for this vine, the stock that your right hand has planted.—℟.	God of hosts, turn again, we implore, look down from heaven and see. Visit the vine and protect it, the vine your right hand has planted.—℟.
But let your hand be upon the one at your right, the one whom you have made strong for yourself. Then we will never turn back from you; give us life, and we will call on your name.—℟. ↓	May your hand be on the one you have chosen, the one you have given your strength. And we shall never forsake you again; give us life that we may call upon your name.—℟. ↓

SECOND READING Heb. 10.5-10   [Doing God's Will]

Jesus said that sacrifices, sin offerings, and burnt offerings did not delight the Lord. But he has come to do the will of God—to establish a second covenant.

A reading from the letter to the Hebrews

WHEN Christ came into the world, he said, "Sacrifices and offerings you have not desired,
 but a body you have prepared for me;
in burnt offerings and sin offerings
 you have taken no pleasure.
Then I said,
 as it is written of me in the scroll of the book,

'See, God, I have come to do your will, O
    God.' "

When Christ said, "You have neither desired
nor taken pleasure in sacrifices and offerings
and burnt offerings and sin offerings" (these
are offered according to the law), then he
added, "See, I have come to do your will." He
abolishes the first in order to establish the second.

And it is by God's will that we have been
sanctified through the offering of the body of
Jesus Christ once for all.—The word of the
Lord. ℟. **Thanks be to God.** ↓

GOSPEL ACCLAMATION Lk. 1.38 [The Lord's Servant]

(If the Alleluia is not sung, the acclamation is omitted.)

℣. Alleluia. ℟. **Alleluia.**
℣. I am the servant of the Lord:
let it be done to me according to your word.
℟. **Alleluia.** ↓

GOSPEL Lk. 1.39-45   [The Visitation]

Mary went to visit Elizabeth who was also blessed by
the Holy Spirit. Elizabeth greeted Mary: "Blessed are
you among women, and blessed is the fruit of your
womb."

℣. The Lord be with you. ℟. **And also with you.**
✠ A reading from the holy gospel according to
Luke. ℟. **Glory to you, Lord.**

MARY set out and went with haste to a
Judean town in the hill country, where she
entered the house of Zechariah and greeted
Elizabeth.

When Elizabeth heard Mary's greeting, the child leaped in her womb. And Elizabeth was filled with the Holy Spirit and exclaimed with a loud cry, "Blessed are you among women, and blessed is the fruit of your womb. And why has this happened to me, that the mother of my Lord comes to me? For as soon as I heard the sound of your greeting, the child in my womb leaped for joy. And blessed is she who believed that there would be a fulfilment of what was spoken to her by the Lord."—The gospel of the Lord. ℟.
Praise to you, Lord Jesus Christ.   ➙ No. 14, p. 18

PRAYER OVER THE GIFTS   [Power of the Spirit]
Lord,
may the power of the Spirit,
which sanctified Mary the mother of your Son,
make holy the gifts we place upon this altar.
Grant this through Christ our Lord.
℟. **Amen.**   ➙ No. 21, p. 24 (Pref. 2)

COMMUNION ANTIPHON Isa. 7.14   [Virgin Mother]
The Virgin is with child and shall bear a son, and she will call him Emmanuel. ↓

PRAYER AFTER COMMUNION [Growth in Holiness]
Lord, in this sacrament
we receive the promise of salvation;
as Christmas draws near
make us grow in faith and love
to celebrate the coming of Christ our Saviour,
who is Lord for ever and ever.
℟. **Amen.**   ➙ No. 32, p. 75

Optional Solemn Blessings, p. 96, and Prayers Over the People, p. 104

The Word is made flesh.

DECEMBER 25

CHRISTMAS

MASS AT MIDNIGHT

ENTRANCE ANTIPHON Ps. 2.7   [Son of God]
The Lord said to me: You are my Son; this day have I begotten you.

OR   [True Peace]
Let us all rejoice in the Lord, for our Saviour is born to the world. True peace has descended from heaven.   → No. 2, p. 10

OPENING PRAYER   [Eternal Joy]
Father,
you make this holy night radiant
with the splendour of Jesus Christ our light.
We welcome him as Lord, the true light of the
    world.
Bring us to eternal joy in the kingdom of heaven,
where he lives and reigns with you and the
    Holy Spirit,
one God, for ever and ever. ℟. **Amen.** ↓

FIRST READING Isa. 9.2-4, 6-7 [The Messiah's Kingdom]

The Messiah is a promise of peace for the world. His
reign shall be vast and filled with justice. The power of
God is revealed through the weakness of humans.

A reading from the book of the prophet Isaiah

THE people who walked in darkness
   have seen a great light;
those who lived in a land of deep darkness—
on them light has shone.
You have multiplied the nation,
you have increased its joy;
they rejoice before you
as with joy at the harvest,
as people exult when dividing plunder.
For the yoke of their burden,
and the bar across their shoulders,
the rod of their oppressor,
you have broken as on the day of Midian.
For a child has been born for us,
a son given to us;
authority rests upon his shoulders;
and he is named
Wonderful Counsellor, Mighty God,
Everlasting Father, Prince of Peace.
His authority shall grow continually,
and there shall be endless peace
for the throne of David and his kingdom.
He will establish and uphold it
with justice and with righteousness
from this time onward and forevermore.
The zeal of the Lord of hosts will do this.
The word of the Lord. ℟. **Thanks be to God.** ↓

RESPONSORIAL PSALM Ps. 95 (96)   [Bless the Lord]

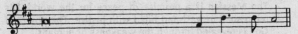

℟. **Today is born our Sav - iour, Christ the Lord.**

(℟. **Today a Saviour has been born to us; he is Christ the Lord.**)

(NRSV Text)	**(GRAIL Text)**
O sing to the Lord a new song; sing to the Lord, all the earth. Sing to the Lord, bless his name; tell of his salvation from day to day.—℟.	O sing a new song to the Lord, sing to the Lord all the earth. O sing to the Lord, bless his name.—℟.
Declare his glory among the nations, his marvellous works among all the peoples. For great is the Lord, and greatly to be praised; he is to be revered above all gods.—℟.	Proclaim his help day by day, tell among the nations his glory and his wonders among all the peoples.—℟.
Let the heavens be glad, and let the earth rejoice; let the sea roar, and all that fills it; let the field exult, and everything in it. Then shall all the trees of the forest sing for joy.—℟.	Let the heavens rejoice and earth be glad, let the sea and all within it thunder praise; let the land and all it bears rejoice.—℟.
Rejoice before the Lord; for he is coming, for he is coming to judge the earth. He will judge the world with righteousness, and the peoples with his truth.—℟. ↓	All the trees of the wood shout for joy. At the presence of the Lord for he comes, he comes to rule the earth. With justice he will rule the world, he will judge the peoples with his truth.—℟. ↓

SECOND READING Titus 2.11-14   [Salvation for All]

God offers salvation to all people. His way asks us to reject worldly desires—to live temperately and justly. He even asked the only Son to sacrifice himself to redeem us.

A reading from the letter of Paul to Titus

THE grace of God has appeared, bringing salvation to all, training us to renounce impiety and worldly passions, and in the present age to live lives that are self-controlled, upright, and godly, while we wait for the blessed hope and the manifestation of the glory of our great God and Saviour, Jesus Christ.

He it is who gave himself for us that he might redeem us from all iniquity and purify for himself a people of his own who are zealous for good deeds.—The word of the Lord. ℟. **Thanks be to God.** ↓

GOSPEL ACCLAMATION Lk. 2.10-11   [News of Joy]
(If the Alleluia is not sung, the acclamation is omitted.)

℣. Alleluia. ℟. **Alleluia.**
℣. Good news and great joy to all the world: today is born our Saviour, Christ the Lord.
℟. **Alleluia.** ↓

GOSPEL Lk. 2.1-16   [Birth of Christ]
Caesar Augustus desired a world census. Joseph and Mary go to Bethlehem where Jesus, the Lord of the universe, is born in a stable. Glory to God and peace on earth!

℣. The Lord be with you. ℟. **And also with you.**
✚ A reading from the holy gospel according to Luke. ℟. **Glory to you, Lord.**

IN those days a decree went out from Emperor Augustus that all the world should be registered. This was the first registration and was taken while Quirinius was governor of Syria. All went to their own towns to be registered. Joseph also went from the town of Nazareth in Galilee to Judea, to the city of

David called Bethlehem, because he was descended from the house and family of David. He went to be registered with Mary, to whom he was engaged and who was expecting a child.

While they were there, the time came for her to deliver her child. And she gave birth to her firstborn son and wrapped him in bands of cloth, and laid him in a manger, because there was no place for them in the inn.

In that region there were shepherds living in the fields, keeping watch over their flock by night. Then an angel of the Lord stood before them, and the glory of the Lord shone around them, and they were terrified. But the angel said to them, "Do not be afraid; for see—I am bringing you good news of great joy for all the people: to you is born this day in the city of David a Saviour, who is the Messiah, the Lord. This will be a sign for you: you will find a child wrapped in bands of cloth and lying in a manger."

And suddenly there was with the angel a multitude of the heavenly host, praising God and saying,

"Glory to God in the highest heaven,
    and on earth peace among those whom he favours!"

When the angels had left them and gone into heaven, the shepherds said to one another, "Let us go now to Bethlehem and see this thing that has taken place, which the Lord has made known to us." So they went with haste and found Mary and Joseph, and the child lying in the manger.—The gospel of the Lord. ℟. **Praise to you, Lord Jesus Christ.**   → No. 14, p. 18

In the profession of faith, all genuflect at the words, and became man.

PRAYER OVER THE GIFTS   [Become Like Christ]
Lord,
accept our gifts on this joyful feast of our salvation.
By our communion with God made man,
may we become more like him
who joins our lives to yours,
for he is Lord for ever and ever.
℟. **Amen.**   ➜ No. 21, p. 24 (Pref. 3-5)

When Eucharistic Prayer I is used, the special Christ-mas form of In union with the whole Church *is said.*

COMMUNION ANTIPHON Jn. 1.14   [Glory of Christ]
The Word of God became man; we have seen his glory. ↓

PRAYER AFTER COMMUNION   [Following Christ]
God our Father,
we rejoice in the birth of our Saviour.
May we share his life completely
by living as he has taught.
We ask this in the name of Jesus the Lord.
℟. **Amen.**   ➜ No. 32, p. 75

Optional Solemn Blessings, p. 96, and Prayers Over the People, p. 104

MASS AT DAWN

ENTRANCE ANTIPHON See Isa. 9.2, 6; Lk. 1.33
[Prince of Peace]

A light will shine on us this day, the Lord is born for us: he shall be called Wonderful God, Prince of peace, Father of the world to come; and his kingship will never end.   ➜ No. 2, p. 10

OPENING PRAYER   [Light of Faith]

Father,
we are filled with the new light
by the coming of your Word among us.
May the light of faith
shine in our words and actions.
Grant this . . . for ever and ever. R̸. **Amen.** ↓

FIRST READING Isa. 62.11-12   [The Saviour's Birth]

**Isaiah foretells the birth of the Saviour who will come to
Zion. These people will be called holy, and they shall be
redeemed.**

A reading from the book of the prophet Isaiah

THE Lord has proclaimed to the end of the
earth:
"Say to daughter Zion,
See, your salvation comes;
his reward is with him,
and his recompense before him.

"They shall be called 'The Holy People,'
'The Redeemed of the Lord';
and you shall be called 'Sought Out,'
'A City Not Forsaken.' "
The word of the Lord. R̸. **Thanks be to God.** ↓

RESPONSORIAL PSALM Ps. 96 (97)   [Be Glad]

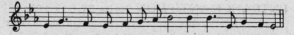

R̸. A light will shine on us this day: the Lord is born for us.

(R̸. **This day new light will shine on the earth; the Lord is
born for us.**)

(NRSV Text)	**(GRAIL Text)**
The Lord is king! Let the earth rejoice; let the many coastlands be glad!	The Lord is king, let earth rejoice, let all the coastlands be glad.
Clouds and thick darkness are all around him;	Cloud and darkness are his raiment; his throne, justice and right.—℟.
righteousness and justice are the foundation of his throne.—℟.	
The mountains melt like wax before the Lord,	The mountains melt like wax before the Lord of all the earth.
before the Lord of all the earth.	The skies proclaim his justice;
The heavens proclaim his righteousness;	all peoples see his glory.—℟.
and all the peoples behold his glory.—℟.	
Light dawns for the righteous,	Light shines forth for the just
and joy for the upright in heart.	and joy for the upright of heart.
Rejoice in the Lord, O you righteous, and give thanks to his holy name!—℟. ↓	Rejoice, you just, in the Lord; give glory to his holy name.—℟. ↓

SECOND READING Titus 3.4-7   [Saved by God's Mercy]

Christians are saved not because of their own merits but because of the mercy of God. We are saved through baptism and renewal in the Holy Spirit.

A reading from the letter of Paul to Titus

WHEN the goodness and loving kindness of God our Saviour appeared, he saved us, not because of any works of righteousness that we had done, but according to his mercy, through the water of rebirth and renewal by the Holy Spirit. This Spirit he poured out on us richly through Jesus Christ our Saviour, so that, having been justified by his grace, we might become heirs according to the hope of eternal life.—The word of the Lord. ℟. **Thanks be to God.** ↓

GOSPEL ACCLAMATION Lk. 2.14 [Glory and Peace]

(If the Alleluia is not sung, the acclamation is omitted.)

℣. Alleluia. ℟. **Alleluia.**
℣. Glory to God in the highest,
peace to God's people on earth.
℟. **Alleluia.** ↓

GOSPEL Lk. 2.15-20 [Jesus, the God-Man]

The shepherds, the poor of the people of God, come to pay homage to Jesus. Mary ponders and prays over the great event of God becoming one of us.

℣. The Lord be with you. ℟. **And also with you.**
✝ A reading from the holy gospel according to Luke. ℟. **Glory to you, Lord.**

WHEN the angels had left them and gone into heaven, the shepherds said to one another, "Let us go now to Bethlehem and see this thing that has taken place, which the Lord has made known to us."

So they went with haste and found Mary and Joseph, and the child lying in the manger. When they saw this, they made known what had been told them about this child; and all who heard it were amazed at what the shepherds told them.

But Mary treasured all these words and pondered them in her heart. The shepherds returned, glorifying and praising God for all they had heard and seen, as it had been told them.— The gospel of the Lord. ℟. **Praise to you, Lord Jesus Christ.**   → No. 14, p. 18

In the profession of faith, all genuflect at the words, and became man.

PRAYER OVER THE GIFTS   [Gift of Divine Life]

Father,
may we follow the example of your Son
who became man and lived among us.
May we receive the gift of divine life
through these offerings here on earth.
We ask this in the name of Jesus the Lord.
℞. **Amen.**   ➔ No. 21, p. 24 (Pref. 3-5)

When Eucharistic Prayer I is used, the special Christ-
mas form of In union with the whole Church *is said.*

COMMUNION ANTIPHON See Zech. 9.9

[The Holy One]

Daughter of Zion, exult; shout aloud, daughter
of Jerusalem! Your King is coming, the Holy
One, the Saviour of the world. ↓

PRAYER AFTER COMMUNION   [Riches of Christ]

Lord,
with faith and joy
we celebrate the birthday of your Son.
Increase our understanding and our love
of the riches you have revealed in him,
who is Lord for ever and ever.
℞. **Amen.**   ➔ No. 32, p. 75

Optional Solemn Blessings, p. 96, and Prayers Over the People, p. 104

MASS DURING THE DAY

ENTRANCE ANTIPHON Isa. 9.6   [Gift of God's Son]

A child is born for us, a son given to us; domin-
ion is laid on his shoulder, and he shall be
called Wonderful Counsellor.   ➔ No. 2, p. 10

OPENING PRAYER   [Share in Christ's Glory]

Lord God,
we praise you for creating man,
and still more for restoring him in Christ.
Your Son shared our weakness:
may we share his glory,
for he lives and reigns with you and the Holy
    Spirit,
one God, for ever and ever. ℟. **Amen.** ↓

FIRST READING Isa. 52.7-10   [Your God Is King]

**God shows salvation to all people. God brings peace
and good news. God comforts and redeems the faithful.**

A reading from the book of the prophet Isaiah

HOW beautiful upon the mountains
    are the feet of the messenger who an-
        nounces peace,
who brings good news,
who announces salvation,
who says to Zion, "Your God reigns."

Listen! Your sentinels lift up their voices,
together they sing for joy;
for in plain sight they see
the return of the Lord to Zion.

Break forth together into singing,
you ruins of Jerusalem;
for the Lord has comforted his people,
he has redeemed Jerusalem.
The Lord has bared his holy arm
before the eyes of all the nations;
and all the ends of the earth shall see the salva-
    tion of our God.
The word of the Lord. ℟. **Thanks be to God.** ↓

RESPONSORIAL PSALM Ps. 97 (98) [Sing a New Song]

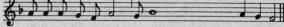

℟. All the ends of the earth have seen the saving   power of God.

(℟. **All the ends of the earth have seen the salvation of our God.**)

(NRSV Text)	(GRAIL Text)
O sing to the Lord a new song, for he has done marvellous things. His right hand and his holy arm have brought him victory.—℟.	Sing a new song to the Lord for he has worked wonders. His right hand and his holy arm have brought salvation.—℟.
The Lord has made known his victory; he has revealed his vindication in the sight of the nations. He has remembered his steadfast love and faithfulness to the house of Israel.—℟.	The Lord has made known his salvation; has shown his justice to the nations. He has remembered his truth and love for the house of Israel.—℟.
All the ends of the earth have seen the victory of our God. Make a joyful noise to the Lord, all the earth; break forth into joyous song and sing praises.—℟.	All the ends of the earth have seen the salvation of our God. Shout to the Lord, all the earth, ring out your joy.—℟.
Sing praises to the Lord with the lyre, with the lyre and the sound of melody. With trumpets and the sound of the horn make a joyful noise before the King, the Lord.—℟. ↓	Sing psalms to the Lord with the harp with the sound of music. With trumpets and the sound of the horn acclaim the King, the Lord.—℟. ↓

SECOND READING Heb. 1.1-6 [God Speaks through Jesus]

God now speaks through Jesus, the Son, who reflects God's glory. The Son cleanses us from sin. Heaven and earth should worship him.

A reading from the letter to the Hebrews

LONG ago God spoke to our ancestors in many and various ways by the prophets,

but in these last days he has spoken to us by a
Son, whom he appointed heir of all things,
through whom he also created the worlds.

He is the reflection of God's glory and the
exact imprint of God's very being, and he sus-
tains all things by his powerful word. When he
had made purification for sins, he sat down at
the right hand of the Majesty on high, having
become as much superior to angels as the name
he has inherited is more excellent than theirs.

For to which of the angels did God ever say,
  "You are my Son;
      today I have begotten you"?
Or again,
  "I will be his Father,
      and he will be my Son"?
And again, when he brings the firstborn into
the world, he says,
  "Let all God's angels worship him."
The word of the Lord. ℟. **Thanks be to God.** ↓

GOSPEL ACCLAMATION   [Adore the Lord]

(If the Alleluia is not sung, the acclamation is omitted.)

℣. Alleluia. ℟. **Alleluia.**
℣. A holy day has dawned upon us.
Come you nations, and adore the Lord.
Today a great light has come upon the earth.
℟. **Alleluia.** ↓

GOSPEL Jn. 1.1-18 or 1.1-5, 9-14   [The True Light]
  John's opening words parallel the Book of Genesis.
  Jesus is the Word made flesh, the light of the world,
  who always was and will ever be.

*[If the "Short Form" is used, the indented text in
brackets is omitted.]*

℣. The Lord be with you. ℟. **And also with you.**
✠ A reading from the holy gospel according to
John. ℟. **Glory to you, Lord.**

IN the beginning was the Word, and the Word
was with God, and the Word was God. He
was in the beginning with God. All things came
into being through him, and without him not
one thing came into being. What has come into
being in him was life, and the life was the light
of all people.

The light shines in the darkness, and the
darkness did not overcome it.

[There was a man sent from God, whose
name was John. He came as a witness to
testify to the light, so that all might believe
through him. He himself was not the light,
but he came to testify to the light.]

The true light, which enlightens everyone,
was coming into the world. He was in the
world, and the world came into being through
him; yet the world did not know him. He came
to what was his own, and his own people did
not accept him. But to all who received him,
who believed in his name, he gave power to become children of God, who were born, not of
blood or of the will of the flesh or of the will of
man, but of God. And the Word became flesh
and lived among us, and we have seen his
glory, the glory as of a father's only son, full of
grace and truth.

[John testified to him and cried out,
"This was he of whom I said, 'He who
comes after me ranks ahead of me because
he was before me.'"]

From his fullness we have all received, grace upon grace. The law indeed was given through Moses; grace and truth came through Jesus Christ. No one has ever seen God. It is God the only Son, who is close to the Father's heart, who has made him known.]

The gospel of the Lord. ℟. **Praise to you, Lord Jesus Christ.** → No. 14, p. 18

In the profession of faith, all genuflect at the words, and became man.

PRAYER OVER THE GIFTS [Peace and Praise]

Almighty God,
the saving work of Christ
made our peace with you.
May our offering today
renew that peace within us
and give you perfect praise.
We ask this in the name of Jesus the Lord.
℟. **Amen.** → No. 21, p. 24 (Pref. 3-5)

When Eucharistic Prayer I is used, the special Christmas form of In union with the whole Church *is said.*

COMMUNION ANTIPHON Ps. 96 (97). 3 [God's Power]

All the ends of the earth have seen the saving power of God. ↓

PRAYER AFTER COMMUNION [Children of God]

Father,
the child born today is the Saviour of the world.
He made us your children.
May he welcome us into your kingdom,
where he lives and reigns with you for ever
and ever.
℟. **Amen.** → No. 32, p. 75

Optional Solemn Blessings, p. 96, and Prayers Over the People, p. 104

"Jesus went down with them and came to Nazareth, and was obedient to them."

DECEMBER 31

HOLY FAMILY

ENTRANCE ANTIPHON Lk. 2.16 [Jesus, Mary, Joseph]

The shepherds hastened to Bethlehem, where they found Mary and Joseph, and the baby lying in a manger. → No. 2, p. 10

OPENING PRAYER [Peace in Families]

Father,
help us to live as the holy family,
united in respect and love.
Bring us to the joy and peace of your eternal
   home.
Grant this . . . for ever and ever. ℟. **Amen.** ↓

FIRST READING 1 Sam. 1.11, 20-22, 24-28

[God's Creative Love]

This reading teaches us that motherhood and life are a gift of God. The presence of children in a family signals the continuation of life and manifests the newness of God's love, which gives origin to ever new creatures.

147

A reading from the first book of Samuel

HANNAH, wife of Elkanah, had no children; she prayed to the Lord and made this vow: "O Lord of hosts, if only you will look on the misery of your servant, and remember me, and not forget your servant, but will give to your servant a male child, then I will set him before you as a nazirite until the day of his death. He shall drink neither wine nor intoxicants, and no razor shall touch his head."

In due time Hannah conceived and bore a son. She named him Samuel, for she said, "I have asked him of the Lord." Elkanah and all his household went up to offer to the Lord the yearly sacrifice, and to pay his vow. But Hannah did not go up, for she said to her husband, "As soon as the child is weaned, I will bring him, that he may appear in the presence of the Lord, and remain there forever; I will offer him as a nazirite for all time."

When she had weaned him, she took him up with her, along with a three-year old bull, a measure of flour, and a skin of wine. She brought him to the house of the Lord at Shiloh; and the child was young. Then they slaughtered the bull, and they brought the child to Eli. And she said, "Oh, my lord! As you live, my lord, I am the woman who was standing here in your presence, praying to the Lord. For this child I prayed; and the Lord has granted me the petition that I made to him. Therefore I have lent him to the Lord; as long as he lives, he is given to the Lord." She left him there for the Lord.—The word of the Lord. ℟. **Thanks be to God.** ↓

RESPONSORIAL PSALM Ps. 83 (84)

[Love for God's House]

℟. **Blessed**   are they who dwell in your house, O Lord.

(NRSV Text)	(GRAIL Text)
How lovely is your dwelling place, O Lord of hosts! My soul longs, indeed it faints for the courts of the Lord; my heart and my flesh sing for joy to the living God.—℟.	How lovely is your dwelling place, Lord, God of hosts. My soul is longing and yearning, is yearning for the courts of the Lord. My heart and my soul ring out their joy to God, the living God.—℟.
Happy are those who live in your house, ever singing your praise. Happy are those whose strength is in you, in whose heart are the highways to Zion.—℟.	They are happy, who dwell in your house, for ever singing your praise. They are happy, whose strength is in you, in whose hearts are the roads to Zion.—℟.
O Lord God of hosts, hear my prayer; give ear, O God of Jacob! Behold our shield, O God; look on the face of your anointed.—℟.	O Lord God of hosts, hear my prayer, give ear, O God of Jacob. Turn your eyes, O God, our shield, look on the face of your anointed.—℟.
For a day in your courts is better than a thousand elsewhere. I would rather be a doorkeeper in the house of my God than live in the tents of wickedness.—℟. ↓	One day within your courts is better than a thousand elsewhere. The threshold of the house of God I prefer to the dwellings of the wicked.—℟. ↓

SECOND READING 1 Jn. 3.1-2, 21-24　[Children of God]

Every family must be a mirror of the divine love because the root of every love is God. Therefore, members of a family should deal lovingly with one another.

A reading from the first letter of John

SEE what love the Father has given us, that we should be called children of God; and that is what we are. The reason the world does not know us is that it did not know him. Beloved, we are God's children now; what we will be has not yet been revealed. What we do know is this: when he is revealed, we will be like him, for we will see him as he is.

Beloved, if our hearts do not condemn us, we have boldness before God; and we receive from him whatever we ask, because we obey his commandments and do what pleases him.

And this is his commandment, that we should believe in the name of his Son Jesus Christ and love one another, just as he has commanded us. All who obey his commandments abide in him, and he abides in them. And by this we know that he abides in us, by the Spirit that he has given us.—The word of the Lord. ℟. **Thanks be to God.** ↓

GOSPEL ACCLAMATION See Acts 16.14b

[Open Hearts]

[If the Alleluia is not sung, the acclamation is omitted.)

℣. Alleluia. ℟. **Alleluia.**
℣. Open our hearts, O Lord,
to listen to the words of your Son.
℟. **Alleluia.** ↓

GOSPEL Lk. 2.41-52   [Jesus Was Obedient to Them]

Jesus and his parents go to Jerusalem for the Passover. Upon returning, Jesus is separated from them. Mary and Joseph find him in the temple teaching. When Mary asks why, Jesus replies that he must be doing his Father's work. Jesus returns with Mary and Joseph to Nazareth.

℣. The Lord be with you. ℟. **And also with you.**
✚ A reading from the holy gospel according to Luke. ℟. **Glory to you, Lord.**

NOW every year the parents of Jesus went to Jerusalem for the festival of the Passover. And when he was twelve years old, they went up as usual for the festival.

When the festival was ended and they started to return, the boy Jesus stayed behind in Jerusalem, but his parents did not know it. Assuming that he was in the group of travellers, they went a day's journey. Then they started to look for him among their relatives and friends. When they did not find him, they returned to Jerusalem to search for him.

After three days they found him in the temple, sitting among the teachers, listening to them and asking them questions. And all who heard him were amazed at his understanding and his answers. When his parents saw him they were astonished; and his mother said to him, "Child, why have you treated us like this? Look, your father and I have been searching for you in great anxiety." He said to them, "Why were you searching for me? Did you not know that I must be in my Father's house?" But they did not understand what he said to them.

Then Jesus went down with them and came to Nazareth, and was obedient to them. His mother treasured all these things in her heart. And Jesus increased in wisdom and in years, and in divine and human favour.—The gospel of the Lord. ℟. **Praise to you, Lord Jesus Christ.**

➜ No. 14, p. 18

PRAYER OVER THE GIFTS   [Unite Our Families]

Lord,
accept this sacrifice
and through the prayers of Mary, the virgin
   Mother of God,
and of her husband, Joseph,
unite our families in peace and love.
We ask this in the name of Jesus the Lord.
℟. **Amen.**   ➜ No. 21, p. 24 (Pref. 3-5)

When Eucharistic Prayer I is used, the special Christmas form of In union with the whole Church *is said.*

COMMUNION ANTIPHON Bar. 3.38   [God with Us]
Our God has appeared on earth, and lived among men. ↓

PRAYER AFTER COMMUNION
[Strength for Families]

Eternal Father,
we want to live as Jesus, Mary, and Joseph,
in peace with you and one another.
May this communion strengthen us
to face the troubles of life.
Grant this through Christ our Lord.
℟. **Amen.**   ➜ No. 32, p. 75

Optional Solemn Blessings, p. 96, and Prayers Over the People, p. 104

"He was called Jesus. . . ."

JANUARY 1, 2007

MARY, MOTHER OF GOD

ENTRANCE ANTIPHON [Hail, Holy Mother]

Hail, holy Mother! The child to whom you gave birth is the King of heaven and earth for ever.

OR See Isa. 9.2, 6; Lk. 1.33 [Wonderful God]

A light will shine on us this day, the Lord is born for us: he shall be called Wonderful God, Prince of peace, Father of the world to come; and his kingship will never end. → No. 2, p. 10

OPENING PRAYER [Mary's Prayers]

God our Father,
may we always profit by the prayers
of the Virgin Mother Mary,
for you bring us life and salvation
through Jesus Christ her Son,
who lives and reigns with you and the Holy
    Spirit,
one God, for ever and ever. ℟. **Amen.** ↓

153

FIRST READING Num. 6.22-27   [The Aaronic Blessing]

Aaron and the Israelites are to pray that God will answer their prayers with blessings.

A reading from the book of Numbers

THE Lord spoke to Moses:
"Speak to Aaron and his sons, saying,
'Thus you shall bless the Israelites:
You shall say to them,

" 'The Lord bless you and keep you;
the Lord make his face to shine upon you,
and be gracious to you;
the Lord lift up his countenance upon you,
and give you peace.'

"So they shall put my name on the Israelites,
and I will bless them."
The word of the Lord. ℟. **Thanks be to God.** ↓

RESPONSORIAL PSALM Ps. 66 (67)   [God Bless Us]

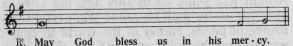

℟. **May God bless us in his mer-cy.**

(℟. **O God, be gracious and bless us, and let your face shine upon us.**)

(NRSV Text)	(GRAIL Text)
May God be gracious to us and bless us and make his face to shine upon us, that your way may be known upon earth, your saving power among all nations.—℟.	O God, be gracious and bless us and let your face shed its light upon us. So will your ways be known upon earth and all nations learn your saving help.—℟.
Let the nations be glad and sing for joy, for you judge the peoples with equity	Let the nations be glad and exult for you rule the world with justice. With fairness you rule the peoples,

and guide the nations upon earth.
Let the peoples praise you, O God;
let all the peoples praise you.—R̟.

The earth has yielded its increase;
God, our God, has blessed us.
May God continue to bless us;
let all the ends of the earth revere
  him.—R̟. ↓

you guide the nations on earth.—R̟.

The earth has yielded its fruit
for God, our God, has blessed us.
May God still give us his blessing
till the ends of the earth revere
  him.—R̟. ↓

SECOND READING Gal. 4.4-7   [Heirs by God's Design]

**God sent Jesus, his Son, born of Mary, to deliver all
people from the bondage of sin and slavery of the law.
By God's choice we are heirs of heaven.**

A reading from the letter of Paul
to the Galatians

WHEN the fullness of time had come, God
sent his Son, born of a woman, born
under the law, in order to redeem those who
were under the law, so that we might receive
adoption as children.

And because you are children, God has sent
the Spirit of his Son into our hearts, crying,
"Abba! Father!" So you are no longer a slave but
a child, and if a child then also an heir, through
God.—The word of the Lord. R̟. **Thanks be to
God.** ↓

GOSPEL ACCLAMATION Heb. 1.1-2   [God Speaks]

(If the Alleluia is not sung, the acclamation is omitted.)

V̟. Alleluia. R̟. **Alleluia.**
V̟. In the past God spoke to our ancestors
  through the prophets;
now God speaks to us through the Son.
R̟. **Alleluia.** ↓

GOSPEL Lk. 2.16-21   [The Name of Jesus]

**When the shepherds came to Bethlehem, they began to
understand the message of the angels. Mary prayed**

about this great event. Jesus received his name according to the Jewish ritual of circumcision.

℣. The Lord be with you. ℟. **And also with you.**
✤ A reading from the holy gospel according to
Luke. ℟. **Glory to you, Lord.**

WHEN the angels had left them the shepherds said to one another, "Let us go now
to Bethlehem and see this thing that has taken
place, which the Lord has made known to us."

So they went with haste and found Mary and
Joseph, and the child lying in the manger.
When they saw this, they made known what
had been told them about this child; and all
who heard it were amazed at what the shepherds told them.

But Mary treasured all these words and pondered them in her heart.

The shepherds returned, glorifying and
praising God for all they had heard and seen,
as it had been told them.

After eight days had passed, it was time to circumcise the child; and he was called Jesus, the
name given by the angel before he was conceived in the womb.—The gospel of the Lord. ℟.
Praise to you, Lord Jesus Christ.   → No. 14, p. 18

PRAYER OVER THE GIFTS   [Salvation Fulfilled]

God our Father,
we celebrate at this season
the beginning of our salvation.
On this feast of Mary, the Mother of God,
we ask that our salvation
will be brought to its fulfilment.
We ask this through Christ our Lord. ℟. **Amen.** ↓

PREFACE (56)   [Mary, Virgin and Mother]

℣. The Lord be with you. ℟. **And also with you.**
℣. Lift up your hearts. ℟. **We lift them up to the
Lord.** ℣. Let us give thanks to the Lord our God.
℟. **It is right to give him thanks and praise.**

Father, all-powerful and ever-living God,
we do well always and everywhere to give you
    thanks
as we celebrate the motherhood of the Blessed
    Virgin Mary.
Through the power of the Holy Spirit,
she became the virgin mother of your only Son,
our Lord Jesus Christ,
who is for ever the light of the world.
Through him the choirs of angels
and all the powers of heaven
praise and worship your glory.
May our voices blend with theirs
as we join in their unending hymn:

                                    ➜ No. 23, p. 25

*When Eucharistic Prayer I is used, the special Christ-
mas form of* In union with the whole Church *is said.*

COMMUNION ANTIPHON Heb. 13.8 [Jesus Forever!]
**Jesus Christ is the same yesterday, today, and
for ever.** ↓

PRAYER AFTER COMMUNION [Mother of Church]
Father,
as we proclaim the Virgin Mary
to be the mother of Christ and the mother of
    the Church,
may our communion with her Son

bring us to salvation.
We ask this in the name of Jesus the Lord.
℟. **Amen.**   ➜ No. 32, p. 75

Optional Solemn Blessings, p. 96, and Prayers Over the People, p. 104

"They knelt down and paid him homage."

JANUARY 7

EPIPHANY OF THE LORD

ENTRANCE ANTIPHON See Mal. 3.1; 1 Chr. 19.12
[Lord and Ruler]

**The Lord and ruler is coming; kingship is his,
and government and power.**   ➜ No. 2, p. 10

OPENING PRAYER   [Light of Faith]
Father,
you revealed your Son to the nations
by the guidance of a star.
Lead us to your glory in heaven
by the light of faith.
We ask this . . . for ever and ever. ℟. **Amen.** ↓

FIRST READING Isa. 60.1-6   [Glory of God's Church]

Jerusalem is favoured by the Lord. Kings and peoples will come there, and the riches of the earth will be placed at its gates.

A reading from the book of the
prophet Isaiah

ARISE, shine, for your light has come,
and the glory of the Lord has risen upon
    you!
For darkness shall cover the earth,
and thick darkness the peoples;
but the Lord will arise upon you,
and his glory will appear over you.

Nations shall come to your light,
and kings to the brightness of your dawn.
Lift up your eyes and look around;
they all gather together, they come to you;
your sons shall come from far away,
and your daughters shall be carried on their
    nurses' arms.

Then you shall see and be radiant;
your heart shall thrill and rejoice,
because the abundance of the sea shall be
    brought to you,
the wealth of the nations shall come to you.
A multitude of camels shall cover you,
the young camels of Midian and Ephah;
all those from Sheba shall come.
They shall bring gold and frankincense,
and shall proclaim the praise of the Lord.
The word of the Lord. ℟. **Thanks be to God.** ↓

RESPONSORIAL PSALM Ps. 71 (72)   [Messiah-King]

R̸. **Lord,   every   nation   on   earth   will adore you.**

(NRSV Text)

Give the king your justice, O God,
and your righteousness to a king's
son.
May he judge your people with righteousness,
and your poor with justice.—R̸.

In his days may righteousness flourish
and peace abound, until the moon is
no more.
May he have dominion from sea to
sea,
and from the River to the ends of the
earth.—R̸.

May the kings of Tarshish and of the
isles render him tribute,
may the kings of Sheba and Seba
bring gifts.
May all kings fall down before him,
all nations give him service.—R̸.

For he delivers the needy when they
call,
the poor and those who have no
helper.
He has pity on the weak and the
needy,
and saves the lives of the needy.—
R̸. ↓

(GRAIL Text)

O God, give your judgment to the
king,
to a king's son your justice,
that he may judge your people in justice
and your poor in right judgment.—
R̸.

In his days justice shall flourish
and peace till the moon fails.
He shall rule from sea to sea,
from the Great River to earth's
bounds.—R̸.

The kings of Tarshish and the sea-
coasts
shall pay him tribute.
The kings of Sheba and Seba
shall bring him gifts.
Before him all rulers shall fall prostrate,
all nations shall serve him.—R̸.

For he shall save the poor when they
cry
and the needy who are helpless.
He will have pity on the weak
and save the lives of the poor.—
R̸. ↓

SECOND READING Eph. 3.2-3a, 5-6 [Good News for All]

**Paul admits that God has revealed the divine plan of
salvation to him. Not only the Jews, but also the whole
world will share in the good news.**

A reading from the letter of Paul
to the Ephesians

SURELY you have already heard of the commission of God's grace that was given me
for you, and how the mystery was made known
to me by revelation.

In former generations this mystery was not
made known to humanity as it has now been
revealed to his holy apostles and prophets by
the Spirit: that is, the Gentiles have become fellow heirs, members of the same body, and
sharers in the promise in Christ Jesus through
the gospel.—The word of the Lord. ℟. **Thanks
be to God.** ↓

GOSPEL ACCLAMATION See Mt. 2.2   [Leading Star]
(If the Alleluia is not sung, the acclamation is omitted.)
℣. Alleluia. ℟. **Alleluia.**
℣. We have seen his star in the east;
and have come to adore the Lord.
℟. **Alleluia.** ↓

GOSPEL Mt. 2.1-12   [Wise Men with Gifts]
**The wise men from the East followed the star to Bethle-
hem, from which a ruler was to come.**

℣. The Lord be with you. ℟. **And also with you.**
✠ A reading from the holy gospel according to
Matthew. ℟. **Glory to you, Lord.**

IN the time of King Herod, after Jesus was
born in Bethlehem of Judea, wise men from
the East came to Jerusalem, asking, "Where is
the child who has been born king of the Jews?
For we observed his star at its rising, and have
come to pay him homage."

When King Herod heard this, he was frightened, and all Jerusalem with him; and calling together all the chief priests and scribes of the people, he inquired of them where the Messiah was to be born. They told him, "In Bethlehem of Judea; for so it has been written by the prophet:
'And you, Bethlehem, in the land of Judah,
    are by no means least among the rulers of
       Judah;
for from you shall come a ruler
    who is to shepherd my people Israel.' "
Then Herod secretly called for the wise men and learned from them the exact time when the star had appeared. Then he sent them to Bethlehem, saying, "Go and search diligently for the child; and when you have found him, bring me word so that I may also go and pay him homage."

When they had heard the king, they set out; and there, ahead of them, went the star that they had seen at its rising, until it stopped over the place where the child was. When they saw that the star had stopped, they were overwhelmed with joy.

On entering the house, they saw the child with Mary his mother; and they knelt down and paid him homage. Then, opening their treasure chests, they offered him gifts of gold, frankincense, and myrrh.

And having been warned in a dream not to return to Herod, they left for their own country by another road.—The gospel of the Lord. ℟.
Praise to you, Lord Jesus Christ. ➜ No. 14, p. 18

PRAYER OVER THE GIFTS   [Offering of Jesus]

Lord,
accept the offerings of your Church,
not gold, frankincense and myrrh,
but the sacrifice and food they symbolize:
Jesus Christ, who is Lord for ever and ever.
℞. **Amen.** ↓

PREFACE (6)   [Jesus Revealed to All]

℣. The Lord be with you. ℞. **And also with you.**
℣. Lift up your hearts. ℞. **We lift them up to the
Lord.** ℣. Let us give thanks to the Lord our God.
℞. **It is right to give him thanks and praise.**

Father, all-powerful and ever-living God,
we do well always and everywhere to give you
    thanks.
Today you revealed in Christ your eternal plan
    of salvation,
and showed him as the light of all peoples.
Now that his glory has shone among us
you have renewed humanity in his immortal
    image.
Now, with angels and archangels,
and the whole company of heaven,
we sing the unending hymn of your praise:

→ No. 23, p. 25

*When Eucharistic Prayer I is used, the special Epiph-
any form of* In union with the whole Church *is said.*

COMMUNION ANTIPHON See Mt. 2.2 [Adore the Lord]

**We have seen his star in the east, and have
come with gifts to adore the Lord.** ↓

PRAYER AFTER COMMUNION [Christ in Eucharist]

Father,
guide us with your light.
Help us to recognize Christ in this eucharist
and welcome him with love,
for he is Lord for ever and ever.
R̸. **Amen.**   → No. 32, p. 75

Optional Solemn Blessings, p. 96, and Prayers Over the People, p. 104

"Jesus said to the servants, 'Fill the jars with water.' "

JANUARY 14

2nd SUNDAY IN ORDINARY TIME

ENTRANCE ANTIPHON Ps. 65 (66).4

[Proclaim His Glory]

May all the earth give you worship and praise, and break into song to your name, O God, Most High.   → No. 2, p. 10

OPENING PRAYER   [Peace in the World]
Father of heaven and earth,
hear our prayers,
and show us the way to peace in the world.
Grant this . . . for ever and ever. ℟. **Amen.** ↓

FIRST READING Isa. 62.1-5   [God's Love for His People]

> "Zion," "Jerusalem," is the people of God and God de-
> scribes deep love and concern for us in terms of the joy
> of a bridegroom.

A reading from the book of the prophet Isaiah

THE Lord says this:
"For Zion's sake I will not keep silent,
and for Jerusalem's sake I will not rest,
until her vindication shines out like the dawn,
and her salvation like a burning torch.

"The nations shall see your vindication,
and all the kings your glory;
and you shall be called by a new name
that the mouth of the Lord will give.
You shall be a crown of beauty in the hand of
    the Lord,
and a royal diadem in the hand of your God.

"You shall no more be termed 'Forsaken,'
and your land shall no more be termed 'Deso-
    late';
but you shall be called 'My Delight Is in Her,'
and your land 'Married';
for the Lord delights in you,
and your land shall be married.

"For as a young man marries a young woman,
so shall your builder marry you,

and as the bridegroom rejoices over the bride,
so shall your God rejoice over you."
The word of the Lord. ℟. **Thanks be to God.** ↓

RESPONSORIAL PSALM Ps. 95 (96)   [God's Deeds]

℟. **Proclaim God's marvellous deeds to all   the   na - tions.**

(℟. **Proclaim the wonders of the Lord among all the peoples.**)

(NRSV Text)	**(GRAIL Text)**
O sing to the Lord a new song; sing to the Lord, all the earth. Sing to the Lord, bless his name; tell of his salvation from day to day.—℟.	O sing a new song to the Lord, sing to the Lord all the earth. O sing to the Lord, bless his name.—℟.
Declare his glory among the nations, his marvellous works among all the peoples. For great is the Lord, and greatly to be praised; he is to be revered above all gods.—℟.	Proclaim his help day by day, tell among the nations his glory and his wonders among all the peoples.—℟. The Lord is great and worthy of all praise, to be feared above all gods.—℟.
Ascribe to the Lord, O families of the peoples, ascribe to the Lord glory and strength. Ascribe to the Lord the glory due his name; bring an offering, and come into his courts.—℟.	Give the Lord, you families of peoples, give the Lord glory and power; give the Lord the glory of his name. Bring an offering and enter his courts.—℟.
Worship the Lord in holy splendour; tremble before him, all the earth. Say among the nations, "The Lord is king! He will judge the peoples with equity."—℟. ↓	Worship the Lord in his temple. O earth, tremble before him. Proclaim to the nations: "God is king!" He will judge the peoples in fairness.—℟. ↓

SECOND READING 1 Cor. 12.4-11   [Gifts of the Spirit]

The gifts of God come from the same Spirit. The gifts are diverse but the Spirit is one; and the gifts are given to unite not separate us.

A reading from the first letter of Paul
to the Corinthians

THERE are varieties of gifts, but the same Spirit; and there are varieties of services, but the same Lord; and there are varieties of activities, but it is the same God who activates all of them in everyone.

To each is given the manifestation of the Spirit for the common good. To one is given through the Spirit the utterance of wisdom, and to another the utterance of knowledge according to the same Spirit, to another faith by the same Spirit, to another gifts of healing by the one Spirit, to another the working of miracles, to another prophecy, to another the discernment of spirits, to another various kinds of tongues, to another the interpretation of tongues.

All these are activated by one and the same Spirit, who allots to each one individually just as the Spirit chooses.—The word of the Lord. ℟. **Thanks be to God.** ↓

GOSPEL ACCLAMATION 2 Thess. 2.14 [We Are Called]

(If the Alleluia is not sung, the acclamation is omitted.)

℣. Alleluia. ℟. **Alleluia.**
℣. God has called us with the gospel,
to share in the glory of our Lord Jesus Christ.
℟. **Alleluia.** ↓

In the place of the Gospel Acclamation given for each Sunday in Ordinary Time, another may be selected.

GOSPEL Jn. 2.1-12   [Jesus Reveals His Glory]

Mary intercedes with her Son for the newlyweds, and Jesus changes water into wine. He thus reveals his glory and indicates that the kingdom of God is at hand.

℣. The Lord be with you. ℟. **And also with you.**
✢ A reading from the holy gospel according to John. ℟. **Glory to you, Lord.**

THERE was a wedding in Cana of Galilee, and the mother of Jesus was there. Jesus and his disciples had also been invited to the wedding.

When the wine gave out, the mother of Jesus said to him, "They have no wine." And Jesus said to her, "Woman, what concern is that to you and to me? My hour has not yet come." His mother said to the servants, "Do whatever he tells you."

Now standing there were six stone water jars for the Jewish rites of purification, each holding about a hundred litres. Jesus said to the servants, "Fill the jars with water." And they filled them up to the brim. He said to them, "Now draw some out, and take it to the chief steward." So they took it.

When the steward tasted the water that had become wine, and did not know where it came from (though the servants who had drawn the water knew), the steward called the bridegroom and said to him, "Everyone serves the good wine first, and then the inferior wine after the guests have become drunk. But you have kept the good wine until now."

Jesus did this, the first of his signs, in Cana of Galilee, and revealed his glory; and his disci-

ples believed in him. After this he went down
to Capernaum with his mother, his brothers,
and his disciples; and they remained there a
few days.—The gospel of the Lord. R̸. **Praise to
you, Lord Jesus Christ.**   → No. 14, p. 18

PRAYER OVER THE GIFTS [Continuing Redemption]
Father,
may we celebrate the eucharist
with reverence and love,
for when we proclaim the death of the Lord
you continue the work of his redemption,
who is Lord for ever and ever.
R̸. **Amen.**   → No. 21, p. 24 (Pref. 29-36)

COMMUNION ANTIPHON Ps. 22 (23).5 [Lord's Feast]
**The Lord has prepared a feast for me: given
wine in plenty for me to drink.** ↓

OR 1 Jn. 4.16   [God's Love]
We know and believe in God's love for us. ↓

PRAYER AFTER COMMUNION   [One in Love]
Lord,
you have nourished us with bread from heaven.
Fill us with your Spirit,
and make us one in peace and love.
We ask this through Christ our Lord.
R̸. **Amen.**   → No. 32, p. 75

Optional Solemn Blessings, p. 96, and Prayers Over the People, p. 104

"The eyes of all in the synagogue were fixed on him."

JANUARY 21

3rd SUNDAY IN ORDINARY TIME

ENTRANCE ANTIPHON Ps. 95 (96).1, 6 [A New Song]

Sing a new song to the Lord! Sing to the Lord, all the earth. Truth and beauty surround him, he lives in holiness and glory. → No. 2, p. 10

OPENING PRAYER [Working for Unity]

All-powerful and ever-living God,
direct your love that is within us,
that our efforts in the name of your Son
may bring the human family to unity and peace.
We ask this . . . for ever and ever. ℟. **Amen.** ↓

FIRST READING Neh. 8.1-4a, 5-6, 8-10 [God's Law]

The people of God return to their homeland, rebuild the temple, and now listen to the proclamation of the law of God.

A reading from the book of Nehemiah

170

ALL the people gathered together into the square before the Water Gate. They told the scribe Ezra to bring the book of the law of Moses, which the Lord had given to Israel. Accordingly, the priest Ezra brought the law before the assembly, both men and women and all who could hear with understanding. This was on the first day of the seventh month. He read from it facing the square before the Water Gate from early morning until midday, in the presence of the men and the women and those who could understand; and the ears of all the people were attentive to the book of the law. The scribe Ezra stood on a wooden platform that had been made for the purpose.

And Ezra opened the book in the sight of all the people, for he was standing above all the people; and when he opened it, all the people stood up. Then Ezra blessed the Lord, the great God, and all the people answered, "Amen, Amen," lifting up their hands. Then they bowed their heads and worshipped the Lord with their faces to the ground.

So the Levites read from the book, from the law of God, with interpretation. They gave the sense, so that the people understood the reading. And Nehemiah, who was the governor, and Ezra the priest and scribe, and the Levites who taught the people said to all the people, "This day is holy to the Lord your God; do not mourn or weep." For all the people wept when they heard the words of the law.

Then Ezra said to them, "Go your way, eat the fat and drink sweet wine and send portions of them to those for whom nothing is prepared, for this day is holy to our Lord; and do not be grieved, for the joy of the Lord is your strength."—The word of the Lord. ℟. **Thanks be to God.** ↓

RESPONSORIAL PSALM Ps. 18 (19)   [Spirit and Life]

℟. Your words, Lord, are Spir - it and life.

(℟. Your words, Lord, are life.)

(NRSV Text)	(GRAIL Text)
The law of the Lord is perfect, reviving the soul; the decrees of the Lord are sure, making wise the simple.—℟.	The law of the Lord is perfect, it revives the soul. The rule of the Lord is to be trusted, it gives wisdom to the simple.—℟.
The precepts of the Lord are right, rejoicing the heart; the commandment of the Lord is clear, enlightening the eyes.—℟.	The precepts of the Lord are right, they gladden the heart. The command of the Lord is clear, it gives light to the eyes.—℟.
The fear of the Lord is pure, enduring forever; the ordinances of the Lord are true and righteous altogether.—℟.	The fear of the Lord is holy, abiding for ever. The decrees of the Lord are truth and all of them just.—℟.
Let the words of my mouth and the meditation of my heart be acceptable to you, O Lord, my rock and my redeemer.—℟. ↓	May the spoken words of my mouth, the thoughts of my heart, win favour in your sight, O Lord, my rescuer, my rock!—℟. ↓

SECOND READING 1 Cor. 12.12-30 or 12.12-14, 27

[One Body]

By baptism we begin to become Christians, Christ takes possession of us, and we must grow with him.

[If "Short Form" is used, omit indented text in brackets.]

A reading from the first letter of Paul
to the Corinthians

JUST as the body is one and has many members, and all the members of the body, though many, are one body, so it is with Christ. For in the one Spirit we were all baptized into one body—Jews or Greeks, slaves or free—and we were all made to drink of one Spirit.

Indeed, the body does not consist of one member but of many.

[If the foot would say, "Because I am not a hand, I do not belong to the body," that would not make it any less a part of the body. And if the ear would say, "Because I am not an eye, I do not belong to the body," that would not make it any less a part of the body. If the whole body were an eye, where would the hearing be? If the whole body were hearing, where would the sense of smell be?

But as it is, God arranged the members in the body, each one of them, as he chose. If all were a single member, where would the body be? As it is, there are many members, yet one body. The eye cannot say to the hand, "I have no need of you," nor again the head to the feet, "I have no need of you."

On the contrary, the members of the body that seem to be weaker are indispensable, and those members of the body that we think less honourable we clothe with greater honour, and our less respectable members are treated with greater respect;

whereas our more respectable members do not need this.

But God has so arranged the body, giving the greater honour to the inferior member, that there may be no dissension within the body, but the members may have the same care for one another. If one member suffers, all suffer together with it; if one member is honoured, all rejoice together with it.]

Now you are the body of Christ and individually members of it.

[And God has appointed in the church first apostles, second prophets, third teachers; then deeds of power, then gifts of healing, forms of assistance, forms of leadership, various kinds of tongues.

Are all apostles? Are all prophets? Are all teachers? Do all work miracles? Do all possess gifts of healing? Do all speak in tongues? Do all interpret?]

The word of the Lord. ℟. **Thanks be to God.** ↓

GOSPEL ACCLAMATION Lk. 4.18-19   [Good News]

(If the Alleluia is not sung, the acclamation is omitted.)

℣. Alleluia. ℟. **Alleluia.**

℣. The Lord sent me to bring good news to the poor

and freedom to prisoners.

℟. **Alleluia.** ↓

GOSPEL Lk. 1.1-4; 4.14-21   [Proclaiming the Good News]

Jesus proclaims the "good news" to the poor, and announces the fulfilment of the prophetic vision of Isaiah.

℣. The Lord be with you. ℞. **And also with you.**
✚ A reading from the holy gospel according to
Luke. ℞. **Glory to you, Lord.**

SINCE many have undertaken to set down an
orderly account of the events that have been
fulfilled among us, just as they were handed on
to us by those who from the beginning were eye-
witnesses and servants of the word, I too decided, after investigating everything carefully
from the very first, to write an orderly account
for you, most excellent Theophilus, so that you
may know the truth concerning the things about
which you have been instructed.

Jesus, filled with the power of the Spirit, returned to Galilee, and a report about him spread
through all the surrounding country. He began to
teach in their synagogues and was praised by
everyone. When he came to Nazareth, where he
had been brought up, Jesus went to the synagogue on the sabbath day, as was his custom.

He stood up to read, and the scroll of the
prophet Isaiah was given to him. He unrolled the
scroll and found the place where it was written:
"The Spirit of the Lord is upon me,
    because he has anointed me to bring good
      news to the poor.
    He has sent me to proclaim release to the
      captives
  and recovery of sight to the blind,
    to let the oppressed go free,
to proclaim the year of the Lord's favour."

And Jesus rolled up the scroll, gave it back to
the attendant, and sat down. The eyes of all in

the synagogue were fixed on him.

Then Jesus began to say to them, "Today this scripture has been fulfilled in your hearing."— The gospel of the Lord. ℟. **Praise to you, Lord Jesus Christ.**   ➜ No. 14, p. 18

PRAYER OVER THE GIFTS   [Offerings of Salvation]

Lord,
receive our gifts.
Let our offerings make us holy
and bring us salvation.
Grant this through Christ our Lord.
℟. **Amen.**   ➜ No. 21, p. 24 (Pref. 29-36)

COMMUNION ANTIPHON Ps. 33 (34).5   [Gladness]

Look up at the Lord with gladness and smile; your face will never be ashamed. ↓

OR Jn. 8.12   [Light of Life]

I am the light of the world, says the Lord; the man who follows me will have the light of life. ↓

PRAYER AFTER COMMUNION   [New Life]

God, all-powerful Father,
may the new life you give us increase our love
and keep us in the joy of your kingdom.
We ask this in the name of Jesus the Lord.
℟. **Amen.**   ➜ No. 32, p. 75

Optional Solemn Blessings, p. 96, and Prayers Over the People, p. 104

"Jesus passed through the midst of them. . . ."

JANUARY 28

4th SUNDAY IN ORDINARY TIME

ENTRANCE ANTIPHON Ps. 105 (106).47   [Save Us]

Save us, Lord our God, and gather us together from the nations, that we may proclaim your holy name and glory in your praise.

➤ No. 2, p. 10

OPENING PRAYER   [Christian Love]

Lord our God,
help us to love you with all our hearts
and to love all people as you love them.
Grant this . . . for ever and ever. ℟. **Amen.** ↓

FIRST READING Jer. 1.4-5, 17-19   [Call of Jeremiah]

Jeremiah is called by the Father to be his spokesman.
He will be rejected but receives the promise of God that
he will support him against his adversaries.

A reading from the book of the prophet
Jeremiah

NOW the word of the Lord came to me saying,

"Before I formed you in the womb, I knew you, and before you were born, I consecrated you; I appointed you a prophet to the nations.

"Therefore, gird up your loins; stand up and tell the people everything that I command you. Do not break down before them, or I will break you before them. And I for my part have made you today a fortified city, an iron pillar, and a bronze wall, against the whole land—against the kings of Judah, its princes, its priests, and the people of the land.

"They will fight against you; but they shall not prevail against you, for I am with you, says the Lord, to deliver you."—The word of the Lord. ℞. **Thanks be to God.** ↓

RESPONSORIAL PSALM Ps. 70 (71) [Sing of Salvation]

℞. I will sing of your sal - va - tion.
(℞. **My lips will tell of your help.**)

(NRSV Text)	**(GRAIL Text)**
In you, O Lord, I take refuge; let me never be put to shame.	In you, O Lord, I take refuge; let me never be put to shame.
In your righteousness, deliver me and rescue me; incline your ear to me and save me.—℞.	In your justice rescue me, free me; pay heed to me and save me.—℞.
Be to me a rock of refuge, a strong fortress, to save me, for you are my rock and my fortress. Rescue me, O my God, from the hand of the wicked.—℞.	Be a rock where I can take refuge, a mighty stronghold to save me; for you are my rock, my stronghold. Free me from the hand of the wicked.—℞.

For you, O Lord, are my hope,
my trust, O Lord, from my youth.
Upon you I have leaned from my birth;
it was you who took me from my
    mother's womb.—R℣.

My mouth will tell of your righteous
    acts,
of your deeds of salvation all day
    long.
O God, from my youth you have
    taught me,
and I still proclaim your wondrous
    deeds.—R℣. ↓

It is you, O Lord, who are my hope,
my trust, O Lord, since my youth.
On you I have leaned from my birth;
from my mother's womb you have
    been my help.—R℣.

My lips will tell of your justice
and day by day of your help.
O God, you have taught me from my
    youth
and I proclaim your wonders still.—
    R℣. ↓

SECOND READING 1 Cor. 12.31—13.13 or 13.4-13

[Power of Love]

Love, the virtue of charity, surpasses all. It rises above everything. All gifts will pass away, but the supernatural virtue of love will never fail.

[If the "Short Form" is used, the indented text in brackets is omitted.]

A reading from the first letter of Paul to the Corinthians

[**B**ROTHERS and sisters, strive for the greater gifts. And I will show you a still more excellent way.

If I speak in the tongues of mortals and of angels, but do not have love, I am a noisy gong or a clanging cymbal. If I have prophetic powers, and understand all mysteries and all knowledge, and if I have all faith, so as to remove mountains, but do not have love, I am nothing. If I give away all my possessions, and if I hand over my body so that I may boast, but do not have love, I gain nothing.]

Love is patient; love is kind; love is not envious or boastful or arrogant or rude. It does not insist on its own way; it is not irritable or resentful; it does not rejoice in wrongdoing, but rejoices in the truth. It bears all things, believes all things, hopes all things, endures all things. Love never ends.

But as for prophecies, they will come to an end; as for tongues, they will cease; as for knowledge, it will come to an end.

For we know only in part, and we prophesy only in part; but when the complete comes, the partial will come to an end.

When I was a child, I spoke like a child, I thought like a child, I reasoned like a child; when I became an adult, I put an end to childish ways.

For now we see in a mirror, dimly, but then we will see face to face. Now I know only in part; then I will know fully, even as I have been fully known.

Now faith, hope, and love abide, these three; and the greatest of these is love.—The word of the Lord. ℟. **Thanks be to God.** ↓

GOSPEL ACCLAMATION Lk. 4.18-19   [Good News]

(If the Alleluia is not sung, the acclamation is omitted.)

℣. Alleluia. ℟. **Alleluia.**

℣. The Lord sent me to bring good news to the poor
and freedom to prisoners.

℟. **Alleluia.** ↓

GOSPEL Lk. 4.21-30   [Preaching Salvation to All People]

Jesus is rejected by his own neighbours. They resented his strong reminder of the past rejections of the prophets. In baptism and the sacraments we are united to Jesus. Like him we must bear our crosses.

℣. The Lord be with you. ℟. **And also with you.**
✠ A reading from the holy gospel according to Luke. ℟. **Glory to you, Lord.**

JESUS, filled with the power of the Spirit, came to Nazareth, where he had been brought up. He went to the synagogue on the sabbath day, as was his custom, and read from the prophet Isaiah. The eyes of all were fixed on him. Then he began to say to them, "Today this scripture has been fulfilled in your hearing." All spoke well of him and were amazed at the gracious words that came from his mouth. They said, "Is not this Joseph's son?"

Jesus said to them, "Doubtless you will quote to me this proverb, 'Doctor, cure yourself!' And you will say, 'Do here also in your hometown the things that we have heard you did at Capernaum.' "

And he said, "Truly I tell you, no prophet is accepted in the prophet's hometown. But the truth is, there were many widows in Israel in the time of Elijah, when the heaven was shut up three years and six months, and there was a severe famine over all the land; yet Elijah was sent to none of them except to a widow at Zarephath in Sidon. There were also many lepers in Israel in the time of the prophet Elisha, and none of them was cleansed except Naaman the Syrian."

When they heard this, all in the synagogue were filled with rage. They got up, drove Jesus out of the town, and led him to the brow of the hill on which their town was built, so that they might hurl him off the cliff. But Jesus passed through the midst of them and went on his way.—The gospel of the Lord. ℟. **Praise to you, Lord Jesus Christ.**   ➜ No. 14, p. 18

PRAYER OVER THE GIFTS   [Sacrament of Salvation]

Lord,
be pleased with the gifts we bring to your altar, and make them the sacrament of our salvation. We ask this through Christ our Lord.

℟. **Amen.**   ➜ No. 21, p. 24 (Pref. 29-36)

COMMUNION ANTIPHON Ps. 30 (31).16-17 [Save Me]

Let your face shine on your servant, and save me by your love. Lord, keep me from shame, for I have called to you. ↓

PRAYER AFTER COMMUNION   [True Faith]

Lord,
you invigorate us with this help to our salvation.
By this eucharist give the true faith continued growth
throughout the world.
We ask this in the name of Jesus the Lord.

℟. **Amen.**   ➜ No. 32, p. 75

Optional Solemn Blessings, p. 96, and Prayers Over the People, p. 104

"They caught so many fish that their nets
were beginning to break."

FEBRUARY 4

5th SUNDAY IN ORDINARY TIME

ENTRANCE ANTIPHON Ps. 94 (95).6-7   [Adoration]

**Come, let us worship the Lord. Let us bow
down in the presence of our maker, for he is
the Lord our God.**   → No. 2, p. 10

OPENING PRAYER   [God's Care]

Father,
watch over your family
and keep us safe in your care,
for all our hope is in you.
Grant this . . . for ever and ever. ℞. **Amen.** ↓

FIRST READING Isa. 6.1-2a, 3-8   [Call of Isaiah]

*The prophet, aware of his own unworthiness, is fearful.
Purged of sin, he accepts the call of the Father.*

A reading from the book of the prophet Isaiah

IN the year that King Uzziah died, I saw the
Lord sitting on a throne, high and lofty; and

the hem of his robe filled the temple. Seraphs were in attendance above him; each had six wings. And one called to another and said:

"Holy, holy, holy is the Lord of hosts;
the whole earth is full of his glory."

The pivots on the thresholds shook at the voices of those who called, and the house filled with smoke.

And I said: "Woe is me! I am lost, for I am a man of unclean lips, and I live among a people of unclean lips; yet my eyes have seen the King, the Lord of hosts!"

Then one of the seraphs flew to me, holding a live coal that had been taken from the altar with a pair of tongs. The seraph touched my mouth with it and said: "Now that this has touched your lips, your guilt has departed and your sin is blotted out."

Then I heard the voice of the Lord saying, "Whom shall I send, and who will go for us?" And I said, "Here am I; send me!"—The word of the Lord. ℞. **Thanks be to God.** ↓

RESPONSORIAL PSALM Ps. 137 (138)   [Gratitude]

℞. **In the sight of the an-gels I will sing your prais-es, Lord.**

(NRSV Text)

I give you thanks, O Lord,
with my whole heart;
before the gods I sing your praise;
I bow down toward your holy temple.

(GRAIL Text)

I thank you, Lord; with all my heart,
you have heard the words of my mouth.
In the presence of the angels I will bless you.
I will adore before your holy temple.—℞.

I give thanks to your name
for your steadfast love and your
  faithfulness.—R̸.

For you have exalted your name
and your word above everything.
On the day I called, you answered me,
you increased my strength of soul.—
  R̸.

All the kings of the earth shall praise
  you, O Lord,
for they have heard the words of your
  mouth.
They shall sing of the ways of the
  Lord,
for great is the glory of the Lord.—R̸.

You stretch out your hand, and your
  right hand delivers me.
The Lord will fulfil his purpose for me;
your steadfast love, O Lord, endures
  forever.
Do not forsake the work of your
  hands.—R̸. ↓

I thank you for your faithfulness and
  love
which excel all we ever knew of you.
On the day I called, you answered;
you increased the strength of my
  soul.—R̸.

All the rulers on earth shall thank
  you
when they hear the words of your
  mouth.
They shall sing of the Lord's ways:
"How great is the glory of the
  Lord!"—R̸.

You stretch out your hand and save
  me,
your hand will do all things for me.
Your love, O Lord, is eternal,
discard not the work of your
  hands.—R̸. ↓

SECOND READING 1 Cor. 15.1-11 or 15.3-8, 11

[Content of Good News]

**Through God's favour, the apostles turned from perse-
cution to preaching the "good news" like Isaiah. Christ
has died, Christ is risen, Christ will come again.**

*[If the "Short Form" is used, the indented text in
brackets is omitted.]*

A reading from the first letter of Paul
to the Corinthians

[I WOULD remind you, brothers and sisters, of the good news that I proclaimed to you, which you in turn received,
in which also you stand. This is the good
news through which also you are being
saved, if you hold firmly to the message

that I proclaimed to you—unless you have come to believe in vain.]

For I handed on to you as of first importance what I in turn had received: that Christ died for our sins in accordance with the scriptures, and that he was buried, and that he was raised on the third day in accordance with the scriptures, and that he appeared to Cephas, then to the twelve.

Then Christ appeared to more than five hundred brothers and sisters at one time, most of whom are still alive, though some have died. Then he appeared to James, then to all the apostles. Last of all, as to one untimely born, Christ appeared also to me.

[For I am the least of the apostles, unfit to be called an apostle, because I persecuted the church of God. But by the grace of God I am what I am, and his grace toward me has not been in vain. On the contrary, I worked harder than any of the apostles—though it was not I, but the grace of God that is with me.]

Whether then it was I or they, so we proclaim and so you have come to believe.—The word of the Lord. ℟. **Thanks be to God.** ↓

GOSPEL ACCLAMATION Mt. 4.19   [Follow Me]
(If the Alleluia is not sung, the acclamation is omitted.)

℣. Alleluia. ℟. **Alleluia.**
℣. Come follow me, says the Lord,
and I will make you fishers of my people.
℟. **Alleluia.** ↓

GOSPEL Lk. 5.1-11   [Call of Peter]

Peter confesses: "I am a sinful man," and is reassured by Christ. Then together with James and John he leaves everything to become his follower.

℣. The Lord be with you. ℟. **And also with you.**
✛ A reading from the holy gospel according to Luke. ℟. **Glory to you, Lord.**

WHILE Jesus was standing beside the lake of Gennesaret, and the crowd was pressing in on him to hear the word of God, he saw two boats there at the shore of the lake; the fishermen had gone out of them and were washing their nets.

Jesus got into one of the boats, the one belonging to Simon, and asked him to put out a little way from the shore. Then he sat down and taught the crowds from the boat. When he had finished speaking, he said to Simon, "Put out into the deep water and let down your nets for a catch." Simon answered, "Master, we have worked all night long but have caught nothing. Yet if you say so, I will let down the nets." When they had done this, they caught so many fish that their nets were beginning to break. So they signalled their partners in the other boat to come and help them. And they came and filled both boats, so that they began to sink.

But when Simon Peter saw it, he fell down at Jesus' knees, saying, "Go away from me, Lord, for I am a sinful man!"

For Simon Peter and all who were with him were amazed at the catch of fish that they had taken; and so also were James and John, sons of Zebedee, who were partners with Simon.

Then Jesus said to Simon, "Do not be afraid; from now on you will be catching people."

When they had brought their boats to shore, they left everything and followed Jesus.—The gospel of the Lord. ℞. **Praise to you, Lord Jesus Christ.**

→ No. 14, p. 18

PRAYER OVER THE GIFTS   [Eternal Life]

Lord our God,
may the bread and wine
you give us for our nourishment on earth
become the sacrament of our eternal life.
We ask this through Christ our Lord.
℞. **Amen.**   → No. 21, p. 24 (Pref. 29-36)

COMMUNION ANTIPHON Ps. 106 (107).8-9   [Praise]

Give praise to the Lord for his kindness, for his wonderful deeds toward men. He has filled the hungry with good things, he has satisfied the thirsty. ↓

OR Mt. 5.5-6   [The Sorrowing]

Blessed are the sorrowing; they shall be consoled. Blessed are those who hunger and thirst for what is right; they shall be satisfied. ↓

PRAYER AFTER COMMUNION   [Salvation and Joy]

God our Father,
you give us a share in the one bread and the
    one cup
and make us one in Christ.
Help us to bring your salvation and joy
to all the world.

We ask this in the name of Jesus the Lord.
℟. **Amen.**   → No. 32, p. 75

Optional Solemn Blessings, p. 96, and Prayers Over the People, p. 104

"Blessed are you who are poor, for yours
is the kingdom of God."

FEBRUARY 11

6th SUNDAY IN ORDINARY TIME

ENTRANCE ANTIPHON Ps. 30 (31).2-3 [Rock of Safety]
**Lord, be my rock of safety, the stronghold that
saves me. For the honour of your name, lead
me and guide me.**   → No. 2, p. 10

OPENING PRAYER   [Living in God's Presence]
God our Father,
you have promised to remain for ever
with those who do what is just and right.
Help us to live in your presence.
We ask this . . . for ever and ever. ℟. **Amen.** ↓

FIRST READING Jer. 17.5-8   [Trust in the Lord]
To put all one's trust in human strength leads to frustra-
tion. Let us trust in the Lord and find fulfilment.

A reading from the book of the
prophet Jeremiah

THUS says the Lord:
"Cursed are those who trust in mere mortals
and make mere flesh their strength,
whose hearts turn away from the Lord.
They shall be like a shrub in the desert,
and shall not see when relief comes.
They shall live in the parched places of the
   wilderness,
in an uninhabited salt land.

"Blessed are those who trust in the Lord,
whose trust is the Lord.
They shall be like a tree planted by water,
sending out its roots by the stream.
This tree shall not fear when heat comes,
and its leaves shall stay green;
in the year of drought it is not anxious,
and it does not cease to bear fruit."
The word of the Lord. ℟. **Thanks be to God.** ↓

RESPONSORIAL PSALM Ps. 1   [Lover of God's Law]

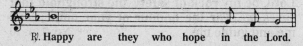

℟. **Happy   are   they   who   hope   in   the   Lord.**

(NRSV Text)	**(GRAIL Text)**
Happy are those who do not follow the advice of the wicked,	Happy indeed are those who follow not the counsel of the wicked,
or take the path that sinners tread, or sit in the seat of scoffers;	nor linger in the way of sinners nor sit in the company of scorners,
but their delight is in the law of the Lord,	but whose delight is the law of the Lord
and on his law they meditate day and night.—℟.	and who ponder his law day and night.—℟.

They are like trees planted by streams of water,
which yield their fruit in its season,
and their leaves do not wither.
In all that they do, they prosper.—
℟.

The wicked are not so,
but are like chaff that the wind drives away.
For the Lord watches over the way of the righteous,
but the way of the wicked will perish.—℟. ↓

They are like a tree that is planted beside the flowing waters,
that yields its fruit in due season
and whose leaves shall never fade;
and all that they do shall prosper.—
℟.

Not so are the wicked, not so!
For they, like winnowed chaff
shall be driven away by the wind.
For the Lord guards the way of the just
but the way of the wicked leads to doom.—℟. ↓

SECOND READING 1 Cor. 15.12, 16-20 [Hope for Eternity]

If our hopes in Christ are limited to this life only, we are the most pitiable of human beings.

A reading from the first letter of Paul
to the Corinthians

IF Christ is proclaimed as raised from the dead, how can some of you say there is no resurrection of the dead?

For if the dead are not raised, then Christ has not been raised. If Christ has not been raised, your faith is futile and you are still in your sins. Then those also who have died in Christ have perished.

If for this life only we have hoped in Christ, we are of all people most to be pitied. But in fact Christ has been raised from the dead, the first fruits of those who have died.—The word of the Lord. ℟. **Thanks be to God.** ↓

GOSPEL ACCLAMATION Lk. 6.23 [Heavenly Reward]

(If the Alleluia is not sung, the acclamation is omitted.)

℣. Alleluia. ℟. **Alleluia.**

℣. Rejoice and be glad;

your reward will be great in heaven.

℞. **Alleluia.** ↓

GOSPEL Lk. 6.17, 20-26   [The Beatitudes]

> Happiness and blessing are the reward of those who accept the Gospel and the Saviour. Sorrow and woe await those who take wealth and pleasure as their goal in life.

℣. The Lord be with you. ℞. **And also with you.**
✚ A reading from the holy gospel according to Luke. ℞. **Glory to you, Lord.**

JESUS came down with the twelve and stood on a level place, with a great crowd of his disciples and a great multitude of people from all Judea, Jerusalem, and the coast of Tyre and Sidon.

Then Jesus looked up at his disciples and said:
"Blessed are you who are poor,
   for yours is the kingdom of God.
Blessed are you who are hungry now,
   for you will be filled.
Blessed are you who weep now,
   for you will laugh.
Blessed are you when people hate you,
   and when they exclude you, revile you,
      and defame you
   on account of the Son of Man.

"Rejoice in that day and leap for joy,
   for surely your reward is great in heaven;
   for that is what their ancestors did to the
      prophets.

"But woe to you who are rich,
   for you have received your consolation.
Woe to you who are full now,
   for you will be hungry.

Woe to you who are laughing now,
 for you will mourn and weep.
Woe to you when all speak well of you,
 for that is what their ancestors did to the
 false prophets."

The gospel of the Lord. ℟. **Praise to you, Lord
Jesus Christ.**   ➥ No. 14, p. 18

PRAYER OVER THE GIFTS   [Obedience]

Lord,
we make this offering in obedience to your
 word.
May it cleanse and renew us,
and lead us to our eternal reward.
We ask this in the name of Jesus the Lord.
℟. **Amen.**   ➥ No. 21, p. 24 (Pref. 29-36)

COMMUNION ANTIPHON Ps. 77 (78).29-30
[God's Food]

**They ate and were filled; the Lord gave them
what they wanted: they were not deprived of
their desire. ↓**

OR Jn. 3.16   [God's Love]

**God loved the world so much, he gave his only
Son, that all who believe in him might not perish, but might have eternal life. ↓**

PRAYER AFTER COMMUNION   [Bread of Life]

Lord,
you give us food from heaven.
May we always hunger
for the bread of life.
Grant this through Christ our Lord.
℟. **Amen.**   ➥ No. 32, p. 75

Optional Solemn Blessings, p. 96, and Prayers Over the People, p. 104

"Do not condemn, and you will not be condemned."

FEBRUARY 18

7th SUNDAY IN ORDINARY TIME

ENTRANCE ANTIPHON Ps. 12 (13).5-6 [God's Mercy]

Lord, your mercy is my hope, my heart rejoices in your saving power. I will sing to the Lord for his goodness to me. → No. 2, p. 10

OPENING PRAYER [Imitating Christ]

Father,
keep before us the wisdom and love
you have revealed in your Son.
Help us to be like him
in word and deed,
for he lives and reigns with you and the Holy
   Spirit,
one God, for ever and ever. R̠. **Amen.** ↓

FIRST READING 1 Sam. 26.2, 7-9, 12-13, 22-25

[David Spares Saul]

King Saul has condemned David and is trying to capture him. David has the opportunity to kill Saul, but refuses to harm the king because Saul is anointed by the Lord.

194

A reading from the first book of Samuel

HAVING heard that David was hiding out in the desert, Saul rose and went down to the Wilderness of Ziph, with three thousand chosen men of Israel, to seek David in the Wilderness of Ziph.

David and Abishai went into Saul's army by night; there Saul lay sleeping within the encampment, with his spear stuck in the ground at his head; and Abner and the army lay around him. Abishai said to David, "God has given your enemy into your hand today; now therefore let me pin him to the ground with one stroke of the spear; I will not strike him twice." But David said to Abishai, "Do not destroy him; for who can raise his hand against the Lord's anointed, and be guiltless?"

So David took the spear that was at Saul's head and the water jar, and they went away. No one saw it, or knew it, nor did anyone awake; for they were all asleep, because a deep sleep from the Lord had fallen upon them.

Then David went over to the other side, and stood on top of a hill far away, with a great distance between them. David called aloud to Saul, "Here is the spear, O king! Let one of the young men come over and get it. The Lord rewards everyone for his righteousness and his faithfulness; for the Lord gave you into my hand today, but I would not raise my hand against the Lord's anointed. As your life was precious today in my sight, so may my life be precious in the sight of the Lord, and may he rescue me from all tribulation."

Then Saul said to David, "Blessed be you, my son David! You will do many things and will succeed in them."

So David went his way, and Saul returned to his place.—The word of the Lord. ℟. **Thanks be to God.** ↓

RESPONSORIAL PSALM Ps. 102 (103)

[The Lord's Mercy]

℟. The   Lord   is   kind and mer-ci-ful.

(NRSV Text)	(GRAIL Text)
Bless the Lord, O my soul, and all that is within me, bless his holy name. Bless the Lord, O my soul, and do not forget all his benefits.—℟.	My soul, give thanks to the Lord all my being, bless his holy name. My soul, give thanks to the Lord and never forget all his blessings.— ℟.
It is the Lord who forgives all your iniquity, who heals all your diseases, who redeems your life from the Pit, who crowns you with steadfast love and mercy.—℟.	It is he who forgives all your guilt, who heals every one of your ills, who redeems your life from the grave, who crowns you with love and compassion.—℟.
The Lord is merciful and gracious, slow to anger and abounding in steadfast love. He does not deal with us according to our sins, nor repay us according to our iniquities.—℟.	The Lord is compassion and love, slow to anger and rich in mercy. He does not treat us according to our sins, nor repay us according to our faults.—℟.
As far as the east is from the west, so far he removes our transgressions from us. As a father has compassion for his children, so the Lord has compassion for those who fear him.—℟. ↓	As far as the east is from the west so far does he remove our sins. As parents have compassion on their children, the Lord has pity on those who fear him.—℟. ↓

SECOND READING 1 Cor. 15.45-50   [Grace and Nature]

Grace builds on nature. In Christ we are formed in the spiritual order.

A reading from the first letter of Paul
to the Corinthians

IT is written: "The first man, Adam, became a living being"; the last Adam became a life-giving spirit. But it is not the spiritual that is first, but the physical, and then the spiritual.

The first was from the earth, made of dust; the second is from heaven. As was the one of dust, so are those who are of the dust; and as is the one of heaven, so are those who are of heaven.

Just as we have borne the image of the one of dust, we will also bear the image of the one of heaven.

What I am saying, brothers and sisters, is this: flesh and blood cannot inherit the kingdom of God, nor does the perishable inherit the imperishable.—The word of the Lord. ℞.
Thanks be to God. ↓

GOSPEL ACCLAMATION Jn. 13.34 [Love One Another]
(If the Alleluia is not sung, the acclamation is omitted.)

℣. Alleluia. ℞. **Alleluia.**
℣. I give you a new commandment:
love one another as I have loved you.
℞. **Alleluia.** ↓

GOSPEL Lk. 6.27-38   [Love for Enemies]

The supernatural virtues go beyond the natural virtues, which even sinners practise.

℣. The Lord be with you. ℞. **And also with you.**
✚ A reading from the holy gospel according to
Luke. ℞. **Glory to you, Lord.**

JESUS addressed a great crowd of his disciples, together with the multitude from Judea, Jerusalem, Tyre and Sidon. "I say to you that listen, Love your enemies, do good to those who hate you, bless those who curse you, pray for those who abuse you. If anyone strikes you on the cheek, offer the other also; and from anyone who takes away your coat do not withhold even your shirt. Give to everyone who begs from you; and if anyone takes away your goods, do not ask for them again. Do to others as you would have them do to you.

"If you love those who love you, what credit is that to you? For even sinners love those who love them. If you do good to those who do good to you, what credit is that to you? For even sinners do the same. If you lend to those from whom you hope to receive, what credit is that to you? Even sinners lend to sinners, to receive as much again. But love your enemies, do good, and lend, expecting nothing in return. Your reward will be great, and you will be children of the Most High; for he is kind to the ungrateful and the wicked. Be merciful, just as your Father is merciful.

"Do not judge, and you will not be judged; do not condemn, and you will not be condemned. Forgive, and you will be forgiven; give, and it will be given to you. A good measure, pressed down, shaken together, running over, will be put into your lap; for the measure you give will be the measure you get back."—The gospel of the Lord. ℞. **Praise to you, Lord Jesus Christ.**

→ No. 14, p. 18

PRAYER OVER THE GIFTS   [Spirit and Truth]

Lord,
as we make this offering,
may our worship in Spirit and truth
bring us salvation.
We ask this in the name of Jesus the Lord.
℟. **Amen.**   → No. 21, p. 24 (Pref. 29-36)

COMMUNION ANTIPHON Ps. 9.1-2   [Joy in God]

**I will tell all your marvellous works. I will re-
joice and be glad in you, and sing to your
name, Most High.** ↓

OR Jn. 11.27   [Belief in Christ]

**Lord, I believe that you are the Christ, the Son
of God, who was to come into this world.** ↓

PRAYER AFTER COMMUNION   [Example of Love]

Almighty God,
help us to live the example of love
we celebrate in this eucharist,
that we may come to its fulfilment in your presence.
We ask this through Christ our Lord.
℟. **Amen.**   → No. 32, p. 75

Optional Solemn Blessings, p. 96, and Prayers Over the People, p. 104

"Whenever you fast, do not look dismal. . . ."

FEBRUARY 21

ASH WEDNESDAY

ENTRANCE ANTIPHON See Wis. 11.24-25, 26

[Repentance]

Lord, you are merciful to all, and hate nothing you have created. You overlook the sins of men to bring them to repentance. You are the Lord our God.

➜ No. 2, p. 10 (Omit Penitential Rite and Gloria)

OPENING PRAYER   [Holiness through Self-Denial]

Lord,
protect us in our struggle against evil.
As we begin the discipline of Lent,
make this day holy by our self-denial.
Grant this . . . for ever and ever. ℟. **Amen.** ↓

FIRST READING Joel 2.12-18   [Rend Your Hearts]

The prophet points to the fact that "works" of penance, if not related to that inner conversion to God in love, are worthless. Whatever has happened in the past, God is merciful and willing to forgive.

A reading from the book of the prophet Joel

"EVEN now," says the Lord,
"return to me with all your heart,
with fasting, with weeping, and with mourning;
rend your hearts and not your clothing.
"Return to the Lord, your God,
for he is gracious and merciful,
slow to anger, and abounding in steadfast love,
and relents from punishing."
Who knows whether the Lord will not turn and
    relent,
and leave a blessing behind him:
a grain offering and a drink offering
to be presented to the Lord, your God?

Blow the trumpet in Zion;
sanctify a fast;
call a solemn assembly;
gather the people.
Sanctify the congregation;
assemble the aged;
gather the children, even infants at the breast.
Let the bridegroom leave his room,
and the bride her canopy.

Between the vestibule and the altar
let the priests, the ministers of the Lord, weep.
Let them say, "Spare your people, O Lord,
and do not make your heritage a mockery,
a byword among the nations.
Why should it be said among the peoples,
'Where is their God?' "
Then the Lord became jealous for his land,
and had pity on his people.
The word of the Lord. ℟. **Thanks be to God.** ↓

RESPONSORIAL PSALM Ps. 50 (51) [Confession of Sin]

℞. **Be merciful,**   **O Lord,**   **for**   **we have sinned.**

(℞. **Have mercy on us, Lord, for we have sinned.**)

(NRSV Text)	(GRAIL Text)
Have mercy on me, O God, according to your steadfast love; according to your abundant mercy blot out my transgressions. Wash me thoroughly from my iniquity, and cleanse me from my sin.—℞.	Have mercy on me, God, in your kindness. In your compassion blot out my offense. O wash me more and more from my guilt and cleanse me from my sin.—℞.
For I know my transgressions, and my sin is ever before me. Against you, you alone, have I sinned, and done what is evil in your sight.—℞.	My offenses truly I know them; my sin is always before me. Against you, you alone, have I sinned; what is evil in your sight I have done.—℞.
Create in me a clean heart, O God, and put a new and right spirit within me. Do not cast me away from your presence, and do not take your holy spirit from me.—℞.	A pure heart create for me, O God, put a steadfast spirit within me. Do not cast me away from your presence, nor deprive me of your holy spirit.—℞.
Restore to me the joy of your salvation, and sustain in me a willing spirit. O Lord, open my lips and my mouth will declare your praise.—℞. ↓	Give me again the joy of your help; with a spirit of fervor sustain me. O Lord, open my lips and my mouth shall declare your praise.—℞. ↓

SECOND READING 2 Cor. 5.20—6.2   [Acceptable Time]

Paul insists on conversion now! "God made Christ to be sin who knew no sin," meaning, Jesus became the Lamb of God who took away our sins. Forgiveness is available. Ask for it now! "Now is the acceptable time."

A reading from the second letter of Paul
to the Corinthians

W E are ambassadors for Christ, since God
is making his appeal through us; we entreat you on behalf of Christ, be reconciled to
God. For our sake God made Christ to be sin
who knew no sin, so that in Christ we might
become the righteousness of God.

As we work together with him, we urge you
also not to accept the grace of God in vain. For
the Lord says,

"At an acceptable time I have listened to you,
and on a day of salvation I have helped
you."

See, now is the acceptable time; see, now is
the day of salvation!—The word of the Lord. ℟.
Thanks be to God. ↓

GOSPEL ACCLAMATION Ps. 94 (95).7-8[God's Voice]
(If the acclamation is not sung, it is omitted.)

℣. Praise to you, Lord Jesus Christ, king of
endless glory!
℟. **Praise to you, Lord Jesus Christ, king of
endless glory!**
℣. If today you hear God's voice,
harden not your hearts.
℟. **Praise to you, Lord Jesus Christ, king of
endless glory!** ↓

GOSPEL Mt. 6.1-6, 16-18   [Almsgiving, Prayer, and Fasting]
The Gospel message is similar to the one in the first
Bible reading. External works of penance have no value
in themselves. We must relate them to the real
penance, our conversion to God.

℣. The Lord be with you. ℟. **And also with you.**
✛ A reading from the holy gospel according to
Matthew. ℟. **Glory to you, Lord.**

JESUS said to the disciples, "Beware of prac-
tising your piety before others in order to be
seen by them; for then you have no reward
from your Father in heaven.

"So whenever you give alms, do not sound a
trumpet before you, as the hypocrites do in the
synagogues and in the streets, so that they may
be praised by others. Truly I tell you, they have
received their reward. But when you give alms,
do not let your left hand know what your right
hand is doing, so that your alms may be done
in secret; and your Father who sees in secret
will reward you.

"And whenever you pray, do not be like the
hypocrites; for they love to stand and pray in
the synagogues and at the street corners, so
that they may be seen by others. Truly I tell
you, they have received their reward. But
whenever you pray, go into your room and shut
the door and pray to your Father who is in secret; and your Father who sees in secret will reward you.

"And whenever you fast, do not look dismal,
like the hypocrites, for they disfigure their
faces so as to show others that they are fasting.
Truly I tell you, they have received their reward. But when you fast, put oil on your head
and wash your face, so that your fasting may
be seen not by others but by your Father who is
in secret; and your Father who sees in secret

will reward you."—The gospel of the Lord. ℟.
Praise to you, Lord Jesus Christ. ➜ No. 14, p. 18

BLESSING AND GIVING OF ASHES

After the homily the priest joins his hands and says:

    Dear friends in Christ, let us ask our Father to bless
these ashes which we will use as the mark of our repentance. ↓

Pause for silent prayer

Lord,   [Blessing of Ashes]
bless the sinner who asks for your forgiveness
and bless ✠ all those who receive these ashes.
May they keep this lenten season
in preparation for the joy of Easter.
We ask this through Christ our Lord.
℟. **Amen.** ↓

OR: [Faithful to the Discipline of Lent]
Lord,
bless these ashes ✠
by which we show that we are dust.
Pardon our sins
and keep us faithful to the discipline of Lent,
for you do not want sinners to die
but to live with the risen Christ,
who reigns with you for ever and ever.
℟. **Amen.** ↓

He sprinkles the ashes with holy water in silence.

*The priest then places ashes on those who come for-
ward, saying to each:*

[Reject Sin]

Turn away from sin and be faithful to the gospel. (Mk.
1.15)

OR: [Dust to Dust]
Remember, man, you are dust
and to dust you will return. (See Gen. 3.19)

Meanwhile some of the following antiphons or other appropriate songs are sung.

ANTIPHON 1 See Joel 2.13   [Turn to God]

Come back to the Lord with all your heart; leave the past in ashes, and turn to God with tears and fasting, for he is slow to anger and ready to forgive.

ANTIPHON 2 See Joel 2.17; Esth. 13.17   [Prayer for Mercy]

Let the priests and ministers of the Lord lament before his altar, and say: Spare us, Lord; spare your people! Do not let us die for we are crying out to you.

ANTIPHON 3 Ps. 50 (51).3   [Remove Our Wickedness]

Lord, take away our wickedness.

These may be repeated after each verse of Psalm 51, Have mercy on me, O God.

RESPONSORY See Bar. 3.5   [Plea for Mercy]

Direct our hearts to better things, O Lord; heal our sin and ignorance. Lord, do not face us suddenly with death, but give us time to repent.

℟. **Turn to us with mercy, Lord; we have sinned against you.**

℣. **Help us, God our saviour, rescue us for the honour of your name.** (Ps. 78 (79).9)

℟. **Turn to us with mercy, Lord; we have sinned against you.**

After the giving of ashes the priest washes his hands; the rite concludes with the General Intercessions or Prayer of the Faithful. The Profession of Faith is not said.

PRAYER OVER THE GIFTS   [Renewal in Spirit]

Lord,
help us to resist temptation
by our lenten works of charity and penance.

By this sacrifice
may we be prepared to celebrate
the death and resurrection of Christ our
   Saviour
and be cleansed from sin and renewed in spirit.
We ask this through Christ our Lord. ℟. **Amen.** ↓

PREFACE (11)   [The Reward of Fasting]

℣. The Lord be with you. ℟. **And also with you.**
℣. Lift up your hearts. ℟. **We lift them up to the
Lord.** ℣. Let us give thanks to the Lord our God.
℟. **It is right to give him thanks and praise.**

Father, all-powerful and ever-living God,
we do well always and everywhere to give you
   thanks.
Through our observance of Lent
you correct our faults and raise our minds to
   you,
you help us grow in holiness,
and offer us the reward of everlasting life
through Jesus Christ our Lord.
Through him the angels and all the choirs of
   heaven
worship in awe before your presence.
May our voices be one with theirs
as they sing with joy the hymn of your glory:

→ No. 23, p. 25

COMMUNION ANTIPHON Ps. 1.2-3   [Meditation]
**The man who meditates day and night on the
law of the Lord will yield fruit in due season.** ↓

PRAYER AFTER COMMUNION   [Fruits of Penance]
Lord,
through this communion

may our lenten penance give you glory
and bring us your protection.
We ask this in the name of Jesus the Lord.
℟. **Amen.**   ➜ No. 32, p. 75

Optional Solemn Blessings, p. 96, and Prayers Over the People, p. 104

"Jesus answered . . . , 'Do not put the Lord
your God to the test.'"

FEBRUARY 25

1st SUNDAY OF LENT

ENTRANCE ANTIPHON Ps. 90 (91).15-16   [Long Life]
**When he calls to me, I will answer; I will res-
cue him and give him honour. Long life and
contentment will be his.**
                              ➜ No. 2, p. 10 (Omit Gloria)

OPENING PRAYER   [Christ's Saving Love]
Father,
through our observance of Lent,
help us to understand the meaning
of your Son's death and resurrection,

and teach us to reflect it in our lives.
Grant this . . . for ever and ever. ℟. **Amen.** ↓

FIRST READING Deut. 26.4-10   [Confession of Faith]

The fruits of our labour are from God. Before we use and enjoy them we should first acknowledge God's bounty with dedication and thanks.

A reading from the book of Deuteronomy

MOSES spoke to the people, saying: "When the priest takes the basket from your hand and sets it down before the altar of the Lord your God, you shall make this response before the Lord your God:

" 'A wandering Aramean was my ancestor; he went down into Egypt and lived there as an alien, few in number, and there he became a great nation, mighty and populous. When the Egyptians treated us harshly and afflicted us, by imposing hard labour on us, we cried to the Lord, the God of our ancestors; the Lord heard our voice and saw our affliction, our toil, and our oppression.

" 'The Lord brought us out of Egypt with a mighty hand and an outstretched arm, with a terrifying display of power, and with signs and wonders; and he brought us into this place and gave us this land, a land flowing with milk and honey. So now I bring the first of the fruit of the ground that you, O Lord, have given me.' "

And Moses continued, "You shall set it down before the Lord your God and bow down before the Lord your God."—The word of the Lord. ℟. **Thanks be to God.** ↓

RESPONSORIAL PSALM Ps. 90 (91)   [Call for Help]

℟. Be with me, Lord, when I am in trou-ble.

(℟. Be with me, Lord, when I am in trouble, be with me, Lord, I pray.)

(NRSV Text)	**(GRAIL Text)**
You who live in the shelter of the Most High,	Those who dwell in the shelter of the Most High
who abide in the shadow of the Almighty,	and abide in the shade of the Almighty
will say to the Lord, "My refuge and my fortress;	say to the Lord, "My refuge, my stronghold, my God in whom I
my God, in whom I trust."—℟.	trust!"—℟.
No evil shall befall you,	Upon you no evil shall fall,
no scourge come near your tent.	no plague approach where you dwell.
For he will command his angels concerning you	For you he has commanded his angels,
to guard you in all your ways.—℟.	to keep you in all your ways.—℟.
On their hands they will bear you up,	They shall bear you upon their hands
so that you will not dash your foot against a stone.	lest you strike your foot against a stone.
You will tread on the lion and the adder,	On the lion and the viper you will tread
the young lion and the serpent you will trample under foot.—℟.	and trample the young lion and the dragon.—℟.
Those who love me, I will deliver;	You set your love on me so I will save you,
I will protect those who know my name.	protect you for you know my name.
When they call to me, I will answer them;	When you call I shall answer: "I am with you."
I will be with them in trouble, I will rescue them and honour them.—℟. ↓	I will save you in distress and give you glory.—℟. ↓

SECOND READING Rom. 10.8-13   [Creed of Christians]
Holiness (justification) is rooted in faith. Believe in your heart that Jesus is raised from the dead.

A reading from the letter of Paul
to the Romans

BROTHERS and sisters, what does scripture
say?
"The word is near you,
    on your lips and in your heart"
(that is, the word of faith that we proclaim); because if you confess with your lips that Jesus is
Lord and believe in your heart that God raised
him from the dead, you will be saved.

For one believes with the heart and so is justified, and one confesses with the mouth and so
is saved.

The scripture says, "No one who believes in
him will be put to shame." For there is no dis-
tinction between Jew and Greek; the same
Lord is Lrd of all and is generous to all who
call on him. For, "Everyone who calls on the
name of the Lord shall be saved."—The word of
the Lord. ℟. **Thanks be to God. ↓**

GOSPEL ACCLAMATION Mt. 4.4   [Source of Life]

(If the acclamation is not sung, it is omitted.)

℣. Praise to you, Lord, king of eternal glory!
℟. **Praise to you, Lord, king of eternal glory!**
℣. No one lives on bread alone,
but on every word that comes from the mouth
    of God.
℟. **Praise to you, Lord, king of eternal glory! ↓**

GOSPEL Lk. 4.1-13   [Practising Our Creed]

Jesus is fully human and overcomes the temptation of
Satan. As Messiah he will not resort to expediency.

℣. The Lord be with you. ℟. **And also with you.**
✛ A reading from the holy gospel according to
Luke. ℟. **Glory to you, Lord.**

JESUS, full of the Holy Spirit, returned from
the Jordan and was led by the Spirit in the
wilderness, where for forty days he was
tempted by the devil. He ate nothing at all during those days, and when they were over, he
was famished.

The devil said to him, "If you are the Son of
God, command this stone to become a loaf of
bread." Jesus answered him, "It is written, 'One
does not live by bread alone.' "

Then the devil led him up and showed him in
an instant all the kingdoms of the world. And
the devil said to him, "To you I will give their
glory and all this authority; for it has been
given over to me, and I give it to anyone I
please. If you, then, will worship me, it will all
be yours." Jesus answered him, "It is written,

'Worship the Lord your God,
   and serve only him.' "

Then the devil took him to Jerusalem, and
placed him on the pinnacle of the temple, saying to him, "If you are the Son of God, throw
yourself down from here, for it is written,

'He will command his angels concerning you,
      to protect you,'

and

'On their hands they will bear you up,
      so that you will not dash your foot against
   a stone.' "

Jesus answered him, "It is said, 'Do not put
the Lord your God to the test.' "

When the devil had finished every test, he departed from him until an opportune time.— The gospel of the Lord. ℞. **Praise to you, Lord Jesus Christ.**   ➡ No. 14, p. 18

PRAYER OVER THE GIFTS   [Better Lives]

Lord,
make us worthy to bring you these gifts.
May this sacrifice
help to change our lives.
We ask this in the name of Jesus the Lord.
℞. **Amen.** ↓

PREFACE (12) (or nos. 8-9, pp. 84-85)   [Christ's Self-Denial]

℣. The Lord be with you. ℞. **And also with you.**
℣. Lift up your hearts. ℞. **We lift them up to the Lord.** ℣. Let us give thanks to the Lord our God.
℞. **It is right to give him thanks and praise.**

Father, all-powerful and ever-living God,
we do well always and everywhere to give you
    thanks
through Jesus Christ our Lord.
His fast of forty days
makes this a holy season of self-denial.
By rejecting the devil's temptations
he has taught us
to rid ourselves of the hidden corruption of evil,
and so share his paschal meal in purity of heart,
until we come to its fulfilment
in the promised land of heaven.
Now we join the angels and the saints
as they sing their unending hymn of praise:
                    ➡ No. 23, p. 25

COMMUNION ANTIPHON Mt. 4.4 [Life-Giving Word]

Man does not live on bread alone, but on every word that comes from the mouth of God. ↓

OR Ps. 90 (91).4   [Refuge in God]

The Lord will overshadow you, and you will find refuge under his wings. ↓

PRAYER AFTER COMMUNION   [Bread of Life]

Father,
you increase our faith and hope,
you deepen our love in this communion.
Help us to live by your words
and to seek Christ, our bread of life,
who is Lord for ever and ever.
℟. **Amen.**   → No. 32, p. 75

Optional Solemn Blessings, p. 96, and Prayers Over the People, p. 104

"They saw . . . Moses and Elijah, talking to Jesus. They appeared in glory."

MARCH 4

2nd SUNDAY OF LENT

ENTRANCE ANTIPHON Ps.24 (25).6, 3, 22

[God's Mercies]

Remember your mercies, Lord, your tenderness from ages past. Do not let our enemies triumph over us; O God, deliver Israel from all her distress.

OR Ps. 26 (27).8-9 [God's Face]

My heart has prompted me to seek your face; I seek it, Lord; do not hide from me.

→ No. 2, p. 10 (Omit Gloria)

OPENING PRAYER [Our Response]

God our Father,
help us to hear your Son.
Enlighten us with your word,
that we may find the way to your glory.
We ask this . . . for ever and ever. ℟. **Amen.** ↓

FIRST READING Gen. 15.5-12, 17-18   [God's Covenant]

By faith Abram finds favour with the Lord. The Lord
makes a covenant, that is, establishes a special relation-
ship, with Abram and his descendants.

A reading from the book of Genesis

THE Lord brought Abram outside and said,
"Look toward heaven and count the stars, if
you are able to count them." Then the Lord
said to him, "So shall your descendants be."
And Abram believed the Lord; and the Lord
reckoned it to him as righteousness.

Then the Lord said to Abram, "I am the Lord
who brought you from Ur of the Chaldeans, to
give you this land to possess."

But Abram said, "O Lord God, how am I to
know that I shall possess it?"

The Lord said to him, "Bring me a heifer
three years old, a female goat three years old, a
ram three years old, a turtledove, and a young
pigeon." Abram brought the Lord all these and
cut them in two, laying each half over against
the other; but he did not cut the birds in two.
And when birds of prey came down on the car-
casses, Abram drove them away.

As the sun was going down, a deep sleep fell
upon Abram, and a deep and terrifying darkness descended upon him. When the sun had
gone down and it was dark, a smoking fire pot
and a flaming torch passed between these
pieces.

On that day the Lord made a covenant with
Abram, saying, "To your descendants I give
this land, from the river of Egypt to the great

river, the river Euphrates."—The word of the
Lord. ℟. **Thanks be to God.** ↓

RESPONSORIAL PSALM Ps. (26) 27 [Union with God]

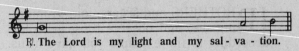

℟. **The Lord is my light and my sal- va- tion.**

(NRSV Text)	**(GRAIL Text)**
The Lord is my light and my salvation; whom shall I fear? The Lord is the stronghold of my life; of whom shall I be afraid?—℟.	The Lord is my light and my help; who shall I fear? The Lord is the stronghold of my life; before whom shall I shrink?—℟.
Hear, O Lord, when I cry aloud, be gracious to me and answer me! "Come," my heart says, "seek his face!" Your face, Lord, do I seek.—℟.	O Lord, hear my voice when I call; have mercy and answer. Of you my heart has spoken: "Seek his face."—℟.
Do not hide your face from me. Do not turn your servant away in anger, you who have been my help. Do not cast me off, do not forsake me, O God of my salvation!—℟.	It is your face, O Lord, that I seek; hide not your face. Dismiss not your servant in anger; you have been my help.—℟.
I believe that I shall see the goodness of the Lord in the land of the living. Wait for the Lord; be strong, and let your heart take courage; wait for the Lord!.—℟. ↓	I am sure I shall see the Lord's goodness in the land of the living. Hope in him, hold firm and take heart. Hope in the Lord!—℟. ↓

SECOND READING Phil. 3.17—4.1 or 3.20—4.1

[Citizenship in Heaven]

**Paul exhorts us to turn away from worldly pleasure and
pride, to reject sin. He reminds us that we are not of
this world.**

[If the "Short Form" is used, the indented text in brackets is omitted.]

A reading from the letter of Paul
to the Philippians

[BROTHERS and sisters, join in imitating me, and observe those who live according to the example you have in us. For many live as enemies of the cross of Christ; I have often told you of them, and now I tell you even with tears. Their end is destruction; their god is the belly; and their glory is in their shame; their minds are set on earthly things.]

But our citizenship is in heaven, and it is from there that we are expecting a Saviour, the Lord Jesus Christ. He will transform the body of our humiliation that it may be conformed to the body of his glory, by the power that also enables him to make all things subject to himself.

Therefore, my brothers and sisters, whom I love and long for, my joy and crown, stand firm, my beloved, in the Lord in this way.—The word of the Lord. ℟. **Thanks be to God.** ↓

GOSPEL ACCLAMATION Lk. 9.35 [Hear Him!]

(If the acclamation is not sung, it is omitted.)

℣. Praise to you, Lord, king of eternal glory!
℟. **Praise to you, Lord, king of eternal glory!**
℣. From the shining cloud the Father's voice is heard:
This is my beloved Son, hear him.
℟. **Praise to you, Lord, king of eternal glory!**

GOSPEL Lk. 9.28b-36   [Glimpse of Christ's Glory]

The glory of Christ is revealed, and God manifests the special mission of Christ.

℣. The Lord be with you. ℟. **And also with you.** ✠ A reading from the holy gospel according to Luke. ℟. **Glory to you, Lord.**

JESUS took with him Peter and John and James, and went up on the mountain to pray. And while he was praying, the appearance of his face changed, and his clothes became dazzling white.

Suddenly they saw two men, Moses and Elijah, talking to Jesus. They appeared in glory and were speaking of his departure, which he was about to accomplish at Jerusalem.

Now Peter and his companions were weighed down with sleep; but since they had stayed awake, they saw his glory and the two men who stood with him.

Just as Moses and Elijah were leaving Jesus, Peter said to him, "Master, it is good for us to be here; let us make three tents, one for you, one for Moses, and one for Elijah." Peter did not know what he was saying.

While Peter was saying this, a cloud came and overshadowed them; and they were terrified as they entered the cloud. Then from the cloud came a voice that said, "This is my Son, my Chosen; listen to him!" When the voice had spoken, Jesus was found alone.

And the disciples kept silent and in those days told no one any of the things they had seen.—The gospel of the Lord. ℟. **Praise to you, Lord Jesus Christ.**   → No. 14, p. 18

PRAYER OVER THE GIFTS   [Holiness]

Lord, make us holy.
May this eucharist take away our sins
that we may be prepared
to celebrate the resurrection.
We ask this in the name of Jesus the Lord.
℟. **Amen.** ↓

PREFACE (13) (or nos. 8-9, pp. 84-85)   [Jesus in Glory]

℣. The Lord be with you. ℟. **And also with you.**
℣. Lift up your hearts. ℟. **We lift them up to the
Lord.** ℣. Let us give thanks to the Lord our God.
℟. **It is right to give him thanks and praise.**

Father, all-powerful and ever-living God,
we do well always and everywhere to give you
    thanks
through Jesus Christ our Lord.
On your holy mountain he revealed himself in
    glory
in the presence of his disciples.
He had already prepared them for his ap-
    proaching death.
He wanted to teach them through the Law and
    the Prophets
that the promised Christ had first to suffer
and so come to the glory of his resurrection.
In our unending joy we echo on earth
the song of the angels in heaven
as they praise your glory for ever: ➜ No. 23, p. 25

COMMUNION ANTIPHON Mt. 17.5   [Son of God]

**This is my Son, my beloved, in whom is all my
delight: listen to him.** ↓

PRAYER AFTER COMMUNION   [Life To Come]

Lord,
we give you thanks for these holy mysteries
which bring to us here on earth
a share in the life to come,
through Christ our Lord.
℟. **Amen.**   → No. 32, p. 75

Optional Solemn Blessings, p. 96, and Prayers Over the People, p. 104

"Let it alone for one more year."

MARCH 11
3rd SUNDAY OF LENT

*The Ritual Mass for the First Scrutiny assigned to this
Sunday in the Rite of Christian Initiation of Adults is
found on p. 227.*

ENTRANCE ANTIPHON Ps. 24 (25).15-16

[Eyes on God]

**My eyes are ever fixed on the Lord, for he re-
leases my feet from the snare. O look at me
and be merciful, for I am wretched and alone.**

OR Ezek. 36.23-26   [A New Spirit]

I will prove my holiness through you. I will
gather you from the ends of the earth; I will
pour clean water on you and wash away all
your sins. I will give you a new spirit within
you, says the Lord. → No. 2, p. 10 (Omit Gloria)

OPENING PRAYER   [Prayer, Fasting, Works]

Father,
you have taught us to overcome our sins
by prayer, fasting and works of mercy.
When we are discouraged by our weakness,
give us confidence in your love.
We ask this . . . for ever and ever. ℟. **Amen.** ↓

FIRST READING Ex. 3.1-8a, 13-15   [The Name of God]

The Lord calls Moses to lead the chosen people, and reveals God's name to Moses.

A reading from the book of Exodus

MOSES was keeping the flock of his father-
in-law Jethro, the priest of Midian; he led
his flock beyond the wilderness, and came to
Horeb, the mountain of God. There the angel of
the Lord appeared to him in a flame of fire out
of a bush; Moses looked, and the bush was
blazing, yet it was not consumed.

Then Moses said, "I must turn aside and look
at this great sight, and see why the bush is not
burned up."

When the Lord saw that Moses had turned
aside to see, God called to him out of the bush,
"Moses, Moses!" And Moses said, "Here I am."
Then God said, "Come no closer! Remove the

sandals from your feet, for the place on which you are standing is holy ground."

God said further, "I am the God of your father, the God of Abraham, the God of Isaac, and the God of Jacob." And Moses hid his face, for he was afraid to look at God.

Then the Lord said, "I have observed the misery of my people who are in Egypt; I have heard their cry on account of their taskmasters. Indeed, I know their sufferings, and I have come down to deliver them from the Egyptians, and to bring them up out of that land to a good and broad land, a land flowing with milk and honey."

But Moses said to God, "If I come to the Israelites and say to them, 'The God of your ancestors has sent me to you,' and they ask me, 'What is his name?' what shall I say to them?"

God said to Moses, "I AM WHO I AM." He said further, "Thus you shall say to the Israelites, 'I AM has sent me to you.' "

God also said to Moses, "Thus you shall say to the Israelites, 'The Lord, the God of your ancestors, the God of Abraham, the God of Isaac, and the God of Jacob, has sent me to you.' This is my name forever, and this my title for all generations."—The word of the Lord. ℟. **Thanks be to God.** ↓

RESPONSORIAL PSALM Ps. 102 (103) [God's Mercy]

℟. **The Lord   is   kind   and   mer - ci - ful.**

(NRSV Text)

Bless the Lord, O my soul,
and all that is within me, bless his holy name.
Bless the Lord, O my soul,
and do not forget all his benefits.—
R̸.

It is the Lord who forgives all your iniquity,
heals all your diseases,
who redeems your life from the Pit,
and crowns you with steadfast love and mercy.—R̸.

The Lord works vindication
and justice for all who are oppressed.
He made known his ways to Moses,
his acts to the people of Israel.—R̸.

The Lord is merciful and gracious,
slow to anger and abounding in steadfast love.
For as the heavens are high above the earth,
so great is his steadfast love toward those who fear him.—R̸. ↓

(GRAIL Text)

My soul, give thanks to the Lord
all my being, bless his holy name.
My soul, give thanks to the Lord
and never forget all his blessings.—
R̸.

It is he who forgives all your guilt,
who heals every one of your ills,
who redeems your life from the grave,
who crowns you with love and compassion.—R̸.

The Lord does deeds of justice,
gives judgment for all who are oppressed.
He made known his ways to Moses
and his deeds to Israel's children.—
R̸.

The Lord is compassion and love,
slow to anger and rich in mercy.
For as the heavens are high above the earth
so strong is his love for those who fear him.—R̸. ↓

SECOND READING 1 Cor. 10.1-6, 10-12   [Firm in Faith]

We must remain steadfast in our faith. We cannot become overconfident even though we are the recipients of God's favour and grace.

A reading from the first letter of Paul to the Corinthians

IDO not want you to be unaware, brothers and sisters, that our ancestors were all under the cloud; all passed through the sea; all were baptized into Moses in the cloud and in the sea; all ate the same spiritual food, and all drank the same spiritual drink. For they drank from the spiritual rock that followed them, and the rock was Christ.

Nevertheless, God was not pleased with most of our ancestors, and they were struck down in the wilderness.

Now these things occurred as examples for us, so that we might not desire evil as they did. And do not complain as some of them did, and were destroyed by the destroyer.

These things happened to our ancestors to serve as an example, and they were written down to instruct us, on whom the ends of the ages have come. So if you think you are standing, watch out that you do not fall.—The word of the Lord. ℟. **Thanks be to God.** ↓

GOSPEL ACCLAMATION Mt. 4.17   [Repent]

(If the acclamation is not sung, it is omitted.)

℣. Praise to you, Lord, king of eternal glory!
℟. **Praise to you, Lord, king of eternal glory!**
℣. Repent, says the Lord;
the kingdom of heaven is at hand.
℟. **Praise to you, Lord, king of eternal glory!** ↓

GOSPEL Lk. 13.1-9   [Time To Reform]

Jesus tells us to repent. Time will run out, and no one can ever count on another year. Now is the time!

℣. The Lord be with you. ℟. **And also with you.**
✚ A reading from the holy gospel according to Luke. ℟. **Glory to you, Lord.**

JESUS was teaching the crowds; some of those present told Jesus about the Galileans whose blood Pilate had mingled with their sacrifices.

Jesus asked them, "Do you think that because these Galileans suffered in this way they were worse sinners than all other Galileans? No, I tell you; but unless you repent, you will all perish as they did. Or those eighteen who were killed when the tower of Siloam fell on them—do you think that they were worse offenders than all the others living in Jerusalem? No, I tell you; but unless you repent, you will all perish just as they did."

Then Jesus told this parable: "A man had a fig tree planted in his vineyard; and he came looking for fruit on it and found none. So he said to the gardener, 'See here! For three years I have come looking for fruit on this fig tree, and still I find none. Cut it down! Why should it be wasting the soil?'

"The gardener replied, 'Sir, let it alone for one more year, until I dig around it and put manure on it. If it bears fruit next year, well and good; but if not, you can cut it down.' "—The gospel of the Lord. R̷. **Praise to you, Lord Jesus Christ.**   → No. 14, p. 18

PRAYER OVER THE GIFTS   [Forgiveness]

Lord,
by the grace of this sacrifice
may we who ask forgiveness
be ready to forgive one another.
We ask this in the name of Jesus the Lord.
R̷. **Amen.**   → No. 21, p. 24 (Pref. 8-9)

COMMUNION ANTIPHON Ps. 83 (84).3-4
[God's House]

The sparrow even finds a home, the swallow finds a nest wherein to place her young, near

to your altars, Lord of hosts, my King, my God!
How happy they who dwell in your house! For
ever they are praising you. ↓

PRAYER AFTER COMMUNION   [Unity and Peace]

Lord,
in sharing this sacrament
may we receive your forgiveness
and be brought together in unity and peace.
We ask this through Christ our Lord.
℟. **Amen.**   → No. 32, p. 75

Optional Solemn Blessings, p. 96, and Prayers Over the People, p. 104

MARCH 11

MASS FOR THE FIRST SCRUTINY

*This Mass is celebrated when the First Scrutiny takes
place during the Rite of Christian Initiation of Adults,
usually on the Third Sunday of Lent.*

ENTRANCE ANTIPHON Ezek. 36.23-26   [A New Spirit]

I will prove my holiness through you. I will gather you
from the ends of the earth; I will pour clean water on
you and wash away all your sins. I will give you a new
spirit within you, says the Lord.

→ No. 2, p. 10 (Omit Gloria)

OPENING PRAYER   [Growth in Wisdom and Love]

Lord,
you call these chosen ones
to the glory of a new birth in Christ, the second Adam.
Help them grow in wisdom and love
as they prepare to profess their faith in you.
Grant this . . . for ever and ever. ℟. **Amen.** ↓

FIRST READING Ex. 17.3-7   [Water from a Rock]

The Israelites murmured against God in their thirst. God directs Moses to strike a rock with his staff, and water issues forth.

A reading from the book of Exodus

IN the wilderness the people thirsted for water; and the people complained against Moses and said, "Why did you bring us out of Egypt, to kill us and our children and livestock with thirst?" So Moses cried out to the Lord, "What shall I do with this people? They are almost ready to stone me."

The Lord said to Moses, "Go on ahead of the people, and take some of the elders of Israel with you; take in your hand the staff with which you struck the Nile, and go. I will be standing there in front of you on the rock at Horeb. Strike the rock, and water will come out of it, so that the people may drink."

Moses did so, in the sight of the elders of Israel. He called the place Massah and Meribah, because the Israelites quarrelled and tested the Lord, saying, "Is the Lord among us or not?"—The word of the Lord. ℞. **Thanks be to God.** ↓

RESPONSORIAL PSALM Ps. 94 (95)   [The Lord Our Rock]

℞. **If today you hear God's voice, harden not your hearts.**

(℞. **O that today you would listen to his voice! Harden not your hearts.**)

(NRSV Text)	(GRAIL Text)
O come, let us sing to the Lord; let us make a joyful noise to the rock of our salvation! Let us come into his presence with thanksgiving; let us make a joyful noise to him with songs of praise!—℞.	Come, ring out your joy to the Lord; hail the rock who saves us. Let us come before him, giving thanks, with songs let us hail the Lord.—℞.

O come, let us worship and bow down, let us kneel before the Lord, our Maker!

For he is our God, and we are the people of his pasture,

and the sheep of his hand.—℟.

O that today you would listen to his voice!

Do not harden your hearts, as at Meribah,

as on the day at Massah in the wilderness,

when your ancestors tested me, and put me to the proof,

though they had seen my work.— ℟. ↓

Come in; let us bow and bend low; let us kneel before the God who made us

for he is our God and we

the people who belong to his pasture,

the flock that is led by his hand.— ℟.

O that today you would listen to his voice!

"Harden not your hearts as at Meribah,

as on the day at Massah in the desert

when your forebears put me to the test;

when they tried me, though they saw my work."—℟. ↓

SECOND READING Rom. 5.1-2, 5-8   [God's Love for Us]

Through Jesus we have received the grace of faith. The love of God has been poured upon us. Jesus laid down his life for us while we were still sinners.

A reading from the letter of Paul
to the Romans

SINCE we are justified by faith, we have peace with God through our Lord Jesus Christ, through whom we have obtained access to this grace in which we stand; and we boast in our hope of sharing the glory of God.

And hope does not disappoint us, because God's love has been poured into our hearts through the Holy Spirit that has been given to us. For while we were still weak, at the right time Christ died for the ungodly. Indeed, rarely will anyone die for a righteous person, though perhaps for a good person someone might actually dare to die. But God proves his love for us in that while we still were sinners Christ died for us.— The word of the Lord. ℟. **Thanks be to God.** ↓

GOSPEL ACCLAMATION Jn. 4.42, 15   [Living Water]

(If the acclamation is not sung, it is omitted.)

℣. Praise to you, Lord, king of eternal glory!
℟. **Praise to you, Lord, king of eternal glory!**
℣. Lord, you are truly the Saviour of the world;
give me living water, that I may never thirst again.
℟. **Praise to you, Lord, king of eternal glory!** ↓

GOSPEL Jn. 4.5-42 or 4.5-15, 19-26, 39, 40-42 [Woman at Well]

**Jesus speaks to the Samaritan woman at the well. He
searches her soul, and she recognizes him as a prophet.
Jesus speaks of the water of eternal life.**

*[If the "Short Form" is used, the indented text in
brackets is omitted.]*

℣. The Lord be with you. ℟. **And also with you.** ✟ A
reading from the holy gospel according to John. ℟.
Glory to you, Lord.

JESUS came to a Samaritan city called Sychar, near
the plot of ground that Jacob had given to his son
Joseph. Jacob's well was there, and Jesus, tired out by
his journey, was sitting by the well. It was about noon.

A Samaritan woman came to draw water, and Jesus
said to her, "Give me a drink." (His disciples had gone
to the city to buy food.)

The Samaritan woman said to him, "How is it that
you, a Jew, ask a drink of me, a woman of Samaria?"
(Jews do not share things in common with Samaritans.) Jesus answered her, "If you knew the gift of God,
and who it is that is saying to you, 'Give me a drink,'
you would have asked him, and he would have given
you living water."

The woman said to him, "Sir, you have no bucket,
and the well is deep. Where do you get that living
water? Are you greater than our ancestor Jacob, who
gave us the well, and, with his children and his flocks,
drank from it?" Jesus said to her, "Everyone who
drinks of this water will be thirsty again, but those

who drink of the water that I will give them will never be thirsty. The water that I will give will become in them a spring of water gushing up to eternal life." The woman said to him, "Sir, give me this water, so that I may never be thirsty or have to keep coming here to draw water."

[Jesus said to her, "Go, call your husband, and come back." The woman answered him, "I have no husband." Jesus said to her, "You are right in saying, 'I have no husband'; for you have had five husbands, and the one you have now is not your husband. What you have said is true!"]

The woman said to him, "Sir, I see that you are a prophet. Our ancestors worshipped on this mountain, but you say that the place where people must worship is in Jerusalem."

Jesus said to her, "Woman, believe me, the hour is coming when you will worship the Father neither on this mountain nor in Jerusalem. You worship what you do not know; we worship what we know, for salvation is from the Jews. But the hour is coming, and is now here, when the true worshippers will worship the Father in spirit and truth, for the Father seeks such as these to worship him. God is spirit, and those who worship him must worship in spirit and truth."

The woman said to him, "I know that the Messiah is coming" (who is called the Christ). "When he comes, he will proclaim all things to us." Jesus said to her, "I am he, the one who is speaking to you."

[Just then his disciples came. They were astonished that he was speaking with a woman, but no one said, "What do you want?" or, "Why are you speaking with her?" Then the woman left her water jar and went back to the city. She said to the people, "Come and see a man who told me everything I have ever done! He cannot be the Messiah, can he?" They left the city and were on their way to him. Meanwhile the disciples were urging him, "Rabbi, eat something."

But he said to them, "I have food to eat that you do not know about." So the disciples said to one another, "Surely no one has brought him something to eat?"

Jesus said to them, "My food is to do the will of him who sent me and to complete his work. Do you not say, 'Four months more, then comes the harvest'? But I tell you, look around you, and see how the fields are ripe for harvesting. The reaper is already receiving wages and is gathering fruit for eternal life, so that sower and reaper may rejoice together. For here the saying holds true, 'One sows and another reaps.' I sent you to reap that for which you did not labour. Others have laboured, and you have entered into their labour."]

Many Samaritans from that city believed in Jesus [because of the woman's testimony, "He told me everything I have ever done."]

So when the Samaritans came to him, they asked him to stay with them; and he stayed there two days. And many more believed because of his word. They said to the woman, "It is no longer because of what you said that we believe, for we have heard for ourselves, and we know that this is truly the Saviour of the world."—The gospel of the Lord. ℟. **Praise to you, Lord Jesus Christ.**   → No. 14, p. 18

PRAYER OVER THE GIFTS   [Faith and Love]

Lord God,
give faith and love to your children
and lead them safely to the banquet
you have prepared for them.
We ask this in the name of Jesus the Lord.
℟.. **Amen.** ↓

PREFACE (14)   [Gift of Faith]

℣. The Lord be with you. ℟. **And also with you.** ℣. Lift up your hearts. ℟. **We lift them up to the Lord.** ℣. Let us give thanks to the Lord our God. ℟. **It is right to give him thanks and praise.**

Father, all-powerful and ever-living God,
we do well always and everywhere to give you thanks
through Jesus Christ our Lord.
When he asked the woman of Samaria for water to
    drink,
Christ had already prepared for her the gift of faith.
In his thirst to receive her faith
he awakened in her heart the fire of your love.
With thankful praise,
in company with the angels,
we glorify the wonders of your power: → No. 23, p. 25

When Eucharistic Prayer I is used, the special Christian Initiation forms of Remember, Lord, your people *and* Father, accept this offering *are said.*

Remember, Lord, these godparents
who will present your chosen men and women for baptism *(the names of the godparents are mentioned).*

Lord, remember all of us . . . (p. 26).
Father,
accept this offering
from your whole family.
We offer it especially for the men and women
you call to share your life
through the living waters of baptism.
[Through Christ our Lord. Amen.]
The rest follows the Roman Canon, pp. 27-30.

COMMUNION ANTIPHON Jn. 4.13-14   [Water of Life]
Whoever drinks the water that I shall give him, says the Lord, will have a spring inside him, welling up for eternal life. ↓

PRAYER AFTER COMMUNION   [God's Protection]
Lord,
be present in our lives

with your gifts of salvation.
Prepare these men and women for your sacraments
and protect them in your love.
We ask this in the name of Jesus the Lord.
℞. **Amen.**   → No. 32, p. 75

Optional Solemn Blessings, p. 96, and Prayers Over the People, p. 104

"Father, I have sinned against heaven and before you."

MARCH 18

4th SUNDAY OF LENT

The Ritual Mass for the Second Scrutiny assigned to this Sunday in the Rite of Christian Initiation of Adults is found on p. 240.

ENTRANCE ANTIPHON See Isa. 66.10-11   [Rejoice]

Rejoice, Jerusalem! Be glad for her, you who love her; rejoice with her, you who mourned for her, and you will find contentment at her consoling breasts.

→ No. 2, p. 10 (Omit Gloria)

OPENING PRAYER   [Faith and Love]

Father of peace,
we are joyful in your Word,
your Son Jesus Christ,
who reconciles us to you.
Let us hasten toward Easter
with the eagerness of faith and love.
We ask this . . . for ever and ever. ℞. **Amen.** ↓

FIRST READING Josh. 5.9a, 10-12 [Food for the Israelites]

**The people of God celebrate the Passover in the prom-
ised land. As a sign that they are "home," the manna
from heaven is no longer provided.**

A reading from the book of Joshua

AFTER the Israelites had crossed over the
Jordan river, and entered the promised
land, the Lord said to Joshua, "Today I have
rolled away from you the disgrace of Egypt."

While the Israelites were camped in Gilgal
they kept the Passover in the evening on the
fourteenth day of the month in the plains of
Jericho.

On the day after the Passover, on that very
day, they ate the produce of the land, unleavened
cakes and parched grain. The manna ceased on
the day they ate the produce of the land, and the
Israelites no longer had manna; they ate the
crops of the land of Canaan that year.—The
word of the Lord. ℞. **Thanks be to God.** ↓

RESPONSORIAL PSALM Ps. 33 (34) [God's Goodness]

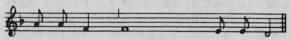

℞. Taste and see   the   goodness   of   the Lord.

(℞. Taste and see that the Lord is good.)

(NRSV Text)	(GRAIL Text)
I will bless the Lord at all times; his praise continually shall be in my mouth. My soul makes its boast in the Lord; let the humble hear and be glad.— Ry.	I will bless the Lord at all times, his praise always on my lips; in the Lord my soul shall make its boast. The humble shall hear and be glad.—Ry.
O magnify the Lord with me, and let us exalt his name together. I sought the Lord, and he answered me, and delivered me from all my fears.—Ry.	Glorify the Lord with me. Together let us praise his name. I sought the Lord and he answered me; from all my terrors he set me free.—Ry.
Look to him, and be radiant; so your faces shall never be ashamed. This poor soul cried, and was heard by the Lord, and was saved from every trouble.—Ry. ↓	Look towards him and be radiant; let your faces not be abashed. When the poor cry out the Lord hears them and rescues them from all their distress.—Ry. ↓

SECOND READING 2 Cor. 5.17-21   [Reconciliation]

Christ, the ambassador, reconciles all to God. Our transgressions find forgiveness in him so that we might become the very holiness of God.

A reading from the second letter of Paul to the Corinthians

IF anyone is in Christ, there is a new creation: everything old has passed away; see, everything has become new! All this is from God, who reconciled us to himself through Christ, and has given us the ministry of reconciliation; that is, in Christ, God was reconciling the world to himself, not counting their trespasses against them, and entrusting the message of reconciliation to us.

So we are ambassadors for Christ, since God is making his appeal through us; we entreat you on behalf of Christ, be reconciled to God. For our sake God made Christ to be sin who knew no sin, so that in Christ we might become the righteousness of God.—The word of the Lord. ℟. **Thanks be to God.** ↓

GOSPEL ACCLAMATION Lk. 15.18   [Return Home]

(If the acclamation is not sung, it is omitted.)

℣. Praise to you, Lord, king of eternal glory!
℟. **Praise to you, Lord, king of eternal glory!**
℣. I will rise and go to my father and tell him: Father, I have sinned against heaven and against you.
℟. **Praise to you, Lord, king of eternal glory!** ↓

GOSPEL Lk. 15.1-3, 11-32   [The Prodigal Son]

Our loving Father is always ready to forgive those who are truly repentant.

℣. The Lord be with you. ℟. **And also with you.**
✠ A reading from the holy gospel according to Luke. ℟. **Glory to you, Lord.**

ALL the tax collectors and sinners were coming near to listen to Jesus. And the Pharisees and the scribes were grumbling and saying, "This fellow welcomes sinners and eats with them."

So he told them a parable: "There was a man who had two sons. The younger of them said to his father, 'Father, give me the share of the property that will belong to me.' So the father divided his property between them. A few days later the younger son gathered all he had and travelled to a distant country, and there he squandered his property in dissolute living.

"When he had spent everything, a severe famine took place throughout that country, and he began to be in need. So he went and hired himself out to one of the citizens of that country, who sent him to his fields to feed the pigs. The young man would gladly have filled himself with the pods that the pigs were eating; and no one gave him anything.

"But when he came to himself he said, 'How many of my father's hired hands have bread enough and to spare, but here I am dying of hunger! I will get up and go to my father, and I will say to him, "Father, I have sinned against heaven and before you; I am no longer worthy to be called your son; treat me like one of your hired hands." '

"So he set off and went to his father. But while he was still far off, his father saw him and was filled with compassion; he ran and put his arms around him and kissed him.

"Then the son said to him, 'Father, I have sinned against heaven and before you; I am no longer worthy to be called your son.' But the father said to his slaves, 'Quickly, bring out a robe—the best one—and put it on him; put a ring on his finger and sandals on his feet. And get the fatted calf and kill it, and let us eat and celebrate; for this son of mine was dead and is alive again; he was lost and is found!' And they began to celebrate.

"Now his elder son was in the field; and when he came and approached the house, he heard music and dancing. He called one of the slaves and asked what was going on. The slave replied, 'Your brother has come, and your father has killed the fatted calf, because he has got him back safe and sound.'

"Then the elder son became angry and refused to go in. His father came out and began to plead with him. But he answered his father, 'Listen! For all these years I have been working like a slave for you, and I have never disobeyed your command; yet you have never given me even a young goat so that I might celebrate with my friends. But when this son of yours came back, who has devoured your property with prostitutes, you killed the fatted calf for him!'

"Then the father said to him, 'Son, you are always with me, and all that is mine is yours. But we had to celebrate and rejoice, because this brother of yours was dead and has come to life; he was lost and has been found.' "—The gospel of the Lord. ℟. **Praise to you, Lord Jesus Christ.**   ➔ No. 14, p. 18

PRAYER OVER THE GIFTS   [Increased Reverence]

Lord,
we offer you these gifts
which bring us peace and joy.
Increase our reverence by this eucharist,
and bring salvation to the world.
We ask this in the name of Jesus the Lord.
℟. **Amen.**   ➔ No. 21, p. 24 (Pref. 8-9)

COMMUNION ANTIPHON Lk. 15.32   [Christian Joy]

My son, you should rejoice, because your brother was dead and has come back to life, he was lost and is found. ↓

PRAYER AFTER COMMUNION [Light of the Gospel]

Father,
you enlighten all who come into the world.
Fill our hearts with the light of your gospel,
that our thoughts may please you,
and our love be sincere.
Grant this through Christ our Lord.
℟. **Amen.**   ➡ No. 32, p. 75

Optional Solemn Blessings, p. 96, and Prayers Over the People, p. 104

MARCH 18

MASS FOR THE SECOND SCRUTINY

This Mass is celebrated when the Second Scrutiny takes place in the Rite of Christian Initiation of Adults, usually on the Fourth Sunday of Lent.

ENTRANCE ANTIPHON Ezek. 36.23-26   [A New Spirit]

I will prove my holiness through you. I will gather you from the ends of the earth; I will pour clean water on you and wash away all your sins. I will give you a new spirit within you, says the Lord.

➡ No. 2, p. 10 (Omit Gloria)

OPENING PRAYER   [Rebirth into the Kingdom]

Almighty and eternal God,
may your Church increase in true joy.
May these candidates for baptism,
and all the family of man,

be reborn into the life of your kingdom.
We ask this . . . for ever and ever. ℟. **Amen.** ↓

FIRST READING 1 Sam. 16.1b, 6-7, 10-13   [God's Anointed]

> **God directs Samuel to anoint David king. God looks into the heart of each person.**

A reading from the first book of Samuel

THE Lord said to Samuel, "Fill your horn with oil and set out; I will send you to Jesse of Bethlehem, for I have provided for myself a king among his sons."

When the sons of Jesse came, Samuel looked on Eliab and thought, "Surely the Lord's anointed is now before the Lord." But the Lord said to Samuel, "Do not look on his appearance or on the height of his stature, because I have rejected him; for the Lord does not see as mortals see; they look on the outward appearance, but the Lord looks on the heart."

Jesse made seven of his sons pass before Samuel, and Samuel said to Jesse, "The Lord has not chosen any of these." Samuel said to Jesse, "Are all your sons here?" And he said, "There remains yet the youngest, but he is keeping the sheep." And Samuel said to Jesse, "Send and bring him; for we will not sit down until he comes here." Jesse sent and brought David in. Now he was ruddy, and had beautiful eyes, and was handsome. The Lord said, "Rise and anoint him; for this is the one."

Then Samuel took the horn of oil, and anointed him in the presence of his brothers; and the spirit of the Lord came mightily upon David from that day forward.—The word of the Lord. ℟. **Thanks be to God.** ↓

RESPONSORIAL PSALM Ps. 22 (23)   [God's Protection]

℟. **The Lord is my shep-herd, there is noth-ing I shall want.**

(NRSV Text)	(GRAIL Text)
The Lord is my shepherd, I shall not want.	The Lord is my shepherd; there is nothing I shall want.
He makes me lie down in green pastures;	Fresh and green are the pastures where he gives me repose.
he leads me beside still waters;	Near restful waters he leads me,
he restores my soul.—℟.	to revive my drooping spirit.—℟.
He leads me in right paths for his name's sake.	He guides me along the right path; he is true to his name.
Even though I walk through the darkest valley, I fear no evil;	If I should walk in the valley of darkness
for you are with me;	no evil would I fear.
your rod and your staff—they comfort me.—℟.	You are there with your crook and your staff; with these you give me comfort.—℟.
You prepare a table before me in the presence of my enemies;	You have prepared a banquet for me in the sight of my foes.
you anoint my head with oil;	My head you have anointed with oil;
my cup overflows.—℟.	my cup is overflowing.—℟.
Surely goodness and mercy shall follow me	Surely goodness and kindness shall follow me
all the days of my life,	all the days of my life.
and I shall dwell in the house of the Lord	In the Lord's own house I shall dwell
my whole life long.—℟. ↓	for ever and ever.—℟. ↓

SECOND READING Eph. 5.8-14   [Children of Light]

We are to walk in the light which shows goodness, justice, and truth. Evil deeds are condemned. Christ gives this light whereby we live.

A reading from the letter of Paul
to the Ephesians

ONCE you were darkness, but now in the Lord you are light. Live as children of light—for the fruit of the light is found in all that is good and right and true.

Try to find out what is pleasing to the Lord. Take no part in the unfruitful works of darkness, but instead expose them. For it is shameful even to mention what such people do secretly; but everything exposed by the light becomes visible, for everything that becomes visible is light. Therefore it is said, "Sleeper, awake! Rise from the dead, and Christ will shine on you."—The word of the Lord. ℟. **Thanks be to God.** ↓

GOSPEL ACCLAMATION Jn. 8.12   [Light of World]

(If the acclamation is not sung, it is omitted.)

℣. Praise to you, Lord, king of eternal glory!
℟. **Praise to you, Lord, king of eternal glory!**
℣. I am the light of the world, says the Lord;
whoever follows me will have the light of life.
℟. **Praise to you, Lord, king of eternal glory!** ↓

GOSPEL Jn. 9.1-41 or 9.1, 6-9, 13-17, 34-38   [The Blind Man]

Jesus is the light. He cures a man born blind by bringing him to see. Jesus identifies himself as the Son of Man.

[If the "Short Form" is used, the indented text in brackets is omitted.]

℣. The Lord be with you. ℟. **And also with you.** ✛ A reading from the holy gospel according to John. ℟. **Glory to you, Lord.**

AS Jesus walked along, he saw a man blind from birth.
[His disciples asked him, "Rabbi, who sinned, this man or his parents, that he was born blind?"

Jesus answered, "Neither this man nor his parents sinned; he was born blind so that God's works might be revealed in him. We must work the works of him who sent me while it is day; night is coming when no one can work. As long as I am in the world, I am the light of the world." When he had said this,]
he spat on the ground and made mud with the saliva and spread the mud on the man's eyes, saying to him, "Go, wash in the pool of Siloam" (which means Sent). Then the man who was blind went and washed, and came back able to see. The neighbours and those who

had seen him before as a beggar began to ask, "Is this not the man who used to sit and beg?" Some were saying, "It is he." Others were saying, "No, but it is someone like him." He kept saying, "I am the man."

[But they kept asking him, "Then how were your eyes opened?" He answered, "The man called Jesus made mud, spread it on my eyes, and said to me, 'Go to Siloam and wash.' Then I went and washed and received my sight." They said to him, "Where is he?" He said, "I do not know."]

They brought to the Pharisees the man who had formerly been blind. Now it was a sabbath day when Jesus made the mud and opened his eyes. Then the Pharisees also began to ask him how he had received his sight. He said to them, "He put mud on my eyes. Then I washed, and now I see." Some of the Pharisees said, "This man is not from God, for he does not observe the sabbath." But others said, "How can a man who is a sinner perform such signs?" And they were divided. So they said again to the blind man, "What do you say about him? It was your eyes he opened." He said, "He is a prophet."

[They did not believe that he had been blind and had received his sight until they called the parents of the man who had received his sight and asked them, "Is this your son, who you say was born blind? How then does he now see?" His parents answered, "We know that this is our son, and that he was born blind; but we do not know how it is that now he sees, nor do we know who opened his eyes. Ask him; he is of age. He will speak for himself." His parents said this because they were afraid of the Jewish authorities, who had already agreed that anyone who confessed Jesus to be the Messiah would be put out of the synagogue. Therefore his parents said, "He is of age; ask him."

So for the second time they called the man who had been blind, and they said to him, "Give glory to God! We know that this man is a sinner." He answered, "I do not know whether he is a sinner. One thing I do know, that though I was blind, now I see." They said to him, "What did he do to you? How did he open your eyes?" He answered them, "I have told you already, and you would not listen. Why do you want to hear it again? Do you also want to become his disciples?" Then they reviled him, saying, "You are his disciple, but we are disciples of Moses. We know that God has spoken to Moses, but as for this man, we do not know where he comes from."

The man answered, "Here is an astonishing thing! You do not know where he comes from, and yet he opened my eyes. We know that God does not listen to sinners, but he does listen to one who worships him and obeys his will. Never since the world began has it been heard that anyone opened the eyes of a person born blind. If this man were not from God, he could do nothing."]

They answered him, "You were born entirely in sins, and are you trying to teach us?" And they drove him out.

Jesus heard that they had driven him out, and when he found him, he said, "Do you believe in the Son of Man?" He answered, "And who is he, sir? Tell me, so that I may believe in him." Jesus said to him, "You have seen him, and the one speaking with you is he." He said, "Lord, I believe." And he worshipped him.

[Jesus said, "I came into this world for judgment so that those who do not see may see, and those who do see may become blind." Some of the Pharisees near him heard this and said to him, "Surely we are not blind, are we?" Jesus said to them, "If you were blind, you would have no sin. But now that you say, 'We see,' your sin remains."]

The gospel of the Lord. ℟. **Praise to you, Lord Jesus Christ.**

→ No. 14, p. 18

PRAYER OVER THE GIFTS   [Faith and Love]

Lord,
we offer these gifts
in joy and thanksgiving for our salvation.
May the example of our faith and love
help your chosen ones on their way to salvation.
Grant this through Christ our Lord. ℟. **Amen.** ↓

PREFACE (15)   [From Darkness to Light]

℣. The Lord be with you. ℟. **And also with you.** ℣. Lift
up your hearts. ℟. **We lift them up to the Lord.** ℣. Let
us give thanks to the Lord our God. ℟. **It is right to
give him thanks and praise.**

Father, all-powerful and ever-living God,
we do well always and everywhere to give you thanks
through Jesus Christ our Lord.
He came among us as a man,
to lead mankind from darkness
into the light of faith.
Through Adam's fall we were born as slaves of sin,
but now through baptism in Christ
we are reborn as your adopted children.
Earth unites with heaven
to sing the new song of creation,
as we adore and praise you for ever: → No. 23, p. 25

*When Eucharistic Prayer I is used, the special Christ-
tian Initiation forms of* Remember, Lord, your people *and* Father, accept this offering *are said:*

Remember, Lord, these godparents
who will present your chosen men and women for bap-
    tism

(the names of the godparents are mentioned).

Lord, remember all of us . . . (p. 26).
Father,
accept this offering
from your whole family.

We offer it especially for the men and women
you call to share your life
through the living waters of baptism.
[Through Christ our Lord. Amen.]

The rest follows the Roman Canon, pp. 27-30.

COMMUNION ANTIPHON See Jn. 9.11   [Spiritual Light]

**The Lord rubbed my eyes: I went away and washed;
then I could see, and I believed in God.** ↓

PRAYER AFTER COMMUNION   [Joy of Salvation]

Lord,
be close to your family.
Rule and guide us on our way to your kingdom
and bring us to the joy of salvation.
Grant this through Christ our Lord.
℟. **Amen.**   → No. 32, p. 75

Optional Solemn Blessings, p. 96, and Prayers Over the People, p. 104

"Go your way, and from now on do not sin again."

MARCH 25

5th SUNDAY OF LENT

The Ritual Mass for the Third Scrutiny assigned to this Sunday in the Rite of Christian Initiation of Adults is found on p. 253.

ENTRANCE ANTIPHON Ps. 42 (43).1-2   [Rescue Me]
Give me justice, O God, and defend my cause against the wicked; rescue me from deceitful and unjust men. You, O God, are my refuge.

→ No. 2, p. 10 (Omit Gloria)

OPENING PRAYER   [Courage To Follow Christ]
Father,
help us to be like Christ your Son,
who loved the world and died for our salvation.
Inspire us by his love,
guide us by his example,
for he lives and reigns with you and the Holy
    Spirit,
one God, for ever and ever. ℟. **Amen.** ↓

FIRST READING Isa. 43.16-21   [Hope for the Future]

A call to look with hope to the future. God is not dead. Look around you and see God's wonderful works.

A reading from the book of the prophet Isaiah

THUS says the Lord,
who makes a way in the sea,
a path in the mighty waters,
who brings out chariot and horse, army and
    warrior;
they lie down, they cannot rise,
they are extinguished, quenched like a wick:
Do not remember the former things,
or consider the things of old.

I am about to do a new thing;
now it springs forth, do you not perceive it?
I will make a way in the wilderness
and rivers in the desert.

The wild animals will honour me,
the jackals and the ostriches;
for I give water in the wilderness, rivers in the
    desert,
to give drink to my chosen people,
the people whom I formed for myself
so that they might declare my praise.
The word of the Lord. ℟. **Thanks be to God.** ↓

RESPONSORIAL PSALM Ps. 125 (126) [Joy of Saved]

℟. **The Lord has done great things for us;   we are filled with joy.**

(℟. **What marvels the Lord worked for us! Indeed we were glad.**)

(NRSV Text)	(GRAIL Text)
When the Lord restored the fortunes of Zion, we were like those who dream. Then our mouth was filled with laughter, and our tongue with shouts of joy.— R̸.	When the Lord delivered Zion from bondage, it seemed like a dream. Then was our mouth filled with laughter, on our lips there were songs.— R̸.
Then it was said among the nations, "The Lord has done great things for them." The Lord has done great things for us, and we rejoiced.— R̸.	The heathens themselves said: "What marvels the Lord worked for them!" What marvels the Lord worked for us! Indeed we were glad.— R̸.
Restore our fortunes, O Lord, like the watercourses in the desert of the Negev. May those who sow in tears reap with shouts of joy.— R̸.	Deliver us, O Lord, from our bondage as streams in dry land. Those who are sowing in tears will sing when they reap.— R̸.
Those who go out weeping, bearing the seed for sowing, shall come home with shouts of joy, carrying their sheaves.— R̸. ↓	They go out, they go out, full of tears, carrying seed for the sowing; they come back, they come back, full of song, carrying their sheaves.— R̸. ↓

SECOND READING Phil. 3.8-14   [Life in Christ]

Faith in Christ is our salvation, but we cannot relax. We must continue, while in this life, to strive for the good things of life in Christ—heaven.

A reading from the letter of Paul to the Philippians

I REGARD everything as loss because of the surpassing value of knowing Christ Jesus my Lord. For his sake I have suffered the loss of all things, and I regard them as rubbish, in order that I may gain Christ and be found in him, not having a righteousness of my own that comes from the law, but one that comes through faith in Christ, the righteousness from God based on faith.

I want to know Christ and the power of his resurrection and the sharing of his sufferings by becoming like him in his death, if somehow I may attain the resurrection from the dead.

Not that I have already obtained this or have already reached the goal; but I press on to make it my own, because Christ Jesus has made me his own.

Beloved, I do not consider that I have made it my own; but this one thing I do: forgetting what lies behind and straining forward to what lies ahead, I press on toward the goal for the prize of the heavenly call of God in Christ Jesus.—The word of the Lord. ℞. **Thanks be to God.** ↓

GOSPEL ACCLAMATION Joel 2.12-13   [Turn to God]

(If the acclamation is not sung, it is omitted.)

℣. Praise to you, Lord, king of eternal glory!
℞. **Praise to you, Lord, king of eternal glory!**
℣. With all your heart turn to me, says the Lord, for I am tender and compassionate.
℞. **Praise to you, Lord, king of eternal glory!** ↓

GOSPEL Jn. 8.1-11   [Christ's Forgiveness]

By his example and works the Lord teaches us that God extends mercy to sinners to free them from slavery to sin.

℣. The Lord be with you. ℞. **And also with you.**
✤ A reading from the holy gospel according to John. ℞. **Glory to you, Lord.**

JESUS went to the Mount of Olives. Early in the morning he came again to the temple.

All the people came to him and he sat down and began to teach them.

The scribes and the Pharisees brought a woman who had been caught in adultery; and making her stand before the people, they said to Jesus, "Teacher, this woman was caught in the very act of committing adultery. In the law, Moses commanded us to stone such women. Now what do you say?" They said this to test Jesus, so that they might have some charge to bring against him.

Jesus bent down and wrote with his finger on the ground. When the scribes and Pharisees kept on questioning him, Jesus straightened up and said to them, "Let anyone among you who is without sin be the first to throw a stone at her." And once again Jesus bent down and wrote on the ground.

When the scribes and Pharisees heard what Jesus had said, they went away, one by one, beginning with the elders; and Jesus was left alone with the woman standing before him.

Jesus straightened up and said to her, "Woman, where are they? Has no one condemned you?" She said, "No one, sir." And Jesus said, "Neither do I condemn you. Go your way, and from now on do not sin again."—The gospel of the Lord. ℟. **Praise to you, Lord Jesus Christ.**   → No. 14, p. 18

PRAYER OVER THE GIFTS   [Take Away Sins]

Almighty God,
may the sacrifice we offer
take away the sins of those

whom you enlighten with the Christian faith.
We ask this in the name of Jesus the Lord.
R̸. **Amen.**   ➜ No. 21, p. 24 (Pref. 8-9)

COMMUNION ANTIPHON Jn. 8.10-11 [Sin No More]
Has no one condemned you? The woman answered: No one, Lord. Neither do I condemn you: go and do not sin again. ↓

PRAYER AFTER COMMUNION   [Union with Jesus]

Almighty Father,
by this sacrifice
may we always remain one with your Son,
  Jesus Christ,
whose body and blood we share,
for he is Lord for ever and ever.
R̸. **Amen.**   ➜ No. 32, p. 75

Optional Solemn Blessings, p. 96, and Prayers Over the People, p. 104

MAR. 25

MASS FOR THE THIRD SCRUTINY

This Mass is celebrated when the Third Scrutiny takes place in the Rite of Christian Initiation of Adults, usually on the Fifth Sunday of Lent.

ENTRANCE ANTIPHON Ezek. 36.23-26   [A New Spirit]
I will prove my holiness through you. I will gather you from the ends of the earth; I will pour clean water on you and wash away all your sins. I will give you a new spirit within you, says the Lord.

                         ➜ No. 2, p. 10 (Omit Gloria)

OPENING PRAYER   [Members of the Church]
Lord,
enlighten your chosen ones with the word of life.

Give them a new birth
in the waters of baptism
and make them living members of the Church.
Grant this . . . for ever and ever. ℟. **Amen.** ↓

FIRST READING Ezek. 37.12-14   [The Lord's Promise]

> **The Lord promises to bring God's people back to their homeland. He will be with them and they will know him.**

A reading from the book of the prophet Ezekiel

THUS says the Lord God: "I am going to open your graves, and bring you up from your graves, O my people; and I will bring you back to the land of Israel. And you shall know that I am the Lord, when I open your graves, and bring you up from your graves, O my people.

"I will put my spirit within you, and you shall live, and I will place you on your own soil; then you shall know that I, the Lord, have spoken and will act," says the Lord.—The word of the Lord. ℟. **Thanks be to God.** ↓

RESPONSORIAL PSALM Ps. 129 (130)   [Redemption]

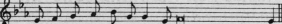

℟. With the Lord there is mer-cy and fullness of redemption.

(NRSV Text)	**(GRAIL Text)**
Out of the depths I cry to you, O Lord, Lord, hear my voice! Let your ears be attentive to the voice of my supplications!—℟.	Out of the depths I cry to you, O Lord, Lord, hear my voice! O let your ears be attentive to the voice of my pleading.—℟.
If you, O Lord, should mark iniquities, Lord, who could stand? But there is forgiveness with you, so that you may be revered.—℟.	If you, O Lord, should mark our guilt, Lord, who would survive? But with you is found forgiveness: for this we revere you.—℟.
I wait for the Lord, my soul waits, and in his word I hope;	My soul is waiting for the Lord. I count on his word.

my soul waits for the Lord
more than those who watch for the
   morning.—R̝.

My soul is longing for the Lord
more than those who watch for daybreak.—R̝.

For with the Lord there is steadfast
   love,
and with him is great power to redeem.
It is he who will redeem Israel
from all its iniquities.—R̝. ↓

Because with the Lord there is mercy
and fullness of redemption,
Israel indeed he will redeem
from all its iniquity.—R̝. ↓

SECOND READING Rom. 8.8-11   [Indwelling Spirit]

**The followers of Jesus live in the Spirit of God. The
same Spirit who brought Jesus back to life will bring
mortal bodies to life since God's Spirit dwells in them.**

A reading from the letter of Paul
to the Romans

THOSE who are in the flesh cannot please God. But
   you are not in the flesh; you are in the Spirit, since
the Spirit of God dwells in you. Anyone who does not
have the Spirit of Christ does not belong to him.

But if Christ is in you, though the body is dead because of sin, the Spirit is life because of righteousness.

If the Spirit of God who raised Jesus from the dead
dwells in you, he who raised Christ from the dead will
give life to your mortal bodies also through his Spirit
that dwells in you.—The word of the Lord. R̝. **Thanks
be to God.** ↓

GOSPEL ACCLAMATION Jn. 11.25, 26   [Eternal Life]

(If the acclamation is not sung, it is omitted.)

V̝. Praise to you, Lord, king of eternal glory!
R̝. **Praise to you, Lord, king of eternal glory!**
V̝. I am the resurrection and the life, says the Lord:
whoever believes in me will not die for ever.
R̝. **Praise to you, Lord, king of eternal glory!** ↓

GOSPEL Jn. 11.1-45 or 11.3-7, 17, 20-27, 33b-45   [Lazarus]

**Jesus, the resurrection and the life, gave life back to
Lazarus, who had died.**

[If the "Short Form" is used, omit indented text.]

℣. The Lord be with you. ℟. **And also with you.** ✢ A reading from the holy gospel according to John. ℟. **Glory to you, Lord.**

[NOW a certain man, Lazarus, was ill. He was from Bethany, the village of Mary and her sister Martha. Mary was the one who anointed the Lord with perfume and wiped his feet with her hair; her brother Lazarus was ill.]

[So] the sisters [of Lazarus] sent a message to Jesus, "Lord, he whom you love is ill." But when Jesus heard this, he said, "This illness does not lead to death; rather it is for God's glory, so that the Son of God may be glorified through it." Accordingly, though Jesus loved Martha and her sister and Lazarus, after having heard that Lazarus was ill, he stayed two days longer in the place where he was.

Then after this Jesus said to the disciples, "Let us go to Judea again."

[The disciples said to him, "Rabbi, the people there were just now trying to stone you, and are you going there again?" Jesus answered, "Are there not twelve hours of daylight? Those who walk during the day do not stumble, because they see the light of this world. But those who walk at night stumble, because the light is not in them."

After saying this, he told them, "Our friend Lazarus has fallen asleep, but I am going there to awaken him." The disciples said to him, "Lord, if he has fallen asleep, he will be all right." Jesus, however, had been speaking about his death, but they thought that he was referring merely to sleep. Then Jesus told them plainly, "Lazarus is dead. For your sake I am glad I was not there, so that you may believe. But let us go to him." Thomas, who was called the Twin, said to his fellow disciples, "Let us also go, that we may die with him."]

When Jesus arrived, he found that Lazarus had already been in the tomb four days.

[Now Bethany was near Jerusalem, some two miles away, and many Jews had come to Martha and Mary to console them about their brother.]
When Martha heard that Jesus was coming, she went and met him, while Mary stayed at home. Martha said to Jesus, "Lord, if you had been here, my brother would not have died. But even now I know that God will give you whatever you ask of him." Jesus said to her, "Your brother will rise again." Martha said to him, "I know that he will rise again in the resurrection on the last day." Jesus said to her, "I am the resurrection and the life. Those who believe in me, even though they die, will live, and everyone who lives and believes in me will never die. Do you believe this?" She said to him, "Yes, Lord, I believe that you are the Messiah, the Son of God, the one coming into the world."

[When she had said this, she went back and called her sister Mary, and told her privately, "The Teacher is here and is calling for you." And when Mary heard it, she got up quickly and went to him. Now Jesus had not yet come to the village, but was still at the place where Martha had met him. The Jews who were with her in the house, consoling her, saw Mary get up quickly and go out. They followed her because they thought that she was going to the tomb to weep there.

When Mary came where Jesus was and saw him, she knelt at his feet and said to him, "Lord, if you had been here, my brother would not have died." When Jesus saw her weeping, and the Jews who came with her also weeping, he]
[Jesus] was greatly disturbed in spirit and deeply moved. He said, "Where have you laid him?" They said to him, "Lord, come and see." Jesus began to weep. So the Jews said, "See how he loved him!" But some of them said, "Could not he who opened the eyes of the blind man have kept this man from dying?"

Then Jesus, again greatly disturbed, came to the tomb. It was a cave, and a stone was lying against it. Jesus said, "Take away the stone." Martha, the sister of the dead man, said to him, "Lord, already there is a stench because he has been dead four days." Jesus said to her, "Did I not tell you that if you believed, you would see the glory of God?" So they took away the stone. And Jesus looked upward and said, "Father, I thank you for having heard me. I knew that you always hear me, but I have said this for the sake of the crowd standing here, so that they may believe that you sent me."

When he had said this, he cried with a loud voice, "Lazarus, come out!" The dead man came out, his hands and feet bound with strips of cloth, and his face wrapped in a cloth. Jesus said to them, "Unbind him, and let him go."

Many of the Jews therefore, who had come with Mary and had seen what Jesus did, believed in him.— The gospel of the Lord. ℟. **Praise to you, Lord Jesus Christ.**
→ No. 14, p. 18

PRAYER OVER THE GIFTS   [Preparing for Baptism]

Almighty God,
hear our prayers for these men and women
who have begun to learn the Christian faith,
and by this sacrifice prepare them for baptism.
We ask this through Christ our Lord. ℟. **Amen.** ↓

PREFACE (16)   [Raised from the Dead]

℣. The Lord be with you. ℟. **And also with you.** ℣. Lift up your hearts. ℟. **We lift them up to the Lord.** ℣. Let us give thanks to the Lord our God. ℟. **It is right to give him thanks and praise.**

Father, all-powerful and ever-living God,
we do well always and everywhere to give you thanks
through Jesus Christ our Lord.
As a man like us, Jesus wept for Lazarus his friend.
As the eternal God, he raised Lazarus from the dead.
In his love for us all,
Christ gives us the sacraments

to lift us up to everlasting life.
Through him the angels of heaven offer their prayer of
    adoration
as they rejoice in your presence for ever.
May our voices be one with theirs
in their triumphant hymn of praise: ➜ No. 23, p. 25

*When Eucharistic Prayer I is used, the special Christ-
tian Initiation forms of* Remember, Lord, your people *and* Father, accept this offering *are said:*

Remember, Lord, these godparents
who will present your chosen men and women for bap-
    tism *(the names of the godparents are mentioned).*
Lord, remember all of us . . . (p. 26).

Father,
accept this offering
from your whole family.
We offer it especially for the men and women
you call to share your life
through the living waters of baptism.
[Through Christ our Lord. Amen.]
The rest follows the Roman Canon, pp. 27-30.

COMMUNION ANTIPHON Jn. 11.26   [Eternal Life]
**He who lives and believes in me will not die for ever,
said the Lord.** ↓

PRAYER AFTER COMMUNION   [God's Children]
Lord,
may your people be one in spirit
and serve you with all their heart.
Free them from all fear.
Give them joy in your gifts
and love for those
who are to be reborn as your children.
We ask this through Christ our Lord.
℟. **Amen.**   ➜ No. 32, p. 75

Optional Solemn Blessings, p. 96, and Prayers Over the People, p. 104

"Blessed are you who have come to us so rich
in love and mercy."

APRIL 1

PASSION SUNDAY
[PALM SUNDAY]

Commemoration of the Lord's Entrance
into Jerusalem

FIRST FORM: THE PROCESSION

*At the scheduled time, the congregation assembles in a
secondary church or chapel or in some other suitable
place distinct from the church to which the procession
will move. The faithful carry palm branches.*

*The priest and ministers put on red vestments for Mass
and go to the place where the people have assembled.
The priest may wear a cope instead of a chasuble; in
this case he removes the cope after the procession.*

*Meanwhile, the following Antiphon or any other ap-
propriate song is sung.*

ANTIPHON Mt. 21.9   [Hosanna]

**Hosanna to the Son of David,
the King of Israel.**

**Blessed is he who comes
in the name of the Lord.
Hosanna in the highest.**

*The priest then greets the people in the usual way and
gives a brief introduction, inviting them to take a full
part in the celebration. He may use these or similar
words:*

Dear friends in Christ, for five weeks of Lent
we have been preparing, by works of charity
and self-sacrifice, for the celebration of our
Lord's paschal mystery. Today we come together to begin this solemn celebration in
union with the whole Church throughout the
world. Christ entered in triumph into his own
city, to complete his work as our Messiah: to
suffer, to die, and to rise again. Let us remember with devotion this entry which began his
saving work and follow him with a lively faith.
United with him in his suffering on the cross,
may we share his resurrection and new life.

*Afterwards the priest, with hands joined, says one of
the following prayers:*

PRAYER   [Following Christ]

Almighty God,
we pray you
bless ✠ these branches
and make them holy.
Today we joyfully acclaim Jesus our Messiah
    and King.
May we reach one day the happiness
of the new and everlasting Jerusalem
by faithfully following him
who lives and reigns for ever and ever.
℞. **Amen.** ↓

OR   [Christ Our King]

Lord,
increase the faith of your people
and listen to our prayers.
Today we honour Christ our triumphant King
by carrying these branches.
May we honour you every day
by living always in him,
for he is Lord for ever and ever. ℟. **Amen.** ↓

*The priest sprinkles the branches with holy water in si-
lence.*

*Then the account of the Lord's entrance is proclaimed
from one of the four gospels. This is done in the usual
way or, if there is no deacon, by the priest.*

GOSPEL Lk. 19.28-40   [Jesus' Triumphal Entry]

**In triumphant glory Jesus comes into Jerusalem. The
people spread their cloaks on the ground for him, wave
olive branches and sing in his honour.**

℣. The Lord be with you. ℟. **And also with you.**
✠ A reading from the holy gospel according to
Luke. ℟. **Glory to you, Lord.**

JESUS went on ahead, going up to Jerusalem. When he had come near Bethphage
and Bethany, at the place called the Mount of
Olives, he sent two of the disciples, saying, "Go
into the village ahead of you, and as you enter
it you will find tied there a colt that has never
been ridden. Untie it and bring it here. If anyone asks you, 'Why are you untying it?' just
say this, 'The Lord needs it.' "
    So those who were sent departed and found
it as Jesus had told them. As they were untying

the colt, its owners asked them, "Why are you untying the colt?" They said, "The Lord needs it."

Then they brought the colt to Jesus; and after throwing their cloaks on the colt, they set Jesus on it.

As he rode along, people kept spreading their cloaks on the road. As he was now approaching the path down from the Mount of Olives, the whole multitude of the disciples began to praise God joyfully, and with a loud voice, for all the deeds of power that they had seen, saying, "Blessed is the king who comes in the name of the Lord! Peace in heaven, and glory in the highest heaven!"

Some of the Pharisees in the crowd said to him, "Teacher, order your disciples to stop."

Jesus answered, "I tell you, if these were silent, the stones would shout out."—The gospel of the Lord. ℟. **Praise to you, Lord Jesus Christ.**

→ No. 14, p. 18

After the gospel, a brief homily may be given. Before the procession begins, the celebrant or other suitable minister may address the people in these or similar words:

Let us go forth in peace,
praising Jesus our Messiah,
as did the crowds who welcomed him to
Jerusalem.

The procession to the church where Mass will be celebrated then begins.

If incense is used, the thurifer goes first with a lighted censer, followed by the cross-bearer (with the cross suitably decorated) between two ministers with lighted candles, then the priest with the ministers, and finally the congregation carrying branches.

During the procession, the choir and people sing the following or other appropriate songs:

ANTIPHON 1 [Hosanna]

The children of Jerusalem/welcomed Christ the King./They carried olive branches/and loudly praised the Lord:/Hosanna in the highest.

The above antiphon may be repeated between verses of Psalm 23 (24).

PSALM 23 (24) [The King of Glory]

The Lord's is the earth and its fullness,
the world and all its peoples.
It is he who set it on the seas;
on the waters he made it firm.
Repeat antiphon 1

Who shall climb the mountain of the Lord?
Who shall stand in his holy place?
Those with clean hands and pure heart,
who desire not worthless things,
(who have not sworn so as to deceive their neighbour.)
Repeat antiphon 1

They shall receive blessings from the Lord
and reward from the God who saves them.

These are the ones who seek him,
seek the face of the God of Jacob. *Repeat antiphon 1*

O gates, lift high your heads;
grow higher, ancient doors.
Let him enter, the king of glory!
Who is the king of glory?
The Lord, the mighty, the valiant,
the Lord, the valiant in war.
Repeat antiphon 1

O gates, lift high your heads;
grow higher, ancient doors.
Let him enter, the king of glory!
Who is he, the king of glory?
He, the Lord of armies,
he is the king of glory.
Repeat antiphon 1

ANTIPHON 2 [Hosanna]

The children of Jerusalem/welcomed Christ the King./They spread their cloaks before him/and loudly praised the Lord:/Hosanna to the Son of David!/ Blessed is he who comes/in the name of the Lord!

The above antiphon may be repeated between the verses of Psalm 46 (47).

PSALM 46 (47)   [The Great King]

All peoples, clap your hands,
cry to God with shouts of joy!
For the Lord, the Most High,
we must fear,
great king over all the earth.
Repeat antiphon 2

He subdues peoples under us
and nations under our feet.
Our inheritance, our glory, is
from him,
given to Jacob out of love.
Repeat antiphon 2

God goes up with shouts of
joy;
the Lord goes up with trumpet blast.
Sing praise for God, sing
praise,

sing praise to our king, sing
praise.
Repeat antiphon 2

God is king of all the earth,
sing praise with all your skill.
God is king over the nations;
God reigns on his holy
throne.
Repeat antiphon 2

The leaders of the people are
assembled
with the people of Abraham's
God.
The rulers of the earth belong
to God,
to God who reigns over all.
Repeat antiphon 2

A hymn in honour of Christ the King, such as All Glory, Laud and Honour, *is sung during the procession. See p. 593.*

As the procession enters the church, the following responsory or another song which refers to the Lord's entrance is sung.

℟. **The children of Jerusalem**   [Hosanna]
welcomed Christ the King.
They proclaimed the resurrection of life,
and, waving olive branches,
they loudly praised the Lord:
Hosanna in the highest.
When the people heard that Jesus
was entering Jerusalem,
they went to meet him

and, waving olive branches,
they loudly praised the Lord:
Hosanna in the highest.

When the priest comes to the altar he venerates it and may also incense it. Then he goes to his chair (removes the cope and puts on the chasuble) and begins immediately the opening prayer of Mass, which concludes the procession. Mass then continues in the usual way.

SECOND FORM: THE SOLEMN ENTRANCE

If the procession cannot be held outside the church, the commemoration of the Lord's entrance may be celebrated before the principal Mass with the solemn entrance, which takes place within the church.

The faithful, holding the branches, assemble either in front of the church door or inside the church. The priest and ministers, with a representative group of the faithful, go to a suitable place in the church outside the sanctuary, so that most of the people will be able to see the rite.

While the priest goes to the appointed place, the antiphon Hosanna *or other suitable song is sung. Then the blessing of branches and proclamation of the gospel about the Lord's entrance into Jerusalem take place, as above. After the gospel the priest, with the ministers and the group of the faithful, moves solemnly through the church to the sanctuary, while the responsory* The children of Jerusalem *or other appropriate song is sung.*

When the priest comes to the altar he venerates it, goes to his chair, and immediately begins the opening prayer of Mass, which then continues in the usual way.

THIRD FORM: THE SIMPLE ENTRANCE

At all other Masses on this Sunday, if the solemn entrance is not held, the Lord's entrance is commemorated with the following simple entrance.

While the priest goes to the altar, the entrance antiphon with its psalm or another song with the same theme is sung. After the priest venerates the altar, he goes to his chair and greets the people. Mass continues in the usual way.

When the entrance antiphon cannot be sung, the priest goes at once to the altar and venerates it. Then he greets the people and reads the entrance antiphon, and Mass continues in the usual way.

ENTRANCE ANTIPHON   [Praise the Lord]

Six days before the solemn passover the Lord came to Jerusalem, and children waving palm branches ran out to welcome him. They loudly praised the Lord: Blessed are you who have come to us so rich in love and mercy.

PSALM 23 (24).9-10   [The King of Glory]

**Open wide the doors and gates.
Lift high the ancient portals.
The King of glory enters.
Who is the King of glory?
He is God the mighty Lord.
Hosanna in the highest.
Blessed are you who have come to us
so rich in love and mercy.**

Where neither the procession nor the solemn entrance can be celebrated, there should be a bible service on the theme of the Lord's messianic entrance and passion, either on Saturday evening or on Sunday at a convenient time.

MASS

After the procession or solemn entrance the priest begins the Mass with the opening prayer.

OPENING PRAYER   [Union with Christ]

Almighty, ever-living God,
you have given the human race Jesus Christ
  our Saviour
as a model of humility.
He fulfilled your will
by becoming man and giving his life on the
  cross.
Help us to bear witness to you
by following his example of suffering
and make us worthy to share in his resurrection.
We ask this . . . for ever and ever. ℞. **Amen.** ↓

FIRST READING Isa. 50.4-7   [Christ's Suffering]

The suffering servant was persecuted and struck by his
own people; he was spit upon and beaten. He proclaims
the true faith and suffers to atone for the sins of his
people. Here we see a foreshadowing of the true servant of God.

A reading from the book of the prophet Isaiah

THE servant of the Lord said:
  "The Lord God has given me the tongue of a
    teacher,
that I may know how to sustain the weary with
  a word.
Morning by morning he wakens—
wakens my ear to listen as those who are
  taught.
The Lord God has opened my ear,
and I was not rebellious,
I did not turn backward.

"I gave my back to those who struck me,
and my cheeks to those who pulled out the
  beard;

I did not hide my face
from insult and spitting.

"The Lord God helps me;
therefore I have not been disgraced;
therefore I have set my face like flint,
and I know that I shall not be put to shame."
The word of the Lord. ℟. **Thanks be to God.** ↓

RESPONSORIAL PSALM Ps. 21 (22) [Abandonment]

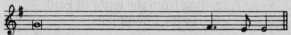

℟. My God, my God, why have you a-ban - doned me?

(℟. **My God, my God, why have you forsaken me?**)

(NRSV Text)	(GRAIL Text)
All who see me mock at me; they make mouths at me, they shake their heads; "Commit your cause to the Lord; let him deliver; let him rescue the one in whom he delights!"—℟.	All who see me deride me. They curl their lips, they toss their heads. "He trusted in the Lord, let him save him: let him release him if this is his friend."—℟.
For dogs are all around me; a company of evildoers encircles me. My hands and feet have shrivelled; I can count all my bones.—℟.	Many dogs have surrounded me, a band of the wicked beset me. They tear holes in my hands and my feet I can count every one of my bones.—℟.
They divide my clothes among themselves, and for my clothing they cast lots. But you, O Lord, do not be far away! O my help, come quickly to my aid!—℟.	They divide my clothing among them. They cast lots for my robe. O Lord, do not leave me alone, my strength, make haste to help me!—℟.
I will tell of your name to my brothers and sisters; in the midst of the congregation I will praise you:	I will tell of your name to my people and praise you where they are assembled. "You who fear the Lord, give him praise;

You who fear the Lord, praise him! All you offspring of Jacob, glorify him; stand in awe of him, all you offspring of Israel!—R. ↓

all children of Jacob, give him glory. Revere him, children of Israel."—R. ↓

SECOND READING Phil. 2.6-11 [Humility]

Paul urges us to be humble like Christ. He put off the majesty of his divinity and became man and humbled himself in obedience to the ignominious death on the cross.

A reading from the letter of Paul to the Philippians

LET the same mind be in you that was in Christ Jesus,
who, though he was in the form of God,
did not regard equality with God
as something to be exploited,
but emptied himself,
taking the form of a slave,
being born in human likeness.
And being found in human form,
he humbled himself
and became obedient to the point of death,
even death on a cross.

Therefore God highly exalted him
and gave him the name that is above every
   name,
so that at the name of Jesus every knee should
   bend,
in heaven and on earth and under the earth,
and every tongue should confess that Jesus
   Christ is Lord,
to the glory of God the Father.
The word of the Lord. R. **Thanks be to God.** ↓

GOSPEL ACCLAMATION Phil. 2.8-9   [Obedience]

(If the acclamation is not sung, it is omitted.)

℣. Praise to you, Lord, king of eternal glory!

℟. **Praise to you, Lord, king of eternal glory!**

℣. Christ became obedient for us even to death,
dying on the cross.

Therefore God raised him on high
and gave him a name above all other names.

℟. **Praise to you, Lord, king of eternal glory!** ↓

GOSPEL Lk. 22.14—23.56 or 23.1-49   [The Passion]

"No one has greater love than this, to lay down one's
life for one's friends. You are my friends" (Jn. 15.13-14).

*Several readers may proclaim the passion narrative
today.* **N.** *indicates the Narrator,* ✚ *the words of Jesus,
and* **S.** *the words of other speakers. The words in
brackets are said only when the Passion is read by one
reader.*

*We participate in the passion narrative in several
ways: by reading it and reflecting on it during the
week ahead; by listening with faith as it is proclaimed;
by singing acclamations at appropriate places in the
text; by respectful posture during the narrative; by reverent silence after the passage about Christ's death.
We do not hold the palms during the reading on Passion Sunday.*

*Who caused the death of Jesus? In listening to God's
word today, we must remember that our Lord died to
save every human person. By our sins we have contributed to his suffering and death. The authorities of
his time bear responsibility for carrying out his execu-
tion; this charge must not be laid against all the Jewish
people of Jesus' day or of our own. We are all responsible for sin and for our Lord's suffering.*

*This week we are challenged by the passion narrative
to reflect on the way we are living up to our baptismal
promises of dying with Christ to sin and living with
him for God.*

Note: A shorter version (23.1-49) is indicated by aster-isks at the beginning and the end (pp. 276-280).

N. THE Passion of our Lord Jesus Christ ac-cording to Luke.

AT THE LAST SUPPER

N. WHEN the hour came, Jesus took his place at the table, and the apostles with him. He said to them, ✠ *"I have eagerly desired to eat this Passover with you before I suffer; for I tell you, I will not eat it until it is fulfilled in the kingdom of God."*

N. Then he took a cup, and after giving thanks he said, ✠ *"Take this and divide it among yourselves; for I tell you that from now on I will not drink of the fruit of the vine until the kingdom of God comes."*

N. Then Jesus took a loaf of bread, and when he had given thanks, he broke it and gave it to them, saying, ✠ *"This is my body, which is given for you. Do this in remembrance of me."* **N.** And he did the same with the cup after sup-per, saying, ✠ *"This cup that is poured out for you is the new covenant in my blood.*

"But see, the one who betrays me is with me, and his hand is on the table. For the Son of Man is going as it has been determined, but woe to that one by whom he is betrayed!" **N.** Then they began to ask one another, which one of them it could be who would do this. A dis-pute also arose among them as to which one of them was to be regarded as the greatest.

But Jesus said to them, ✠ *"The kings of the Gentiles lord it over them; and those in author-ity over them are called benefactors.*

"But not so with you; rather the greatest among you must become like the youngest, and the leader like one who serves. For who is greater, the one who is at the table or the one who serves? Is it not the one at the table? But I am among you as one who serves.

"You are those who have stood by me in my trials; and I confer on you, just as my Father has conferred on me, a kingdom, so that you may eat and drink at my table in my kingdom, and you will sit on thrones judging the twelve tribes of Israel.

"Simon, Simon, listen! Satan has demanded to sift all of you like wheat, but I have prayed for you that your own faith may not fail; and you, when once you have turned back, strengthen your brothers." **N.** And Peter said to Jesus, **S₁.** **"Lord, I am ready to go with you to prison and to death!"** [**N.** Jesus said,] ✝ *"I tell you, Peter, the cock will not crow this day, until you have denied three times that you know me."*

N. Then Jesus said to the disciples, ✝ *"When I sent you out without a purse, bag, or sandals, did you lack anything?"* [**N.** The apostles said,] **S₁.** **"No, not a thing."** [**N.** Jesus said to them,] ✝ *"But now, the one who has a purse must take it, and likewise a bag. And the one who has no sword must sell his cloak and buy one. For I tell you, this scripture must be fulfilled in me, 'And he was counted among the lawless'; and indeed what is written about me is being fulfilled."*
[**N.** The apostles said,] **S₁.** **"Lord, look, here are two swords."** [**N.** Jesus replied,] ✝ *"It is enough."*

At this point all may join in singing an appropriate acclamation.

JESUS IN THE GARDEN

N. JESUS came out and went, as was his custom, to the Mount of Olives; and the disciples followed him. When he reached the place, he said to his disciples, ✠ *"Pray that you may not come into the time of trial."*

N. Then Jesus withdrew from them about a stone's throw, knelt down, and prayed, ✠ *"Father, if you are willing, remove this cup from me; yet, not my will but yours be done."*

N. Then an angel from heaven appeared to Jesus and gave him strength. In his anguish he prayed more earnestly, and his sweat became like great drops of blood falling down on the ground. When Jesus got up from prayer, he came to the disciples and found them sleeping because of grief, and he said to them, ✠ *"Why are you sleeping? Get up and pray that you may not come into the time of trial."*

JESUS ARRESTED

N. WHILE Jesus was still speaking, suddenly a crowd came, and the one called Judas, one of the twelve, was leading them. He approached Jesus to kiss him; but Jesus said to him, ✠ *"Judas, is it with a kiss that you are betraying the Son of Man?"*

N. When those who were around Jesus saw what was coming, they asked, **S1. "Lord, should we strike with the sword?" N.** Then one of the disciples struck the slave of the high priest and cut off his right ear. But Jesus said, ✠ *"No more of this!"* **N.** And Jesus touched the slave's ear and healed him.

Then Jesus said to the chief priests, the officers of the temple police, and the elders who had come for him, ✠ *"Have you come out with swords and clubs as if I were a bandit? When I was with you day after day in the temple, you did not lay hands on me. But this is your hour, and the power of darkness!"*

PETER DENIES THE LORD JESUS

N. THEN they seized Jesus and led him away, bringing him into the high priest's house. But Peter was following at a distance. When they had kindled a fire in the middle of the courtyard and sat down together, Peter sat among them. Then a servant girl, seeing him in the firelight, stared at him and said, **S₃. "This man also was with him."**

N. But Peter denied it, saying, **S₁. "Woman, I do not know him."** **N.** A little later someone else, on seeing him, said, **S₃. "You also are one of them."** **N.** But Peter said, **S₁. "Man, I am not!"** **N.** Then about an hour later still another kept insisting, **S₃. "Surely this man also was with him; for he is a Galilean."** **N.** But Peter said, **S₁. "Man, I do not know what you are talking about!"** **N.** At that moment, while he was still speaking, the cock crowed. The Lord turned and looked at Peter. Then Peter remembered the word of the Lord, how he had said to him, "Before the cock crows today, you will deny me three times." And Peter went out and wept bitterly.

TRIAL IN THE HIGH PRIEST'S HOUSE

N. **N**OW the men who were holding Jesus began to mock him and beat him; they also blindfolded him and kept asking him, **S2. "Prophesy! Who is it that struck you?"** N. They kept heaping many other insults on him.

★ When day came, the assembly of the elders of the people, both chief priests and scribes, gathered together, and they brought Jesus to their council. They said, **S2. "If you are the Messiah, tell us."** [N. Jesus replied,] ✝ *"If I tell you, you will not believe; and if I question you, you will not answer. But from now on the Son of Man will be seated at the right hand of the power of God."* N. All of them asked, **S2. "Are you, then, the Son of God?"** [N. Jesus said to them,] *"You say that I am."* [N. Then they said,] **S2. "What further testimony do we need? We have heard it ourselves from his own lips!"**

At this point all may join in singing an appropriate acclamation.

JESUS BEFORE PILATE

N. **T**HEN the assembly rose as a body and brought Jesus before Pilate. They began to accuse him, saying, **S2. "We found this man perverting our nation, forbidding us to pay taxes to the emperor, and saying that he himself is the Messiah, a king."**

N. Then Pilate asked Jesus, **S3. "Are you the king of the Jews?"** [N. He answered,] ✝ *"You* *say so.*" **N.** Then Pilate said to the chief priests and the crowds, **S3. "I find no basis for an accusation against this man."** **N.** But they were insistent and said, **S2. "He stirs up the people by teaching throughout all Judea, from Galilee where he began even to this place."** **N.** When Pilate heard this, he asked whether the man was a Galilean. And when he learned that he was under Herod's jurisdiction, he sent him off to Herod, who was himself in Jerusalem at that time.

When Herod saw Jesus, he was very glad, for he had been wanting to see him for a long time, because he had heard about him and was hoping to see Jesus perform some sign. Herod questioned him at some length, but Jesus gave him no answer. The chief priests and the scribes stood by, vehemently accusing him. Even Herod with his soldiers treated him with contempt and mocked him; then he put an elegant robe on him, and sent him back to Pilate. That same day Herod and Pilate became friends with each other; before this they had been enemies.

Pilate then called together the chief priests, the leaders, and the people, and said to them, **S3. "You brought me this man as one who was perverting the people; and here I have examined him in your presence and have not found this man guilty of any of your charges against him. Neither has Herod, for he sent him back to us. Indeed, he has done nothing to deserve death. I will therefore have him flogged and release him."**

N. Now Pilate was obliged to release someone for them at the festival. Then they all shouted out together, **S2. "Away with this fellow! Release Barabbas for us." N.** (This was a man who had been put in prison for an insurrection that had taken place in the city, and for murder.) Pilate, wanting to release Jesus, addressed them again; but they kept shouting, **S2. "Crucify, crucify him!" N.** A third time Pilate said to them, **S3. "Why, what evil has he done? I have found in him no ground for the sentence of death; I will therefore have him flogged and then release him."**

N. But they kept urgently demanding with loud shouts that he should be crucified; and their voices prevailed. So Pilate gave his verdict that their demand should be granted. He released the man they asked for, the one who had been put in prison for insurrection and murder, and he handed Jesus over as they wished.

ON THE WAY TO CALVARY

N. **A**S they led Jesus away, they seized a man, Simon of Cyrene, who was coming from the country, and they laid the cross on him, and made him carry it behind Jesus.

A great number of the people followed him, and among them were women who were beating their breasts and wailing for him. But Jesus turned to them and said, ✠ *"Daughters of Jerusalem, do not weep for me, but weep for yourselves and for your children. For the days are surely coming when they will say, 'Blessed are the barren, and the wombs that never bore, and the breasts that never nursed.' Then they will begin to say to the mountains, 'Fall on us,' and to the hills, 'Cover us.' For if they do this when the wood is green, what will happen when it is dry?"*

At this point all may join in singing an appropriate acclamation.

JESUS IS CRUCIFIED AND DIES FOR US

N. TWO others also, who were criminals, were led away to be put to death with Jesus. When they came to the place that is called The Skull, they crucified Jesus there with the criminals, one on his right and one on his left.

Then Jesus said, ✝ *"Father, forgive them; for they do not know what they are doing."* **N.** And they cast lots to divide his clothing.

And the people stood by, watching; but the leaders scoffed at him, saying, **S2. "He saved others; let him save himself if he is the Messiah of God, his chosen one!"**

N. The soldiers also mocked Jesus, coming up and offering him sour wine, and saying, **S3. "If you are the King of the Jews, save yourself!"** **N.** There was also an inscription over him, "This is the King of the Jews."

One of the criminals who were hanged there kept deriding him and saying, **S2. "Are you not the Messiah? Save yourself and us!"** **N.** But the other criminal rebuked the first, saying, **S3. "Do you not fear God, since you are under the same sentence of condemnation? And we indeed have been condemned justly, for we are**

**getting what we deserve for our deeds, but this
man has done nothing wrong."** N. Then he said,
**S₃. "Jesus, remember me when you come into
your kingdom."** [N. Jesus replied,] ✢ *"Truly I tell
you, today you will be with me in Paradise."*

N. It was now about noon, and darkness
came over the whole land until three in the af-
ternoon, while the sun's light failed; and the
curtain of the temple was torn in two.

Then Jesus, crying with a loud voice, said, ✢
"Father, into your hands I commend my spirit."
N. Having said this, he breathed his last.

All may kneel for a period of silence.

EVENTS AFTER JESUS' DEATH

N. WHEN the centurion saw what had
taken place, he praised God and said,
S₃. "Certainly this man was innocent." N. And
when all the crowds who had gathered there
for this spectacle saw what had taken place,
they returned home, beating their breasts.

But all his acquaintances, including the
women who had followed him from Galilee,
stood at a distance, watching these things.★

JESUS' BODY IS PLACED IN THE TOMB

N. NOW there was a good and righteous
man named Joseph, who, though a
member of the council, had not agreed to their
plan and action. He came from the Jewish
town of Arimathea, and he was waiting expec-
tantly for the kingdom of God. This man went
to Pilate and asked for the body of Jesus. Then
he took it down, wrapped it in a linen cloth,

and laid it in a rock-hewn tomb where no one had ever been laid.

It was the day of Preparation, and the sabbath was beginning. The women who had come with Jesus from Galilee followed, and they saw the tomb and how his body was laid. Then they returned, and prepared spices and ointments. On the sabbath these women rested according to the commandment. ➜ No. 14, p. 18

PRAYER OVER THE GIFTS   [Pleasing to God]

Lord,
may the suffering and death of Jesus, your only
    Son,
make us pleasing to you.
Alone we can do nothing,
but may this perfect sacrifice
win us your mercy and love.
We ask this in the name of Jesus the Lord.
℟. **Amen.** ↓

PREFACE (19)   [Raised to Holiness of Life]

℣. The Lord be with you. ℟. **And also with you.**
℣. Lift up your hearts. ℟. **We lift them up to the Lord.** ℣. Let us give thanks to the Lord our God.
℟. **It is right to give him thanks and praise.**

Father, all-powerful and ever-living God,
we do well always and everywhere to give you
    thanks
through Jesus Christ our Lord.
Though he was sinless, he suffered willingly
    for sinners.
Though innocent, he accepted death to save the
    guilty.

By his dying, he has destroyed our sins.
By his rising, he has raised us up to holiness of
   life.
Glory and honour are his
as heaven and earth, angels and archangels,
cry out in unending praise: ➙ No. 23, p. 25

COMMUNION ANTIPHON Mt. 26.42   [God's Will]

**Father, if this cup may not pass, but I must
drink it, then your will be done. ↓**

PRAYER AFTER COMMUNION   [Perseverance]

Lord,
you have satisfied our hunger with this eucharistic food.
The death of your Son gives us hope and
   strengthens our faith.
May his resurrection give us perseverance
and lead us to salvation.
We ask this through Christ our Lord.
℟. **Amen.**   ➙ No. 32, p. 75

Optional Solemn Blessings, p. 96, and Prayers Over the People, p. 104

"This is my body that is for you.
Do this in remembrance of me."

APRIL 5
HOLY THURSDAY
EVENING MASS OF THE LORD'S SUPPER

*The Mass of the Lord's Supper is celebrated in the
evening, at a convenient hour, with the full participation of the whole local community and with all the
priests and clergy exercising their ministry.*

Introductory Rites and Liturgy of the Word

ENTRANCE ANTIPHON See Gal. 6.14 [Glory in Cross]

**It is our duty to glory in the cross of our Lord
Jesus Christ. He saves us and sets us free;
through him we find salvation, life, and resurrection.** → No. 2, p. 10

OPENING PRAYER [Fullness of Love]

God our Father,
we are gathered here to share in the supper
which your only Son left to his Church to re-
    veal his love.
He gave it to us when he was about to die

283

and commanded us to celebrate it
as the new and eternal sacrifice.
We pray that in this eucharist
we may find the fullness of love and life.
Grant this . . . for ever and ever. ℟. **Amen.** ↓

FIRST READING Ex. 12.1-8, 11-14   [The First Passover]

The people are instructed to prepare for the Passover meal. By the blood of the lamb they are saved from death.

A reading from the book of Exodus

THE Lord said to Moses and Aaron in the land of Egypt: This month shall mark for you the beginning of months; it shall be the first month of the year for you. Tell the whole congregation of Israel that on the tenth of this month they are to take a lamb for each family, a lamb for each household. If a household is too small for a whole lamb, it shall join its closest neighbour in obtaining one; the lamb shall be divided in proportion to the number of people who eat of it.

Your lamb shall be without blemish, a year-old male; you may take it from the sheep or from the goats. You shall keep it until the fourteenth day of this month; then the whole assembled congregation of Israel shall slaughter it at twilight. They shall take some of the blood and put it on the two doorposts and the lintel of the houses in which they eat it. They shall eat the lamb that same night; they shall eat it roasted over the fire with unleavened bread and bitter herbs.

This is how you shall eat it: your loins girded, your sandals on your feet, and your staff in your hand; and you shall eat it hurriedly. It is the Passover of the Lord. For I will pass through the land of Egypt that night, and I will strike down every firstborn in the land of Egypt, both human beings and animals; on all the gods of Egypt I will execute judgments: I am the Lord.

The blood shall be a sign for you on the houses where you live: when I see the blood, I will pass over you, and no plague shall destroy you when I strike the land of Egypt.

This day shall be a day of remembrance for you. You shall celebrate it as a festival to the Lord; throughout your generations you shall observe it as a perpetual ordinance.—The word of the Lord. ℟. **Thanks be to God.** ↓

RESPONSORIAL PSALM Ps. 115 (116) [Thanksgiving]

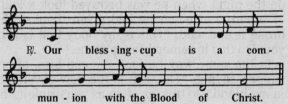

℟. Our bless-ing-cup is a com-mun-ion with the Blood of Christ.

(℟. **The blessing-cup that we bless is a communion with the blood of Christ.**)

(NRSV Text)	(GRAIL Text)
What shall I return to the Lord for all his bounty to me? I will lift up the cup of salvation and call on the name of the Lord.— ℟.	How can I repay the Lord for his goodness to me? The cup of salvation I will raise; I will call on the Lord's name.— ℟.
Precious in the sight of the Lord is the death of his faithful ones. O Lord, I am your servant; I am your servant, the child of your serving girl.	O precious in the eyes of the Lord is the death of his faithful. Your servant, Lord, your servant am I; You have loosened my bonds.— ℟.

You have loosed my bonds.—R̶.

I will offer to you a thanksgiving sacrifice
and call on the name of the Lord.
I will pay my vows to the Lord
in the presence of all his people.—
R̶. ↓

A thanksgiving sacrifice I make;
I will call on the Lord's name.
My vows to the Lord I will fulfill
before all his people.—R̶. ↓

SECOND READING 1 Cor. 11.23-26 [The Lord's Supper]

Paul recounts the events of the Last Supper which were handed down to him. The changing of bread and wine into the body and blood of the Lord proclaims again his death. It is a sacrificial meal.

A reading from the first letter of Paul
to the Corinthians

BELOVED: I received from the Lord what I also handed on to you, that the Lord Jesus on the night when he was betrayed took a loaf of bread, and when he had given thanks, he broke it and said, "This is my body that is for you. Do this in remembrance of me."

In the same way he took the cup also, after supper, saying, "This cup is the new covenant in my blood. Do this, as often as you drink it, in remembrance of me." For as often as you eat this bread and drink the cup, you proclaim the Lord's death until he comes.—The word of the Lord. R̶. **Thanks be to God.** ↓

GOSPEL ACCLAMATION Jn. 13.34 [Love One Another]

(If the acclamation is not sung, it is omitted.)

V̶. Praise to you, Lord, king of eternal glory!
R̶. **Praise to you, Lord, king of eternal glory!**
V̶. I give you a new commandment:
love one another as I have loved you.
R̶. **Praise to you, Lord, king of eternal glory!** ↓

GOSPEL Jn. 13.1-15   [Love and Service]

Jesus washes the feet of his disciples to prove to them his sincere love and great humility which they should imitate.

℣. The Lord be with you. ℟. **And also with you.**
✠ A reading from the holy gospel according to John. ℟. **Glory to you, Lord.**

NOW before the festival of the Passover, Jesus knew that his hour had come to depart from this world and go to the Father. Having loved his own who were in the world, he loved them to the end.

The devil had already put it into the heart of Judas, son of Simon Iscariot, to betray him. And during supper Jesus, knowing that the Father had given all things into his hands, and that he had come from God and was going to God, got up from the table, took off his outer robe, and tied a towel around himself. Then he poured water into a basin and began to wash the disciples' feet and to wipe them with the towel that was tied around him.

He came to Simon Peter, who said to him, "Lord, are you going to wash my feet?" Jesus answered, "You do not know now what I am doing, but later you will understand." Peter said to him, "You will never wash my feet." Jesus answered, "Unless I wash you, you have no share with me." Simon Peter said to him, "Lord, not my feet only but also my hands and my head!" Jesus said to him, "One who has bathed does not need to wash, except for the feet, but is entirely clean. And you are clean, though not all of you." For he knew who was to betray him; for this reason he said, "Not all of you are clean."

After he had washed their feet, put on his robe, and returned to the table, Jesus said to them, "Do you know what I have done to you? You call me Teacher and Lord—and you are right, for that is what I am. So if I, your Lord and Teacher, have washed your feet, you also ought to wash one another's feet. For I have set you an example, that you also should do as I have done to you."—The gospel of the Lord. ℟. **Praise to you, Lord Jesus Christ.**

The homily should explain the principal mysteries which are commemorated in this Mass: the institution of the eucharist, the institution of the priesthood, and Christ's commandment to love one another.

Washing of Feet

Depending on pastoral circumstances, the washing of feet follows the homily.

The people who have been chosen are led by the ministers to chairs prepared in a suitable place. Then the priest (removing his chasuble if necessary) goes to each one. With the help of the ministers, he pours water over each one's feet and dries them.

Meanwhile some of the following antiphons or other appropriate songs are sung.

ANTIPHON 1 See Jn. 13.4, 5, 15   [Jesus' Example]

**The Lord Jesus,
when he had eaten with his disciples,
poured water into a basin
and began to wash their feet, saying:
This example I leave you.**

ANTIPHON 2 Jn. 13.6, 7, 8   [Peter's Understanding]

℟. Lord, do you wash my feet?
Jesus said to him:
If I do not wash your feet,
you can have no part with me.

℟. Lord, do you wash my feet?
So he came to Simon Peter,
who said to him:

℟. Lord, do you wash my feet?
Now you do not know what I am doing,
but later you will understand.

℟. Lord, do you wash my feet?

ANTIPHON 3 See Jn. 13.14   [Service]

If I, your Lord and Teacher, have washed your
    feet,
then surely you must wash one another's feet.

ANTIPHON 4 Jn. 13.35   [Identified by Love]

If there is this love among you,
all will know that you are my disciples.
Jesus said to his disciples:
If there is this love among you,
all will know that you are my disciples.

ANTIPHON 5 Jn. 13.34   [New Commandment]

I give you a new commandment:
love one another as I have loved you.

ANTIPHON 6 1 Cor. 13.13   [Greatest Is Love]

Faith, hope, and love,
let these endure among you;
and the greatest of these is love.

*The general intercessions follow the washing of feet,
or, if this does not take place, they follow the homily.
The profession of faith is not said in this Mass.*

The Liturgy of the Eucharist

*At the beginning of the liturgy of the eucharist, there
may be a procession of the faithful with gifts for the
poor. During the procession the following may be sung,
or another appropriate song.*

[Christ's Love]

℟. **Where charity and love are found, there is
God.**

The love of Christ has gathered us together
  into one.
Let us rejoice and be glad in him.
Let us fear and love the living God
and love each other from the depths of our
  heart.

℟. **Where charity and love are found, there is
God.**

Therefore when we are together,
let us take heed not to be divided in mind.
Let there be an end to bitterness and quarrels,
  an end to strife,
and in our midst be Christ our God.

℟. **Where charity and love are found, there is
God.**

And, in company with the blessed, may we see
your face in glory, Christ our God,
pure and unbounded joy
for ever and ever.

℟. **Where charity and love are found, there is
God.**   → No. 17, p. 22

PRAYER OVER THE GIFTS   [Work of Redemption]

Lord,
make us worthy to celebrate these mysteries.
Each time we offer this memorial sacrifice,
the work of our redemption is accomplished.
We ask this in the name of Jesus the Lord.
R̸. **Amen.**   ➜ No. 21, p. 24 (Pref. 47)

*When Eucharistic Prayer I is used, the special Holy
Thursday forms of* In union with the whole Church,
Father, accept this offering, *and* The day before he
suffered *are said:*

In union with the whole Church
we celebrate that day
when Jesus Christ, our Lord,
was betrayed for us.
We honour Mary,
the ever-virgin mother of Jesus Christ our Lord
    and God.
We honour Joseph, her husband,
the apostles and martyrs
Peter and Paul, Andrew,
and all the saints.
May their merits and prayers
gain us your constant help and protection.

Father, accept this offering
from your whole family
in memory of the day when Jesus Christ, our
    Lord,
gave the mysteries of his body and blood
for his disciples to celebrate.

Grant us your peace in this life,
save us from final damnation,
and count us among those you have chosen.

Bless and approve our offering;
make it acceptable to you,
an offering in spirit and in truth.
Let it become for us
the body and blood of Jesus Christ,
your only Son, our Lord.

The day before he suffered
to save us and all people,
that is today,
he took bread in his sacred hands
and looking up to heaven,
to you, his almighty Father,
he gave you thanks and praise.
He broke the bread,
gave it to his disciples, and said:

Take this, all of you, and eat it:
this is my body which will be given up for you.

The rest follows the Roman canon, pp. 28-30.

COMMUNION ANTIPHON 1 Cor. 11.24-25
[In Remembrance of Christ]

**This body will be given for you. This is the cup
of the new covenant in my blood; whenever
you receive them, do so in remembrance of
me. ↓**

*After the distribution of communion, the ciborium with
hosts for Good Friday is left on the altar.*

*A period of silence may be observed after communion,
or a psalm or song of praise may be sung.*

PRAYER AFTER COMMUNION   [New Life]

Almighty God,
we receive new life
from the supper your Son gave us in this world.

May we find full contentment
in the meal we hope to share
in your eternal kingdom.
We ask this through Christ our Lord. ℟. **Amen.**

The Mass concludes with this prayer.

Transfer of the Holy Eucharist

After the prayer the priest stands before the altar and puts incense in the thurible. Kneeling, he incenses the Blessed Sacrament three times. Then he receives the humeral veil, takes the ciborium, and covers it with the ends of the veil.

The Blessed Sacrament is carried through the church in procession, led by a cross-bearer and accompanied by candles and incense, to the place of reposition prepared in a chapel suitably decorated for the occasion. During the procession the hymn Pange, lingua *(Sing, My Tongue, no. 55) (exclusive of the last two stanzas) or some other eucharistic song is sung.*

When the procession reaches the place of reposition, the priest sets the ciborium down. Then he puts incense in the thurible and, kneeling, incenses the Blessed Sacrament, while Tantum ergo sacramentum *(no. 55) is sung. The tabernacle of reposition is then closed.*

After a period of silent adoration, the priest and ministers genuflect and return to the sacristy.

Then the altar is stripped and, if possible, the crosses are removed from the church. It is desirable to cover any crosses which remain in the church.

The faithful should be encouraged to continue adoration before the Blessed Sacrament for a suitable period of time during the night, according to local circumstances, but there should be no solemn adoration after midnight.

"He bowed his head and gave up his spirit."

APRIL 6

GOOD FRIDAY

CELEBRATION OF THE LORD'S PASSION

This week, on Good Friday and Holy Saturday, the people of God are called to observe a solemn paschal fast. In this way, they are in union with the Christians of every century, and will be ready to receive the joys of the Lord's resurrection with uplifted and responsive hearts.

The priest and deacon, wearing red Mass vestments, go to the altar. There they make a reverence and prostrate themselves, or they may kneel. All kneel and pray silently for a while. Then the priest goes to the chair with the ministers. He faces the people and sings or says one of the following prayers.

PRAYER   [Make Us Holy]

Lord,
by shedding his blood for us,
your Son, Jesus Christ,
established the paschal mystery.
In your goodness, make us holy

and watch over us always.
We ask this through Christ our Lord. ℟. **Amen.**

OR   [Likeness of Christ]

Lord,
by the suffering of Christ your Son
you have saved us all from the death
we inherited from sinful Adam.
By the law of nature
we have borne the likeness of his manhood.
May the sanctifying power of grace
help us to put on the likeness of our Lord in
    heaven,
who lives and reigns for ever and ever.
℟. **Amen.**

LITURGY OF THE WORD

FIRST READING Isa. 52.13—53.12   [Suffering and Glory]

The Suffering Servant shall be raised up and exalted. The doctrine of expiatory suffering finds supreme expression in these words.

A reading from the book of the prophet Isaiah

Sᴇᴇ, my servant shall prosper;
   he shall be exalted and lifted up,
and shall be very high.

Just as there were many who were astonished
    at him
—so marred was his appearance, beyond
    human semblance,
and his form beyond that of mortals—
so he shall startle many nations;
kings shall shut their mouths because of him;
for that which had not been told them they
    shall see,

and that which they had not heard they shall
   contemplate.
Who has believed what we have heard?
And to whom has the arm of the Lord been revealed?

For he grew up before the Lord like a young
   plant,
and like a root out of dry ground;
he had no form or majesty that we should look
   at him,
nothing in his appearance that we should desire him.
He was despised and rejected by others;
a man of suffering and acquainted with infirmity;
and as one from whom others hide their faces
he was despised,
and we held him of no account.

Surely he has borne our infirmities and carried
   our diseases;
yet we accounted him stricken,
struck down by God, and afflicted.
But he was wounded for our transgressions,
crushed for our iniquities;
upon him was the punishment that made us
   whole,
and by his bruises we are healed.
All we like sheep have gone astray;
we have all turned to our own way,
and the Lord has laid on him
the iniquity of us all.

He was oppressed, and he was afflicted,
yet he did not open his mouth;
like a lamb that is led to the slaughter,
and like a sheep that before its shearers is silent,

so he did not open his mouth.
By a perversion of justice he was taken away.
Who could have imagined his future?
For he was cut off from the land of the living,
stricken for the transgression of my people.
They made his grave with the wicked
and his tomb with the rich,
although he had done no violence,
and there was no deceit in his mouth.

Yet it was the will of the Lord to crush him
    with pain.
When you make his life an offering for sin,
he shall see his offspring, and shall prolong his
    days;
through him the will of the Lord shall prosper.
Out of his anguish he shall see light;
he shall find satisfaction through his knowledge.
The righteous one, my servant, shall make
    many righteous,
and he shall bear their iniquities.

Therefore I will allot him a portion with the great,
and he shall divide the spoil with the strong;
because he poured out himself to death,
and was numbered with the transgressors;
yet he bore the sin of many,
and made intercession for the transgressors.
The word of the Lord. ℟. **Thanks be to God.** ↓

RESPONSORIAL PSALM Ps. 30 (31)   [Trust in God]

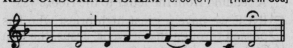

℟. Fa - ther,   I put my life__ in your hands.

(℟. Into your hands, O Lord, I commend my spirit.)

(NRSV Text)	(GRAIL Text)
In you, O Lord, I seek refuge; do not let me ever be put to shame; in your righteousness deliver me. Into your hand I commit my spirit; you have redeemed me, O Lord, faithful God.—℟.	In you, O Lord, I take refuge. Let me never be put to shame. In your justice, set me free. Into your hands I commend my spirit. It is you who will redeem me, Lord.— ℟.
I am the scorn of all my adversaries, a horror to my neighbours, an object of dread to my acquaintances. Those who see me in the street flee from me. I have passed out of mind like one who is dead; I have become like a broken vessel.—℟.	In the face of all my foes I am a reproach, an object of scorn to my neighbours and of fear to my friends.—℟. Those who see me in the street run far away from me. I am like the dead, forgotten by all, like a thing thrown away.—℟.
But I trust in you, O Lord, I say, "You are my God." My times are in your hand; deliver me from the hand of my enemies and persecutors.—℟.	But as for me, I trust in you, Lord; I say: "You are my God. My life is in your hands, deliver me from the hands of those who hate me."—℟.
Let your face shine upon your servant; save me in your steadfast love. Be strong, and let your heart take courage, all you who wait for the Lord.—℟. ↓	"Let your face shine on your servant. Save me in your love." Be strong, let your heart take courage, all who hope in the Lord.—℟. ↓

SECOND READING Heb. 4.14-16; 5.7-9

[Access to Christ]

The theme of the compassionate high priest appears again in this passage. In him Christians can approach God confidently and without fear.

A reading from the letter to the Hebrews

SINCE we have a great high priest who has passed through the heavens, Jesus, the Son of God, let us hold fast to our confession. For we do not have a high priest who is unable to sympathize with our weaknesses, but we have one who in every respect has been tested as we are, yet without sin. Let us therefore approach the throne of grace with boldness, so that we may receive mercy and find grace to help in time of need.

In the days of his flesh, Jesus offered up prayers and supplications, with loud cries and tears, to the one who was able to save him from death, and he was heard because of his reverent submission. Although he was a Son, he learned obedience through what he suffered; and having been made perfect, he became the source of eternal salvation for all who obey him.—The word of the Lord. ℟. **Thanks be to God.** ↓

GOSPEL ACCLAMATION Phil. 2.8-9 [Obedient for Us]
(If the acclamation is not sung, it is omitted.)

℣. Praise to you, Lord, king of eternal glory!
℟. **Praise to you, Lord, king of eternal glory!**
℣. Christ became obedient for us even to death, dying on the cross.
Therefore God raised him on high
and gave him a name above all other names.
℟. **Praise to you, Lord, king of eternal glory!** ↓

GOSPEL Jn. 18.1—19.42   [Christ's Passion]
The passion is read in the same way as on the preceding Sunday. The narrator is noted by **N**, *the words of Jesus by a* ✝ *and the words of others by* **S**.

It is important for us to understand the meaning of Christ's sufferings today. See the note on p. 271.

The beginning scene is Christ's agony in the garden. Our Lord knows what is to happen. The Scriptures recount the betrayal, the trial, the condemnation, and the crucifixion of Jesus.

N. **T**HE Passion of our Lord Jesus Christ according to John.

JESUS IS ARRESTED

N. **A**FTER [they had eaten] the supper, Jesus went out with his disciples across the Kidron valley to a place where there was a garden, which he and his disciples entered. Now Judas, who betrayed him, also knew the place, because Jesus often met there with his disciples. So Judas brought a detachment of soldiers together with police from the chief priests and the Pharisees, and they came there with lanterns and torches and weapons. Then Jesus, knowing all that was to happen to him, came forward and asked them, ✠ *"Whom are you looking for?"* **N.** They answered, **S2.** **"Jesus of Nazareth."** [**N.** Jesus replied,] ✠ *"I am he."* **N.** Judas, who betrayed him, was standing with them. When Jesus said to them, "I am he," they stepped back and fell to the ground. Again he asked them, ✠ *"Whom are you looking for?"* [**N.** And they said,] **S2.** **"Jesus of Nazareth."** [**N.** Jesus answered,] ✠ *"I told you that I am he. So if you are looking for me, let these men go."* **N.** This was to fulfil the word that he had spoken, "I did not lose a single one of those whom you gave me."

Then Simon Peter, who had a sword, drew it, struck the high priest's slave, and cut off his right ear. The slave's name was Malchus. Jesus said to Peter, ✠ *"Put your sword back into its sheath. Am I not to drink the cup that the Father has given me?"*

TRIAL BEFORE ANNAS

N. **S**O the soldiers, their officer, and the Jewish police arrested Jesus and bound him. First they took him to Annas, who was the father-in-law of Caiaphas, the high priest that year. Caiaphas was the one who had advised the Jewish leaders that it was better to have one person die for the people.

Simon Peter and another disciple followed Jesus. Since that disciple was known to the high priest, he went with Jesus into the courtyard of the high priest, but Peter was standing outside at the gate. So the other disciple, who was known to the high priest, went out, spoke to the woman who guarded the gate, and brought Peter in. The woman said to Peter, **S₃.** **"You are not also one of this man's disciples, are you?"** **N.** Peter said, **S₁.** **"I am not."** **N.** Now the slaves and the police had made a charcoal fire because it was cold, and they were standing around it and warming themselves. Peter also was standing with them and warming himself.

Then the high priest questioned Jesus about his disciples and about his teaching. Jesus answered, ✠ *"I have spoken openly to the world; I have always taught in synagogues and in the temple, where all the Jews come together. I have said nothing in secret. Why do you ask me? Ask those who heard what I said to them; they know what I said."*

N. When he had said this, one of the police standing nearby struck Jesus on the face, saying,

S₃. "Is that how you answer the high priest?" [N. Jesus answered,] ✠ *"If I have spoken wrongly, testify to the wrong. But if I have spoken rightly, why do you strike me?"* **N.** Then Annas sent him bound to Caiaphas the high priest.

PETER DENIES THE LORD JESUS

N. **N**OW Simon Peter was standing and warming himself. They asked him, **S₂. "You are not also one of his disciples, are you?"** N. He denied it and said, **S₁. "I am not."** N. One of the slaves of the high priest, a relative of the man whose ear Peter had cut off, asked, **S₂. "Did I not see you in the garden with him?"** N. Again Peter denied it, and at that moment the cock crowed.

At this point all may join in singing an acclamation.

TRIAL BEFORE PILATE

N. **T**HEN they took Jesus from Caiaphas to Pilate's headquarters. It was early in the morning. They themselves did not enter the headquarters, so as to avoid ritual defilement and to be able to eat the Passover. So Pilate went out to them and said, **S₃. "What accusation do you bring against this man?"** N. They answered, **S₂. "If this man were not a criminal, we would not have handed him over to you."** N. Pilate said to them, **S₃. "Take him yourselves and judge him according to your law."** N. They replied, **S₂. "We are not permitted to put anyone to death."** N. (This was to fulfil what Jesus had said when he indicated the kind of death he was to die.)

Then Pilate entered the headquarters again, summoned Jesus, and asked him, **S3. "Are you the King of the Jews?"** [**N.** Jesus answered,] ✤ *"Do you ask this on your own, or did others tell you about me?"* [**N.** Pilate replied,] **S3. "I am not a Jew, am I? Your own nation and the chief priests have handed you over to me. What have you done?"** [**N.** Jesus answered,] ✤ *"My kingdom is not from this world. If my kingdom were from this world, my followers would be fighting to keep me from being handed over to the Jewish authorities. But as it is, my kingdom is not from here."* [**N.** Pilate asked him,] **S2. "So you are a king?"** [**N.** Jesus answered,] ✤ *"You say that I am a king. For this I was born, and for this I came into the world, to testify to the truth. Everyone who belongs to the truth listens to my voice."* [**N.** Pilate asked him,] **S2. "What is truth?"**

N. After he had said this, Pilate went out to the Jewish leaders again and told them, **S3. "I find no case against him. But you have a custom that I release someone for you at the Passover. Do you want me to release for you the King of the Jews?"** **N.** They shouted in reply, **S2. "Not this man, but Barabbas!"** **N.** Now Barabbas was a bandit.

Then Pilate took Jesus and had him flogged. And the soldiers wove a crown of thorns and put it on his head, and they dressed him in a purple robe. They kept coming up to him, saying, **S2. "Hail, King of the Jews!"** **N.** and they struck him on the face.

Pilate went out again and said to them, S3. **"Look, I am bringing him out to you to let you know that I find no case against him."** N. So Jesus came out, wearing the crown of thorns and the purple robe. Pilate said to them, S3. **"Here is the man!"**

N. When the chief priests and the police saw him, they shouted, S2. **"Crucify him! Crucify him!"** N. Pilate said to them, S3. **"Take him yourselves and crucify him; I find no case against him."** N. They answered him, S2. **"We have a law, and according to that law he ought to die because he has claimed to be the Son of God."**

N. Now when Pilate heard this, he was more afraid than ever. He entered his headquarters again and asked Jesus, S3. **"Where are you from?"** N. But Jesus gave him no answer. Pilate therefore said to him, S3. **"Do you refuse to speak to me? Do you not know that I have power to release you, and power to crucify you?"** [N. Jesus answered him,] ✠ *"You would have no power over me unless it had been given you from above; therefore the one who handed me over to you is guilty of a greater sin."* N. From then on Pilate tried to release him, but the Jewish leaders cried out, S2. **"If you release this man, you are no friend of the emperor. Everyone who claims to be a king sets himself against the emperor."** N. When Pilate heard these words, he brought Jesus outside and sat on the judge's bench at a place called "The Stone Pavement," or in Hebrew "Gabbatha."

Now it was the day of Preparation for the Passover; and it was about noon. Pilate said to the Jewish leaders, S3. **"Here is your King!"** N. They cried out, S2. **"Away with him! Away with him! Crucify him!"** N. Pilate asked them, S3. **"Shall I crucify your King?"** N. The chief priests answered, S2. **"We have no king but the emperor."** N. Then Pilate handed Jesus over to them to be crucified.

At this point all may join in singing an appropriate acclamation.

JESUS IS CRUCIFIED AND DIES FOR US

N. SO they took Jesus; and carrying the cross by himself, he went out to what is called The Place of the Skull, which in Hebrew is called Golgotha. There they crucified him, and with him two others, one on either side, with Jesus between them.

Pilate also had an inscription written and put on the cross. It read, "Jesus of Nazareth, the King of the Jews." Many of the people read this inscription, because the place where Jesus was crucified was near the city; and it was written in Hebrew, in Latin, and in Greek. Then the chief priests of the Jews said to Pilate, S2. **"Do not write, 'The King of the Jews,' but, 'This man said, I am King of the Jews.' "** N. Pilate answered, S3. **"What I have written I have written."**

N. When the soldiers had crucified Jesus, they took his clothes and divided them into four parts, one for each soldier. They also took his tunic; now the tunic was seamless, woven in one piece from the top. So they said to one another, **S₂. "Let us not tear it, but cast lots for it to see who will get it." N.** This was to fulfil what the scripture says,

"They divided my clothes among themselves,
and for my clothing they cast lots."

And that is what the soldiers did.

Meanwhile, standing near the cross of Jesus were his mother, and his mother's sister, Mary the wife of Clopas, and Mary Magdalene. When Jesus saw his mother and the disciple whom he loved standing beside her, he said to his mother, ✠ *"Woman, here is your son."* **N.** Then he said to the disciple, ✠ *"Here is your mother."* **N.** And from that hour the disciple took her into his own home.

After this, when Jesus knew that all was now finished, he said (in order to fulfil the scripture), ✠ *"I am thirsty."* **N.** A jar full of sour wine was standing there. So they put a sponge full of the wine on a branch of hyssop and held it to his mouth. When Jesus had received the wine, he said, ✠ *"It is finished."* **N.** Then he bowed his head and gave up his spirit.

All may kneel for a period of silence.

EVENTS AFTER JESUS' DEATH

N. SINCE it was the day of Preparation, the Jewish leaders did not want the bodies left on the cross during the sabbath, especially because that sabbath was a day of great solemnity. So they asked Pilate to have the legs of the crucified men broken and the bodies removed.

Then the soldiers came and broke the legs of the first and of the other who had been crucified with him. But when they came to Jesus and saw that he was already dead, they did not break his legs. Instead, one of the soldiers pierced his side with a spear, and at once blood and water came out.

He who saw this has testified so that you also may believe. His testimony is true, and he knows that he tells the truth. These things occurred so that the scripture might be fulfilled, "None of his bones shall be broken." And again another passage of scripture says, "They will look on the one whom they have pierced."

JESUS' BODY IS PLACED IN THE TOMB

N. **A**FTER these things, Joseph of Arimathea, who was a disciple of Jesus, though a secret one because of his fear of the Jewish authorities, asked Pilate to let him take away the body of Jesus. Pilate gave him permission; so he came and removed his body.

Nicodemus, who had at first come to Jesus by night, also came, bringing a mixture of myrrh and aloes, weighing about a hundred grams. They took the body of Jesus and wrapped it with the spices in linen cloths, according to the burial custom of the Jews. Now there was a garden in the place where he was crucified, and in the garden there was a new tomb in which no one had ever been buried. And so, because it was the Jewish day of Preparation, and the tomb was nearby, they laid Jesus there.

After the reading of the passion there may be a brief homily.

GENERAL INTERCESSIONS

The general intercessions conclude the liturgy of the word. The priest stands at the chair, or he may be at the lectern or altar. With his hands joined, he sings or says the introduction in which each intention is stated. All kneel and pray silently for some period of time, and then the priest, with hands extended, sings or says the prayer. The people may either kneel or stand throughout the entire period of the general intercessions.

1. For the Church

Let us pray, dear friends,
for the holy Church of God throughout the
　world,
that God the almighty Father
guide it and gather it together
so that we may worship him
in peace and tranquility.

Deacon or cantor (or celebrant):

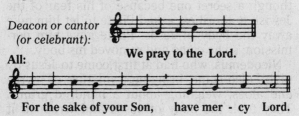

We pray to the Lord.

All:

For the sake of your Son,　have mer - cy Lord.

Silent prayer. Then the priest sings or says:

Almighty and eternal God,
you have shown your glory to all nations
in Christ, your Son.
Guide the work of your Church.
Help it to persevere in faith,
proclaim your name,
and bring your salvation to people everywhere.

We ask this through Christ our Lord.

All:

A - men.

2. For the Pope

Let us pray
for our Holy Father, Pope N.,
that God who chose him to be bishop
may give him health and strength
to guide and govern God's holy people.

*Deacon or cantor
(or celebrant):*

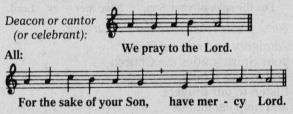

We pray to the Lord.

All:

For the sake of your Son,　have mer - cy Lord.

Silent prayer. Then the priest sings or says:

Almighty and eternal God,
you guide all things by your word,
you govern all Christian people.
In your love protect the Pope you have chosen
　for us.
Under his leadership deepen our faith
and make us better Christians.
We ask this through Christ our Lord.

All:

A - men.

3. For the clergy and laity of the Church

Let us pray
for N., our bishop;
for all bishops, priests, and deacons;
for all who have a special ministry in the Church
and for all God's people.

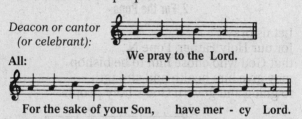

*Deacon or cantor
(or celebrant):*

All:

We pray to the Lord.

For the sake of your Son,   have mer - cy Lord.

Silent prayer. Then the priest sings or says:

Almighty and eternal God,
your Spirit guides the Church
and makes it holy.
Listen to our prayers
and help each of us
in his own vocation
to do your work more faithfully.
We ask this through Christ our Lord.

All:

A - men.

4. For those preparing for baptism

Let us pray
for those [among us] preparing for baptism,
that God in his mercy
make them responsive to his love,

forgive their sins through the waters of new
    birth,
and give them life in Jesus Christ our Lord.

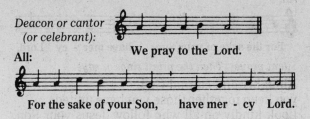

*Deacon or cantor
    (or celebrant):*   **We pray to the Lord.**

All:

For the sake of your Son,   have mer - cy Lord.

Silent prayer. Then the priest sings or says:

Almighty and eternal God,
you continually bless your Church with new
    members.
Increase the faith and understanding
of those [among us] preparing for baptism.
Give them a new birth in these living waters
and make them members of your chosen family.
We ask this through Christ our Lord.

All:

A - men.

5. For the unity of Christians

Let us pray
for all our brothers and sisters
who share our faith in Jesus Christ,
that God may gather and keep together in one
    Church
all those who seek the truth with sincerity.

Deacon or cantor
(or celebrant):

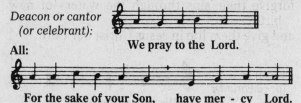

We pray to the Lord.

All:

For the sake of your Son,   have mer - cy   Lord.

Silent prayer. Then the priest sings or says:

Almighty and eternal God,
you keep together those you have united.
Look kindly on all who follow Jesus your Son.
We are all consecrated to you by our common
    baptism.
Make us one in the fullness of faith,
and keep us one in the fellowship of love.
We ask this through Christ our Lord.

All:

A - men.

6. For the Jewish people

Let us pray
for the Jewish people,
the first to hear the word of God,
that they may continue to grow in the love of
    his name
and in faithfulness to his covenant.

Deacon or cantor
(or celebrant):

We pray to the Lord.

All:

For the sake of your Son, have mer - cy Lord.

Silent prayer. Then the priest sings or says:

Almighty and eternal God,
long ago you gave your promise
to Abraham and his posterity.
Listen to your Church as we pray
that the people you first made your own
may arrive at the fullness of redemption.
We ask this through Christ our Lord.

All:

A - men.

7. For those who do not believe in Christ.

Let us pray
for those who do not believe in Christ,
that the light of the Holy Spirit
may show them the way to salvation.

Deacon or cantor
(or celebrant):

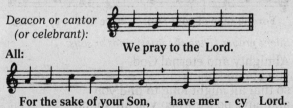

We pray to the Lord.

All:

For the sake of your Son, have mer - cy Lord.

Silent prayer. Then the priest sings or says:

Almighty and eternal God,
enable those who do not acknowledge Christ
to find the truth
as they walk before you in sincerity of heart.

Help us to grow in love for one another,
to grasp more fully the mystery of your godhead,
and to become more perfect witnesses of your
   love
in the sight of men.
We ask this through Christ our Lord.

All:

A - men.

8. For those who do not believe in God

Let us pray
for those who do not believe in God,
that they may find him
by sincerely following all that is right.

*Deacon or cantor
   (or celebrant):*

We pray to the Lord.

All:

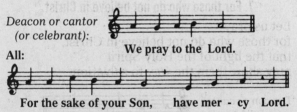

For the sake of your Son,   have mer - cy Lord.

Silent prayer. Then the priest sings or says:

Almighty and eternal God,
you created mankind
so that all might long to find you
and have peace when you are found.
Grant that, in spite of the hurtful things
that stand in their way,
they may all recognize in the lives of Christians
the tokens of your love and mercy,
and gladly acknowledge you

as the one true God and Father of us all.
We ask this through Christ our Lord.

All:

A - men.

9. For all in public office

Let us pray
for those who serve us in public office,
that God may guide their minds and hearts,
so that all men may live in true peace and freedom.

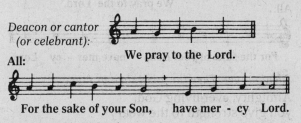

*Deacon or cantor
(or celebrant):*

We pray to the Lord.

All:

For the sake of your Son,   have mer - cy Lord.

Silent prayer. Then the priest sings or says:
Almighty and eternal God,
you know the longings of men's hearts
and you protect their rights.
In your goodness
watch over those in authority,
so that people everywhere may enjoy
religious freedom, security and peace.
We ask this through Christ our Lord.

All:

A - men.

10. For those in special need

Let us pray, dear friends,
that God the almighty Father
may heal the sick,
comfort the dying,
give safety to travellers,
free those unjustly deprived of liberty,
and rid the world of falsehood,
hunger and disease.

*Deacon or cantor
(or celebrant):*

We pray to the Lord.

All:

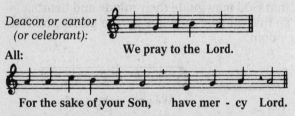

For the sake of your Son,   have mer - cy Lord.

Silent prayer. Then the priest sings or says:

Almighty, ever-living God,
you give strength to the weary
and new courage to those who have lost heart.
Hear the prayers of all who call on you in any
    trouble
that they may have the joy
of receiving your help in their need.
We ask this through Christ our Lord.

All:

A - men.

VENERATION OF THE CROSS

After the general intercessions, the veneration of the cross takes place. Pastoral demands will determine which of the two forms is more effective and should be chosen. The deacon or choir may assist the priest in the singing.

I

The veiled cross is carried to the altar, accompanied by two ministers with lighted candles. Standing at the altar, the priest takes the cross, uncovers the upper part of it, then elevates it and begins the invitation, This is the wood of the cross. *All respond:* Come, let us worship. *At the end of the singing all kneel and venerate the cross briefly in silence; the priest remains standing and holds the cross high.*

Then the priest uncovers the right arm of the cross, lifts it up, and again begins the invitation, This is the wood of the cross, *and the rite is repeated as before.*

Finally he uncovers the entire cross, lifts it up, and again begins the invitation, This is the wood of the cross, *a third time, and the rite is repeated as before.*

Accompanied by two ministers with lighted candles, the priest then carries the cross to the entrance of the sanctuary or to another suitable place. There he lays the cross down or hands it to the ministers to hold. Candles are placed on either side of the cross, and the veneration follows.

II

The priest or deacon, accompanied by the ministers or by another suitable minister, goes to the church door. There he takes the uncovered cross, and the ministers take lighted candles. They go in procession through the church to the sanctuary. Near the entrance of the church, in the middle of the church, and at the entrance to the sanctuary, the one carrying the cross stops, lifts it up, and sings the invitation, This is the wood of the cross. *All respond:* Come, let us worship. *After each response all kneel and venerate the cross briefly in silence as above.*

Then the cross and candles are placed at the entrance to the sanctuary.

INVITATION

Celebrant:

This is the wood of the cross,
on which hung the Saviour of the world.

People:

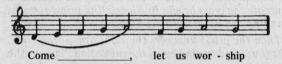

Come _____,   let us wor - ship

VENERATION OF THE CROSS

The priest, clergy, and faithful approach to venerate the cross in a kind of procession. They make a simple genuflection or perform some other appropriate sign of reverence according to local custom, for example, kissing the cross.

During the veneration the antiphon, We worship you, Lord, *the reproaches or other suitable songs are sung. All who have venerated the cross return to their places and sit.*

Only one cross should be used for the veneration. If the number of people makes it impossible for everyone to venerate the cross individually, the priest may take the cross, after some of the faithful have venerated it, and stand in the center in front of the altar. In a few words he invites the people to venerate the cross and then holds it up briefly for them to worship in silence.

After the veneration, the cross is carried to its place at the altar, and the lighted candles are placed around the altar or near the cross.

SONGS AT THE VENERATION OF THE CROSS

Individual parts are indicated by no. 1 (first choir) and no. 2 (second choir); parts sung by both choirs together are indicated by nos. 1 and 2.

1 and 2: Antiphon   [Holy Cross]

**We worship you, Lord,
we venerate your cross,
we praise your resurrection.
Through the cross you brought joy to the
    world.**

1: Psalm 66 (67).2

**May God be gracious and bless us;
and let his face shed its light upon us.**

1 and 2:

**We worship you, Lord,
we venerate your cross,
we praise your resurrection.
Through the cross you brought joy to the
    world.**

I

REPROACHES

1 and 2: **My people, what have I done to you?
    How have I offended you? Answer me!**
1:   **I led you out of Egypt, from slavery to freedom,
    but you led your Saviour to the cross.**
2:   **My people, what have I done to you?
    How have I offended you? Answer me!**

1: **Holy is God!**
2: **Holy and strong!**
1: **Holy immortal One,
    have mercy on us!**

1 and 2: For forty years I led you safely through the
         desert.
         I fed you with manna from heaven,
         and brought you to a land of plenty;
         but you led your Saviour to the cross.

1: **Holy is God!**
2: **Holy and strong!**
1: **Holy immortal One,
    have mercy on us!**

1 and 2: What more could I have done for you?
         I planted you as my fairest vine,
         but you yielded only bitterness:
         when I was thirsty you gave me vinegar to drink,
         and you pierced your Saviour with a lance.

1: **Holy is God!**
2: **Holy and strong!**
1: **Holy immortal One,
    have mercy on us!**

II

1: For your sake I scourged your captors and their
       firstborn sons,
    but you brought your scourges down on me.
2: My people, what have I done to you?
    How have I offended you? Answer me!
1: I led you from slavery to freedom
    and drowned your captors in the sea,
    but you handed me over to your high priests.

2: **My people, what have I done to you?
How have I offended you? Answer me!**

1: **I opened the sea before you,
but you opened my side with a spear.**

2: **My people, what have I done to you?
How have I offended you? Answer me!**

1: **I led you on your way in a pillar of cloud,
but you led me to Pilate's court.**

2: **My people, what have I done to you?
How have I offended you? Answer me!**

1: **I bore you up with manna in the desert,
but you struck me down and scourged me.**

2: **My people, what have I done to you?
How have I offended you? Answer me!**

1: **I gave you saving water from the rock,
but you gave me gall and vinegar to drink.**

2: **My people, what have I done to you?
How have I offended you? Answer me!**

1: **For you I struck down the kings of Canaan,
but you struck my head with a reed.**

2: **My people, what have I done to you?
How have I offended you? Answer me!**

1: **I gave you a royal sceptre,
but you gave me a crown of thorns.**

2: **My people, what have I done to you?
How have I offended you? Answer me!**

1: **I raised you to the height of majesty,
but you have raised me high on a cross.**

2: **My people, what have I done to you?
How have I offended you? Answer me!**

*A hymn in honour of the cross, or of Christ crucified,
may be sung.*

HOLY COMMUNION

The altar is covered with a cloth and the corporal and book are placed on it. Then the deacon or, if there is no deacon, the priest brings the ciborium with the Blessed Sacrament from the place of reposition to the altar without any procession, while all stand in silence. Two ministers with lighted candles accompany him and they place their candles near the altar or on it.

The deacon places the ciborium on the altar and uncovers it. Meanwhile the priest comes from his chair, genuflects, and goes up to the altar. With hands joined he says aloud:

Let us pray with confidence to the Father
in the words our Saviour gave us:

He extends his hands and continues, with all present:

**Our Father, who art in heaven,
hallowed be thy name;
thy kingdom come,
thy will be done
on earth as it is in heaven.
Give us this day our daily bread;
and forgive us our trespasses
as we forgive those who trespass against us;
and lead us not into temptation,
but deliver us from evil.**

With hands extended, the priest continues alone:

Deliver us, Lord, from every evil,
and grant us peace in our day.
In your mercy keep us free from sin
and protect us from all anxiety
as we wait in joyful hope
for the coming of our Saviour, Jesus Christ.

He joins his hands. The people end the prayer with the acclamation:

**For the kingdom, the power, and the glory are
   yours, now and for ever.**

Then the priest joins his hands and says quietly:

Lord Jesus Christ, with faith in your love and
mercy I eat your body and drink your blood.
Let it not bring me condemnation, but health in
mind and body.

*The priest genuflects. Taking the host, he raises it
slightly over the ciborium and, facing the people, says
aloud:*

This is the Lamb of God
who takes away the sins of the world.
Happy are those who are called to his supper.

He adds, once only, with the people:

**Lord, I am not worthy to receive you,
but only say the word and I shall be healed.**

*Facing the altar, he reverently consumes the body of
Christ.*

*Then communion is distributed to the faithful. Any
appropriate song may be sung during communion.*

*When the communion has been completed, a suitable
minister may take the ciborium to a place prepared
outside the church or, if circumstances require, may
place it in the tabernacle.*

*A period of silence may now be observed. The priest
then says the following prayer:*

[Serving God]

Almighty and eternal God,
you have restored us to life
by the triumphant death and resurrection of
   Christ.

Continue this healing work within us.
May we who participate in this mystery
never cease to serve you.
We ask this in the name of Jesus the Lord.
℟. **Amen.**

*For the dismissal the priest faces the people, extends
his hands toward them, and says the following prayer
over the people:*

PRAYER OVER THE PEOPLE   [Salvation Assured]

Lord,
send down your abundant blessing upon your
    people
who have devoutly recalled the death of your
    Son
in the sure hope of the resurrection.
Grant them pardon; bring them comfort.
May their faith grow stronger
and their eternal salvation be assured.
We ask this through Christ our Lord. ℟. **Amen.**

*All depart in silence. The altar is stripped at a conve-
nient time.*

APRIL 7

HOLY SATURDAY

*On Holy Saturday the Church waits at the Lord's
tomb, meditating on his suffering and death. The altar
is left bare, and the sacrifice of the Mass is not celebrated. Only after the solemn vigil during the night,
held in anticipation of the resurrection, does the
Easter celebration begin, with a spirit of joy that over-
flows into the following period of fifty days.*

*On this day holy communion may be given only as
viaticum.*

"He is not here, but has risen."

APRIL 7
EASTER VIGIL

In accord with ancient tradition, this night is one of vigil for the Lord (Ex. 12.42). The Gospel of Luke (12.35-48) is a reminder to the faithful to have their lamps burning ready, awaiting their master's return so that when he arrives he will find them wide awake and will seat them at his table.

The night vigil is arranged in four parts: a) a brief service of light; b) the liturgy of the word, when the Church meditates on all the wonderful things God has done for his people from the beginning; c) the liturgy of baptism, when new members of the Church are reborn as the day of resurrection approaches; and d) the liturgy of the eucharist, when the whole Church is called to the table which the Lord prepared for his people through his death and resurrection.

SOLEMN BEGINNING OF THE VIGIL:
THE SERVICE OF LIGHT

BLESSING OF THE FIRE AND LIGHTING
OF THE CANDLE   [The Fire of Christ]

All the lights in the church are put out.

I

A large fire is prepared in a suitable place outside the church. When the people have assembled, the priest goes there with the ministers, one of whom carries the Easter candle.

If it is not possible to light the fire outside the church, the rite is carried out as in II below.

The priest greets the congregation in the usual manner and briefly instructs them about the vigil in these or similar words:

Dear friends in Christ,   [Honouring Christ's Memory]
on this most holy night,
when our Lord Jesus Christ passed from death to life,
the Church invites her children throughout the world
to come together in vigil and prayer.
This is the passover of the Lord:
if we honour the memory of his death and resurrection
by hearing his word and celebrating his mysteries,
then we may be confident
that we shall share his victory over death
and live with him for ever in God.

Then the fire is blessed.

Let us pray.

Pause for silent prayer.

Father,   [Light of the World]
we share in the light of your glory
through your Son, the light of the world.
Make this new fire ✢ holy, and inflame us with new hope.

Purify our minds by this Easter celebration
and bring us one day to the feast of eternal light.
We ask this through Christ our Lord.
R̸. **Amen.**

The Easter candle is lighted from the new fire.

PREPARATION OF THE CANDLE
[The Easter Candle]

*Depending on the nature of the congregation, it may
seem appropriate to stress the dignity and significance
of the Easter candle with other symbolic rites. This
may be done as follows:*

*a) After the blessing of the new fire, an acolyte or
one of the ministers brings the Easter candle to the celebrant, who cuts a cross in the wax with a stylus. Then
he traces the Greek letter alpha above the cross, the
letter omega below, and the numerals of the current
year between the arms of the cross. Meanwhile he says:*

1. Christ yesterday and today *(as he traces the
   vertical arm of the cross)*
2. the beginning and the end *(the horizontal
   arm)*
3. Alpha *(alpha, above the cross)*
4. and Omega *(omega below the cross)*
5. all time belongs to him *(the first numeral, in
   the upper left corner of the cross)*
6. and all the ages *(the second numeral in the
   upper right corner)*
7. to him be glory and power *(the third numeral in the lower left corner)*
8. through every age for ever. Amen. *(the last
   numeral in the lower right corner)*

b) When the cross and other marks have been made, the priest may insert five grains of incense in the candle. He does this in the form of a cross, saying:

1. By his holy   1
2. and glorious wounds
3. may Christ our Lord   4   2   5
4. guard us   3
5. and keep us. Amen.

c) The priest lights the candle from the new fire, saying:

May the light of Christ, rising in glory,
dispel the darkness of our hearts and minds.

Any or all of the preceding rites may be used, depending on local pastoral circumstances. The conferences of bishops may also determine other rites better adapted to the culture of the people.

II

Where it may be difficult to have a large fire, the blessing of the fire is adapted to the circumstances. When the people have assembled in the church as on other occasions, the priest goes with the ministers (carrying the Easter candle) to the church door. If possible, the people turn to face the priest.

The greeting and brief instruction take place as above. Then the fire is blessed and, if desired, the candle is prepared and lighted as above.

PROCESSION   [Praise of Christ Our Light]

Then the deacon, or, if there is no deacon, the priest takes the Easter candle, lifts it high, and sings alone:

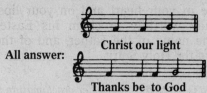

Christ our light

All answer:

Thanks be to God

Then all enter the church, led by the deacon with the Easter candle. At the church door, he raises the candle and sings in a higher tone.

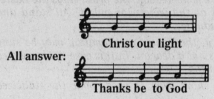

Christ our light

All answer:

Thanks be to God

All light their candles from the Easter candle and continue in the procession. When the deacon arrives before the altar, he faces the people and sings a third time, in a higher tone.

Christ our light

All answer:

Thanks be to God

EASTER PROCLAMATION

When he comes to the altar, the priest goes to his chair. The deacon places the Easter candle on a stand in the middle of the sanctuary or near the lectern. If incense is used, the priest puts some in the censer, as at the gospel of Mass. Then the deacon asks the blessing of the priest, who says in a low voice:

The Lord be in your heart and on your lips, that you may worthily proclaim his Easter praise. In the name of the Father, and of the Son, ✠ and of the Holy Spirit.

The deacon answers: Amen.

This blessing is omitted if the Easter proclamation is sung by one who is not a deacon.

The book and candle may be incensed. Then the deacon or, if there is no deacon, the priest sings the Easter proclamation at the lectern or pulpit. All stand and hold lighted candles.

If necessary, the Easter proclamation may be sung by one who is not a deacon. In this case the bracketed words are omitted.

When the short form is used, omit the italicized parts.

Rejoice, heavenly powers! Sing, choirs of angels!
  Exult, all creation around God's throne!
  Jesus Christ, our King, is risen!
  Sound the trumpet of salvation!

Rejoice, O earth, in shining splendour,
  radiant in the brightness of your King!
  Christ has conquered! Glory fills you!
  Darkness vanishes for ever!

Rejoice, O Mother Church! Exult in glory!
  The risen Saviour shines upon you!
  Let this place resound with joy,
  echoing the mighty song of all God's people!

[My dearest friends, standing with me in this holy light,
  join me in asking God for mercy,

that he may give his unworthy minister
grace to sing his Easter praises.]

[℣. The Lord be with you. ℟. **And also with you.]**
℣. Lift up your hearts. ℟. **We lift them up to the**
Lord. ℣. Let us give thanks to the Lord our God.
℟. **It is right to give him thanks and praise.**

It is truly right
that with full hearts and minds and voices
we should praise the unseen God,
the all-powerful Father,
and his only Son, our Lord Jesus Christ.
For Christ has ransomed us with his blood,
    and paid for us the price of Adam's sin
    to our eternal Father!

This is our passover feast,
    when Christ, the true Lamb, is slain,
    whose blood consecrates the homes of all be-
        lievers.

This is the night when first you saved our fa-
        thers:
    you freed the people of Israel from their slav-
        ery
    and led them dry-shod through the sea.

This is the night when the pillar of fire
    destroyed the darkness of sin!

This is the night when Christians everywhere,
    washed clean of sin
    and freed from all defilement,
    are restored to grace and grow together in
        holiness.

This is the night when Jesus Christ
    broke the chains of death
    and rose triumphant from the grave.

What good would life have been to us,
    had Christ not come as our Redeemer?

Father, how wonderful your care for us!
    How boundless your merciful love!
    To ransom a slave
    you gave away your Son.

O happy fault, O necessary sin of Adam,
    which gained for us so great a Redeemer!

Most blessed of all nights, chosen by God
    to see Christ rising from the dead!

Of this night scripture says:
    "The night will be as clear as day:
    it will become my light, my joy."

The power of this holy night
    dispels all evil, washes guilt away,
    restores lost innocence, brings mourners joy;
    it casts out hatred, brings us peace, and hum-
        bles earthly pride.

Night truly blessed when heaven is wedded to
        earth
    and man is reconciled with God!

Therefore, heavenly Father, in the joy of this
        night,
    receive our evening sacrifice of praise,
    your Church's solemn offering.

Accept this Easter candle,
    a flame divided but undimmed,
    a pillar of fire that glows to the honour of God.

Short form only:
    May it always dispel the darkness of this night!

Let it mingle with the lights of heaven
  and continue bravely burning
    to dispel the darkness of this night!

May the Morning Star which never sets
  find this flame still burning:
  Christ, that Morning Star,
  who came back from the dead,
  and shed his peaceful light on all mankind,
  your Son who lives and reigns for ever and
    ever.

All answer:

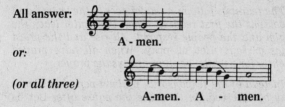

or:

(or all three)

LITURGY OF THE WORD

*In this vigil, the mother of all vigils, nine readings
are provided, seven from the Old Testament and two
from the New Testament (the epistle and gospel).*

*The number of readings from the Old Testament may
be reduced for pastoral reasons, but it must always be
borne in mind that the reading of the word of God is
the fundamental element of the Easter vigil. At least
three readings from the Old Testament should be read,
although for more serious reasons the number may be
reduced to two. The reading of Exodus 14, however, is
never to be omitted.*

*After the Easter proclamation, the candles are put
aside and all sit down. Before the readings begin, the
priest speaks to the people in these or similar words:*

Dear friends in Christ,   [Attentive Listening]
we have begun our solemn vigil.
Let us now listen attentively to the word of
   God,
recalling how he saved his people throughout
   history
and, in the fullness of time,
sent his own Son to be our Redeemer.
Through this Easter celebration,
may God bring to perfection
the saving work he has begun in us.

*The readings follow. A reader goes to the lectern and
proclaims the first reading. Then the cantor leads the
psalm and the people respond. All rise and the priest
sings or says,* Let us pray. *When all have prayed
silently for a while, he sings or says the prayer.*

*Instead of the responsorial psalm a period of silence
may be observed. In this case the pause after* Let us
pray *is omitted.*

FIRST READING Gen. 1.1—2.2 or 1.1, 26-31a [Our Creator]

**God created the world and all that is in it, and saw that
it was good. This reading from the first book of the
Bible shows that God made and loves all that exists.**

*[If the "Short Form" is used, the indented text in
brackets is omitted.]*

   A reading from the book of Genesis

IN the beginning [when] God created the
heavens and the earth,
   [the earth was a formless void and darkness covered the face of the deep, while
   the spirit of God swept over the face of the

waters. Then God said, "Let there be light"; and there was light. And God saw that the light was good; and God separated the light from the darkness. God called the light "Day," and the darkness he called "Night." And there was evening and there was morning, the first day.

And God said, "Let there be a dome in the midst of the waters, and let it separate the waters from the waters." So God made the dome and separated the waters that were under the dome from the waters that were above the dome. And it was so. God called the dome "Sky." And there was evening and there was morning, the second day.

And God said, "Let the waters under the sky be gathered together into one place, and let the dry land appear." And it was so. God called the dry land "Earth," and the waters that were gathered together he called "Seas." And God saw that it was good.

Then God said, "Let the earth put forth vegetation: plants yielding seed, and fruit trees of every kind on earth that bear fruit with the seed in it." And it was so. The earth brought forth vegetation: plants yielding seed of every kind, and trees of every kind bearing fruit with the seed in it. And God saw that it was good. And there was evening and there was morning, the third day.

And God said, "Let there be lights in the dome of the sky to separate the day from the night; and let them be for signs and for seasons and for days and years, and let them be lights in the dome of the sky to give light upon the earth." And it was so.

God made the two great lights—the greater light to rule the day and the lesser light to rule the night—and the stars. God set them in the dome of the sky to give light upon the earth, to rule over the day and over the night, and to separate the light from the darkness. And God saw that it was good. And there was evening and there was morning, the fourth day.

And God said, "Let the waters bring forth swarms of living creatures, and let birds fly above the earth across the dome of the sky." So God created the great sea monsters and every living creature that moves, of every kind, with which the waters swarm, and every winged bird of every kind. And God saw that it was good. God blessed them, saying, "Be fruitful and multiply and fill the waters in the seas, and let birds multiply on the earth." And there was evening and there was morning, the fifth day.

And God said, "Let the earth bring forth living creatures of every kind: cattle and creeping things and wild animals of the earth of every kind." And it was so. God made the wild animals of the earth of every kind, and the cattle of every kind, and everything that creeps upon the ground of every kind. And God saw that it was good.]

[Then] God said, "Let us make human beings in our image, according to our likeness; and let them have dominion over the fish of the sea, and over the birds of the air, and over the cattle, and over all the wild animals of the earth, and over every creeping thing that creeps upon the earth."

So God created human beings in his image,
in the image of God he created them;
male and female he created them.

God blessed them, and God said to them, "Be fruitful and multiply, and fill the earth and subdue it; and have dominion over the fish of the sea and over the birds of the air and over every living thing that moves upon the earth."

God said, "See, I have given you every plant yielding seed that is upon the face of all the earth, and every tree with seed in its fruit; you shall have them for food. And to every beast of the earth, and to every bird of the air, and to everything that creeps on the earth, everything that has the breath of life, I have given every green plant for food." And it was so.

God saw everything that he had made, and indeed, it was very good.

[And there was evening and there was morning, the sixth day.

Thus the heavens and the earth were finished, and all their multitude. And on the seventh day God finished the work that he had done, and he rested on the seventh day from all the work that he had done.]

The word of the Lord. ℟. **Thanks be to God.** ↓

RESPONSORIAL PSALM Ps. (103) 104 [Creator Spirit]

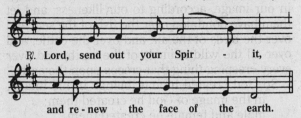

℟. Lord, send out your Spir - it,
and re - new the face of the earth.

(℟. **Send forth your Spirit, O Lord, and renew the face of the earth.**)

(NRSV Text)	(GRAIL Text)
Bless the Lord, O my soul.	Bless the Lord, my soul!
O Lord my God, you are very great.	Lord God, how great you are,
You are clothed with honour and majesty,	clothed in majesty and glory,
wrapped in light as with a garment.—℟.	wrapped in light as in a robe.—℟.
You set the earth on its foundations, so that it shall never be shaken.	You founded the earth on its base, to stand firm from age to age.
You cover it with the deep as with a garment;	You wrapped it with the ocean like a cloak;
the waters stood above the mountains.—℟.	the waters higher than the mountains.—℟.
You make springs gush forth in the valleys;	You make springs gush forth in the valleys;
they flow between the hills.	they flow in between the hills.
By the streams the birds of the air have their habitation;	On their banks dwell the birds of heaven;
they sing among the branches.—℟.	from the branches they sing their song.—℟.
From your lofty abode you water the mountains;	From your dwelling place you water the hills;
the earth is satisfied with the fruit of your work.	each drinks its fill of your gift.
You cause the grass to grow for the cattle,	You make the grass grow for the cattle
and plants for people to use, to bring forth food from the earth.—℟.	and plants to serve our needs.—℟.

O Lord, how manifold are your works!	How many are your works, O Lord!
In wisdom you have made them all;	In wisdom you have made them all.
the earth is full of your creatures.	The earth is full of your riches.
Bless the Lord, O my soul.—℟. ↓	Bless the Lord, my soul.—℟. ↓

OR

RESPONSORIAL PSALM Ps. 32 (33)　[God's Goodness]

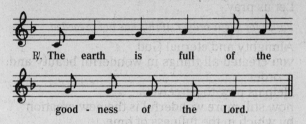

℟. The earth is full of the good-ness of the Lord.

(℟. **The earth is full of the goodness of our God.**)

(NRSV Text)	**(GRAIL Text)**
The word of the Lord is upright, and all his work is done in faithfulness. He loves righteousness and justice; the earth is full of the steadfast love of the Lord.—℟.	For the word of the Lord is faithful and all his works to be trusted. The Lord loves justice and right and fills the earth with his love.— ℟.
By the word of the Lord the heavens were made, and all their host by the breath of his mouth. He gathered the waters of the sea as in a bottle; he put the deeps in storchouses.— ℟.	By his word the heavens were made, by the breath of his mouth all the stars. He collects the waves of the ocean; he stores up the depths of the sea.— ℟.
Happy is the nation whose God is the Lord, the people whom he has chosen as his heritage. The Lord looks down from heaven; he sees all human beings.—℟.	They are happy, whose God is the Lord, the people he has chosen as his own. From the heavens the Lord looks forth, he sees all the peoples of the earth.—℟.

Our soul waits for the Lord;
he is our help and shield.
Let your steadfast love, O Lord, be
  upon us,
even as we hope in you.—℟. ↓

Our soul is waiting for the Lord.
The Lord is our help and our shield.
May your love be upon us, O Lord,
as we place all our hope in you.—
  ℟. ↓

PRAYER   [New Creation]

Let us pray.

Pause for silent prayer, if this has not preceded.

Almighty and eternal God,
you created all things in wonderful beauty and
  order.
Help us now to perceive
how still more wonderful is the new creation
by which in the fullness of time
you redeemed your people
through the sacrifice of our passover, Jesus
  Christ,
who lives and reigns for ever and ever.
℟. **Amen.** ↓

OR

PRAYER (on the creation of the human race)

Lord God,   [Our Redemption]
the creation of man was a wonderful work,
his redemption still more wonderful.
May we persevere in right reason
against all that entices to sin
and so attain to everlasting joy.
We ask this through Christ our Lord.
℟. **Amen.** ↓

SECOND READING Gen. 22.1-18 or 22.1-2, 9-13, 15-18
[Obedience to God]

Abraham is obedient to the will of God. Because God asks him, without hesitation he prepares to sacrifice his son Isaac. In the new order, God sends the only Son to redeem us by his death on the cross.

[If the "Short Form" is used, the indented text in brackets is omitted.]

A reading from the book of Genesis

GOD tested Abraham. He said to him, "Abraham!" And Abraham said, "Here I am." God said, "Take your son, your only son Isaac, whom you love, and go to the land of Moriah, and offer him there as a burnt offering on one of the mountains that I shall show you."

[So Abraham rose early in the morning, saddled his donkey, and took two of his young men with him, and his son Isaac; he cut the wood for the burnt offering, and set out and went to the place in the distance that God had shown him.

On the third day Abraham looked up and saw the place far away. Then Abraham said to his young men, "Stay here with the donkey; the boy and I will go over there; we will worship, and then we will come back to you." Abraham took the wood of the burnt offering and laid it on his son Isaac, and he himself carried the fire and the knife. So the two of them walked on together.

Isaac said to his father Abraham, "Father!" And Abraham said, "Here I am, my son." Isaac said, "The fire and the wood are here, but where is the lamb for a burnt offering?" Abraham said, "God himself will provide the lamb for a burnt offering, my son." So the two of them walked on together.]

When Abraham and Isaac came to the place that God had shown him, Abraham built an altar there and laid the wood in order. He bound his son Isaac, and laid him on the altar, on top of the wood. Then Abraham reached out his hand and took the knife to kill his son.

But the angel of the Lord called to him from heaven, and said, "Abraham, Abraham!" And he said, "Here I am." The angel said, "Do not lay your hand on the boy or do anything to him; for now I know that you fear God, since you have not withheld your son, your only son, from me." And Abraham looked up and saw a ram, caught in a thicket by its horns. Abraham went and took the ram and offered it up as a burnt offering instead of his son.

[So Abraham called that place "The Lord will provide"; as it is said to this day, "On the mount of the Lord it shall be provided."]

The angel of the Lord called to Abraham a second time from heaven, and said, "By myself I have sworn, says the Lord: Because you have done this, and have not withheld your son, your only son, I will indeed bless you, and I will make your offspring as numerous as the stars of heaven and as the sand that is on the seashore. And your offspring shall possess the gate of their enemies, and by your offspring shall all the nations of the earth gain blessing for themselves, because you have obeyed my voice."—The word of the Lord. ℟. **Thanks be to God.** ↓

RESPONSORIAL PSALM Ps. 15 (16)   [God Our Hope]

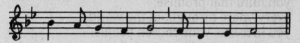

℟. **Keep me safe, O God, you are my hope.**

(NRSV Text)

The Lord is my chosen portion and my cup;
you hold my lot.
I keep the Lord always before me;
because he is at my right hand, I shall not be moved.—℟.

Therefore my heart is glad, and my soul rejoices;
my body also rests secure.
For you do not give me up to Sheol, or let your faithful one see the Pit.—℟.

You show me the path of life.
In your presence there is fullness of joy;
in your right hand are pleasures forevermore.—℟. ↓

(GRAIL Text)

O Lord, it is you who are my portion and cup,
it is you yourself who are my prize.
I keep you, Lord, ever in my sight;
since you are at my right hand, I shall stand firm.—℟.

And so my heart rejoices, my soul is glad;
even my body shall rest in safety.
For you will not leave my soul among the dead,
nor let your beloved know decay.—℟.

You will show me the path of life,
the fullness of joy in your presence,
at your right hand happiness for ever.—℟. ↓

PRAYER   [Response to God's Call]

Let us pray.

Pause for silent prayer, if this has not preceded.

God and Father of all who believe in you,
you promised Abraham
that he would become the father of all nations,
and through the death and resurrection of
   Christ
you fulfil that promise:
everywhere throughout the world
you increase your chosen people.
May we respond to your call
by joyfully accepting your invitation to the new
   life of grace.
We ask this in the name of Jesus the Lord.
℟. **Amen.** ↓

THIRD READING Ex. 14.15-31; 15.20, 1   [Exodus]

**God saved the chosen people from slavery and death by
leading them through the waters of the sea; now our
God saves us by leading us through the waters of baptism, by which we come to share in the death and rising
of Jesus.**

A reading from the book of Exodus

THE Lord said to Moses, "Why do you cry
out to me? Tell the Israelites to go forward.
But you, lift up your staff, and stretch out your
hand over the sea and divide it, that the Israelites may go into the sea on dry ground.
Then I will harden the hearts of the Egyptians
so that they will go in after them; and so I will
gain glory for myself over Pharaoh and all his
army, his chariots, and his chariot drivers. And
the Egyptians shall know that I am the Lord,

when I have gained glory for myself over Pharaoh, his chariots, and his chariot drivers."

The angel of God who was going before the Israelite army moved and went behind them; and the pillar of cloud moved from in front of them and took its place behind them. It came between the army of Egypt and the army of Israel. And so the cloud was there with the darkness, and it lit up the night; one did not come near the other all night. Then Moses stretched out his hand over the sea. The Lord drove the sea back by a strong east wind all night, and turned the sea into dry land; and the waters were divided. The Israelites went into the sea on dry ground, the waters forming a wall for them on their right and on their left.

The Egyptians pursued, and went into the sea after them, all of Pharaoh's horses, chariots, and chariot drivers. At the morning watch, the Lord in the pillar of fire and cloud looked down upon the Egyptian army, and threw the Egyptian army into panic. He clogged their chariot wheels so that they turned with difficulty. The Egyptians said, "Let us flee from the Israelites, for the Lord is fighting for them against Egypt."

Then the Lord said to Moses, "Stretch out your hand over the sea, so that the water may come back upon the Egyptians, upon their chariots and chariot drivers." So Moses stretched out his hand over the sea, and at dawn the sea returned to its normal depth. As the Egyptians fled before it, the Lord tossed the

Egyptians into the sea. The waters returned and covered the chariots and the chariot drivers, the entire army of Pharaoh that had followed them into the sea; not one of them remained.

But the Israelites walked on dry ground through the sea, the waters forming a wall for them on their right and on their left. Thus the Lord saved Israel that day from the Egyptians; and Israel saw the Egyptians dead on the seashore. Israel saw the great work that the Lord did against the Egyptians. So the people feared the Lord and believed in the Lord and in his servant Moses.

The prophet Miriam, Aaron's sister, took a tambourine in her hand; and all the women went out after her with tambourines and with dancing. Moses and the Israelites sang this song to the Lord: ↓

RESPONSORIAL CANTICLE Ex. 15 [God the Saviour]

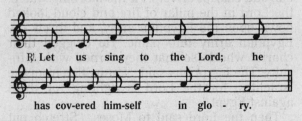

℟. Let us sing to the Lord; he has cov-ered him-self in glo - ry.

(NRSV Text)	(GRAIL Text)
I will sing to the Lord, for he has triumphed gloriously;	I will sing to the Lord, glorious his triumph!
horse and rider he has thrown into the sea.	Horse and rider he has thrown into the sea!
The Lord is my strength and my might,	The Lord is my strength, my song, my salvation.

and he has become my salvation;
this is my God, and I will praise him,
my father's God, and I will exalt
   him.—℟.

The Lord is a warrior;
the Lord is his name.
Pharaoh's chariots and his army he
   cast into the sea;
his picked officers were sunk in the
   Red Sea.
The floods covered them;
they went down into the depths like a
   stone.—℟.

Your right hand, O Lord, glorious in
   power;
your right hand, O Lord, shattered
   the enemy.
In the greatness of your majesty
you overthrew your adversaries;
you sent out your fury,
it consumed them like stubble.—℟.

You brought your people in
and planted them
on the mountain of your own possession,
the place, O Lord, that you made your
   abode,
the sanctuary, O Lord, that your
   hands have established.
The Lord will reign forever and
   ever.—℟. ↓

This is my God and I extol him,
my father's God, and I give him
   praise.—℟.

The Lord is a warrior! The Lord is his
   name.
The chariots of Pharaoh he hurled
   into the sea,
the flower of his army is drowned in
   the sea.
The deeps hide them; they sank like
   a stone.—℟.

Your right hand, Lord, glorious in its
   power,
your right hand, Lord, has shattered
   the enemy.
In the greatness of your glory you
   crushed the foe.—℟.

You will lead them and plant them
   on your mountain,
the place, O Lord, where you have
   made your home,
the sanctuary, Lord, which your
   hands have made.
The Lord will reign for ever and
   ever.—℟. ↓

PRAYER   [Children of Abraham]

Let us pray.

Pause for silent prayer, if this has not preceded.

Father,
even today we see the wonders
of the miracles you worked long ago.

You once saved a single nation from slavery,
and now you offer that salvation to all through
  baptism.
May the peoples of the world become true sons
  of Abraham
and prove worthy of the heritage of Israel.
Grant this through Christ our Lord.
℟. **Amen.** ↓

OR

PRAYER   [New Birth]
Lord God,
in the new covenant
you shed light on the miracles you worked in
  ancient times:
the Red Sea is a symbol of our baptism,
and the nation you freed from slavery
is a sign of your Christian people.
May every nation
share the faith and privilege of Israel
and come to new birth in the Holy Spirit.
Grant this through Christ our Lord.
℟. **Amen.** ↓

FOURTH READING Isa. 54.5-14   [God's Love]

> For a time, God hid from the chosen people, but God's
> love for this people is everlasting. God takes pity on
> them and promises them prosperity.

 A reading from the book of the prophet Isaiah

THUS says the Lord, the God of hosts.
  Your Maker is your husband,
the Lord of hosts is his name;
the Holy One of Israel is your Redeemer,

the God of the whole earth he is called.
For the Lord has called you
like a wife forsaken and grieved in spirit,
like the wife of a man's youth when she is cast
off,
says your God.

For a brief moment I abandoned you,
but with great compassion I will gather you.
In overflowing wrath for a moment
I hid my face from you,
but with everlasting love I will have compassion on you,
says the Lord, your Redeemer.

This is like the days of Noah to me:
Just as I swore that the waters of Noah
would never again go over the earth,
so I have sworn that I will not be angry with you
and will not rebuke you.
For the mountains may depart
and the hills be removed,
but my steadfast love shall not depart from you,
and my covenant of peace shall not be removed,
says the Lord, who has compassion on you.

O afflicted one, storm-tossed, and not comforted,
I am about to set your stones in antimony,
and lay your foundations with sapphires.
I will make your pinnacles of rubies,
your gates of jewels,
and all your wall of precious stones.
All your children shall be taught by the Lord,
and great shall be the prosperity of your children.

In righteousness you shall be established;
you shall be far from oppression, for you shall
 not fear;
and from terror, for it shall not come near you.
The word of the Lord. ℟. **Thanks be to God.** ↓

RESPONSORIAL PSALM Ps. 29 (30)   [God Our Help]

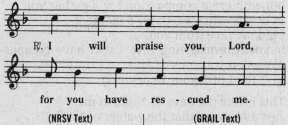

℟. I will praise you, Lord,
for you have res - cued me.

(NRSV Text)	**(GRAIL Text)**
I will extol you, O Lord, for you have drawn me up,	I will praise you, Lord, you have rescued me
and did not let my foes rejoice over me.	and have not let my enemies rejoice over me.
O Lord, you brought up my soul from Sheol,	O Lord, you have raised my soul from the dead,
restored me to life from among those gone down to the Pit.—℟.	restored me to life from those who sink into the grave.—℟.
Sing praises to the Lord, O you his faithful ones,	Sing psalms to the Lord, you who love him,
and give thanks to his holy name.	give thanks to his holy name.
For his anger is but for a moment; his favour is for a lifetime.	His anger lasts a moment; his favour all through life.
Weeping may linger for the night, but joy comes with the morning.— ℟.	At night there are tears, but joy comes with dawn.—℟.
Hear, O Lord, and be gracious to me!	The Lord listened and had pity.
O Lord, be my helper!	The Lord came to my help.
You have turned my mourning into dancing.	For me you have changed my mourning into dancing,
O Lord my God, I will give thanks to you forever.—℟. ↓	O Lord my God, I will thank you for ever.—℟. ↓

PRAYER   [Fulfilment of God's Promise]

Let us pray.

Pause for silent prayer, if this has not preceded.

Almighty and eternal God,
glorify your name by increasing your chosen
    people
as you promised long ago.
In reward for their trust,
may we see in the Church the fulfilment of
    your promise.
We ask this through Christ our Lord.
℟. **Amen.** ↓

*Prayers may also be chosen from those given after the
following readings, if the readings are omitted.*

FIFTH READING Isa. 55.1-11   [God of Forgiveness]

> God is a loving Father, calling all people to come back.
> Our God promises an everlasting covenant with them.
> God is merciful, generous, and forgiving.

A reading from the book of the prophet Isaiah

EVERYONE who thirsts,
    come to the waters;
and you that have no money,
come, buy and eat!
Come, buy wine and milk
without money and without price.
Why do you spend your money for that which
    is not bread,
and your labour for that which does not sat-
    isfy?
Listen carefully to me, and eat what is good,

and delight yourselves in rich food.
Incline your ear, and come to me;
listen, so that you may live.
I will make with you an everlasting covenant,
my steadfast, sure love for David.

See, I made him a witness to the peoples,
a leader and commander for the peoples.
See, you shall call nations that you do not
   know,
and nations that do not know you shall run to
   you,
because of the Lord your God, the Holy One of
   Israel,
for he has glorified you.

Seek the Lord while he may be found,
call upon him while he is near;
let the wicked forsake their way,
and the unrighteous their thoughts;
let them return to the Lord, that he may have
   mercy on them,
and to our God, for he will abundantly pardon.

For my thoughts are not your thoughts,
nor are your ways my ways, says the Lord.
For as the heavens are higher than the earth,
so are my ways higher than your ways
and my thoughts than your thoughts.

For as the rain and the snow come down from
   heaven,
and do not return there until they have watered
   the earth,
making it bring forth and sprout,
giving seed to the sower and bread to the eater,

so shall my word be that goes out from my
    mouth;
it shall not return to me empty,
but it shall accomplish that which I purpose,
and succeed in the thing for which I sent it.
The word of the Lord. ℟. **Thanks be to God.** ↓

RESPONSORIAL CANTICLE Isa. 12   [God's Deeds]

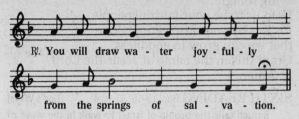

℟. You will draw wa - ter joy - ful - ly
from the springs of sal - va - tion.

(NRSV Text)	(GRAIL Text)
Surely God is my salvation; I will trust, and will not be afraid, for the Lord God is my strength and my might; he has become my salvation. With joy you will draw water from the wells of salvation.—℟.	Truly, God is my salvation, I trust, I shall not fear. For the Lord is my strength, my song, he became my saviour. With joy you will draw water from the wells of salvation.—℟.

Give thanks to the Lord,
call on his name;
make known his deeds among the
  nations;
proclaim that his name is exalted.—
  ℟.
	Give thanks to the Lord, give praise
	  to his name!
	Make his mighty deeds known to the
	  peoples!
	Declare the greatness of his
	  name.—℟.

Sing praises to the Lord,
for he has done gloriously;
let this be known in all the earth.
Shout aloud and sing for joy, O royal
  Zion,
for great in your midst
is the Holy One of Israel.—℟. ↓
	Sing a psalm to the Lord
	for he has done glorious deeds,
	make them known to all the earth!
	People of Zion, sing and shout for joy
	for great in your midst is the Holy
	  One of Israel.—℟. ↓

PRAYER   [Growth in Goodness]

Let us pray.

Pause for silent prayer, if this has not preceded.

Almighty, ever-living God,
only hope of the world,
by the preaching of the prophets
you proclaimed the mysteries we are celebrat-
　ing tonight.
Help us to be your faithful people,
for it is by your inspiration alone
that we can grow in goodness.
Grant this in the name of Jesus the Lord.
℟. **Amen.** ↓

SIXTH READING Bar. 3.9-15, 32—4.4   [God's Ways]

**Baruch tells the people of Israel to walk in the ways of
God. They have to learn prudence, wisdom, understanding. Then they will have peace forever.**

A reading from the book of the prophet Baruch

HEAR the commandments of life, O Israel;
　give ear, and learn wisdom!
Why is it, O Israel,
why is it that you are in the land of your ene-
　mies,
that you are growing old in a foreign country,
that you are defiled with the dead,
that you are counted among those in Hades?
You have forsaken the fountain of wisdom.
If you had walked in the way of God,
you would be living in peace forever.
Learn where there is wisdom,
where there is strength,
where there is understanding,

so that you may at the same time discern
where there is length of days, and life,
where there is light for the eyes, and peace.
Who has found her place?
And who has entered her storehouses?

But the one who knows all things knows her,
he found her by his understanding.
The one who prepared the earth for all time
filled it with four-footed creatures;
the one who sends forth the light, and it goes;
he called it, and it obeyed him, trembling;
the stars shone in their watches, and were glad;
he called them, and they said, "Here we are!"
They shone with gladness for him who made
  them.

This is our God;
no other can be compared to him.
He found the whole way to knowledge,
and gave her to his servant Jacob
and to Israel, whom he loved.
Afterward she appeared on earth
and lived with humanity.

She is the book of the commandments of God,
the law that endures forever.
All who hold her fast will live,
and those who forsake her will die.
Turn, O Jacob, and take her;
walk toward the shining of her light.
Do not give your glory to another,
or your advantages to an alien people.
Happy are we, O Israel,
for we know what is pleasing to God.

The word of the Lord. ℟. **Thanks be to God.** ↓

RESPONSORIAL PSALM Ps. 18 (19)   [Words of Life]

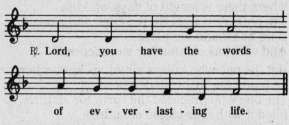

℟. Lord, you have the words of ev-ver-last-ing life.

(NRSV Text)	(GRAIL Text)

The law of the Lord is perfect,
reviving the soul;
the decrees of the Lord are sure,
making wise the simple.—℟.

The law of the Lord is perfect,
it revives the soul.
The rule of the Lord is to be trusted,
it gives wisdom to the simple.—℟.

The precepts of the Lord are right,
rejoicing the heart;
the commandment of the Lord is
clear,
enlightening the eyes.—℟.

The precepts of the Lord are right,
they gladden the heart.
The command of the Lord is clear,
it gives light to the eyes.—℟.

The fear of the Lord is pure,
enduring forever;
the ordinances of the Lord are true
and righteous altogether.—℟.

The fear of the Lord is holy,
abiding for ever.
The decrees of the Lord are truth
and all of them just.—℟.

More to be desired are they than
gold,
even much fine gold;
sweeter also than honey,
and drippings of the honeycomb.—
℟. ↓

They are more to be desired than
gold,
than the purest of gold
and sweeter are they than honey,
than honey from the comb.—℟. ↓

PRAYER   [Hear Our Prayer]

Let us pray.

Pause for silent prayer, if this has not preceded.

Father,
you increase your Church

by continuing to call all people to salvation.
Listen to our prayers
and always watch over those you cleanse in baptism.
We ask this through Christ our Lord.
℟. **Amen.** ↓

SEVENTH READING Ezek. 36.16-17a, 18-28

[God's Name]

God wants the chosen people to respect God's holy name. All shall know the holiness of God, who will cleanse this people from idol worship and bring them home again.

A reading from the book of the prophet Ezekiel

THE word of the Lord came to me: Mortal, when the house of Israel lived on their own soil, they defiled it with their ways and their deeds; their conduct in my sight was unclean. So I poured out my wrath upon them for the blood that they had shed upon the land, and for the idols with which they had defiled it. I scattered them among the nations, and they were dispersed through the countries; in accordance with their conduct and their deeds I judged them.

But when they came to the nations, wherever they came, they profaned my holy name, in that it was said of them, "These are the people of the Lord, and yet they had to go out of his land."

But I had concern for my holy name, which the house of Israel had profaned among the nations to which they came. Therefore say to the house of Israel, Thus says the Lord God: It is not for your sake, O house of Israel, that I am about to act, but for the sake of my holy name, which you have profaned among the nations to which you came.

I will sanctify my great name, which has been profaned among the nations, and which you have profaned among them; and the nations shall know that I am the Lord, says the Lord God, when through you I display my holiness before their eyes.

I will take you from the nations, and gather you from all the countries, and bring you into your own land. I will sprinkle clean water upon you, and you shall be clean from all your uncleanness, and from all your idols I will cleanse you. A new heart I will give you, and a new spirit I will put within you; and I will remove from your body the heart of stone and give you a heart of flesh. I will put my spirit within you, and make you follow my statutes and be careful to observe my ordinances. Then you shall live in the land that I gave to your ancestors; and you shall be my people, and I will be your God.— The word of the Lord. ℟. **Thanks be to God.** ↓

RESPONSORIAL PSALM Ps. 41—42 (42—43) [Longing]

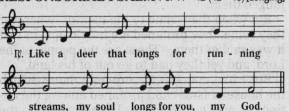

℟. Like a deer that longs for run-ning streams, my soul longs for you, my God.

(℟. **Like the deer that yearns for running streams, so my soul is yearning for you, my God.**)

(NRSV Text)

My soul thirsts for God, for the living God.
When shall I come and behold the face of God?—℟.

I went with the throng,
and led them in procession to the house of God,
with glad shouts and songs of thanksgiving,
a multitude keeping festival.—℟.

O send out your light and your truth;
let them lead me;
let them bring me to your holy mountain
and to your dwelling.—℟.

Then I will go to the altar of God,
to God my exceeding joy;
and I will praise you with the harp,
O God, my God.—℟. ↓

(GRAIL Text)

My soul is thirsting for God,
the God of my life;
when can I enter and see
the face of God?—℟.

These things will I remember
as I pour out my soul:
how I would lead the rejoicing crowd
into the house of God,
amid cries of gladness and thanksgiving,
the throng wild with joy.—℟.

O send forth your light and your truth;
let these be my guide.
Let them bring me to your holy mountain
to the place where you dwell.—℟.

And I will come to your altar, O God,
the God of my joy.
My redeemer, I will thank you on the harp,
O God, my God.—℟. ↓

OR

When baptism is celebrated, Isaiah 12 (after Fifth Reading, p. 353) may be used.

OR

RESPONSORIAL PSALM Ps. (50) 51   **[A Clean Heart]**

℟. Cre - ate a clean heart in me, O God.

(℟. Create for me, O God, a pure and humble heart.)

(NRSV Text)	(GRAIL Text)
Create in me a clean heart, O God, and put a new and steadfast spirit within me. Do not cast me away from your presence, and do not take your holy spirit from me.—℞. Restore to me the joy of your salvation, and sustain in me a willing spirit. Then I will teach transgressors your ways, and sinners will return to you.—℞. For you have no delight in sacrifice; if I were to give a burnt offering, you would not be pleased. The sacrifice acceptable to God is a broken spirit; a broken and contrite heart, O God, you will not despise.—℞. ↓	A pure heart create for me, O God, put a steadfast spirit within me. Do not cast me away from your presence, nor deprive me of your holy spirit.—℞. Give me again the joy of your help; with a spirit of fervor sustain me, that I may teach transgressors your ways and sinners may return to you.—℞. For in sacrifice you take no delight, burnt offering from me you would refuse; my sacrifice, a contrite spirit, a humbled, contrite heart you will not spurn.—℞. ↓

PRAYER   [Confirm Our Hope]

Let us pray.

Pause for silent prayer, if this has not preceded.

Father,
you teach us in both the Old and the New Testament
to celebrate this passover mystery.
Help us to understand your great love for us.
May the goodness you now show us
confirm our hope in your future mercy.
We ask this in the name of Jesus the Lord.
℞. **Amen.** ↓

OR   [Lasting Salvation]

God of unchanging power and light,
look with mercy and favour on your entire
  Church.
Bring lasting salvation to mankind,
so that the world may see
the fallen lifted up,
the old made new,
and all things brought to perfection,
through him who is their origin,
our Lord Jesus Christ,
who lives and reigns for ever and ever.
℞. **Amen.** ↓

OR

(if there are candidates to be baptized)

PRAYER   [Born Again in Baptism]

Let us pray.
Pause for silent prayer, if this has not preceded.

Almighty and eternal God,
be present in this sacrament of your love.
Send your Spirit of adoption
on those to be born again in baptism.
And may the work of our humble ministry
be brought to perfection by your mighty power.
We ask this in the name of Jesus the Lord.
℞. **Amen.** ↓

GLORY TO GOD   [Hymn of Praise]

*After the last reading from the Old Testament with its
responsory and prayer, the altar candles are lighted,
and the priest intones the Glory to God which is taken
up by all present (p. 14). The church bells are rung, according to local custom.*

OPENING PRAYER   [Renewed in Mind and Body]

Let us pray.

(Pause for silent prayer)

Lord God,
you have brightened this night
with the radiance of the risen Christ.
Quicken the spirit of sonship in your Church;
renew us in mind and body
to give you whole-hearted service.
Grant this through our Lord Jesus Christ, your
    Son,
who lives and reigns with you and the Holy
    Spirit,
one God, for ever and ever. ℟. **Amen.** ↓

EPISTLE Rom. 6.3-11   [Alive in Christ]

In baptism we are united to Christ, and we begin to be
formed in him. Christ has died; we will die. Christ is
risen; we will rise.

A reading from the letter of Paul
to the Romans

DO you not know that all of us who have
been baptized into Christ Jesus were baptized into his death? Therefore we have been
buried with him by baptism into death, so that,
just as Christ was raised from the dead by the
glory of the Father, so we too might walk in
newness of life. For if we have been united with
him in a death like his, we will certainly be
united with him in a resurrection like his.

We know that our old self was crucified with
him so that the body of sin might be destroyed,

and we might no longer be enslaved to sin. For whoever has died is freed from sin. But if we have died with Christ, we believe that we will also live with him.

We know that Christ, being raised from the dead, will never die again; death no longer has dominion over him. The death he died, he died to sin, once for all; but the life he lives, he lives to God. So you also must consider yourselves dead to sin and alive to God in Christ Jesus.—The word of the Lord. ℟. **Thanks be to God.** ↓

RESPONSORIAL PSALM Ps. (117) 118 [God's Mercy]

After the epistle all rise, and the priest solemnly intones the Alleluia, *which is repeated by all present. The cantor sings the psalm and the people answer,* Alleluia.

℟. **Al-le - lu - ia.**

(NRSV Text)	(GRAIL Text)
O give thanks to the Lord, for he is good; his steadfast love endures forever. Let Israel say, "His steadfast love endures forever"—℟.	Give thanks to the Lord for he is good, for his love endures for ever. Let the family of Israel say: "His love endures for ever."—℟.
"The right hand of the Lord is exalted; the right hand of the Lord does valiantly." I shall not die, but I shall live, and recount the deeds of the Lord.—℟.	The Lord's right hand has triumphed; his right hand raised me. I shall not die, I shall live and recount his deeds.—℟.

The stone that the builders rejected has become the chief cornerstone. This is the Lord's doing; it is marvellous in our eyes.—℟. ↓

The stone which the builders rejected has become the corner stone. This is the work of the Lord, a marvel in our eyes.—℟. ↓

GOSPEL Lk. 24.1-12   [The Resurrection]

**Christ has died, Christ has risen, Christ will come again!
God's mercy brings us forgiveness and salvation.**

℣. The Lord be with you. ℟. **And also with you.**
✛ A reading from the holy gospel according to
Luke. ℟. **Glory to you, Lord.**

ON the first day of the week, at early dawn, the women who had accompanied Jesus from Galilee came to the tomb, taking the spices that they had prepared. They found the stone rolled away from the tomb, but when they went in, they did not find the body.

While they were perplexed about this, suddenly two men in dazzling clothes stood beside them. The women were terrified and bowed their faces to the ground, but the men said to them, "Why do you look for the living among the dead? He is not here, but has risen. Remember how he told you, while he was still in Galilee, that the Son of Man must be handed over to sinners, and be crucified, and on the third day rise again."

Then the women remembered Jesus' words, and returning from the tomb, they told all this to the eleven and to all the rest. Now it was Mary Magdalene, Joanna, Mary the mother of James, and the other women with them who told this to the apostles.

These words seemed to the apostles an idle tale, and they did not believe the women. But

Peter got up and ran to the tomb; stooping and looking in, he saw the linen cloths by themselves; then he went home, amazed at what had happened.—The gospel of the Lord. ℟. **Praise to you, Lord Jesus Christ.**

The homily follows the gospel, and then the Liturgy of Sacraments of Initiation.

LITURGY OF SACRAMENTS OF INITIATION

The following is taken from the Rite of Christian Initiation of Adults.

Celebration of Baptism

PRESENTATION OF THE CANDIDATES

An assisting deacon or other minister calls the candidates for baptism forward and their godparents present them. The invitation to prayer and the Litany of the Saints follow.

INVITATION TO PRAYER   [Supportive Prayer]

The celebrant addresses the following or a similar invitation for the assembly to join in prayer for the candidates for baptism.

Dear friends, let us pray to almighty God for our brothers and sisters, N. and N., who are asking for baptism. He has called them and brought them to this moment; may he grant them light and strength to follow Christ with resolute hearts and to profess the faith of the Church. May he give them the new life of the Holy Spirit, whom we are about to call down on this water.

LITANY OF THE SAINTS   [Petitioning the Saints]

The singing of the Litany of the Saints is led by cantors and may include, at the proper place, names of other saints (for example, the titular of the church, the patron saints of the place or of those to be baptized) or petitions suitable to the occasion.

Cantor: All:

Lord, have mer - cy.   **Lord, have mer - cy.**

Christ, have mer - cy.   **Christ, have mer - cy.**

Lord, have mer - cy.   **Lord, have mer - cy.**

Holy Mary, Mother of God,   **pray for us.**
Saint Michael,
Holy angels of God,
Saint John the Baptist,
Saint Joseph,
Saint Peter and Saint Paul,
Saint Andrew,
Saint John,

Saint Mary Magdalene,
Saint Stephen,
Saint Ignatius,
Saint Lawrence,
Saint Perpetua and Saint Felicity,
Saint Agnes,
Saint Gregory,
Saint Augustine,
Saint Athanasius,
Saint Basil,
Saint Martin,
Saint Benedict,
Saint Francis and Saint Dominic,
Saint Francis Xavier,
Saint John Vianney,
Saint Catherine,
Saint Theresa,
(Other saints)
All holy men and women,
Lord, be merciful,
From all evil,
From every sin,

Lord, save your peo-ple.

From everlasting death,
By your coming as man,
By your death and rising to new life,
By your gift of the Holy Spirit,

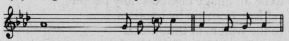

Be merciful to   us sin - ers **Lord, hear our prayer.**

Give new life to these chosen ones
by the grace of baptism,
Jesus, Son of the living God.

Christ, hear us. **Christ, hear us.**

Lord Je - sus hear our prayer. **Lord Je-sus hear our prayer.**

BLESSING OF THE WATER   [Grace-Filled Water]

Facing the font (or vessel) containing the water, the celebrant sings the following:

Father,
you give us grace through sacramental signs,
which tell us the wonders of your unseen power.
In baptism we use your gift of water,
which you have made a rich symbol of the grace
you give us in this sacrament.
At the very dawn of creation
your Spirit breathed on the waters,
making them the wellspring of all holiness.
The waters of the great flood
you made a sign of the waters of baptism,
that make an end of sin
and a new beginning of goodness.
Through the waters of the Red Sea
you led Israel out of slavery,
to be an image of God's holy people,
set free from sin by baptism.
In the waters of the Jordan
your Son was baptized by John
and anointed with the Spirit.
Your Son willed that water and blood should flow from his side
as he hung upon the cross.

After his resurrection he told his disciples:
"Go out and teach all nations,
baptizing them in the name of the Father and
  of the Son and of the Holy Spirit."
Father,
look now with love upon your Church,
and unseal for it the fountain of baptism.
By the power of the Holy Spirit
give to this water the grace of your Son,
so that in the sacrament of baptism
all those whom you have created in your likeness
may be cleansed from sin
and rise to a new birth of innocence
by water and the Holy Spirit.

*Here, if this can be done conveniently, the celebrant
before continuing lowers the Easter candle into the
water once or three times, then holds it there until the
acclamation at the end of the blessing.*

We ask you, Father, with your Son
to send the Holy Spirit upon the waters of this
  font.
May all who are buried with Christ in the death
  of baptism
rise also with him to newness of life.
We ask this through Christ our Lord.

All:

A - men.

If the Easter candle has been held in the water, the celebrant then raises it and the people sing the following or another suitable acclamation.

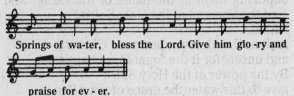

Springs of wa-ter, bless the Lord. Give him glo-ry and

praise for ev - er.

RENUNCIATION OF SIN   [Reject Evil]

Using one of the following formularies, the celebrant questions all the elect together; or, after being informed of each candidate's name by the godparents, he may use the same formularies to question the candidates individually.

A.

Do you reject sin so as to live in the freedom of God's children? **I do.**

Do you reject the glamour of evil, and refuse to be mastered by sin? **I do.**

Do you reject Satan, father of sin and prince of darkness? **I do.**

B.

Do you reject Satan, and all his works, and all his empty promises? **I do.**

C.

Do you reject Satan? **I do.**

And all his works? **I do.**

And all his empty promises? **I do.**

ANOINTING OF CATECHUMENS WITH OIL

[Oil of Salvation]

We anoint you with the oil of salvation
in the name of Christ our Saviour.
May he strengthen you with his power,
who lives and reigns for ever and ever. **Amen.**

*The celebrant anoints each candidate with the oil of
catechumens on both hands, on the breast, or, if this
seems desirable, on other parts of the body.*

PROFESSION OF FAITH

[We Do Believe]

*Then the celebrant, informed again of each candi-
date's name by the godparents, questions each candidate individually. Each candidate is baptized immediately after his or her profession of faith.*

Celebrant: N., do you believe in God, the
     Father almighty,
   creator of heaven and earth?
Candidate: **I do.**
Celebrant: Do you believe in Jesus Christ, his
     only Son, our Lord,
   who was born of the Virgin Mary,
   was crucified, died, and was buried,
   rose from the dead,
   and is now seated at the right hand of the
     Father?
Candidate: **I do.**
Celebrant: Do you believe in the Holy Spirit,
   the holy catholic Church, the communion
     of saints,

the forgiveness of sins, the resurrection of
   the body,
   and the life everlasting?
Candidate: **I do.**

BAPTISM [Children of God]

The celebrant baptizes each candidate either by immersion or by the pouring of water.

N., I baptize you in the name of the Father, and
of the Son, and of the Holy Spirit.

ANOINTING AFTER BAPTISM [Chrism of Salvation]

*If the confirmation of those baptized is separated
from their baptism, the celebrant anoints them with
chrism immediately after baptism.*

The God of power and Father of our Lord Jesus
   Christ
has freed you from sin
and brought you to new life
through water and the Holy Spirit.

He now anoints you with the chrism of salvation,
so that, united with his people,
you may remain for ever a member of Christ
who is Priest, Prophet, and King.

Newly baptized: **Amen.**

*In silence each of the newly baptized is anointed
with chrism on the crown of the head.*

CLOTHING WITH A BAPTISMAL GARMENT
[Clothed in Christ]

*The garment used in this rite may be white or of a
color that conforms to local custom. If circumstances
suggest, this rite may be omitted.*

N. and N., you have become a new creation
and have clothed yourselves in Christ.
Receive this baptismal garment
and bring it unstained to the judgment seat of
   our Lord Jesus Christ,
so that you may have everlasting life.

Newly baptized: **Amen.**

PRESENTATION OF A LIGHTED CANDLE

[Light of Christ]

The celebrant takes the Easter candle in his hands
or touches it, saying:

Godparents, please come forward to give to the
newly baptized the light of Christ.

A godparent of each of the newly baptized goes to
the celebrant, lights a candle from the Easter candle,
then presents it to the newly baptized.

You have been enlightened by Christ.
Walk always as children of the light
and keep the flame of faith alive in your hearts.
When the Lord comes, may you go out to meet
   him
with all the saints in the heavenly kingdom.

Newly baptized: **Amen.**

BLESSING OF THE WATER

If no one is to be baptized and the font is not to be
blessed, the priest blesses the water:

My brothers and sisters,
let us ask the Lord our God
to bless this water he has created,
which we shall use to recall our baptism.
May he renew us

and keep us faithful to the Spirit
we have all received.

All pray silently for a short while. With hands joined the priest continues:

Lord our God,
this night your people keep prayerful vigil.
Be with us as we recall the wonder of our creation
and the greater wonder of our redemption.
Bless this water: it makes the seed grow,
it refreshes us and makes us clean.
You have made of it a servant of your loving kindness:
through water you set your people free,
and quenched their thirst in the desert.
With water the prophets announced a new covenant
that you would make with man.
By water, made holy by Christ in the Jordan,
you made our sinful nature new
in the bath that gives rebirth.
Let this water remind us of our baptism;
let us share the joys of our brothers and sisters
who are baptized this Easter.
We ask this through Christ our Lord. ℟. **Amen.**

Renewal of Baptismal Promises

INVITATION   [Call to Renewal]

After the celebration of baptism, the celebrant addresses the community, in order to invite those present to the renewal of their baptismal promises; the candidates for reception into full communion join the rest of the community in this renunciation of sin and profession of faith. All stand and hold lighted candles. The celebrant may use the following or similar words.

Dear friends, through the paschal mystery we have been buried with Christ in baptism, so that we may rise with him to a new life. Now that we have completed our Lenten observance, let us renew the promises we made in baptism, when we rejected Satan and his works, and promised to serve God faithfully in his holy catholic Church.

RENUNCIATION OF SIN   [Reject Evil]

A.

Celebrant: Do you reject sin, so as to live in the freedom of God's children?

All: **I do.**

Celebrant: Do you reject the glamour of evil, and refuse to be mastered by sin?

All: **I do.**

Celebrant: Do you reject Satan, father of sin and prince of darkness?

All: **I do.**

B.

Celebrant: Do you reject Satan?

All: **I do.**

Celebrant: And all his works?

All: **I do.**

Celebrant: And all his empty promises?

All: **I do.**

PROFESSION OF FAITH   [We Do Believe]

Then the celebrant continues:

Celebrant: Do you believe in God, the Father almighty, creator of heaven and earth?

All: **I do.**

Celebrant: Do you believe in Jesus Christ, his
    only Son, our Lord,
  who was born of the virgin Mary,
  was crucified, died, and was buried,
  rose from the dead,
  and is now seated at the right hand of the
    Father?

All: **I do.**

Celebrant: Do you believe in the Holy Spirit,
    the holy Catholic Church, the communion
    of saints,
  the forgiveness of sins, the resurrection of
    the body,
  and the life everlasting?

All: **I do.**

SPRINKLING WITH BAPTISMAL WATER
[Water of Life]

*The celebrant sprinkles all the people with the
blessed baptismal water, while all sing the following
song or any other that is baptismal in character.*

Antiphon See Ezek. 47.1-2, 9

**I saw water flowing
from the right side of the temple, alleluia.
It brought God's life and his salvation,
and the people sang in joyful praise:
alleluia, alleluia.**

*The celebrant then concludes with the following
prayer.*

[Remaining Faithful]

God, the all-powerful Father of our Lord Jesus
    Christ,
has given us a new birth by water and the Holy
    Spirit,

and forgiven all our sins.
May he also keep us faithful to our Lord Jesus
 Christ
for ever and ever.
All: **Amen.**

Celebration of Reception

INVITATION   [Call To Come Forward]

*If baptism has been celebrated at the font, the cele-
brant, the assisting ministers, and the newly baptized
with their godparents proceed to the sanctuary. As
they do so the assembly may sing a suitable song.*

*Then in the following or similar words the celebrant
invites the candidates for reception, along with their
sponsors, to come into the sanctuary and before the
community to make a profession of faith.*

N. and N., of your own free will you have
asked to be received into the full communion
of the Catholic Church. You have made your
decision after careful thought under the guidance of the Holy Spirit. I now invite you to
come forward with your sponsors and in the
presence of this community to profess the
Catholic faith. In this faith you will be one with
us for the first time at the eucharistic table of
the Lord Jesus, the sign of the Church's unity.

PROFESSION BY THE CANDIDATES
[Belief in the Church]

*When the candidates for reception and their spon-
sors have taken their places in the sanctuary, the celebrant asks the candidates to make the following profession of faith. The candidates say:*

**I believe and profess all that the holy Catholic
Church believes, teaches, and proclaims to be
revealed by God.**

ACT OF RECEPTION   [Full Communion]

Then the candidates with their sponsors go individu-
ally to the celebrant, who says to each candidate (lay-
ing his right hand on the head of any candidate who is
not to receive confirmation):

N., the Lord receives you into the Catholic
   Church.
His loving kindness has led you here,
so that in the unity of the Holy Spirit
you may have full communion with us
in the faith that you have professed in the presence of his family.

Celebration of Confirmation

INVITATION   [Strength in the Spirit]

The newly baptized with their godparents and, if
they have not received the sacrament of confirmation,
the newly received with their sponsors, stand before
the celebrant. He first speaks briefly to the newly bap-
tized and the newly received in these or similar words.

My dear candidates for confirmation, by your
baptism you have been born again in Christ
and you have become members of Christ and
of his priestly people. Now you are to share in
the outpouring of the Holy Spirit among us, the
Spirit sent by the Lord upon his apostles at
Pentecost and given by them and their succes-
sors to the baptized.

The promised strength of the Holy Spirit, which
you are to receive, will make you more like
Christ and help you to be witnesses to his suffering, death, and resurrection. It will strengthen
you to be active members of the Church and to
build up the Body of Christ in faith and love.

My dear friends, let us pray to God our Father, that he will pour out the Holy Spirit on these candidates for confirmation to strengthen them with his gifts and anoint them to be more like Christ, the Son of God.

All pray briefly in silence.

LAYING ON OF HANDS   [Gifts of the Spirit]

The celebrant holds his hands outstretched over the entire group of those to be confirmed and says the following prayer.

All-powerful God, Father of our Lord Jesus Christ,
by water and the Holy Spirit
you freed your sons and daughters from sin
and gave them new life.
Send your Holy Spirit upon them
to be their helper and guide.

Give them the spirit of wisdom and understanding,
the spirit of right judgment and courage,
the spirit of knowledge and reverence.
Fill them with the spirit of wonder and awe in your presence.
We ask this through Christ our Lord.
℟. **Amen.**

ANOINTING WITH CHRISM   [Sealed in the Spirit]

Either or both godparents and sponsors place the right hand on the shoulder of the candidate; a godparent or a sponsor of the candidate gives the candidate's name to the minister of the sacrament. During the conferral of the sacrament an appropriate song may be sung.

The minister of the sacrament dips his right thumb in the chrism and makes the sign of the cross on the forehead of the one to be confirmed as he says:

N., be sealed with the Gift of the Holy Spirit.
Newly confirmed: **Amen.**

Minister: Peace be with you.
Newly confirmed: **And also with you.**

After all have received the sacrament, the newly confirmed as well as the godparents and sponsors are led to their places in the assembly.

Since the profession of faith is not said, the general intercessions (no. 15, p. 20) begin immediately and for the first time the neophytes take part in them.

LITURGY OF THE EUCHARIST

The priest goes to the altar and begins the liturgy of the eucharist in the usual way. It is fitting that the bread and wine be brought forward by the newly baptized.

PRAYER OVER THE GIFTS   [God's Saving Work]

Lord,
accept the prayers and offerings of your people.
With your help
may this Easter mystery of our redemption
bring to perfection the saving work you have begun in us.
We ask this through Christ our Lord.
℟. **Amen.**

➜ No. 21, p. 24 (Pref. 21: on this Easter night)

When Eucharistic Prayer I is used, the special Easter forms of In union with the whole Church *and* Father, accept this offering *are said.*

COMMUNION ANTIPHON 1 Cor. 5.7-8   [Sincerity]

Christ has become our paschal sacrifice; let us feast with the unleavened bread of sincerity and truth, alleluia. ↓

PRAYER AFTER COMMUNION   [Peace and Love]

Lord,
you have nourished us with your Easter sacraments.
Fill us with your Spirit,
and make us one in peace and love.
We ask this through Christ our Lord.
℟. **Amen.** ↓

The deacon (or priest) sings or says the dismissal as follows:

Go in the peace of Christ,
alleluia, alleluia.

or

Go in peace to love and serve the Lord,
alleluia, alleluia.

or

The Mass is ended, go in peace,
alleluia, alleluia.

The people answer:

Thanks be to God. Al-le-lu-ia, Al-le - lu - ia.

Optional Solemn Blessings, p. 96, and Prayers Over the People, p. 104

"I have risen: I am with you once more."

APRIL 8

EASTER SUNDAY

ENTRANCE ANTIPHON Ps. 138 (139).18, 5-6

[Resurrection]

I have risen: I am with you once more; you placed your hand on me to keep me safe. How great is the depth of your wisdom!

OR Lk. 24.34; see Rev. 1.6   [King and Lord]

The Lord has indeed risen, alleluia. Glory and kingship be his for ever and ever. ➜ No. 2, p. 10

OPENING PRAYER   [Renewal]

God our Father,
by raising Christ your Son
you conquered the power of death
and opened for us the way to eternal life.
Let our celebration today
raise us up and renew our lives
by the Spirit that is within us.

Grant this through our Lord Jesus Christ, your Son,

who lives and reigns with you and the Holy Spirit,

one God, for ever and ever. ℟. **Amen.** ↓

FIRST READING Acts 10.34a, 36-43 [Salvation in Christ]

In his sermon Peter sums up the good news, the Gospel. Salvation comes through Christ, the beloved Son of the Father, and the anointed of the Holy Spirit.

A reading from the Acts of the Apostles

PETER began to speak to those assembled in the house of Cornelius. "You know the message God sent to the people of Israel, preaching peace by Jesus Christ—he is Lord of all. That message spread throughout Judea, beginning in Galilee after the baptism that John announced: how God anointed Jesus of Nazareth with the Holy Spirit and with power; how he went about doing good and healing all who were oppressed by the devil, for God was with him.

"We are witnesses to all that he did both in Judea and in Jerusalem. They put him to death by hanging him on a tree; but God raised him on the third day and allowed him to appear, not to all the people but to us who were chosen by God as witnesses, and who ate and drank with him after he rose from the dead.

"He commanded us to preach to the people and to testify that he is the one ordained by God as judge of the living and the dead. All the prophets testify about him that everyone who believes in him receives forgiveness of sins

through his name."—The word of the Lord. ℟.
Thanks be to God. ↓

RESPONSORIAL PSALM Ps. 117 (118)

[Day of the Lord]

℟. This is the day the Lord has made;
let us re - joice and be glad.

℟. Or: **Alleluia! Alleluia! Alleluia!**

(NRSV Text)	(GRAIL Text)
O give thanks to the Lord, for he is good;	Give thanks to the Lord for he is good,
his steadfast love endures forever.	for his love endures for ever.
Let Israel say,	Let the family of Israel say:
"His steadfast love endures forever."—℟.	"His love endures for ever."—℟.
"The right hand of the Lord is exalted;	The Lord's right hand has triumphed;
the right hand of the Lord does valiantly."	his right hand raised me.
I shall not die, but I shall live,	I shall not die, I shall live
and recount the deeds of the Lord.—℟.	and recount his deeds.—℟.
The stone that the builders rejected has become the chief cornerstone.	The stone which the builders rejected has become the corner stone.
This is the Lord's doing;	This is the work of the Lord,
it is marvellous in our eyes.—℟. ↓	a marvel in our eyes.—℟. ↓

One of the following texts may be chosen as the Second Reading.

SECOND READING Col. 3.1-4　　[Seek Heavenly Things]
Look to the glory of Christ in which we share because
our lives are hidden in him through baptism, and we are
destined to share in his glory.

A reading from the letter of Paul
to the Colossians

IF you have been raised with Christ, seek the
things that are above, where Christ is, seated
at the right hand of God. Set your minds on
things that are above, not on things that are on
earth, for you have died, and your life is hidden
with Christ in God. When Christ who is your
life is revealed, then you also will be revealed
with him in glory.—The word of the Lord. R̸.
Thanks be to God. ↓

OR

SECOND READING 1 Cor. 5.6b-8   [Change of Heart]

**Turn away from your old ways, from sin. Have a change
of heart; be virtuous.**

A reading from the first letter of Paul
to the Corinthians

DO you not know that a little yeast leavens
the whole batch of dough? Clean out the
old yeast so that you may be a new batch, as
you really are unleavened. For our paschal
lamb, Christ, has been sacrificed. Therefore, let
us celebrate the festival, not with the old yeast,
the yeast of malice and evil, but with the unleavened bread of sincerity and truth.—The
word of the Lord. R̸. **Thanks be to God.** ↓

SEQUENCE   [Hymn to the Victor]

1. **Christians, praise the paschal victim!**
   Offer thankful sacrifice!
2. **Christ the Lamb has saved the sheep,**
   Christ the just one paid the price,

Reconciling sinners to the Father.

3. **Death and life fought bitterly**
   For this wondrous victory;
   The Lord of life who died reigns glorified!
4. **O Mary, come and say**
   what you saw at break of day.
5. **"The empty tomb of my living Lord!"**
   I saw Christ Jesus risen and adored!
6. **Bright angels testified,**
   Shroud and grave clothes side by side!
7. **"Yes, Christ my hope rose gloriously.**
   He goes before you into Galilee."
8. **Share the Good News, sing joyfully:**
   His death is victory!
   Lord Jesus, Victor King, show us mercy. ↓

GOSPEL ACCLAMATION 1 Cor. 5.7-8 [Joy in the Lord]
(If the Alleluia is not sung, the acclamation is omitted.)

℣. Alleluia. ℟. **Alleluia.**
℣. Christ has become our paschal sacrifice;
let us feast with joy in the Lord.
℟. **Alleluia.** ↓

(FOR MORNING MASS)

GOSPEL Jn. 20.1-18 or 20.1-9   [Renewed Faith]
   Let us ponder this mystery of Christ's rising, and like
   Christ's first followers be strengthened in our faith.

[If "Short Form" is used, omit indented text in brackets.]

℣. The Lord be with you. ℟. **And also with you.**
✠ A reading from the holy gospel according to
John. ℟. **Glory to you, Lord.**

EARLY on the first day of the week, while it
was still dark, Mary Magdalene came to the

tomb and saw that the stone had been removed from the tomb. So she ran and went to Simon Peter and the other disciple, the one whom Jesus loved, and said to them, "They have taken the Lord out of the tomb, and we do not know where they have laid him."

Then Peter and the other disciple set out and went toward the tomb. The two were running together, but the other disciple outran Peter and reached the tomb first. He bent down to look in and saw the linen wrappings lying there, but he did not go in.

Then Simon Peter came, following him, and went into the tomb. He saw the linen wrappings lying there, and the cloth that had been on Jesus' head, not lying with the linen wrappings but rolled up in a place by itself. Then the other disciple, who reached the tomb first, also went in, and he saw and believed; for as yet they did not understand the scripture, that he must rise from the dead.

[Then the disciples returned to their homes. But Mary Magdalene stood weeping outside the tomb. As she wept, she bent over to look into the tomb; and she saw two angels in white, sitting where the body of Jesus had been lying, one at the head and the other at the feet. They said to her, "Woman, why are you weeping?" She said to them, "They have taken away my Lord, and I do not know where they have laid him."

When she had said this, she turned around and saw Jesus standing there, but she did not know that it was Jesus. Jesus said to her, "Woman, why are you weeping? Whom are you looking for?" Supposing him to be the gardener, she said to him, "Sir, if you have carried him away, tell me where you have laid him, and I will take him away."

Jesus said to her, "Mary!" She turned and said to him in Hebrew, "Rabbouni!" which means Teacher. Jesus said to her, "Do not hold on to me, because I have not yet ascended to the Father. But go to my brothers and say to them, 'I am ascending to my Father and your Father, to my God and your God.' "

Mary Magdalene went and announced to the disciples, "I have seen the Lord," and she told them that he had said these things to her.]

The gospel of the Lord. ℟. **Praise to you, Lord Jesus Christ.**

OR

GOSPEL Lk. 24.1-12   [The Resurrection]

See p. 364.

(FOR AN AFTERNOON OR EVENING MASS)

GOSPEL Lk. 24.13-35   [The Messiah's Need To Suffer]

Let us accept the testimony of these two witnesses that our hearts may burn with the fire of faith.

℣. The Lord be with you. ℟. **And also with you.** ✠ A reading from the holy gospel according to Luke. ℟. **Glory to you, Lord.**

ON the first day of the week, two of the disciples were going to a village called Emmaus, about eleven kilometres from Jerusalem, and talking with each other about all these things that had happened. While they were talking and discussing, Jesus himself came near and went with them, but their eyes were kept from recognizing him.

And Jesus said to them, "What are you discussing with each other while you walk along?" They stood still, looking sad. Then one of them, whose name was Cleopas, answered him, "Are you the only stranger in Jerusalem who does not know the things that have taken place there in these days?"

Jesus asked them, "What things?" They replied, "The things about Jesus of Nazareth, who was a prophet mighty in deed and word before God and all the people, and how our chief priests and leaders handed him over to be condemned to death and crucified him. But we had hoped that he was the one to redeem Israel. Yes, and besides all this, it is now the third day since these things took place. Moreover, some women of our group astounded us. They were at the tomb early this morning, and when they did not find his body there, they came back and told us that they had indeed seen a vision of angels who said that Jesus was alive. Some of those who were with us went to the tomb and found it just as the women had said; but they did not see Jesus."

Then Jesus said to them, "Oh, how foolish you are, and how slow of heart to believe all that the prophets have declared! Was it not necessary that the Messiah should suffer these things and then enter into his glory?"

Then beginning with Moses and all the prophets, Jesus interpreted to them the things about himself in all the scriptures. As they came near the village to which they were going, Jesus walked ahead as if he were going on. But they urged him strongly, saying, "Stay with us, because it is almost evening and the day is now nearly over." So Jesus went in to stay with them.

When he was at the table with them, he took bread, blessed and broke it, and gave it to them. Then their eyes were opened, and they recognized Jesus; and he vanished from their sight.

The two disciples said to each other, "Were not our hearts burning within us while he was talking to us on the road, while he was opening the scriptures to us?"

That same hour they got up and returned to Jerusalem; and they found the eleven and their companions gathered together. These were saying, "The Lord has risen indeed, and he has appeared to Simon!"

Then the two disciples told what had happened on the road, and how the Lord had been made known to them in the breaking of the bread.—The gospel of the Lord. ℟. **Praise to you, Lord Jesus Christ.**

Renewal of Baptismal Promises, p. 374 (omit Creed).

PRAYER OVER THE GIFTS   [Renewing Sacrifice]

Lord,
with Easter joy we offer you the sacrifice
by which your Church is reborn and nourished
through Christ our Lord.
R/. **Amen.**

→ No. 21, p. 24 (Pref. 21: on this Easter day)

*When Eucharistic Prayer I is used, the special Easter
forms of* In union with the whole Church *and*
Father, accept this offering *are said.*

COMMUNION ANTIPHON 1 Cor. 5.7-8   [Sincerity]

**Christ has become our paschal sacrifice; let us
celebrate the feast with the unleavened bread
of sincerity and truth, alleluia.** ↓

PRAYER AFTER COMMUNION
[Glory of Resurrection]

Father of love,
watch over your Church
and bring us to the glory of the resurrection
promised by this Easter sacrament.
We ask this in the name of Jesus the Lord.
R/. **Amen.** ↓

Dismissal: see p. 381.

"Thomas answered him, 'My Lord and my God!' "

APRIL 15

2nd SUNDAY OF EASTER

ENTRANCE ANTIPHON 1 Pet. 2.2   [Spiritual Milk]

Like newborn children you should thirst for milk, on which your spirit can grow to strength, alleluia.

OR   [Give Thanks]

Rejoice to the full in the glory that is yours, and give thanks to God who called you to his kingdom, alleluia.   → No. 2, p. 10

OPENING PRAYER   [Renewed Gift of Life]

God of mercy,
you wash away our sins in water,
you give us new birth in the Spirit,
and redeem us in the blood of Christ.
As we celebrate Christ's resurrection
increase our awareness of these blessings,
and renew your gift of life within us.
We ask this through our Lord Jesus Christ,
  your Son,

who lives and reigns with you and the Holy
  Spirit,
one God, for ever and ever. ℟. **Amen.** ↓

FIRST READING Acts 5.12-16   [Signs and Wonders]

**Through signs and wonders—miracles—the Lord sup-
ports the work of the apostles and leads people to the
Faith.**

A reading from the Acts of the Apostles

Many signs and wonders were done among
the people through the apostles. And the
believers were all together in Solomon's Por-
tico. None of the rest dared to join them, but the
people held them in high esteem.
  Yet more than ever believers were added to
the Lord, great numbers of both men and
women, so that they even carried out the sick
into the streets, and laid them on cots and
mats, in order that Peter's shadow might fall on
some of them as he came by. A great number
of people would also gather from the towns
around Jerusalem, bringing the sick and those
tormented by unclean spirits, and they were all
cured.—The word of the Lord. ℟. **Thanks be to
God.** ↓

RESPONSORIAL PSALM Ps. 117 (118)

[God's Goodness]

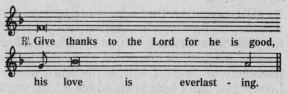

℟. Give thanks to the Lord for he is good,
his love is everlast - ing.

℟. Or: **Alleluia! Alleluia! Alleluia!**

(NRSV Text)

Let Israel say,
"His steadfast love endures forever."
Let the house of Aaron say,
"His steadfast love endures forever."
Let those who fear the Lord say,
"His steadfast love endures forever."—℟.

The stone that the builders rejected
has become the chief cornerstone.
This is the Lord's doing;
it is marvellous in our eyes.
This is the day that the Lord has made;
let us rejoice and be glad in it.—℟.

Save us, we beseech you, O Lord!
O Lord, we beseech you, give us success!
Blessed is the one who comes in the name of the Lord.
We bless you from the house of the Lord.
The Lord is God,
and he has given us light.—℟. ↓

(GRAIL Text)

Let the family of Israel say:
"His love endures for ever."
Let the family of Aaron say:
"His love endures for ever."
Let those who fear the Lord say:
"His love endures for ever."—℟.

The stone which the builders rejected
has become the corner stone.
This is the work of the Lord,
a marvel in our eyes.
This day was made by the Lord;
we rejoice and are glad.—℟.

O Lord, grant us salvation;
O Lord, grant success.
Blessed in the name of the Lord
is the one who comes.
We bless you from the house of the Lord;
the Lord God is our light.—℟. ↓

SECOND READING Rev. 1.9-11a, 12-13, 17-19

[The First and the Last]

In symbol and allegory the glory of the Lord is depicted. It is he, Jesus Christ, who shares power with God the Father.

A reading from the book of Revelation

I, JOHN, your brother who share with you in Jesus the persecution and the kingdom and the patient endurance, was on the island called Patmos because of the word of God and the testimony of Jesus. I was in the spirit on the Lord's day, and I heard behind me a loud voice like a trumpet saying, "Write in a book what you see and send it to the seven churches."

Then I turned to see whose voice it was that spoke to me, and on turning I saw seven golden lampstands, and in the midst of the lampstands I saw one like the Son of Man, clothed with a long robe and with a golden sash across his chest.

When I saw him, I fell at his feet as though dead. But he placed his right hand on me, saying, "Do not be afraid; I am the first and the last, and the living one. I was dead, but see, I am alive forever and ever; and I have the keys of Death and of Hades. Now write what you have seen, what is, and what is to take place after this."—The word of the Lord. ℟. **Thanks be to God.** ↓

GOSPEL ACCLAMATION See Jn. 20.29 [Blessed Faith]

(If the Alleluia is not sung, the acclamation is omitted.)

℣. Alleluia. ℟. **Alleluia.**

℣. You believed in me, Thomas, because you have seen me;

happy those who have not seen me, but still believe!

℟. **Alleluia.** ↓

GOSPEL Jn. 20.19-31   [Living Faith]

Jesus is risen; he comes and stands before his disciples. He encourages them and strengthens their faith.

℣. The Lord be with you. ℟. **And also with you.**
✝ A reading from the holy gospel according to John. ℟. **Glory to you, Lord.**

IT was evening on the day Jesus rose from the dead, the first day of the week, and the doors of the house where the disciples had met were locked for fear of the authorities. Jesus came and stood among them and said, "Peace be with you." After he said this, he showed them his hands and his side. Then the disciples rejoiced when they saw the Lord.

Jesus said to them again, "Peace be with you. As the Father has sent me, so I send you." When he had said this, he breathed on them and said to them, "Receive the Holy Spirit. If you forgive the sins of any, they are forgiven them; if you retain the sins of any, they are retained."

But Thomas, who was called the Twin, one of the twelve, was not with them when Jesus came. So the other disciples told him, "We have seen the Lord." But he said to them, "Unless I see the mark of the nails in his hands, and put my finger in the mark of the nails and my hand in his side, I will not believe."

A week later his disciples were again in the house, and Thomas was with them. Although the doors were shut, Jesus came and stood among them and said, "Peace be with you." Then he said to Thomas, "Put your finger here and see my hands. Reach out your hand and put it in my side. Do not doubt but believe." Thomas answered him, "My Lord and my God!" Jesus said to him, "Have you believed because you have seen me? Blessed are those who have not seen and yet have come to believe."

Now Jesus did many other signs in the presence of his disciples, which are not written in this book. But these are written so that you may come to believe that Jesus is the Messiah, the Son of God, and that through believing you may have life in his name.—The gospel of the Lord. ℟. **Praise to you, Lord Jesus Christ.**

➜ No. 14, p. 18

PRAYER OVER THE GIFTS   [New Creation]

Lord,
through faith and baptism
we have become a new creation.
Accept the offerings of your people
(and of those born again in baptism)
and bring us to eternal happiness.
Grant this through Christ our Lord.
℟. **Amen.**   ➜ No. 21, p. 24 (Pref. 21)

When Eucharistic Prayer I is used, the special Easter forms of In union with the whole Church *and* Father, accept this offering *are said.*

COMMUNION ANTIPHON See Jn. 20.27   [Believe]

Jesus spoke to Thomas: Put your hand here, and see the place of the nails. Doubt no longer, but believe, alleluia. ↓

PRAYER AFTER COMMUNION [Devout Reception]

Almighty God,
may the Easter sacraments we have received
live for ever in our minds and hearts.
We ask this in the name of Jesus the Lord.
℟. **Amen.**   ➜ No. 32, p. 75

Optional Solemn Blessings, p. 96, and Prayers Over the People, p. 104

"Cast the net to the right side of the boat,"
Jesus suggested.

APRIL 22

3rd SUNDAY OF EASTER

ENTRANCE ANTIPHON Ps. 65 (66).1-2

[Praise the Lord]

Let all the earth cry out to God with joy; praise the glory of his name; proclaim his glorious praise, alleluia. → No. 2, p. 10

OPENING PRAYER [Hope of Resurrection]

God our Father,
may we look forward with hope to our resur-
    rection,
for you have made us your sons and daughters,
and restored the joy of our youth.
We ask this . . . for ever and ever. ℟. **Amen.** ↓

FIRST READING Acts 5.27-32, 40b-41

[Preaching the Name]

With a strong faith the apostles persevere in the mission that Christ gave them.

398

A reading from the Acts of the Apostles

THE captain went with the temple police and brought the apostles, who were teaching in the temple, and had them stand before the council. The high priest questioned the apostles, saying, "We gave you strict orders not to teach in this name, yet here you have filled Jerusalem with your teaching and you are determined to bring this man's blood on us."

But Peter and the apostles answered, "We must obey God rather than any human authority. The God of our ancestors raised up Jesus, whom you had killed by hanging him on a tree. God exalted him at his right hand as Leader and Saviour that he might give repentance to Israel and forgiveness of sins. And we are witnesses to these things, and so is the Holy Spirit whom God has given to those who obey him."

Then the council ordered the apostles not to speak in the name of Jesus, and let them go. As they left the council, they rejoiced that they were considered worthy to suffer dishonour for the sake of the name.—The word of the Lord. ℟. **Thanks be to God.** ↓

RESPONSORIAL PSALM Ps. 29 (30)   [Divine Security]

℟. **I will praise you, Lord, for you have res-cued me.**

℟. Or: **Alleluia! Alleluia! Alleluia!**

(NRSV Text)	(GRAIL Text)
I will extol you, O Lord, for you have drawn me up,	I will praise you, Lord, you have rescued me
and did not let my foes rejoice over me.	and have not let my enemies rejoice over me.

O Lord, you brought up my soul from Sheol,
restored me to life from among those gone down to the Pit.—℟.

Sing praises to the Lord, O you his faithful ones,
and give thanks to his holy name.
For his anger is but for a moment; his favour is for a lifetime.
Weeping may linger for the night,
but joy comes with the morning.—℟.

Hear, O Lord, and be gracious to me!
O Lord, be my helper!
You have turned my mourning into dancing.
O Lord my God, I will give thanks to you forever.—℟. ↓

O Lord, you have raised my soul from the dead,
restored me to life from those who sink into the grave.—℟.

Sing psalms to the Lord, you who love him,
give thanks to his holy name.
His anger lasts a moment; his favour all through life.
At night there are tears, but joy comes with dawn.—℟.

The Lord listened and had pity.
The Lord came to my help.
For me you have changed my mourning into dancing,
O Lord my God, I will thank you for ever.—℟. ↓

SECOND READING Rev. 5.11-14 **[The Throne of God]**

The power and the glory of God are acclaimed by all creation.

A reading from the book of Revelation

I, JOHN, looked, and I heard the voice of many angels surrounding the throne and the living creatures and the elders; they numbered myriads of myriads and thousands of thousands, singing with full voice,

"Worthy is the Lamb that was slaughtered
to receive power and wealth and wisdom and might
and honour and glory and blessing!"

Then I heard every creature in heaven and on earth and under the earth and in the sea, and all that is in them, singing,

"To the one seated on the throne and to the Lamb

be blessing and honour and glory and might forever and ever!"

And the four living creatures said, "Amen!" And the elders fell down and worshipped.— The word of the Lord. ℟. **Thanks be to God.** ↓

GOSPEL ACCLAMATION   [Lord of All Creation]

(If the Alleluia is not sung, the acclamation is omitted.)

℣. Alleluia. ℟. **Alleluia.**

℣. Christ is risen, the Lord of all creation; he has shown pity on all people.

℟. **Alleluia.** ↓

GOSPEL Jn. 21.1-19   [Christ Is Lord]

Again the risen Saviour appears to his disciples in a very human way. Peter in three affirmations rejects his triple denial and again hears the call "Follow me."

℣. The Lord be with you. ℟. **And also with you.**

✜ A reading from the holy gospel according to John. ℟. **Glory to you, Lord.**

JESUS showed himself again to the disciples by the Sea of Tiberias; and he showed himself in this way. Gathered there together were Simon Peter, Thomas called the Twin, Nathanael of Cana in Galilee, the sons of Zebedee, and two others of his disciples. Simon Peter said to them, "I am going fishing." They said to him, "We will go with you." They went out and got into the boat, but that night they caught nothing.

Just after daybreak, Jesus stood on the beach; but the disciples did not know that it was Jesus. Jesus said to them, "Children, you have no fish, have you?" They answered him, "No." He said to them, "Cast the net to the right side of the boat, and you will find some." So they cast it, and now they were not able to haul it in because there were so many fish.

That disciple whom Jesus loved said to Peter, "It is the Lord!" When Simon Peter heard that it was the Lord, he put on some clothes, for he was naked, and jumped into the sea. But the other disciples came in the boat, dragging the net full of fish, for they were not far from the land, only about ninety metres off.

When they had gone ashore, they saw a charcoal fire there, with fish on it, and bread. Jesus said to them, "Bring some of the fish that you have just caught." So Simon Peter went aboard and hauled the net ashore, full of large fish, a hundred fifty-three of them; and though there were so many, the net was not torn. Jesus said to them, "Come and have breakfast." Now none of the disciples dared to ask him, "Who are you?" because they knew it was the Lord. Jesus came and took the bread and gave it to them, and did the same with the fish. This was now the third time that Jesus appeared to the disciples after he was raised from the dead.

When they had finished breakfast, Jesus said to Simon Peter, "Simon son of John, do you love me more than these?" He said to him, "Yes, Lord; you know that I love you." Jesus said to him, "Feed my lambs."

A second time he said to him, "Simon son of John, do you love me?" He said to him, "Yes, Lord; you know that I love you." Jesus said to him, "Tend my sheep."

He said to him the third time, "Simon son of John, do you love me?" Peter felt hurt because he said to him the third time, "Do you love me?" And he said to him, "Lord, you know everything; you know that I love you." Jesus said to him, "Feed my sheep.

"Very truly, I tell you, when you were younger, you used to fasten your own belt and go wherever you wished. But when you grow old, you will stretch out your hands, and someone else will fasten a belt around you and take you where you do not wish to go."

He said this to indicate the kind of death by which he would glorify God. After this he said to him, "Follow me."—The gospel of the Lord. ℟.
Praise to you, Lord Jesus Christ. ➔ No. 14, p. 18

PRAYER OVER THE GIFTS   [Perfect Joy]

Lord,
receive these gifts from your Church.
May the great joy you give us
come to perfection in heaven.
Grant this through Christ our Lord.
℟. **Amen.**   ➔ No. 21, p. 24 (Pref. 22-25)

COMMUNION ANTIPHON See Jn. 21.12-13
[Come and Eat]

Jesus said to his disciples: Come and eat. And he took the bread, and gave it to them, alleluia. ↓

PRAYER AFTER COMMUNION [The Lord's Kindness]

Lord,
look on your people with kindness
and by these Easter mysteries
bring us to the glory of the resurrection.
We ask this in the name of Jesus the Lord.
℟. **Amen.**   ➔ No. 32, p. 75

Optional Solemn Blessings, p. 96, and Prayers Over the People, p. 104

"My sheep hear my voice."

APRIL 29

4th SUNDAY OF EASTER

ENTRANCE ANTIPHON Ps. 32 (33).5-6

[God the Creator]

The earth is full of the goodness of the Lord; by the word of the Lord the heavens were made, alleluia.   ➔ No. 2, p. 10

OPENING PRAYER   [Strengthened in Christ]

Almighty and ever-living God,
give us new strength
from the courage of Christ our shepherd,
and lead us to join the saints in heaven,
where he lives and reigns with you and the
  Holy Spirit,
one God, for ever and ever. ℟. **Amen.** ↓

FIRST READING Acts 13.14, 43-52   [Salvation in Jesus]

As missionaries, Paul and Barnabas meet with some success and encounter strong opposition. Steadfastness in faith is a source of joy.

A reading from the Acts of the Apostles

PAUL and Barnabas went on from Perga and came to Antioch in Pisidia. On the sabbath day they went into the synagogue and sat down.

When the meeting of the synagogue broke up, many Jews and devout converts to Judaism followed Paul and Barnabas, who spoke to them and urged them to continue in the grace of God.

The next sabbath almost the whole city gathered to hear the word of the Lord. But when the Jewish officials saw the crowds, they were filled with jealousy; and blaspheming, they contradicted what was spoken by Paul.

Then both Paul and Barnabas spoke out boldly, saying, "It was necessary that the word of God should be spoken first to you. Since you reject it and judge yourselves to be unworthy of eternal life, we are now turning to the Gentiles. For so the Lord has commanded us, saying, 'I have set you to be a light for the Gentiles, so that you may bring salvation to the ends of the earth.' " When the Gentiles heard this, they were glad and praised the word of the Lord; and as many as had been destined for eternal life became believers.

Thus the word of the Lord spread throughout the region. But the officials incited the devout women of high standing and the leading men of the city, and stirred up persecution against Paul and Barnabas, and drove them out of their region. So they shook the dust off their feet in protest against them, and went to Iconium. And the disciples were filled with joy and with

the Holy Spirit.—The word of the Lord. ℟.
Thanks be to God. ↓

RESPONSORIAL PSALM Ps. 99 (100) [The Lord Is God]

℟. **We are God's peo - ple, the sheep of his flock.**

(℟. **We are his people, the flock of the Lord.**)

℟. Or: **Alleluia! Alleluia! Alleluia!**

(NRSV Text)	(GRAIL Text)
Make a joyful noise to the Lord, all the earth.	Cry out with joy to the Lord, all the earth.
Worship the Lord with gladness; come into his presence with singing.—℟.	Serve the Lord with gladness. Come before him, singing for joy.— ℟.
Know that the Lord is God. It is he that made us, and we are his; we are his people, and the sheep of his pasture.—℟.	Know that he, the Lord, is God. He made us, we belong to him, we are his people, the sheep of his flock.—℟.
For the Lord is good; his steadfast love endures forever, and his faithfulness to all generations.—℟. ↓	Indeed, how good is the Lord, eternal his merciful love. He is faithful from age to age.— ℟. ↓

SECOND READING Rev. 7.9, 14b-17 [Blood of the Lamb]

Those who remain faithful despite severe persecution will find their reward is to be with God and restored to peace.

A reading from the book of Revelation

AFTER this I, John, looked, and there was a great multitude that no one could count, from every nation, from all tribes and peoples and languages, standing before the throne and before the Lamb, robed in white, with palm branches in their hands.

And one of the elders then said to me, "These are they who have come out of the great ordeal; they have washed their robes and made them white in the blood of the Lamb.

"For this reason they are before the throne of God,
and worship him day and night within his temple,
and the one who is seated on the throne will shelter them.
They will hunger no more, and thirst no more;
the sun will not strike them, nor any scorching heat;
for the Lamb at the centre of the throne will be their shepherd,
and he will guide them to springs of the water of life,
and God will wipe away every tear from their eyes."

The word of the Lord. ℟. **Thanks be to God.** ↓

GOSPEL ACCLAMATION Jn. 10.14   [Know the Lord]

(If the Alleluia is not sung, the acclamation is omitted.)

℣. Alleluia. ℟. **Alleluia.**
℣. I am the good shepherd, says the Lord;
I know my sheep, and mine know me.
℟. **Alleluia.** ↓

GOSPEL Jn. 10.27-30   [The Good Shepherd]

Jesus proclaims his oneness with the Father. His love for us is so great that he brings us eternal life.

℣. The Lord be with you. ℟. **And also with you.**
✝ A reading from the holy gospel according to John. ℟. **Glory to you, Lord.**

JESUS said: "My sheep hear my voice. I know them, and they follow me. I give them eternal life, and they will never perish. No one will snatch them out of my hand. What my Father has given me is greater than all else, and no one can snatch it out of the Father's hand. The Father and I are one."—The gospel of the Lord. ℞. **Praise to you, Lord Jesus Christ.**   ➔ No. 14, p. 18

PRAYER OVER THE GIFTS   [Eternal Joy]

Lord,
restore us by these Easter mysteries.
May the continuing work of our redeemer
bring us eternal joy.
We ask this through Christ our Lord.
℞. **Amen.**   ➔ No. 21, p. 24 (Pref. 22-25)

COMMUNION ANTIPHON   [The Risen Shepherd]

The Good Shepherd is risen! He who laid down his life for his sheep, who died for his flock, he is risen, alleluia. ↓

PRAYER AFTER COMMUNION   [Eternal Shepherd]

Father, eternal shepherd,
watch over the flock redeemed by the blood of
   Christ
and lead us to the promised land.
Grant this through Christ our Lord.
℞. **Amen.**   ➔ No. 32, p. 75

Optional Solemn Blessings, p. 96, and Prayers Over the People, p. 104

"I give you a new commandment. . . . Just as I have loved you, you also should love one another."

MAY 6

5th SUNDAY OF EASTER

ENTRANCE ANTIPHON Ps. 97 (98).1-2

[Marvellous Deeds]

Sing to the Lord a new song, for he has done marvellous deeds; he has revealed to the nations his saving power, alleluia. ➔ No. 2, p. 10

OPENING PRAYER   [True Freedom]

God our Father,
look upon us with love.
You redeem us and make us your children in
 Christ.
Give us true freedom
and bring us to the inheritance you promised.
We ask this through our Lord Jesus Christ,
 your Son,
who lives and reigns with you and the Holy
 Spirit,
one God, for ever and ever. ℟. **Amen.** ↓

FIRST READING Acts 14.21b-27 [Conversion of Gentiles]

The life we have through faith is not easy; we must struggle against many difficulties, even temptations, on our journey to eternal life.

A reading from the Acts of the Apostles

PAUL and Barnabas returned to Lystra, then on to Iconium and Antioch. There they strengthened the souls of the disciples and encouraged them to continue in the faith, saying, "It is through many persecutions that we must enter the kingdom of God." And after they had appointed elders for them in each church, with prayer and fasting they entrusted them to the Lord in whom they had come to believe.

Then they passed through Pisidia and came to Pamphylia. When they had spoken the word in Perga, they went down to Attalia. From there they sailed back to Antioch, where they had been commended to the grace of God for the work that they had completed.

When they arrived, they called the church together and related all that God had done with them, and how he had opened a door of faith for the Gentiles.—The word of the Lord. ℟. **Thanks be to God.** ↓

RESPONSORIAL PSALM Ps. 144 (145)

[God's Kingdom]

℟. I will praise your name for-ev - er my King and my God.

℟. Or: **Alleluia! Alleluia! Alleluia!**

(NRSV Text)	(GRAIL Text)
The Lord is gracious and merciful, slow to anger and abounding in steadfast love. The Lord is good to all, and his compassion is over all that he has made.—R̸.	You are kind and full of compassion, slow to anger, abounding in love. How good you are, Lord, to all, compassionate to all your creatures.—R̸.
All your works shall give thanks to you, O Lord, and all your faithful shall bless you. They shall speak of the glory of your kingdom, and tell of your power.—R̸.	All your creatures shall thank you, O Lord, and your friends shall repeat their blessing. They shall speak of the glory of your reign and declare your might, O God.—R̸.
To make known to all people your mighty deeds, and the glorious splendour of your kingdom. Your kingdom is an everlasting kingdom, and your dominion endures throughout all generations.—R̸. ↓	They shall make known to all your mighty deeds and the glorious splendour of your reign. Yours is an everlasting kingdom; your rule lasts from age to age.— R̸. ↓

SECOND READING Rev. 21.1-5a   [God's Dwelling]

In the Kingdom of God all things are made new.

A reading from the book of Revelation

THEN I, John, saw a new heaven and a new earth; for the first heaven and the first earth had passed away, and the sea was no more.

And I saw the holy city, the new Jerusalem, coming down out of heaven from God, prepared as a bride adorned for her husband.

And I heard a loud voice from the throne saying,

"See, the home of God is among mortals.
He will dwell with them as their God;
they will be his peoples,
and God himself will be with them;

he will wipe every tear from their eyes.
Death will be no more;
mourning and crying and pain will be no
    more,
for the first things have passed away."
And the one who was seated on the throne
said,
    "See, I am making all things new."
The word of the Lord. ℟. **Thanks be to God.** ↓

GOSPEL ACCLAMATION See Jn. 13.34   [Love]

(If the Alleluia is not sung, the acclamation is omitted.)

℣. Alleluia. ℟. **Alleluia.**
℣. I give you a new commandment:
love one another as I have loved you.
℟. **Alleluia.** ↓

GOSPEL Jn. 13.1, 31-33a, 34-35   [The New Commandment]

**Jesus is about to be betrayed yet he teaches us the way
to glory—the way he will go. It is the way of love.**

℣. The Lord be with you. ℟. **And also with you.**
✤ A reading from the holy gospel according to
John. ℟. **Glory to you, Lord.**

BEFORE the festival of the Passover, Jesus
knew that his hour had come to depart
from this world and go to the Father. Having
loved his own who were in the world, he loved
them to the end.

During the supper, when Judas had gone out,
Jesus said, "Now the Son of Man has been glorified, and God has been glorified in him. If
God has been glorified in him, God will also
glorify him in himself and will glorify him at
once.

"Little children, I am with you only a little longer. I give you a new commandment, that you love one another. Just as I have loved you, you also should love one another. By this everyone will know that you are my disciples, if you have love for one another."—The gospel of the Lord. R̷. **Praise to you, Lord Jesus Christ.**   ➔ No. 14, p. 18

PRAYER OVER THE GIFTS   [Guided by God's Truth]

Lord God,
by this holy exchange of gifts
you share with us your divine life.
Grant that everything we do
may be directed by the knowledge of your
    truth.
We ask this in the name of Jesus the Lord.
R̷. **Amen.**   ➔ No. 21, p. 24 (Pref. 22-25)

COMMUNION ANTIPHON Jn. 15.1, 5

[Union with Christ]

I am the vine and you are the branches, says the Lord: he who lives in me, and I in him, will bear much fruit, alleluia. ↓

PRAYER AFTER COMMUNION   [New Life]

Merciful Father,
may these mysteries give us new purpose
and bring us to a new life in you.
Grant this through Christ our Lord.
R̷. **Amen.**   ➔ No. 32, p. 75

Optional Solemn Blessings, p. 96, and Prayers Over the People, p. 104

"The Advocate, the Holy Spirit, whom the Father
will send in my name. . . ."

MAY 13

6th SUNDAY OF EASTER

ENTRANCE ANTIPHON See Isa. 48.20

[Spiritual Freedom]

**Speak out with a voice of joy; let it be heard to
the ends of the earth: The Lord has set his people free, alleluia.**   → No. 2, p. 10

OPENING PRAYER   [Operative Faith]

Ever-living God,
help us to celebrate our joy
in the resurrection of the Lord
and to express in our lives
the love we celebrate.
Grant this . . . for ever and ever. ℟. **Amen.** ↓

FIRST READING Acts 15.1-2, 22-29   [Settling a Dispute]

The Church faces its first test caused by inner dissen-
sions and shows how, guided by the Spirit, charity will
prevail.

A reading from the Acts of the Apostles

CERTAIN individuals came down from Judea and were teaching the brothers, "Unless you are circumcised according to the custom of Moses, you cannot be saved." And after Paul and Barnabas had no small dissension and debate with them, Paul and Barnabas and some of the others were appointed to go up to Jerusalem to discuss this question with the apostles and the elders.

Then the apostles and the elders, with the consent of the whole church, decided to choose men from among their members and to send them to Antioch with Paul and Barnabas. They sent Judas called Barsabbas, and Silas, leaders among the brothers, with the following letter:

"The brothers, both the apostles and the elders, to the believers of Gentile origin in Antioch and Syria and Cilicia, greetings. Since we have heard that certain persons who have gone out from us, though with no instructions from us, have said things to disturb you and have unsettled your minds, we have decided unanimously to choose representatives and send them to you, along with our beloved Barnabas and Paul, who have risked their lives for the sake of our Lord Jesus Christ. We have therefore sent Judas and Silas, who themselves will tell you the same things by word of mouth.

"For it has seemed good to the Holy Spirit and to us to impose on you no further burden than these essentials: that you abstain from what has been sacrificed to idols, and from blood and from what is strangled, and from fornication. If you keep yourselves from these, you will do well. Farewell."—The word of the Lord. ℟. **Thanks be to God.** ↓

RESPONSORIAL PSALM Ps. 66 (67)   [Praise of God]

    ℟. **O God, let all the na‑tions praise you!**

(℟. **Let the peoples praise you, O God; let all the peoples praise you.**)

℟. Or: **Alleluia! Alleluia! Alleluia!**

(NRSV Text)	(GRAIL Text)
May God be gracious to us and bless us and make his face to shine upon us, that your way may be known upon earth, your saving power among all nations.—℟.	O God, be gracious and bless us and let your face shed its light upon us. So will your ways be known upon earth and all nations learn your saving help.—℟.
Let the nations be glad and sing for joy, for you judge the peoples with equity and guide the nations upon earth. Let the peoples praise you, O God.—℟.	Let the nations be glad and exult for you rule the world with justice. With fairness you rule the peoples, you guide the nations on earth.—℟.
The earth has yielded its increase; God, our God, has blessed us. May God continue to bless us; let all the ends of the earth revere him.—℟. ↓	Let the peoples praise you, O God; let all the peoples praise you. May God still give us his blessing till the ends of the earth revere him.—℟. ↓

SECOND READING Rev. 21.10-14, 22-23   [City of God]
In symbolic language the Church is depicted as a wonderful glorious city, caught up in the glory of God.

A reading from the book of Revelation

IN the spirit the angel carried me away to a great, high mountain and showed me the holy city Jerusalem coming down out of heaven from God. It has the glory of God and a radiance like a very rare jewel, like jasper, clear as crystal.

It has a great, high wall with twelve gates, and at the gates twelve angels, and on the gates are inscribed the names of the twelve tribes of the Israelites; on the east there were three gates, on the north three gates, on the south three gates, and on the west three gates. And the wall of the city has twelve foundations, and on them are the twelve names of the twelve apostles of the Lamb.

I saw no temple in the city, for its temple is the Lord God the Almighty and the Lamb. And the city has no need of sun or moon to shine on it, for the glory of God is its light, and its lamp is the Lamb.—The word of the Lord. ℟. **Thanks be to God.** ↓

GOSPEL ACCLAMATION Jn. 14.23   [Love in Deed]

(If the Alleluia is not sung, the acclamation is omitted.)

℣. Alleluia. ℟. **Alleluia.**
℣. All who love me will keep my words,
and my Father will love them, and we will
  come to them.
℟. **Alleluia.** ↓

GOSPEL Jn. 14.23-29   [Promise of the Spirit]

In saying farewell Jesus has not deserted us. In his name the Father sends the Holy Spirit that we may drink in his power and live in peace.

℣. The Lord be with you. ℟. **And also with you.**
✛ A reading from the holy gospel according to John. ℟. **Glory to you, Lord.**

JESUS said to his disciples: "Those who love me will keep my word, and my Father will

love them, and we will come to them and make
our home with them. Whoever does not love
me does not keep my words; and the word that
you hear is not mine, but is from the Father
who sent me.

"I have said these things to you while I am
still with you. But the Advocate, the Holy
Spirit, whom the Father will send in my name,
will teach you everything, and remind you of
all that I have said to you.

"Peace I leave with you; my peace I give to
you. I do not give to you as the world gives. Do
not let your hearts be troubled, and do not let
them be afraid.

"You heard me say to you, 'I am going away,
and I am coming to you.' If you loved me, you
would rejoice that I am going to the Father, because the Father is greater than I. And now I
have told you this before it occurs, so that
when it does occur, you may believe."—The
gospel of the Lord. ℟. **Praise to you, Lord Jesus
Christ.**   ➔ No. 14, p. 18

PRAYER OVER THE GIFTS   [Forgiveness]

Lord,
accept our prayers and offerings.
Make us worthy of your sacraments of love
by granting us your forgiveness.
We ask this in the name of Jesus the Lord.
℟. **Amen.**   ➔ No. 21, p. 24 (Pref. 22-25)

COMMUNION ANTIPHON Jn. 14.15-16 [Role of Spirit]

**If you love me, keep my commandments, says
the Lord. The Father will send you the Holy
Spirit, to be with you for ever, alleluia.** ↓

PRAYER AFTER COMMUNION

[Eucharistic Strength]

Almighty and ever-living Lord,
you restored us to life
by raising Christ from death.
Strengthen us by this Easter sacrament;
may we feel its saving power in our daily life.
We ask this through Christ our Lord.
℟. **Amen.**   → No. 32, p. 75

Optional Solemn Blessings, p. 96, and Prayers Over the People, p. 104

"Go and teach all people my gospel."

MAY 20

ASCENSION OF THE LORD

ENTRANCE ANTIPHON Acts 1.11   [Lord Will Return]
**Men of Galilee, why do you stand looking in
the sky? The Lord will return, just as you have
seen him ascend, alleluia.**   → No. 2, p. 10

OPENING PRAYER   [Joy in the Ascension]

God our Father,
make us joyful in the ascension of your Son
   Jesus Christ.
May we follow him into the new creation,
for his ascension is our glory and our hope.
We ask this . . . for ever and ever. ℟. **Amen.** ↓

FIRST READING Acts 1.1-11   [Christ's Ascension]

Christ is divine! He will come again! Our faith affirms this for us. We live in the era of the Holy Spirit.

A reading from the Acts of the Apostles

IN the first book, Theophilus, I wrote about all that Jesus did and taught from the beginning until the day when he was taken up to heaven, after giving instructions through the Holy Spirit to the apostles whom he had chosen. After his suffering he presented himself alive to them by many convincing proofs, appearing to them during forty days and speaking about the kingdom of God.

While staying with them, he ordered them not to leave Jerusalem, but to wait there for the promise of the Father. "This," he said, "is what you have heard from me; for John baptized with water, but you will be baptized with the Holy Spirit not many days from now."

So when they had come together, they asked him, "Lord, is this the time when you will restore the kingdom to Israel?" He replied, "It is not for you to know the times or periods that the Father has set by his own authority. But you will receive power when the Holy Spirit has come upon you; and you will be my witnesses in Jerusalem, in all Judea and Samaria, and to the ends of the earth."

When he had said this, as they were watching, he was lifted up, and a cloud took him out of their sight. While he was going and they were gazing up toward heaven, suddenly two men in white robes stood by them. They said, "Men of Galilee, why do you stand looking up toward heaven? This Jesus, who has been taken up from you into heaven, will come in the same way as you saw him go into heaven."—The word of the Lord. ℟. **Thanks be to God.** ↓

RESPONSORIAL PSALM Ps.46 (47) [Praise to the Lord]

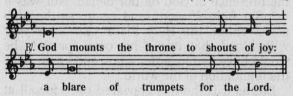

℟. God mounts the throne to shouts of joy: a blare of trumpets for the Lord.

(℟. **God goes up with shouts of joy; the Lord goes up with trumpet blast.**)

℟. Or: **Alleluia! Alleluia! Alleluia!**

(NRSV Text)	(GRAIL Text)
Clap your hands, all you peoples; shout to God with loud songs of joy. For the Lord, the Most High, is awesome, a great king over all the earth.—℟.	All peoples, clap your hands, cry to God with shouts of joy! For the Lord, the Most High, we must fear, great king over all the earth.—℟.
God has gone up with a shout, the Lord with the sound of a trumpet. Sing praises to God, sing praises; sing praises to our King, sing praises.—℟.	God goes up with shouts of joy; the Lord goes up with trumpet blast. Sing praise for God, sing praise, sing praise to our king, sing praise.—℟.

For God is the king of all the earth;	God is king of all the earth,
sing praises with a psalm.	sing praise with all your skill.
God is king over the nations;	God is king over the nations;
God sits on his holy throne.—℟. ↓	God reigns on his holy throne.—℟. ↓

SECOND READING Heb. 9.24-28; 10.19-23

[Divine Access]

Christ has entered the heavenly sanctuary, where he is now our Intercessor. Through him, we have confident access to the Father. We should approach with sincerity, faith, and hope.

A reading from the letter to the Hebrews

CHRIST did not enter a sanctuary made by human hands, a mere copy of the true one, but he entered into heaven itself, to appear in the presence of God on our behalf. Nor was it to offer himself again and again, as the high priest enters the Holy Place year after year with blood that is not his own; for then he would have had to suffer again and again since the foundation of the world.

But as it is, he has appeared once for all at the end of the age to remove sin by the sacrifice of himself. Just as it is appointed for mortals to die once, and after that comes the judgment, so Christ, having been offered once to bear the sins of many, will appear a second time, not to deal with sin, but to save those who are eagerly waiting for him.

Therefore, my friends, since we have confidence to enter the sanctuary by the blood of Jesus, by the new and living way that he opened for us through the curtain, that is, through his flesh, and since we have a great priest over the house of God, let us approach with a true heart in full assurance of faith, with our hearts sprinkled clean from an evil conscience and our bodies washed with pure water. Let us hold fast to the confession of our hope without wavering, for he who has promised is faithful.—The word of the Lord. ℟. **Thanks be to God.** ↓

GOSPEL ACCLAMATION Mt. 28.19, 20 [Go and Teach]
(*If the Alleluia is not sung, the acclamation is omitted.*)

℣. Alleluia. ℟. **Alleluia.**
℣. Go and teach all people my gospel;
I am with you always, until the end of the world.
℟. **Alleluia.** ↓

GOSPEL Lk. 24.46-53   [The Ascension]
    We are called to penance for the remission of sins.

℣. The Lord be with you. ℟. **And also with you.**
✠ A reading from the holy gospel according to Luke. ℟. **Glory to you, Lord.**

JESUS said to the disciples, "These are my words that I spoke to you while I was still with you—that everything written about me in the law of Moses, the prophets, and the psalms must be fulfilled."

Then he opened their minds to understand the scriptures, and he said to them, "Thus it is written, that the Messiah is to suffer and to rise from the dead on the third day, and that repentance and forgiveness of sins is to be proclaimed in his name to all nations, beginning from Jerusalem. You are witnesses of these things.

"And see, I am sending upon you what my Father promised; so stay here in the city until you have been clothed with power from on high."

Then he led them out as far as Bethany, and, lifting up his hands, he blessed them. While he was blessing them, he withdrew from them and was carried up into heaven. And they worshipped him, and returned to Jerusalem with great joy; and they were continually in the temple blessing God.—The gospel of the Lord. ℟. **Praise to you, Lord Jesus Christ.** ➜ No. 14, p. 18

PRAYER OVER THE GIFTS   [Rise to Heavenly Joy]

Lord,
receive our offering
as we celebrate the ascension of Christ your Son.
May his gifts help us rise with him
to the joys of heaven,
where he lives and reigns for ever and ever.
℟. **Amen.**   ➜ No. 21, p. 24 (Pref. 26-27)

When Eucharistic Prayer I is used, the special Ascension form of In union with the whole Church *is said.*

COMMUNION ANTIPHON Mt. 28.20 [Christ's Presence]

I, the Lord, am with you always, until the end of the world, alleluia. ↓

PRAYER AFTER COMMUNION   [Following Christ]

Father,
in this eucharist
we touch the divine life you give to the world.
Help us to follow Christ with love
to eternal life where he is Lord for ever and ever.
℟. **Amen.**   ➜ No. 32, p. 75

Optional Solemn Blessings, p. 96, and Prayers Over the People, p. 104

"All of them were filled with the Holy Spirit."

MAY 27

PENTECOST SUNDAY

ENTRANCE ANTIPHON Wis. 1.7 [Spirit in the World]
The Spirit of the Lord fills the whole world. It holds all things together and knows every word spoken by man, alleluia.

OR Rom. 5.5; 8.11 [God's Love for Us]
The love of God has been poured into our hearts by his Spirit living in us, alleluia.

→ No. 2, p. 10

OPENING PRAYER [Work of the Spirit]
God our Father,
let the Spirit you sent on your Church
to begin the teaching of the gospel
continue to work in the world
through the hearts of all who believe.
We ask this . . . for ever and ever. ℟. **Amen.** ↓

FIRST READING Acts 2.1-11 [Coming of the Spirit]
As promised by Jesus, the Holy Spirit fills the faithful, and, inspired, they proclaim the good news.

A reading from the Acts of the Apostles

WHEN the day of Pentecost had come, they were all together in one place. And suddenly from heaven there came a sound like the rush of a violent wind, and it filled the entire house where they were sitting. Divided tongues, as of fire, appeared among them, and a tongue rested on each of them. All of them were filled with the Holy Spirit and began to speak in other languages, as the Spirit gave them ability.

Now there were devout Jews from every nation under heaven living in Jerusalem. And at this sound the crowd gathered and was bewildered, because all heard them speaking in their own languages. Amazed and astonished, they asked, "Are not all these who are speaking Galileans? And how is it that we hear, each of us, in our own language? Parthians, Medes, Elamites, and residents of Mesopotamia, Judea and Cappadocia, Pontus and Asia, Phrygia and Pamphylia, Egypt and the parts of Libya belonging to Cyrene, and visitors from Rome, both Jews and converts, Cretans and Arabs—in our own languages we hear them speaking about God's deeds of power."—The word of the Lord. ℟. **Thanks be to God.** ↓

RESPONSORIAL PSALM Ps. 103 (104)   [Renewal]

℟. **Send forth your Spirit, O Lord, and re-new the face of the earth.**

℟. Or: **Alleluia! Alleluia! Alleluia!**

(NRSV Text)	(GRAIL Text)
Bless the Lord, O my soul.	Bless the Lord, my soul!
O Lord my God, you are very great.	Lord God, how great you are!
O Lord, how manifold are your works!	How many are your works, O Lord!
the earth is full of your creatures.—R̸.	The earth is full of your riches.—R̸.
When you take away their breath, they die	You take back your spirit, they die, returning to the dust from which they came.
and return to their dust.	
When you send forth your spirit, they are created;	You send forth your spirit, they are created;
and you renew the face of the earth.—R̸.	and you renew the face of the earth.—R̸.
May the glory of the Lord endure forever;	May the glory of the Lord last for ever!
may the Lord rejoice in his works.	May the Lord rejoice in his works!
May my meditation be pleasing to him, for I rejoice in the Lord.—R̸. ↓	May my thoughts be pleasing to him. I find my joy in the Lord.—R̸. ↓

SECOND READING Rom. 8.8-17   [Children of God]

We should live by the Spirit. For those who are led by the Spirit are children of God, heirs of God and joint heirs with Christ.

A reading from the letter of Paul
to the Romans

THOSE who are in the flesh cannot please God. But you are not in the flesh; you are in the Spirit, since the Spirit of God dwells in you. Anyone who does not have the Spirit of Christ does not belong to him.

But if Christ is in you, though the body is dead because of sin, the Spirit is life because of righteousness. If the Spirit of God who raised Jesus from the dead dwells in you, he who raised Christ from the dead will give life to your mortal bodies also through his Spirit that dwells in you.

So then, brothers and sisters, we are debtors, not to the flesh, to live according to the flesh—for if you live according to the flesh, you will die; but if by the Spirit you put to death the deeds of the body, you will live.

For all who are led by the Spirit of God are children of God. For you did not receive a spirit of slavery to fall back into fear, but you have received a spirit of adoption. When we cry, "Abba! Father!" it is that very Spirit bearing witness with your spirit that we are children of God, and if children, then heirs, heirs of God and joint heirs with Christ—if, in fact, we suffer with him so that we may also be glorified with him.—The word of the Lord. ℞. **Thanks be to God.** ↓

SEQUENCE

[Come, Holy Spirit]

1. Holy Spirit, Lord divine,
Come, from heights of heav'n and shine,
Come with blessed radiance bright!

2. Come, O Father of the poor,
Come, whose treasured gifts ensure,
Come, our heart's unfailing light!

3. Of consolers, wisest, best,
And our soul's most welcome guest,
Sweet refreshment, sweet repose.

4. In our labour rest most sweet,
Pleasant coolness in the heat,
Consolation in our woes.

5. Light most blessed, shine with grace
In our heart's most secret place,
Fill your faithful through and through.

6. Left without your presence here,
Life itself would disappear,
Nothing thrives apart from you!

7. Cleanse our soiled hearts of sin,
Arid souls refresh within,
Wounded lives to health restore.

8. Bend the stubborn heart and will,
Melt the frozen, warm the chill,

Guide the wayward home
    once more!
9. On the faithful who are
    true
And profess their faith in you,
In your sev'nfold gift de-
    scend!

10. Give us virtue's sure re-
    ward,
Give us your salvation,
    Lord,
Give us joys that never end! ↓

GOSPEL ACCLAMATION   [Fire of Love]

(If the Alleluia is not sung, the acclamation is omitted.)

℣. Alleluia. ℟. **Alleluia.**
℣. Come, Holy Spirit, fill the hearts of your
    faithful
and kindle in them the fire of your love.
℟. **Alleluia.** ↓

GOSPEL Jn. 14.15-16, 23b-26   [Our Teacher]

**The Holy Spirit, whom the Father will send in the name
of Jesus, will teach Christians everything. He will be
their Advocate forever.**

℣. The Lord be with you. ℟. **And also with you.**
✛ A reading from the holy gospel according to
John. ℟. **Glory to you, Lord.**

JESUS spoke to the disciples: "If you love me,
you will keep my commandments. And I will
ask the Father, and he will give you another
Advocate, to be with you forever.

"Those who love me will keep my word, and
my Father will love them, and we will come to
them and make our home with them. Whoever
does not love me does not keep my words; and
the word that you hear is not mine, but is from
the Father who sent me.

"I have said these things to you while I am still with you. But the Advocate, the Holy Spirit, whom the Father will send in my name, will teach you everything, and remind you of all that I have said to you."—The gospel of the Lord. ℟. **Praise to you, Lord Jesus Christ.**

➜ No. 14, p. 18

PRAYER OVER THE GIFTS　　　　[Spirit of Jesus]

Lord,
may the Spirit you promised
lead us into all truth
and reveal to us the full meaning of this sacri-
　fice.
Grant this through Christ our Lord. ℟. **Amen.** ↓

PREFACE (28)　　　　[Coming of the Spirit]

℣. The Lord be with you. ℟. **And also with you.**
℣. Lift up your hearts. ℟. **We lift them up to the Lord.** ℣. Let us give thanks to the Lord our God.
℟. **It is right to give him thanks and praise.**

Father, all-powerful and ever-living God,
we do well always and everywhere to give you
　thanks.
Today you sent the Holy Spirit
on those marked out to be your children
by sharing the life of your only Son,
and so you brought the paschal mystery to its
　completion.
Today we celebrate the great beginnings of
　your Church
when the Holy Spirit made known to all peo-
　ples the one true God,

and created from the many languages of
   man
one voice to profess one faith.
The joy of the resurrection renews the whole
   world,
while the choirs of heaven sing for ever to your
   glory: ➝ No. 23, p. 25

*When Eucharistic Prayer I is used, the special Pente-
cost form of* In union with the whole Church *is
said.*

COMMUNION ANTIPHON Acts 2.4, 11 [Spirit-Filled]

**They were all filled with the Holy Spirit, and
they spoke of the great things God had done,
alleluia.** ↓

PRAYER AFTER COMMUNION [Vigour of the Spirit]

Father,
may the food we receive in the eucharist
help our eternal redemption.
Keep within us the vigour of your Spirit
and protect the gifts you have given to your
   Church.
We ask this in the name of Jesus the Lord.
℞. **Amen.**   ➝ No. 32, p. 75

Optional Solemn Blessings, p. 96, and Prayers Over the People, p. 104

"Glory to the Father, the Son, and the Holy Spirit."

JUNE 3
TRINITY SUNDAY

ENTRANCE ANTIPHON　　　　[Blessed Trinity]

Blessed be God the Father and his only-begotten Son and the Holy Spirit: for he has shown that he loves us.　➡ No. 2, p. 10

OPENING PRAYER　　　　[Witnessing to the Trinity]

Father,
you sent your Word to bring us truth
and your Spirit to make us holy.
Through them we come to know the mystery of
　your life.
Help us to worship you, one God in three Persons,
by proclaiming and living our faith in you.
Grant this . . . for ever and ever. ℞. **Amen.** ↓

FIRST READING Prov. 8.22-31　　　　[God's Wisdom]

In a messianic application the "Wisdom of God" who speaks in this reading foreshadows the revelation of the Second Person of the Trinity.

A reading from the book of Proverbs

THUS says the wisdom of God:
  "The Lord created me at the beginning of
    his work,
the first of his acts of long ago.
Ages ago I was set up,
at the first, before the beginning of the earth.
When there were no depths I was brought forth,
when there were no springs abounding with
    water.

"Before the mountains had been shaped,
before the hills, I was brought forth—
when he had not yet made earth and fields,
or the world's first bits of soil.

"When he established the heavens, I was there,
when he drew a circle on the face of the deep,
when he made firm the skies above,
when he established the fountains of the deep,
when he assigned to the sea its limit,
so that the waters might not transgress his
    command,
when he marked out the foundations of the earth,
then I was beside him, like a master worker;
and I was daily his delight,
rejoicing before him always,
rejoicing in his inhabited world
and delighting in the human race."
The word of the Lord. ℟. **Thanks be to God.** ↓

RESPONSORIAL PSALM Ps. 8   [The Power of God]

℟. O Lord, our God, how wonderful your name in all the earth!

(NRSV Text)	(GRAIL Text)
When I look at your heavens, the work of your fingers,	When I see the heavens, the work of your hands,
the moon and the stars that you have established;	the moon and the stars which you arranged,
what are human beings that you are mindful of them,	what are we that you should keep us in mind,
mortals that you care for them?—℟.	men and women that you care for us?—℟.
Yet you have made them a little lower than God,	Yet you have made us little less than gods;
and crowned them with glory and honour.	and crowned us with glory and honour,
You have given them dominion over the works of your hands;	gave us power over the works of your hands,
you have put all things under their feet.—℟.	put all things under our feet.—℟.
All sheep and oxen,	All of them, sheep and cattle,
and also the beasts of the field,	yes, even the savage beasts,
the birds of the air, and the fish of the sea,	birds of the air, and fish
whatever passes along the paths of the seas.—℟. ↓	that make their way through the waters.—℟. ↓

SECOND READING Rom. 5.1-5 [Justification by Faith]

Our hope, our faith, will be fulfilled because the Holy Spirit has been given to us.

A reading from the letter of Paul to the Romans

SINCE we are justified by faith, we have peace with God through our Lord Jesus Christ, through whom we have obtained access to this grace in which we stand; and we boast in our hope of sharing the glory of God.

And not only that, but we also boast in our sufferings, knowing that suffering produces endurance, and endurance produces character, and character produces hope, and hope does not disappoint us, because God's love has been poured into our hearts through the Holy Spirit that has been given to us.—The word of the Lord. ℟. **Thanks be to God.** ↓

GOSPEL ACCLAMATION See Rev. 1.8 [Glory to God]

(If the Alleluia is not sung, the acclamation is omitted.)

℣. Alleluia. ℟. **Alleluia.**
℣. Glory to the Father, the Son, and the Holy Spirit:
to God who is, who was, and who is to come.
℟. **Alleluia.** ↓

GOSPEL Jn. 16.12-15   [The Spirit of Truth]

All that the Father has belongs to Jesus. The Spirit of truth will guide us and announce to us the things to come.

℣. The Lord be with you. ℟. **And also with you.**
✠ A reading from the holy gospel according to John. ℟. **Glory to you, Lord.**

JESUS said to his disciples: "I still have many things to say to you, but you cannot bear them now. When the Spirit of truth comes, he will guide you into all the truth; for he will not speak on his own, but will speak whatever he hears, and he will declare to you the things that are to come. He will glorify me, because he will take what is mine and declare it to you. All that the Father has is mine. For this reason I said that he will take what is mine and declare it to you."—The gospel of the Lord. ℟. **Praise to you, Lord Jesus Christ.** ➙ No. 14, p. 18

PRAYER OVER THE GIFTS   [Perfect Offering]

Lord our God,
make these gifts holy,

and through them
make us a perfect offering to you.
We ask this in the name of Jesus the Lord.
℟. **Amen.** ↓

PREFACE (43)   [Mystery of the One Godhead]

℣. The Lord be with you. ℟. **And also with you.**
℣. Lift up your hearts. ℟. **We lift them up to the
Lord.** ℣. Let us give thanks to the Lord our God.
℟. **It is right to give him thanks and praise.**

Father, all-powerful and ever-living God,
we do well always and everywhere to give you
   thanks.
We joyfully proclaim our faith
in the mystery of your Godhead.
You have revealed your glory
as the glory also of your Son
and of the Holy Spirit:
three Persons equal in majesty,
undivided in splendour,
yet one Lord, one God,
ever to be adored in your everlasting glory.
And so, with all the choirs of angels in heaven
we proclaim your glory
and join in their unending hymn of praise:

→ No. 23, p. 25

COMMUNION ANTIPHON Gal. 4.6   [Abba, Father]
**You are the sons of God, so God has given you
the Spirit of his Son to form your hearts and
make you cry out: Abba, Father.** ↓

PRAYER AFTER COMMUNION   [Eternal God]

Lord God,
we worship you, a Trinity of Persons, one eternal God.
May our faith and the sacrament we receive
bring us health of mind and body.
We ask this through Christ our Lord.
℟. **Amen.**   → No. 32, p. 75

Optional Solemn Blessings, p. 96, and Prayers Over the People, p. 104

"Jesus . . . looked up to heaven, and blessed
and broke [the loaves]."

JUNE 10

BODY AND BLOOD OF CHRIST
(CORPUS CHRISTI)

ENTRANCE ANTIPHON Ps.80 (81).16 [Finest Wheat]
**The Lord fed his people with the finest wheat
and honey; their hunger was satisfied.**

→ No. 2, p. 10

OPENING PRAYER   [Memorial of Christ]

Lord Jesus Christ,
you gave us the eucharist
as the memorial of your suffering and death.
May our worship of this sacrament of your
  body and blood
help us to experience the salvation you won for
  us
and the peace of the kingdom
where you live with the Father and the Holy
  Spirit,
one God, for ever and ever. ℟. **Amen.** ↓

FIRST READING Gen. 14.18-20 [Blessing of Melchizedek]

**Sharing bread and wine, a foreshadowing of the eu-
charistic elements, Abram is blessed and God is praised.**

A reading from the book of Genesis

W HEN Abram heard that his nephew, Lot,
had been taken captive, he led forth his
trained men, and routed the abductors.

After Abram's return King Melchizedek of
Salem brought out bread and wine; he was priest
of God Most High. He blessed Abram and said,
  "Blessed be Abram by God Most High,
    maker of heaven and earth;
  and blessed be God Most High,
    who has delivered your enemies into your
    hand!"
And Abram gave him one tenth of everything.—
The word of the Lord. ℟. **Thanks be to God.** ↓

RESPONSORIAL PSALM Ps. 109 (110) [Eternal Priest]

℟. You are a priest for ev - er , in the line of Mel-chi-ze-dek.

(NRSV Text)	(GRAIL Text)
The Lord says to my lord, "Sit at my right hand until I make your enemies your footstool."—Ry.	The Lord's revelation to my Master: "Sit on my right: your foes I will put beneath your feet."—Ry.
The Lord sends out from Zion your mighty sceptre. Rule in the midst of your foes.—Ry.	The Lord will wield from Zion your scepter of power; rule in the midst of all your foes.— Ry.
Your people will offer themselves willingly on the day you lead your forces on the holy mountains. From the womb of the morning, like dew, your youth will come to you.—Ry.	A prince from the day of your birth on the holy mountains; from the womb before the dawn I begot you.—Ry.
The Lord has sworn and will not change his mind, "You are a priest forever according to the order of Melchizedek."—Ry. ↓	The Lord has sworn an oath he will not change. "You are a priest for ever, a priest like Melchizedek of old."— Ry. ↓

SECOND READING 1 Cor. 11.23-26 [The First Eucharist]

When we eat this bread and drink this cup, we proclaim your glory, Lord Jesus, until you come again.

A reading from the first letter of to Paul to the Corinthians

BELOVED, I received from the Lord what I also handed on to you, that the Lord Jesus on the night when he was betrayed took a loaf of bread, and when he had given thanks, he broke it and said, "This is my body that is for you. Do this in remembrance of me."

In the same way he took the cup also, after supper, saying, "This cup is the new covenant in my blood. Do this, as often as you drink it, in remembrance of me."

For as often as you eat this bread and drink the cup, you proclaim the Lord's death until he comes.—The word of the Lord. ℟. **Thanks be to God.** ↓

SEQUENCE   [Praise of the Eucharist]

This optional sequence is intended to be sung; otherwise it is better omitted. The shorter version begins at the asterisk.

1. Praise, O Zion, Christ our glory;
To the Shepherd let us sing,
Tell to all the world the story.
Laud with all our might the King.
Bread of life and source of living!
Lacking, still our praises ring.

2. This our special theme for singing,
Christ the Lamb for us was slain.
At the paschal meal he taught us,
To the twelve he made it plain:
Flesh as food for us was giving,
Therefore let your faith not wane.

3. On this day of Christian feasting,
With full voices we delight:
Instituting our salvation,
In the sacred meal that night,
Christ the ancient law fulfilling,
Fills all people with new sight.

4. In the memory of Jesus,
Gathered we as chosen band.
Bread and wine Christ is transforming,
Flesh and Blood are now at hand.
From his words and actions learning;
Love we share at his command.

5. Gathered at this solemn table,
Darkness now has taken flight.
In the bread and wine partaking,
Christ is for each one the light,
Then as food to us disciples,
Gives our souls a new delight.

6. To all people Christ is giving,
Truth in word and sacrament.
By the sacrifice redeeming,
All into one covenant.
One in Jesus' name assembling:
Faith and love our testament.

7. To our minds these signs disclosing,
To our senses must unfold:
Bread is broken, Blood outpouring;
Christ the myst'ry, awe untold!
Flesh and Blood to sight revealing:
This the story to be told.

8. Undivided is his body,
Yet Christ gives himself to all.
Word made flesh with us abiding,
For without him we must fall.
Christ the Pasch we are consuming,
One in spirit is our call.

9. Good and evil are all sharing,
Seeds of destiny are sown.
To new life our Saviour guides us;
Death prevails when on our own.
Life immortal, for those seeking,
Is fulfilled in Christ alone.

10. When the sacred bread is broken,
All receive the Christ as one.
By his love Christ is transforming,
Though so many we are one;

All the scattered are united,
All the lonely welcomed home.

*11. Come, behold, the bread of angels,
This our strength on pilgrims' way.
For the children God is giving,
Manna for our bread each day.
Now the sign of Isaac telling:
Christ has conquered on this day.

12. Hear our prayers, O kindly Shepherd,
Be for us true living bread.
Grant us peace in all our doings,
To our resting place be led;
Forth with all the saints now dwelling,
We the body, you the Head. ↓

GOSPEL ACCLAMATION Jn. 6.51   [Living Bread]
(If the Alleluia is not sung, the acclamation is omitted.)

℣. Alleluia. ℟. **Alleluia.**

℣. I am the living bread from heaven, says the Lord;

whoever eats this bread will live for ever.

℟. **Alleluia.** ↓

GOSPEL Lk. 9.11b-17   [Loaves and Fishes]

The compassion of Jesus is limitless. He pronounces a blessing and gives nourishment to the crowd. In the eucharist he gives us his body and blood and unites us to himself.

℣. The Lord be with you. ℟. **And also with you.**
✠ A reading from the holy gospel according to Luke. ℟. **Glory to you, Lord.**

J ESUS spoke to the crowds about the kingdom of God, and healed those who needed
to be cured.

The day was drawing to a close, and the
twelve came to him and said, "Send the crowd
away, so that they may go into the surrounding
villages and countryside, to lodge and get pro-
visions; for we are here in a deserted place."

But Jesus said to them, "You give them something to eat." They said, "We have no more than
five loaves and two fish—unless we are to go
and buy food for all these people." For there
were about five thousand men.

And Jesus said to his disciples, "Make the
people sit down in groups of about fifty each."
They did so and made them all sit down.

And taking the five loaves and the two fish,
he looked up to heaven, and blessed and broke
them, and gave them to the disciples to set before the crowd.

And all ate and were filled. What was left
over was gathered up, twelve baskets of broken
pieces.—The gospel of the Lord. ℞. **Praise to
you, Lord Jesus Christ.**   ➥ No. 14, p. 18

PRAYER OVER THE GIFTS   [Unity and Peace]
Lord,
may the bread and cup we offer
bring your Church the unity and peace they
   signify.
We ask this in the name of Jesus the Lord.
℞. **Amen.**   ➥ No. 21, p. 24 (Pref. 47-48)

COMMUNION ANTIPHON Jn. 6.57 [Eucharistic Life]
**Whoever eats my flesh and drinks my blood
will live in me and I in him, says the Lord.** ↓

PRAYER AFTER COMMUNION   [Divine Life]

Lord Jesus Christ,
you give us your body and blood in the eucharist
as a sign that even now we share your life.
May we come to possess it completely in the
    kingdom
where you live for ever and ever.
℟. **Amen.**   → No. 32, p. 75

Optional Solemn Blessings, p. 96, and Prayers Over the People, p. 104

"Your faith has saved you; go in peace."

JUNE 17

11th SUNDAY IN ORDINARY TIME

ENTRANCE ANTIPHON Ps. 26 (27).7, 9 [Hear My Voice]

**Lord, hear my voice when I call to you. You are
my help; do not cast me off, do not desert me,
my Saviour God.**   → No. 2, p. 10

OPENING PRAYER   [Following Christ]

Almighty God,
our hope and our strength,
without you we falter.
Help us to follow Christ
and to live according to your will.
We ask this through our Lord Jesus Christ,
   your Son,
who lives and reigns with you and the Holy
   Spirit,
one God, for ever and ever. ℟. **Amen.** ↓

FIRST READING 2 Sam. 12.7-10, 13 [David's Repentance]

The prophet Nathan rebukes King David for having
sinned grievously after God had been so good to him.
Whenever we have been weak, we should repent and
ask God for forgiveness.

A reading from the second book of Samuel

DAVID did what displeased the Lord, and
   the Lord sent the prophet Nathan to David.
Nathan said to David, "Thus says the Lord, the
God of Israel: I anointed you king over Israel,
and I rescued you from the hand of Saul; I gave
you your master's house, and your master's
wives into your bosom, and gave you the house
of Israel and of Judah; if that had been too little, I would have added as much more.

"Why have you despised the word of the Lord,
to do what is evil in his sight? You have struck
down Uriah the Hittite with the sword, and have
taken his wife to be your wife, and have killed
Uriah with the sword of the Ammonites.

"Now therefore the sword shall never depart
from your house, for you have despised me, and

have taken the wife of Uriah the Hittite to be your wife."

David said to Nathan, "I have sinned against the Lord." Nathan said to David, "Now the Lord has put away your sin; you shall not die."—The word of the Lord. ℟. **Thanks be to God.** ↓

RESPONSORIAL PSALM Ps. 31 (32) [God's Kindness]

℟. Lord forgive the wrong I have done.

(℟. Forgive, Lord, the guilt of my sin.)

(NRSV Text)	(GRAIL Text)
Happy are those whose transgression is forgiven,	Happy those whose offense is forgiven,
whose sin is covered.	whose sin is remitted.
Happy are those to whom the Lord imputes no iniquity,	O happy those to whom the Lord imputes no guilt,
and in whose spirit there is no deceit.—℟.	in whose spirit is no guile.—℟.
I acknowledged my sin to you,	But now I have acknowledged my sins;
and I did not hide my iniquity;	my guilt I did not hide.
I said, "I will confess my transgressions to the Lord,"	I said: "I will confess my offense to the Lord."
and you forgave the guilt of my sin.—℟.	And you, Lord, have forgiven the guilt of my sin.—℟.
You are a hiding place for me;	You are my hiding place, O Lord;
you preserve me from trouble;	you save me from distress.
you surround me with glad cries of deliverance,	You surround me with cries of deliverance—℟.
for steadfast love surrounds those who trust in the Lord.—℟.	Rejoice, rejoice in the Lord,
Be glad in the Lord	exult, you just!
and rejoice, O righteous,	O come, ring out your joy,
and shout for joy,	all you upright of heart.—℟. ↓
all you upright in heart.—℟. ↓	

SECOND READING Gal. 2.16, 19-21

[Justification by Faith]

In faith we are united and all distinctions are transcended. We look upon Abraham as our father in faith.

A reading from the letter of Paul
to the Galatians

WE know that a person is justified not by the works of the law but through faith in Jesus Christ. And we have come to believe in Christ Jesus, so that we might be justified by faith in Christ, and not by doing the works of the law, because no one will be justified by the works of the law. For through the law I died to the law, so that I might live to God.

I have been crucified with Christ; and it is no longer I who live, but it is Christ who lives in me. And the life I now live in the flesh I live by faith in the Son of God, who loved me and gave himself for me. I do not nullify the grace of God; for if justification comes through the law, then Christ died for nothing.—The word of the Lord. ℟. **Thanks be to God.** ↓

GOSPEL ACCLAMATION 1 Jn. 4.10

[God's Forgiving Love]

(If the Alleluia is not sung, the acclamation is omitted.)

℣. Alleluia. ℟. **Alleluia.**
℣. God first loved us
   and sent his Son to take away our sins.
℟. **Alleluia.** ↓

GOSPEL Lk. 7.36—8.3 or 7.36-50   [Unselfish Love]

Jesus rebukes Simon for his ungracious and self-satisfied behaviour, but grants forgiveness to the sinner who

sincerely repents for her sins. He is always ready to
grant pardon for true repentance.

*[If the "Short Form" is used, the indented text in
brackets is omitted.]*

℣. The Lord be with you. ℟. **And also with you.**
✠ A reading from the holy gospel according to
Luke. ℟. **Glory to you, Lord.**

ONE of the Pharisees asked Jesus to eat with
him, and he went to the Pharisee's house
and took his place at table.

A woman in the city, who was a sinner, having
learned that Jesus was eating in the Pharisee's
house, brought an alabaster jar of ointment. She
stood behind Jesus at his feet, weeping, and
began to bathe his feet with her tears and to
dry them with her hair. Then she continued
kissing his feet and anointing them with the
ointment.

Now when the Parisee who had invited Jesus
saw it, he said to himself, "If this man were a
prophet, he would have known who and what
kind of woman this is who is touching him—that
she is a sinner."

Jesus spoke up and said to him, "Simon, I have
something to say to you." "Teacher," he replied,
"speak."

"A certain creditor had two debtors; one owed
five hundred denarii, and the other fifty. When
they could not pay, he cancelled their debts for
both of them. Now which one of them will love
him more?" Simon answered, "I suppose the one
for whom he cancelled the greater debt." And
Jesus said to him, "You have judged rightly."

Then turning toward the woman, he said to Simon, "Do you see this woman? I entered your house; you gave me no water for my feet, but she has bathed my feet with her tears and dried them with her hair.

"You gave me no kiss, but from the time I came in she has not stopped kissing my feet. You did not anoint my head with oil, but she has anointed my feet with ointment.

"Therefore, I tell you, her sins, which were many, have been forgiven; hence she has shown great love. But the one to whom little is forgiven, loves little." Then Jesus said to her, "Your sins are fogiven."

But those who were at the table with him began to say among themselves, "Who is this who even forgives sins?" And Jesus said to the woman, "Your faith has saved you; go in peace."

[Soon afterwards Jesus went on through cities and villages, proclaiming and bringing the good news of the kingdom of God. The twelve were with him, as well as some women who had been cured of evil spirits and infirmities: Mary, called Magdalene, from whom seven demons had gone out, and Joanna, the wife of Herod's steward Chuza, and Susanna, and many others, who provided for them out of their resources.]

The gospel of the Lord. ℟. **Praise to you, Lord Jesus Christ.**   → No. 14, p. 18

PRAYER OVER THE GIFTS

[Health of Mind and Body]

Lord, God,
in this bread and wine
you give us food for body and spirit.
May the eucharist renew our strength
and bring us health of mind and body.
℟. **Amen.**   ➔ No. 21, p. 24 (Pref. 29-36)

COMMUNION ANTIPHON Ps. 26 (27).4

[Dwelling with the Lord]

**One thing I seek: to dwell in the house of the
Lord all the days of my life.** ↓

OR Jn. 17.11   [One with God]

**Father, keep in your name those you have
given me, that they may be one as we are one,
says the Lord.** ↓

PRAYER AFTER COMMUNION   [Church Unity]

Lord,
may this eucharist
accomplish in your Church
the unity and peace it signifies.
Grant this through Christ our Lord.
℟. **Amen.**   ➔ No. 32, p. 75

Optional Solemn Blessings, p. 96, and Prayers Over the People, p. 104

John "lived in the wilderness until the day he appeared publicly to Israel."

JUNE 24

BIRTH OF ST. JOHN THE BAPTIST

VIGIL MASS

ENTRANCE ANTIPHON Lk. 1.15, 14   [Spirit-Filled]

From his mother's womb, he will be filled with the Holy Spirit; he will be great in the sight of the Lord, and many will rejoice at his birth.

➔ No. 2, p. 10

OPENING PRAYER   [Following St. John]

All-powerful God,
help your people to walk the path to salvation.
By following the teaching of John the Baptist,
may we come to your Son, our Lord Jesus Christ,
who lives and reigns with you and the Holy
  Spirit,
one God, for ever and ever. ℟. **Amen.** ↓

FIRST READING Jer. 1.4-10   [God's Call]

Just as Jeremiah was selected, John the Baptist was appointed even before his birth to announce the coming of the Saviour. Thus, he helped to bring the old to an end and build the new.

A reading from the book of the
prophet Jeremiah

THE word of the Lord came to me saying,
"Before I formed you in the womb I knew
you;
and before you were born I consecrated you;
I appointed you a prophet to the nations."
Then I said, "Ah, Lord God! Truly I do not
know how to speak: I am only a boy." But the
Lord said to me,
"Do not say 'I am only a boy';
for you shall go to all to whom I send you,
and you shall speak whatever I command
you.
Do not be afraid of them,
for I am with you to deliver you,
says the Lord."
Then the Lord put out his hand and touched
my mouth; and the Lord said to me,
"Now I have put my words in your mouth.
See, today I appoint you over nations and
over kingdoms,
to pluck up and to pull down,
to destroy and to overthrow,
to build and to plant."
The word of the Lord. ℟. **Thanks be to God.** ↓

RESPONSORIAL PSALM Ps. 70 (71) [God Our Strength]

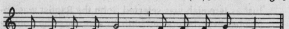

℟. **Since my moth-er's womb, you have been my strength.**

(NRSV Text)	(GRAIL Text)

(NRSV Text)

In you, O Lord, I take refuge;
let me never be put to shame.
In your righteousness deliver me and
   rescue me;
incline your ear to me and save
   me.—℟.

Be to me a rock of refuge,
a strong fortress to save me,
for you are my rock and my fortress.
Rescue me, O my God, from the hand
   of the wicked.—℟.

For you , O Lord, are my hope,
my trust, O Lord, from my youth.
Upon you I have leaned from my birth;
it was you who took me from my
   mother's womb.—℟.

My mouth will tell of your righteous
   acts,
of your deeds of salvation all day long.
O God, from my youth you have
   taught me,
and I still proclaim your wondrous
   deeds.—℟. ↓

(GRAIL Text)

In you, O Lord, I take refuge;
let me never be put to shame.
In your justice rescue me, free me;
pay heed to me and save me.—℟.

Be a rock where I can take refuge,
a mighty stronghold to save me;
for you are my rock, my stronghold.
Free me from the hand of the
   wicked.—℟.

It is you, O Lord, who are my hope,
my trust, O Lord, since my youth.
On you I have leaned from my birth,
from my mother's womb you have
   been my help.—℟.

My lips will tell of your justice
and day by day of your help.
O God, you have taught me from my
   youth
and I proclaim your wonders still.—
   ℟. ↓

SECOND READING 1 Pet. 1.3, 8-13 [Faith and Life]

**John the Baptist is numbered among the Old Testament
prophets. He pointed to Christ, but did not live to see
the entire work of Jesus. John spent his life directing his
followers to Christ and to the fullness of faith and life.**

A reading from the first letter of Peter

BLESSED be the God and Father of our Lord
Jesus Christ! By his great mercy he has given

us a new birth into a living hope through the resurrection of Jesus Christ from the dead.

Although you have not seen Jesus Christ, you love him; and even though you do not see him now, you believe in him and rejoice with an indescribable and glorious joy, for you are receiving the outcome of your faith, the salvation of your souls.

The prophets who prophesied of the grace that was to be yours concerning this salvation made careful search and inquiry, inquiring about the person or time that the Spirit of Christ within them indicated when it testified in advance to the sufferings and the subsequent glory destined for Christ.

It was revealed to the prophets that they were serving not themselves but you, in regard to the things that have now been announced to you through those who brought you good news by the Holy Spirit sent from heaven—things into which angels long to look! Therefore prepare your minds for action; discipline yourselves; set all your hope on the grace that Jesus Christ will bring you when he is revealed.—The word of the Lord. ℟. **Thanks be to God.** ↓

GOSPEL ACCLAMATION Jn. 1.7; Lk. 1.17   [Witness]

℣. Alleluia. ℟. **Alleluia.**

℣. John came to bear witness to the light,
   to prepare an upright people for the Lord.

℟. **Alleluia.** ↓

GOSPEL Lk. 1.5-17   [Preparation for Christ]

Luke tells of the announcement of the birth and the mission of John the Baptist. In the Scriptures, the birth of persons selected to play an important role in the history of salvation is often announced by a special heavenly message. John is to be like a new Elijah.

℣. The Lord be with you. ℟. **And also with you.**
✠ A reading from the holy gospel according to Luke. ℟. **Glory to you, Lord.**

IN the days of King Herod of Judea there was a priest called Zechariah, who belonged to the priestly order of Abijah. His wife was a descendant of Aaron, and her name was Elizabeth. Both of them were righteous before God, living blamelessly according to all the commandments and regulations of the Lord. But they had no children, because Elizabeth was barren, and both were getting on in years.

Once when Zechariah was serving as priest before God and his section was on duty, he was chosen by lot, according to the custom of the priesthood, to enter the sanctuary of the Lord and offer incense. Now at the time of the incense offering, the whole assembly of the people was praying outside.

Then there appeared to him the angel of the Lord, standing at the right side of the altar of incense. When Zechariah saw him, he was terrified; and fear overwhelmed him.

But the angel said to him, "Do not be afraid, Zechariah, for your prayer has been heard. Your wife Elizabeth will bear you a son, and you will name him John.

"You will have joy and gladness and many will rejoice at his birth, for he will be great in the sight of the Lord. He must never drink wine or strong drink; even before his birth he will be filled with the Holy Spirit.

"He will turn many of the people of Israel to the Lord their God. With the spirit and power of Elijah, he will go before him, to turn the hearts of parents to their children, and the disobedient to the wisdom of the righteous, to make ready a people prepared for the Lord."—The gospel of the Lord. ℟. **Praise to you, Lord Jesus Christ.**

➜ No. 14, p. 18

PRAYER OVER THE GIFTS   [Living the Mass]

Lord, look with favour on the gifts we bring
on this feast of John the Baptist.
Help us put into action
the mystery we celebrate in this sacrament.
We ask this in the name of Jesus the Lord.
℟. **Amen.** ↓

PREFACE (61)   [John: Witness to Christ]

℣. The Lord be with you. ℟. **And also with you.**
℣. Lift up your hearts. ℟. **We lift them up to the Lord.** ℣. Let us give thanks to the Lord our God.
℟. **It is right to give him thanks and praise.**

Father, all-powerful and ever-living God,
we do well always and everywhere to give you thanks
through Jesus Christ our Lord.
We praise your greatness
as we honour the prophet
who prepared the way before your Son.
You set John the Baptist apart from other men,
marking him out with special favour.
His birth brought great rejoicing:

even in the womb he leapt for joy,
so near was man's salvation.
You chose John the Baptist from all the prophets
to show the world its redeemer,
the lamb of sacrifice.
He baptized Christ, the giver of baptism,
in waters made holy by the one who was bap-
    tized.
You found John worthy of a martyr's death,
his last and greatest act of witness to your Son.
In our unending joy we echo on earth
the song of the angels in heaven
as they praise your glory for ever:

➤ No. 23, p. 25

COMMUNION ANTIPHON Lk. 1.68 [God Has Visited Us]
Blessed be the Lord God of Israel, for he has visited and redeemed his people. ↓

PRAYER AFTER COMMUNION [The Mercy of Christ]
Father,
may the prayers of John the Baptist
lead us to the Lamb of God.
May this eucharist bring us the mercy of Christ,
who is Lord for ever and ever.
℟. **Amen.**   ➤ No. 32, p. 75

Optional Solemn Blessings, p. 96, and Prayers Over the People, p. 104

MASS DURING THE DAY

ENTRANCE ANTIPHON Jn. 1.6-7; Lk. 1.17   [Witness]
There was a man sent from God whose name was John. He came to bear witness to the light, to prepare an upright people for the Lord.

➤ No. 2, p. 10

OPENING PRAYER   [Joy and Peace]

God our Father,
you raised up John the Baptist
to prepare a perfect people for Christ the Lord.
Give your Church joy in spirit
and guide those who believe in you
into the way of salvation and peace.
We ask this through our Lord Jesus Christ,
  your Son,
who lives and reigns with you and the Holy
  Spirit,
one God, for ever and ever. ℟. **Amen.** ↓

FIRST READING Is. 49.1-6   [A Suffering Messiah]

The Lord chose the people of Israel as servants and to
make the Lord's name known to all. The words of Isaiah
find their fulfillment in the nations, but especially in the
Messiah, who will come from among the chosen people.

A reading from the book of the prophet Isaiah

L ISTEN to me, O coastlands,
  pay attention, you peoples from far away!
The Lord called me before I was born,
while I was in my mother's womb he named me.

He made my mouth like a sharp sword,
in the shadow of his hand he hid me;
he made me a polished arrow,
in his quiver he hid me away.

And the Lord said to me, "You are my servant,
  Israel,
in whom I will be glorified."
But I said, "I have laboured in vain,
I have spent my strength for nothing and vanity;
yet surely my cause is with the Lord,

and my reward with my God."

And now the Lord says,
who formed me in the womb to be his servant,
to bring Jacob back to him,
and that Israel might be gathered to him,
for I am honoured in the sight of the Lord,
and my God has become my strength.

The Lord says,
"It is too small a thing that you should be my
    servant,
to raise up the tribes of Jacob
and to restore the survivors of Israel;
I will give you as a light to the nations,
that my salvation may reach to the end of the
    earth."

The word of the Lord. ℟. **Thanks be to God.** ↓

RESPONSORIAL PSALM Ps.138 (139)

[The Lord Our Maker]

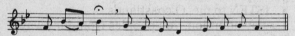

℟. **I praise you for I am won-der-ful-ly made.**

(NRSV Text)	(GRAIL Text)
O Lord, you have searched me and known me.	O Lord, you search me and you know me,
You know when I sit down and when I rise up;	you know my resting and my rising, you discern my purpose from afar.
you discern my thoughts from far away.	You mark when I walk or lie down. all my ways lie open to you.—℟.
You search out my path and my lying down,	For it was you who created my being, knit me together in my mother's womb.
and are aquainted with all my ways.—℟.	I thank you for the wonder of my being,
For it was you who formed my inward parts;	for the wonders of all your creation.—℟.

you knit me together in my mother's womb.
I praise you,
for I am fearfully and wonderfully made.—R̪.

Wonderful are your works; that I know very well.
My frame was not hidden from you, when I was being made in secret. intricately woven in the depths of the earth.—R̪. ↓

Already you knew my soul.
my body held no secret from you
when I was being fashioned in secret
and moulded in the depths of the earth.—R̪. ↓

SECOND READING Acts 13.22-26   [John, Herald of Jesus]

Luke quotes Paul as applying the prophecies of the Old Testament to Jesus Christ, the son of David and the Saviour of Israel. John proclaimed his coming to Jew and Gentile alike.

A reading from the Acts of the Apostles

ON the sabbath, Paul and his companion went to the synagogue, and the officials of the synagogue invited them to address the people. So Paul stood up and began to speak. "You Israelites, and all who fear God, listen. God made David king of our ancestors. In his testimony about him God said, 'I have found David, son of Jesse, to be a man after my heart, who will carry out all my wishes.'

"Of this man's posterity God has brought to Israel a Saviour, Jesus, as he promised; before the coming of Jesus John had already proclaimed a baptism of repentance to all the people of Israel. And as John was finishing his work, he said, 'What do you suppose that I am? I am not he. No, but one is coming after me; I am not worthy to untie the thong of the sandals on his feet.'

"You descendants of Abraham's family, and others who fear God, to us the message of this salvation has been sent."—The word of the Lord. ℟. **Thanks be to God.** ↓

GOSPEL ACCLAMATION Lk. 1.76 [Prepare the Way]

℣. Alleluia. ℟. **Alleluia.**

℣. You, child, shall be called the prophet of the Most High;

for you will go before the Lord to prepare his way.

℟. **Alleluia.** ↓

GOSPEL Lk. 1.57-66, 80 [Birth of John]

The birth of John and the birth of Jesus are alike in some details. Both are chosen from their first moment of life; both receive names assigned by an angel. Both come out of the desert—John to announce, and Jesus to fulfil.

℣. The Lord be with you. ℟. **And also with you.**
✝ A reading from the holy gospel according to Luke. ℟. **Glory to you, Lord.**

THE time came for Elizabeth to give birth, and she bore a son. Her neighbours and relatives heard that the Lord had shown his great mercy to her, and they rejoiced with her.

On the eighth day they came to circumcise the child, and they were going to name him Zechariah after his father. But his mother said, "No; he is to be called John." They said to her, "None of your relatives has this name." Then they began motioning to his father to find out what name he wanted to give him.

He asked for a writing tablet and wrote, "His name is John." And all of them were amazed.

Immediately his mouth was opened and his tongue freed, and he began to speak, praising God.

Fear came over all their neighbours, and all these things were talked about throughout the entire hill country of Judea. All who heard them pondered them and said, "What then will this child become?" For, indeed, the hand of the Lord was with him.

The child grew and became strong in spirit, and he was in the wilderness until the day he appeared publicly to Israel.—The gospel of the Lord. ℟. **Praise to you, Lord Jesus Christ.**

→ No. 14, p. 18

PRAYER OVER THE GIFTS   [John Manifested Christ]

Father,
accept the gifts we bring to your altar
to celebrate the birth of John the Baptist,
who foretold the coming of our Saviour
and made him known when he came.
We ask this in the name of Jesus the Lord.
℟. **Amen.**   → Pref. (61), p 455

COMMUNION ANTIPHON Lk. 1.78

[Dawn from On High]

Through the tender compassion of our God, the dawn from on high shall break upon us. ↓

PRAYER AFTER COMMUNION   [Welcoming Jesus]

Lord,
you have renewed us with this eucharist,
as we celebrate the feast of John the Baptist,
who foretold the coming of the Lamb of God.

May we welcome your Son as our Saviour,
for he gives us new life,
and is Lord for ever and ever.
℟. **Amen.**   ➜ No. 32, p. 75

Optional Solemn Blessings, p. 96, and Prayers Over the People, p. 104

"No one who puts a hand to the plough and looks back
is fit for the kingdom of God."

JULY 1

13th SUNDAY IN ORDINARY TIME

ENTRANCE ANTIPHON Ps. 46 (47).1 [Shout with Joy]
**All nations, clap your hands. Shout with a
voice of joy to God.**   ➜ No. 2, p. 10

OPENING PRAYER   [Walk in Christ's Light]
Father,
you call your children,

to walk in the light of Christ.
Free us from darkness
and keep us in the radiance of your truth.
We ask this through our Lord Jesus Christ,
  your Son,
who lives and reigns with you and the Holy
  Spirit,
one God, for ever and ever. ℟. **Amen.** ↓

FIRST READING 1 Kings 19.16b, 19-21   [Call of Elisha]

**Elisha receives the divine call and leaves all his posses-
sions. Our dedication should also be total.**

A reading from the first book of Kings

THE Lord spoke to the prophet Elijah and
said, "You shall anoint Elisha, son of
Shaphat, as prophet in your place."

So Elijah set out from there, and found Elisha, who was ploughing. There were twelve
yoke of oxen ahead of him, and he was with
the twelfth.

Elijah passed by Elisha and threw his mantle
over him. Elisha left the oxen, ran after Elijah,
and said, "Let me kiss my father and my
mother, and then I will follow you."

Then Elijah said to him, "Go back again; for
what have I done to you?" Elisha returned from
following Elijah, took the yoke of oxen, and
slaughtered them; using the equipment from
the oxen, he boiled their flesh, and gave it to
the people, and they ate. Then Elisha set out
and followed Elijah, and became his servant.—
The word of the Lord. ℟. **Thanks be to God.** ↓

RESPONSORIAL PSALM Ps. 15 (16) [Refuge in God]

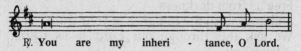

℟. You are my inheri - tance, O Lord.

(℟. **O Lord, it is you who are my portion and cup; you yourself who are my prize.**)

(NRSV Text)	**(GRAIL Text)**
Protect me, O God, for in you I take refuge.	Preserve me, God, I take refuge in you.
I say to the Lord, "You are my Lord; I have no good apart from you."	I say to the Lord, "You are my God."
The Lord is my chosen portion and my cup; you hold my lot.—℟.	O Lord, it is you who are my portion and cup;
	it is you yourself who are my prize.—℟.
I bless the Lord who gives me counsel;	I will bless you, Lord, you give me counsel,
in the night also my heart instructs me.	and even at night direct my heart.
I keep the Lord always before me;	I keep you, Lord, ever in my sight;
because he is at my right hand, I shall not be moved.—℟.	since you are at my right hand, I shall stand firm.—℟.
Therefore my heart is glad, and my soul rejoices;	And so my heart rejoices, my soul is glad;
my body also rests secure.	even my body shall rest in safety.
For you do not give me up to Sheol, or let your faithful one see the Pit.—℟.	For you will not leave my soul among the dead,
	nor let your beloved know decay.—℟.
You show me the path of life.	You will show me the path of life,
In your presence there is fullness of joy;	the fullness of joy in your presence,
in your right hand are pleasures forevermore.—℟. ↓	at your right hand happiness for ever.—℟. ↓

SECOND READING Gal. 5.1, 13-18 [Freedom in Christ]

We are called to be at one another's service and to love others as we love ourselves.

A reading from the letter of Paul to the Galatians

FOR freedom Christ has set us free. Stand firm, therefore, and do not submit again to a yoke of slavery. For you were called to freedom, brothers and sisters; only do not use your freedom as an opportunity for self-indulgence, but through love become slaves to one another.

For the whole law is summed up in a single commandment, "You shall love your neighbour as yourself." If, however, you bite and devour one another, take care that you are not consumed by one another.

Live by the Spirit, I say, and do not gratify the desires of the flesh. For what the flesh desires is opposed to the Spirit, and what the Spirit desires is opposed to the flesh; for these are opposed to each other, to prevent you from doing what you want. But if you are led by the Spirit, you are not subject to the law.—The word of the Lord. ℟. **Thanks be to God.** ↓

GOSPEL ACCLAMATION 1 Sam. 3.9; Jn. 6.69b [Listen]

(If the Alleluia is not sung, the acclamation is omitted.)

℣. Alleluia. ℟. **Alleluia.**
℣. Speak, O Lord, your servant is listening;
you have the words of everlasting life.
℟. **Alleluia.** ↓

GOSPEL Lk. 9.51-62   [Following Christ]

> To follow Jesus we must be ready to give of ourselves totally.

℣. The Lord be with you. ℟. **And also with you.**
✚ A reading from the holy gospel according to Luke. ℟. **Glory to you, Lord.**

WHEN the days drew near for him to be taken up, Jesus set his face to go to Jerusalem.

And he sent messengers ahead of him. On their way they entered a village of the Samaritans to make ready for Jesus; but the Samaritans did not receive him, because his face was set toward Jerusalem.

When his disciples James and John saw it, they said, "Lord, do you want us to command fire to come down from heaven and consume them?" But Jesus turned and rebuked them. Then they went on to another village.

As they were going along the road, someone said to him, "I will follow you wherever you go." And Jesus said to him, "Foxes have holes, and birds of the air have nests; but the Son of Man has nowhere to lay his head."

To another Jesus said, "Follow me." But he replied, "Lord, first let me go and bury my father." But Jesus said to him, "Let the dead bury their own dead; but as for you, go and proclaim the kingdom of God."

Another said, "I will follow you, Lord; but let me first say farewell to those at my home." Jesus said to him, "No one who puts a hand to the plough and looks back is fit for the kingdom of God."—The gospel of the Lord. ℟.
Praise to you, Lord Jesus Christ. ➔ No. 14, p. 18

PRAYER OVER THE GIFTS   [Faithful Service]

Lord God,
through your sacraments

you give us the power of your grace.
May this eucharist
help us to serve you faithfully.
We ask this in the name of Jesus the Lord.
℟. **Amen.**   → No. 21, p. 24 (Pref. 29-36)

COMMUNION ANTIPHON Ps. 102 (103).1

[Bless the Lord]

**O, bless the Lord, my soul, and all that is
within me, bless his holy name.** ↓

OR Jn. 17.20-21   [One in God]

**Father, I pray for them: may they be one in us,
so that the world may believe it was you who
sent me.** ↓

PRAYER AFTER COMMUNION   [Christ's Love]

Lord,
may this sacrifice and communion
give us a share in your life
and help us bring your love to the world.
Grant this through Christ our Lord.
℟. **Amen.**   → No. 32, p. 75

Optional Solemn Blessings, p. 96, and Prayers Over the People, p. 104

"He said to them, 'The harvest is plentiful,
but the labourers are few.' "

JULY 8

14th SUNDAY IN ORDINARY TIME

ENTRANCE ANTIPHON Ps. 47 (48).9-10

[God's Kindness]

Within your temple, we ponder your loving
kindness, O God. As your name, so also your
praise reaches to the ends of the earth; your
right hand is filled with justice. → No. 2, p. 10

OPENING PRAYER [Forgiveness]

Father,
through the obedience of Jesus,
your servant and your Son,
you raised a fallen world.
Free us from sin
and bring us the joy that lasts for ever.
Grant this . . . for ever and ever. R̸. **Amen.** ↓

FIRST READING Isa. 66.10-14   [God's Goodness]

We may apply this reading to the Church. The Church is Jerusalem, a loving protecting mother, who receives the blessing of God.

A reading from the book of the prophet Isaiah

REJOICE with Jerusalem,
and be glad for her,
all you who love her;
rejoice with her in joy,
all you who mourn over her—
that you may nurse and be satisfied
from her consoling breast;
that you may drink deeply with delight
from her glorious bosom.

For thus says the Lord:
"I will extend prosperity to her like a river,
and the wealth of the nations like an overflowing stream;
and you shall nurse and be carried on her arm,
and dandled on her knees.
As a mother comforts her child,
so I will comfort you;
you shall be comforted in Jerusalem.

"You shall see, and your heart shall rejoice;
your bodies shall flourish like the grass;
and it shall be known
that the hand of the Lord is with his servants."
The word of the Lord. ℟. **Thanks be to God. ↓**

RESPONSORIAL PSALM Ps. 65 (66)   [Praise of God]

℟. Let   all   the   earth   cry   out   to   God with joy.
(℟. Cry out with joy to God, all the earth.)

(NRSV Text)	(GRAIL Text)
Make a joyful noise to God, all the earth;	Cry out with joy to God all the earth, O sing to the glory of his name.
sing the glory of his name;	O render him glorious praise.
give to him glorious praise.	Say to God: "How tremendous your deeds!"—℟.
Say to God, "How awesome are your deeds!"—℟.	
"All the earth worships you; they sing praises to you, sing praises to your name."	"Before you all the earth shall bow, shall sing to you, sing to your name!"
Come and see what God has done: he is awesome in his deeds among mortals.—℟.	Come and see the works of God, tremendous his deeds among the peoples.—℟.
He turned the sea into dry land; they passed through the river on foot.	He turned the sea into dry land, they passed through the river dry-shod.
There we rejoiced in him, who rules by his might forever.—℟.	Let our joy then be in him; he rules for ever by his might.—℟.
Come and hear, all you who fear God, and I will tell what he has done for me.	Come and hear, all who fear God, I will tell what he did for my soul.
Blessed be God, because he has not rejected my prayer	Blessed be God who did not reject my prayer
or removed his steadfast love from me.—℟. ↓	nor withhold his love from me.—℟. ↓

SECOND READING Gal. 6.14-18   [Boasting in the Lord]

Through the cross of Christ we are created anew.

A reading from the letter of Paul to the Galatians

MAY I never boast of anything except the cross of our Lord Jesus Christ, by which the world has been crucified to me, and I to the world. For neither circumcision nor uncircumcision is anything; but a new creation is everything!

As for those who will follow this rule—peace be upon them, and mercy, and upon the Israel of God. From now on, let no one make trouble for me; for I carry the marks of Jesus branded on my body.

May the grace of our Lord Jesus Christ be with your spirit, brothers and sisters. Amen.— The word of the Lord. ℟. **Thanks be to God. ↓**

GOSPEL ACCLAMATION Col. 3.15a,16a

[Peace of Christ]

(If the Alleluia is not sung, the acclamation is omitted.)

℣. Alleluia. ℟. **Alleluia.**

℣. May the peace of Christ rule in your hearts, and the fullness of his message live within you. ℟. **Alleluia. ↓**

GOSPEL Lk. 10.1-12, 17-20 or 10.1-9   [Spreading the Word]

Even though our good works may be fruitful, we rejoice not in them but in our perseverance in grace.

[If the "Short Form" is used, the indented text in brackets is omitted.]

℣. The Lord be with you. ℟. **And also with you.**
✠ A reading from the holy gospel according to Luke. ℟. **Glory to you, Lord.**

THE Lord appointed seventy others and sent them on ahead of him in pairs to every town and place where he himself intended to go.

He said to them, "The harvest is plentiful, but the labourers are few; therefore ask the Lord of the harvest to send out labourers into his harvest. Go on your way. See, I am sending you out like lambs into the midst of wolves. Carry no purse, no bag, no sandals; and greet no one on the road.

"Whatever house you enter, first say, 'Peace to this house!' And if anyone is there who shares in peace, your peace will rest on that person; but if not, it will return to you. Remain in the same house, eating and drinking whatever they provide, for the labourer deserves to be paid. Do not move about from house to house.

"Whenever you enter a town and its people welcome you, eat what is set before you; cure the sick who are there, and say to them, 'The kingdom of God has come near to you.'

["But whenever you enter a town and they do not welcome you, go out into its streets and say, 'Even the dust of your town that clings to our feet, we wipe off in protest against you. Yet know this: the kingdom of God has come near.' I tell you, on that day it will be more tolerable for Sodom than for that town."

The seventy returned with joy, saying, "Lord, in your name even the demons submit to us!" Jesus said to them, "I watched Satan fall from heaven like a flash of lightning. See, I have given you authority to tread on snakes and scorpions, and over all the power of the enemy; and nothing will hurt you.

"Nevertheless, do not rejoice at this, that the spirits submit to you, but rejoice that your names are written in heaven."]

The gospel of the Lord. ℟. **Praise to you, Lord Jesus Christ.**   ➜ No. 14, p. 18

PRAYER OVER THE GIFTS [God's Glory]

Lord,
let this offering to the glory of your name
purify us and bring us closer to eternal life.
We ask this in the name of Jesus the Lord.
℟. **Amen.**   → No. 21, p. 24 (Pref. 29-36)

COMMUNION ANTIPHON Ps. 33 (34).8

[God's Goodness]

**Taste and see the goodness of the Lord;
blessed is he who hopes in God.** ↓

PRAYER AFTER COMMUNION [Life and Salvation]

Lord,
may we never fail to praise you
for the fullness of life and salvation
you give us in this eucharist.
We ask this through Christ our Lord.
℟. **Amen.**   → No. 32, p. 75

Optional Solemn Blessings, p. 96, and Prayers Over the People, p. 104

"He went to him and bandaged his wounds."

JULY 15

15th SUNDAY IN ORDINARY TIME

ENTRANCE ANTIPHON Ps. 16 (17).15   [God's Face]

In my justice I shall see your face, O Lord; when your glory appears, my joy will be full.
→ No. 2, p.10

OPENING PRAYER   [Rule of Life]

God our Father,
your light of truth
guides us to the way of Christ.
May all who follow him
reject what is contrary to the gospel.
We ask this . . . for ever and ever. ℟. **Amen.** ↓

FIRST READING Deut. 30.10-14   [Obeying the Law]

> We heed the word of the Lord by keeping the commandments. God's word is not foreign to us.

A reading from the book of Deuteronomy

MOSES spoke to the people, saying, "Obey the Lord your God by observing his commandments and decrees that are written in this book of the law; turn to the Lord your God with all your heart and with all your soul.

"Surely this commandment that I am commanding you today is not too hard for you, nor is it too far away. It is not in heaven, that you should say, 'Who will go up to heaven for us, and get it for us so that we may hear it and observe it?'

"Neither is it beyond the sea, that you should say, 'Who will cross to the other side of the sea for us, and get it for us so that we may hear it and observe it?'

"No, the word is very near to you; it is in your mouth and in your heart for you to observe."—The word of the Lord. ℟. **Thanks be to God.** ↓

RESPONSORIAL PSALM Ps. 68 (69) [God's Salvation]

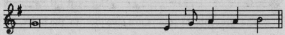

℟. **Turn to the Lord in your need, and you will live.**

(℟. Seek the Lord, you who are poor, and your hearts will revive.)

(NRSV Text)	(GRAIL Text)
As for me, my prayer is to you, O Lord. At an acceptable time, O God, in the abundance of your steadfast love, answer me. With your steadfast help, rescue me. Answer me, O Lord, for your steadfast love is good; according to your abundant mercy, turn to me.—℟.	This is my prayer to you. my prayer for your favour. In your great love, answer me, O God, with your help that never fails; Lord, answer, for your love is kind; in your compassion, turn towards me.—℟.
But I am lowly and in pain; let your salvation, O God, protect me.	As for me in my poverty and pain, let your help, O God, lift me up. I will praise God's name with a song;

I will praise the name of God with a song;
I will magnify him with thanksgiving.—R̶.

Let the oppressed see it and be glad;
you who seek God, let your hearts revive.
For the Lord hears the needy,
and does not despise his own that are in bonds.—R̶.

For God will save Zion
and rebuild the cities of Judah;
the children of his servants shall inherit it,
those who love his name shall live in it.—R̶. ↓

I will glorify him with thanksgiving.—R̶.

The poor when they see it will be glad
and God-seeking hearts will revive;
for the Lord listens to the needy
and does not spurn his servants in their chains.—R̶.

For God will bring help to Zion
and rebuild the cities of Judah.
The children of his servants shall inherit it;
those who love his name shall dwell there.—R̶. ↓

OR

RESPONSORIAL PSALM Ps. 18 (19)   [God's Law]

R̶. **The precepts of the Lord give joy to the heart.**

(NRSV Text)

The law of the Lord is perfect,
reviving the soul;
the decrees of the Lord are sure,
making wise the simple.—R̶.

The precepts of the Lord are right,
rejoicing the heart;
the commandment of the Lord is clear,
enlightening the eyes.—R̶.

The fear of the Lord is pure,
enduring forever;
the ordinances of the Lord are true
and righteous altogether.—R̶.

More to be desired are they than gold,

(GRAIL Text)

The law of the Lord is perfect,
it revives the soul.
The rule of the Lord is to be trusted,
it gives wisdom to the simple.—R̶.

The precepts of the Lord are right,
they gladden the heart.
The command of the Lord is clear,
it gives light to the eyes.—R̶.

The fear of the Lord is holy,
abiding for ever.
The decrees of the Lord are truth
and all of them just.—R̶.

They are more to be desired than gold,

even much fine gold;
sweeter also than honey,
and drippings of the honeycomb.—
℞. ↓

than the purest of gold
and sweeter are they than honey,
than honey from the comb.—℞. ↓

SECOND READING Col. 1.15-20 [The Primacy of Christ]

The glory of Christ is proclaimed for all to know.

A reading from the letter of Paul
to the Colossians

CHRIST is the image of the invisible God,
the firstborn of all creation; for in him all
things in heaven and on earth were created,
things visible and invisible, whether thrones or
dominions or rulers or powers—all things have
been created through him and for him.

Christ is before all things, and in him all
things hold together. He is the head of the
body, the church; he is the beginning, the firstborn from the dead, so that he might come to
have first place in everything.

For in Christ all the fullness of God was
pleased to dwell, and through him God was
pleased to reconcile to himself all things,
whether on earth or in heaven, by making
peace through the blood of his cross.—The
word of the Lord. ℞. **Thanks be to God.** ↓

GOSPEL ACCLAMATION Jn. 6.63, 69 [Spirit and Life]

(If the Alleluia is not sung, the acclamation is omitted.)

℣. Alleluia. ℞. **Alleluia.**
℣. Your words, Lord, are spirit and life;
you have the words of everlasting life.
℞. **Alleluia.** ↓

GOSPEL Lk. 10.25-37   [The Good Samaritan]

A man is mugged. Who cares? How do we love others as we love ourselves?

℣. The Lord be with you. ℟. **And also with you.**
✤ A reading from the holy gospel according to Luke. ℟. **Glory to you, Lord.**

A LAWYER stood up to test Jesus. "Teacher," he said, "what must I do to inherit eternal life?"

Jesus said to him, "What is written in the law? What do you read there?" The lawyer answered, "You shall love the Lord your God with all your heart, and with all your soul, and with all your strength, and with all your mind; and your neighbour as yourself."

And Jesus said to him, "You have given the right answer; do this, and you will live." But wanting to justify himself, the lawyer asked Jesus, "And who is my neighbour?"

Jesus replied, "A man was going down from Jerusalem to Jericho, and fell into the hands of robbers, who stripped him, beat him, and went away, leaving him half dead. Now by chance a priest was going down that road; and when he saw him, he passed by on the other side. So likewise a Levite, when he came to the place and saw him, passed by on the other side.

"But a Samaritan while travelling came near him; and when he saw him, he was moved with pity. He went to him and bandaged his wounds, having poured oil and wine on them. Then he put him on his own animal, brought him to an inn, and took care of him.

"The next day the Samaritan took out two denarii, gave them to the innkeeper, and said,

'Take care of him; and when I come back, I will repay you whatever more you spend.' "

Jesus asked, "Which of these three, do you think, was a neighbour to the man who fell into the hands of the robbers?" The lawyer said, "The one who showed him mercy." Jesus said to him, "Go and do likewise."—The gospel of the Lord. ℞. **Praise to you, Lord Jesus Christ.**

➜ No. 14, p. 18

PRAYER OVER THE GIFTS   [Growth in Faith]

Lord,
accept the gifts of your Church.
May this eucharist
help us grow in holiness and faith.
We ask this in the name of Jesus the Lord.
℞. **Amen.**   ➜ No. 21, p. 24 (Pref. 29-36)

COMMUNION ANTIPHON   Ps. 83 (84).3-4   [Our Home]

The sparrow even finds a home, the swallow finds a nest wherein to place her young, near to your altars, Lord of hosts, my King, my God! How happy they who dwell in your house! For ever they are praising you. ↓

OR Jn. 6.57   [Life in Jesus]

Whoever eats my flesh and drinks my blood will live in me and I in him, says the Lord. ↓

PRAYER AFTER COMMUNION   [God's Love]

Lord,
by our sharing in the mystery of this eucharist,
let your saving love grow within us.
Grant this through Christ our Lord.
℞. **Amen.**   ➜ No. 32, p. 75

Optional Solemn Blessings, p. 96, and Prayers Over the People, p. 104

"Mary has chosen the better part, which will not be taken away from her."

JULY 22

16th SUNDAY IN ORDINARY TIME

ENTRANCE ANTIPHON Ps. 53 (54).4, 6 [God Our Help]

God himself is my help. The Lord upholds my life. I will offer you a willing sacrifice; I will praise your name, O Lord, for its goodness.

→ No. 2, p. 10

OPENING PRAYER [Faithful Service]

Lord,
be merciful to your people.
Fill us with your gifts
and make us always eager to serve you
in faith, hope, and love.
Grant this . . . for ever and ever. ℟. **Amen.** ↓

FIRST READING Gen. 18.1-10a [Hospitality]

Abraham extends hospitality and the Lord reveals that the promise to Abraham will be fulfilled.

480

A reading from the book of Genesis

THE Lord appeared to Abraham by the oaks of Mamre, as Abraham sat at the entrance of his tent in the heat of the day. Abraham looked up and saw three men standing near him. When he saw them, he ran from the tent entrance to meet them, and bowed down to the ground.

He said, "My lord, if I find favour with you, do not pass by your servant. Let a little water be brought, and wash your feet, and rest yourselves under the tree. Let me bring a little bread, that you may refresh yourselves, and after that you may pass on—since you have come to your servant." So they said, "Do as you have said."

And Abraham hastened into the tent to Sarah, and said, "Make ready quickly three measures of choice flour, knead it, and make cakes." Abraham ran to the herd, and took a calf, tender and good, and gave it to the servant, who hastened to prepare it. Then he took curds and milk and the calf that he had prepared, and set it before them; and he stood by them under the tree while they ate.

They said to Abraham, "Where is your wife Sarah?" And he said, "There, in the tent."

Then one said, "I will surely return to you in due season, and your wife Sarah shall have a son."—The word of the Lord. ℟. **Thanks be to God.** ↓

RESPONSORIAL PSALM Ps. 14 (15) [The Just]

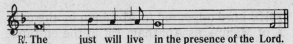

℟. The just will live in the presence of the Lord.

(℟. **Lord, who shall be admitted to your tent?**)

(NRSV Text)	(GRAIL Text)
O Lord, who may dwell on your holy hill?	Lord, who shall dwell on your holy mountain?
Those who walk blamelessly, and do what is right,	Those who walk without fault, those who act with justice
and speak the truth from their heart;	and speak the truth from their hearts,
who do not slander with their tongue.—℟.	those who do not slander with their tongue.—℟.
Those who do no evil to their friends,	Those who do no wrong to their kindred,
nor take up a reproach against their neighbours;	who cast no slur on their neighbours,
in whose eyes the wicked are despised,	who hold the godless in disdain,
but who honour those who fear the Lord.—℟.	but honour those who fear the Lord.—℟.
Those who stand by their oath even to their hurt;	Those who keep their word, come what may,
who do not lend money at interest,	who take no interest on a loan
and do not take a bribe against the innocent.	and accept no bribes against the innocent.
Those who do these things shall never be moved.—℟. ↓	Such people will stand firm for ever. —℟. ↓

SECOND READING Col. 1.24-28 [The Mystery of Christ]

The word of God in its fullness is now revealed in the mystery of Christ.

A reading from the letter of Paul to the Colossians

I AM now rejoicing in my sufferings for your sake, and in my flesh I am completing what is lacking in Christ's afflictions for the sake of his body, that is, the church.

I became its servant according to God's commission that was given to me for you, to make the word of God fully known, the mystery that has been hidden throughout the ages and generations but has now been revealed to his saints.

To them God chose to make known how great among the Gentiles are the riches of the glory of this mystery, which is Christ in you, the hope of glory. It is Christ whom we proclaim, warning everyone and teaching everyone in all wisdom, so that we may present everyone mature in Christ.—The word of the Lord. ℟. **Thanks be to God.** ↓

GOSPEL ACCLAMATION Lk. 8.15   [Perseverance]

(If the Alleluia is not sung, the acclamation is omitted.)

℣. Alleluia. ℟. **Alleluia.**
℣. Blessed are they who have kept the word
   with a generous heart,
and yield a harvest through perseverance.
℟. **Alleluia.** ↓

GOSPEL Lk. 10.38-42   [Martha and Mary]

Strive for a sense of proportion—maintain a balance in all things.

℣. The Lord be with you. ℟. **And also with you.**
✙ A reading from the holy gospel according to Luke. ℟. **Glory to you, Lord.**

NOW as Jesus and his disciples went on their way, he entered a certain village, where a woman named Martha welcomed him into her home. She had a sister named Mary, who sat at the Lord's feet and listened to what he was saying.

But Martha was distracted by her many tasks; so she came to Jesus and asked, "Lord, do you not care that my sister has left me to do all the work by myself? Tell her then to help me."

But the Lord answered her, "Martha, Martha, you are worried and distracted by many things; there is need of only one thing. Mary has chosen the better part, which will not be taken away from her."—The gospel of the Lord. ℟.
Praise to you, Lord Jesus Christ. → No. 14, p. 18

PRAYER OVER THE GIFTS   [Saving Gifts]

Lord,
bring us closer to salvation
through these gifts which we bring in your honour.
Accept the perfect sacrifice you have given us,
bless it as you blessed the gifts of Abel.
We ask this through Christ our Lord.
℟. **Amen.**   → No. 21, p. 24 (Pref. 29-36)

COMMUNION ANTIPHON Ps. 110 (111).4-5
[God Provides]

The Lord keeps in our minds the wonderful things he has done. He is compassion and love; he always provides for his faithful. ↓

OR Rev. 3.20   [Jesus Knocks]

I stand at the door and knock, says the Lord. If anyone hears my voice and opens the door, I

will come in and sit down to supper with him,
and he with me. ↓

PRAYER AFTER COMMUNION [New Life]

Merciful Father,
may these mysteries
give us new purpose
and bring us to a new life in you.
We ask this in the name of Jesus the Lord.
℟. **Amen.** → No. 32, p. 75

Optional Solemn Blessings, p. 96, and Prayers Over the People, p. 104

"Lord, teach us to pray, as John taught
his disciples."

JULY 29

17th SUNDAY IN ORDINARY TIME

ENTRANCE ANTIPHON Ps. 67 (68).5-6, 35

[Our Strength]

God is in his holy dwelling; he will give a home
to the lonely, he gives power and strength to
his people. → No. 2, p. 10

OPENING PRAYER   [Wise Use of Gifts]

God our Father and protector,
without you nothing is holy,
nothing has value.
Guide us to everlasting life
by helping us to use wisely
the blessings you have given to the world.
We ask . . . for ever and ever. ℟. **Amen.** ↓

FIRST READING Gen. 18.20-21, 23-32 [Persevering Prayer]

The Lord is just and merciful. He will hear our prayers and give us strength to handle any situation in life.

A reading from the book of Genesis

THE Lord appeared to Abraham by the oaks of Mamre and said, "How great is the outcry against Sodom and Gomorrah and how very grave their sin! I must go down and see whether they have done altogether according to the outcry that has come to me; and if not, I will know."

Then Abraham came near and said, "Will you indeed sweep away the righteous with the wicked? Suppose there are fifty righteous within the city; will you then sweep away the place and not forgive it for the fifty righteous who are in it? Far be it from you to do such a thing, to slay the righteous with the wicked, so that the righteous fare as the wicked! Far be that from you! Shall not the Judge of all the earth do what is just?" And the Lord said, "If I find at Sodom fifty righteous in the city, I will forgive the whole place for their sake."

Abraham answered, "Let me take it upon myself to speak to the Lord, I who am but dust and ashes. Suppose five of the fifty righteous are lacking? Will you destroy the whole city for lack of five?" And the Lord said, "I will not destroy it if I find forty-five there."

Again Abraham spoke to the Lord, "Suppose forty are found there." He answered, "For the sake of forty I will not do it."

Then Abraham said, "Oh do not let the Lord be angry if I speak. Suppose thirty are found there." The Lord answered, "I will not do it, if I find thirty there."

Abraham said, "Let me take it upon myself to speak to the Lord. Suppose twenty are found there." The Lord answered, "For the sake of twenty I will not destroy it."

Then Abraham said, "Oh do not let the Lord be angry if I speak just once more. Suppose ten are found there." The Lord answered, "For the sake of ten I will not destroy it."—The word of the Lord. ℟. **Thanks be to God.** ↓

RESPONSORIAL PSALM Ps. 137 (138)   [God's Help]

℟. **Lord, on the day I called for help, you an - swered me.**

(NRSV Text)	**(GRAIL Text)**
I give you thanks, O Lord, with my whole heart, before the gods I sing your praise; I bow down toward your holy temple. I give thanks to your name for your steadfast love and your faithfulness.—℟.	I thank you, Lord, with all my heart, you have heard the words of my mouth. In the presence of the angels I will bless you. I will adore before your holy temple.—℟.

For you have exalted your name
and your word above everything.
On the day I called, you answered
  me;
you increased my strength of soul.—
  ℟.

For though the Lord is high, he re-
  gards the lowly;
but the haughty he perceives from
  far away.
Though I walk in the midst of trouble,
you preserve me against the wrath of
  my enemies.—℟.

You stretch out your hand and your
  right hand delivers me.
The Lord will fulfil his purpose for
  me;
your steadfast love, O Lord, endures
  forever.
Do not forsake the work of your
  hands.—℟. ↓

I thank you for your faithfulness and
  love
which excel all we ever knew of you.
On the day I called, you answered;
you increased the strength of my
  soul.—℟.

The Lord is high yet he looks on the
  lowly
and the haughty he knows from afar.
Though I walk in the midst of affliction
you give me life and frustrate my
  foes.—℟.

You stretch out your hand and save
  me,
your hand will do all things for me.
Your love, O Lord, is eternal,
discard not the work of your
  hands.—℟. ↓

SECOND READING   Col. 2.6-14   [New Life from God]

**The merciful Lord cancels our debt, pardons all our sins.
He has given us new life in Christ.**

A reading from the letter of Paul
to the Colossians

BROTHERS and sisters, as you have received Christ Jesus the Lord, continue to
live your lives in him, rooted and built up in
him and established in the faith, just as you
were taught, abounding in thanksgiving. For in
him the whole fullness of deity dwells bodily,
and you have come to fullness in him, who is
the head of every ruler and authority.

In him also you were circumcised with a
spiritual circumcision, by putting off the body

of flesh in the circumcision of Christ. When you were buried with Christ in baptism, you were also raised with him through faith in the power of God, who raised Christ from the dead.

And when you were dead in trespasses and the uncircumcision of your flesh, God made you alive together with him, when he forgave us all our trespasses, erasing the record that stood against us with its legal demands. He set this aside, nailing it to the cross.—The word of the Lord. ℟. **Thanks be to God.** ↓

GOSPEL ACCLAMATION Rom. 8.15 [God's Children]

(If the Alleluia is not sung, the acclamation is omitted.)

℣. Alleluia. ℟. **Alleluia.**
℣. You have received the Spirit which makes us God's children,
and in that Spirit we call God our Father.
℟. **Alleluia.** ↓

GOSPEL Lk. 11.1-13   [The Lord's Prayer]

In the Lord's Prayer Jesus urges us to persevere in prayer and trust in the goodness of our loving Father.

℣. The Lord be with you. ℟. **And also with you.**
✣ A reading from the holy gospel according to Luke. ℟. **Glory to you, Lord.**

JESUS was praying in a certain place, and after he had finished, one of his disciples said to him, "Lord, teach us to pray, as John taught his disciples."

He said to them, "When you pray, say:
'Father, hallowed be your name.

Your kingdom come.
Give us each day our daily bread.
And forgive us our sins,
for we ourselves forgive everyone indebted
to us.
And do not bring us to the time of trial.' "

And Jesus said to the disciples, "Suppose one of you has a friend, and you go to him at midnight and say to him, 'Friend, lend me three loaves of bread; for a friend of mine has arrived, and I have nothing to set before him.' And your friend answers from within, 'Do not bother me; the door has already been locked, and my children are with me in bed; I cannot get up and give you anything.'

"I tell you, even though he will not get up and give him anything because he is his friend, at least because of his persistence he will get up and give him whatever he needs.

"So I say to you: Ask, and it will be given you; search, and you will find; knock, and the door will be opened for you. For everyone who asks receives, and everyone who searches finds, and for everyone who knocks, the door will be opened.

"Is there anyone among you who, if your child asks for a fish, will give a snake instead of a fish? Or if the child asks for an egg, will give a scorpion?

"If you then, who are evil, know how to give good gifts to your children, how much more will the heavenly Father give the Holy Spirit to

those who ask him!"—The gospel of the Lord.
℟. **Praise to you, Lord Jesus Christ.**

→ No. 14, p. 18

PRAYER OVER THE GIFTS   [Sanctifying Mysteries]

Lord,
receive these offerings
chosen from your many gifts.
May these mysteries make us holy
and lead us to eternal joy.
Grant this through Christ our Lord.
℟. **Amen.**   → No. 21, p. 24 (Pref. 29-36)

COMMUNION ANTIPHON Ps. 101 (102):2

[Bless the Lord]

**O, bless the Lord, my soul, and remember all
his kindness.** ↓

OR Mt. 5.7-8   [Blessed Are the Pure of Heart]

**Blessed are those who show mercy; mercy
shall be theirs. Blessed are the pure of heart,
for they shall see God.** ↓

PRAYER AFTER COMMUNION [Memorial of Christ]

Lord,
we receive the sacrament
which celebrates the memory
of the death and resurrection of Christ your
   Son.
May this gift bring us closer to our eternal salvation.
We ask this through Christ our Lord.
℟. **Amen.**   → No. 32, p. 75

Optional Solemn Blessings, p. 96, and Prayers Over the People, p. 104

"Be on your guard against all kinds of greed. . . ."

AUGUST 5

18th SUNDAY IN ORDINARY TIME

ENTRANCE ANT. Ps. 69 (70). 1, 5   [God's Help]

God, come to my help. Lord, quickly give me
assistance. You are the one who helps me and
sets me free. Lord, do not be long in coming.

→ No. 2, p. 10

OPENING PRAYER   [God's Forgiveness]

Father of everlasting goodness,
our origin and guide,
be close to us
and hear the prayers of all who praise you.
Forgive our sins and restore us to life.
Keep us safe in your love.
Grant this . . . for ever and ever. ℟. **Amen.** ↓

FIRST READING Eccl. 1. 2; 2. 21-23   [Folly of Vanity]

Without our faith all our strivings lead to nothing.

A reading from the book of Ecclesiastes

VANITY of vanities, says the Teacher,
vanity of vanities! All is vanity!

Sometimes one who has toiled with wisdom
and knowledge and skill
must leave all to be enjoyed by another
who did not toil for it.
This also is vanity and a great evil.

What do mortals get from all the toil and strain
with which they toil under the sun?
For all their days are full of pain,
and their work is a vexation;
even at night their minds do not rest.
This also is vanity.

The word of the Lord. ℟. **Thanks be to God.** ↓

RESPONSORIAL PSALM Ps. 89 (90)   [Our Refuge]

℟. In ev-er-y age, O Lord, you have been our refuge.

(℟. **O Lord, you have been our refuge from one generation to the next.**)

(NRSV Text)	(GRAIL Text)
You turn us back to dust, and say, "Turn back, you mortals."	You turn us back into dust and say: "Go back, children of the earth."
For a thousand years in your sight are like yesterday when it is past, or like a watch in the night.—℟.	To your eyes a thousand years are like yesterdays, come and gone, no more than a watch in the night.—℟.
You sweep them away; they are like a dream, like grass that is renewed in the morning; in the morning it flourishes and is renewed; in the evening it fades and withers.—℟.	You sweep us away like a dream, like grass which springs up in the morning. In the morning it springs up and flowers;

So teach us to count our days
that we may gain a wise heart.
Turn, O Lord! How long?
Have compassion on your servants!—℟.

Satisfy us in the morning with your steadfast love,
so that we may rejoice and be glad all our days.
Let the favour of the Lord our God be upon us,
and prosper for us the work of our hands.—℟. ↓

by evening it withers and fades.—℟.

Make us know the shortness of our life
that we may gain wisdom of heart.
Lord, relent! Is your anger for ever?
Show pity to your servants.—℟.

In the morning, fill us with your love;
we shall exult and rejoice all our days.
Let the favor of the Lord be upon us:
give success to the work of our hands.—℟. ↓

SECOND READING Col. 3.1-5, 9-11 [Heavenly Things]

In baptism the Christian is to die to the old self and to sin in order to live with Christ. When he appears, all who have been faithful will appear with him in glory.

A reading from the letter of Paul
to the Colossians

S O if you have been raised with Christ, seek the things that are above, where Christ is, seated at the right hand of God.

Set your minds on things that are above, not on things that are on earth, for you have died, and your life is hidden with Christ in God. When Christ who is your life is revealed, then you also will be revealed with him in glory.

Put to death, therefore, whatever in you is earthly: fornication, impurity, passion, evil desire, and greed, which is idolatry.

Do not lie to one another, seeing that you have stripped off the old self with its practices and have clothed yourselves with the new self, which is being renewed in knowledge according to the image of its creator.

In that renewal there is no longer Greek and Jew, circumcised and uncircumcised, barbarian, Scythian, slave and free; but Christ is all and in all.—The word of the Lord. ℟. **Thanks be to God.** ↓

GOSPEL ACCLAMATION Mt. 5.3 [Heirs of Heaven]

(If the Alleluia is not sung, the acclamation is omitted.)

℣. Alleluia. ℟. **Alleluia.**
℣. Blessed are the poor in spirit;
the kingdom of God is theirs!
℟. **Alleluia.** ↓

GOSPEL Lk. 12. 13-21   [True Wealth in God]

How foolish and vain are those who put all their trust in their own devices.

℣. The Lord be with you. ℟. **And also with you.**
✙ A reading from the holy gospel according to Luke. ℟. **Glory to you, Lord.**

SOMEONE in the crowd said to Jesus, "Teacher, tell my brother to divide the family inheritance with me." But Jesus said to him, "Friend, who set me to be a judge or arbitrator over you?"

And Jesus said to the crowd, "Take care! Be on your guard against all kinds of greed; for one's life does not consist in the abundance of possessions."

Then Jesus told them a parable: "The land of a rich man produced abundantly. And he thought to himself, 'What should I do, for I have no place to store my crops?' Then he said, 'I will do this: I will pull down my barns and build larger ones, and there I will store all my grain and my goods. And I will say to my soul, "Soul, you have ample goods laid up for many years; relax, eat, drink, be merry." '

"But God said to him, 'You fool! This very night your life is being demanded of you. And the things you have prepared, whose will they be?' So it is with those who store up treasures for themselves but are not rich toward God."— The gospel of the Lord. ℞. **Praise to you, Lord Jesus Christ.** → No. 14, p. 18

PRAYER OVER THE GIFTS   [Spiritual Sacrifice]

Merciful Lord,
make these gifts holy,
and let our spiritual sacrifice
make us an everlasting gift to you.
We ask this in the name of Jesus the Lord.
℞. **Amen.**   → No. 21, p. 22 (Pref. P 29-36)

COMMUNION ANT. Wis. 16.20   [Bread from Heaven]

You gave us bread from heaven, Lord: a sweet-tasting bread that was very good to eat. ↓

PRAYER AFTER COMMUNION   [Divine Strength]

Lord,
you give us the strength of new life
by the gift of the eucharist.
Protect us with your love
and prepare us for eternal redemption.
We ask this through Christ our Lord.
℞. **Amen.**   → No. 32, p. 75

Optional Solemn Blessings, p. 96, and Prayers Over the People, p. 104

"Be dressed for action and have your lamps lit."

AUGUST 12

19th SUNDAY IN ORDINARY TIME

ENTRANCE ANTIPHON Ps. 73 (74).20, 19, 22, 23

[Rise Up]

Lord, be true to your covenant, forget not the life of your poor ones for ever. Rise up, O God, and defend your cause; do not ignore the shouts of your enemies. → No. 2, p. 10

OPENING PRAYER [Growth in God's Love]

Almighty and ever-living God,
your Spirit made us your children,
confident to call you Father.
Increase your Spirit within us
and bring us to our promised inheritance.
Grant this through our Lord Jesus Christ, your
    Son,
who lives and reigns with you and the Holy
    Spirit,
one God, for ever and ever. ℟. **Amen.** ↓

FIRST READING Wis. 18.6-9   [Salvation of the Just]

The first Passover is recalled, when the faithful people of God prayed behind closed doors, and the angel of death struck at the firstborn of Egypt.

A reading from the book of Wisdom

THE night of the deliverance from Egypt
was made known beforehand to our ances-
        tors,
so that they might rejoice in sure knowledge of
    the oaths
in which they trusted.

The deliverance of the righteous
and the destruction of their enemies
were expected by your people.
For by the same means
by which you punished our enemies
you called us to yourself and glorified us.

For in secret
the holy children of good people offered sacri-
        fices,
and with one accord agreed to the divine law,
so that the saints would share alike the same
    things,
both blessings and dangers;
and already they were singing the praises of
    the ancestors.
The word of the Lord. ℟. **Thanks be to God. ↓**

RESPONSORIAL PSALM Ps. 32 (33)   [Refuge in God]

℟. Hap-py the peo-ple   the Lord has chosen to be his own.

(NRSV Text)	(GRAIL Text)
Rejoice in the Lord, O you righteous. Praise befits the upright.	Ring out your joy to the Lord, O you just; for praise is fitting for loyal hearts.
Happy is the nation whose God is the Lord, the people whom he has chosen as his heritage.—R̸.	They are happy, whose God is the Lord, the people he has chosen as his own.—R̸.
Truly the eye of the Lord is on those who fear him, on those who hope in his steadfast love, to deliver their soul from death, and to keep them alive in famine.— R̸.	The Lord looks on those who revere him, on those who hope in his love, to rescue their souls from death, to keep them alive in famine.—R̸.
Our soul waits for the Lord; he is our help and shield. Let your steadfast love, O Lord, be upon us, even as we hope in you.—R̸. ↓	Our soul is waiting for the Lord. The Lord is our help and our shield. May your love be upon us, O Lord, as we place all our hope in you.— R̸. ↓

SECOND READING Heb. 11.1-2, 8-19 or 11.1-2, 8-12

[Courageous Faith]

Abraham, our father in faith, relies on the confident assurance of what he hopes for. May we take courage from his example.

[If the "Short Form" is used, the indented text in brackets is omitted.]

A reading from the letter to the Hebrews

NOW faith is the assurance of things hoped for, the conviction of things not seen. Indeed, by faith our ancestors received approval.
By faith Abraham obeyed when he was called to set out for a place that he was to receive as an inheritance; and he set out, not knowing where he was going. By faith he stayed for a time in the land he had been prom-

ised, as in a foreign land, living in tents, as did Isaac and Jacob, who were heirs with him of the same promise.

For Abraham looked forward to the city that has foundations, whose architect and builder is God. By faith Sarah herself, though barren, received power to conceive, even when she was too old, because she considered him faithful who had promised.

Therefore from one person, and this one as good as dead, descendants were born, "as many as the stars of heaven and as the innumerable grains of sand by the seashore."

[All of these died in faith without having received the promises, but from a distance they saw and greeted them. They confessed that they were strangers and foreigners on the earth, for people who speak in this way make it clear that they are seeking a homeland. If they had been thinking of the land that they had left behind, they would have had opportunity to return.

But as it is, they desire a better country, that is, a heavenly one. Therefore God is not ashamed to be called their God; indeed, he has prepared a city for them.

By faith Abraham, when put to the test, offered up Isaac. He who had received the promises was ready to offer up his only son, of whom he had been told, "It is through Isaac that descendants shall be named for you." Abraham considered the fact that God is able even to raise someone from the dead—and figuratively speaking, he did receive Isaac back.]

The word of the Lord. ℟. **Thanks be to God.** ↓

GOSPEL ACCLAMATION Mt. 24.42, 44   [Be Ready]

(If the Alleluia is not sung, the acclamation is omitted.)

℣. Alleluia. ℟. **Alleluia.**

℣. Be watchful and ready:

you know not when the Son of Man is coming.

℟. **Alleluia.** ↓

GOSPEL Lk. 12.32-48 or 12.35-40   [Awaiting the Lord]

As the faithful people of God, we must act in accordance with our faith. We must be constant.

[If the "Short Form" is used, the indented text in brackets is omitted.]

℣. The Lord be with you. ℟. **And also with you.**
✠ A reading from the holy gospel according to Luke. ℟. **Glory to you, Lord.**

JESUS said to his disciples,
　　["Do not be afraid, little flock, for it is your Father's good pleasure to give you the kingdom. Sell your possessions, and give alms. Make purses for yourselves that do not wear out, an unfailing treasure in heaven, where no thief comes near and no moth destroys. For where your treasure is, there your heart will be also.]

"Be dressed for action and have your lamps lit; be like those who are waiting for their master to return from the wedding banquet, so that they may open the door for him as soon as he comes and knocks. Blessed are those slaves

whom the master finds alert when he comes;
truly I tell you, he will fasten his belt and have
them sit down to eat, and he will come and
serve them. If he comes during the middle of
the night, or near dawn, and finds them so,
blessed are those slaves.

"But know this: if the owner of the house had
known at what hour the thief was coming, he
would not have let his house be broken into.
You also must be ready, for the Son of Man is
coming at an unexpected hour."

[Peter said, "Lord, are you telling this
parable for us or for everyone?" And the
Lord said, "Who then is the faithful and
prudent manager whom his master will
put in charge of his slaves, to give them
their allowance of food at the proper time?
Blessed is that slave whom his master will
find at work when he arrives. Truly I tell
you, he will put that one in charge of all
his possessions. But if that slave says to
himself, 'My master is delayed in coming,'
and if he begins to beat the other slaves,
men and women, and to eat and drink and
get drunk, the master of that slave will
come on a day when he does not expect
him and at an hour that he does not know,
and will cut him in pieces, and put him
with the unfaithful.

"That slave who knew what his master
wanted, but did not prepare himself or do
what was wanted, will receive a severe
beating. But the one who did not know and

did what deserved a beating will receive a light beating.

"From everyone to whom much has been given, much will be required; and from the one to whom much has been entrusted, even more will be demanded."]

The gospel of the Lord. ℟. **Praise to you, Lord Jesus Christ.**   → No. 14, p. 18

PRAYER OVER THE GIFTS   [Sacrament of Salvation]

God of power,
giver of the gifts we bring,
accept the offering of your Church
and make it the sacrament of our salvation.
We ask this through Christ our Lord.
℟. **Amen.**   → No. 21, p. 24 (Pref. 29-36)

COMMUNION ANTIPHON Ps. 147.12, 14

[Praise God]

Praise the Lord, Jerusalem; he feeds you with the finest wheat. ↓

PRAYER AFTER COMMUNION   [Faithful to God]

Lord,
may the eucharist you give us
bring us to salvation
and keep us faithful to the light of your truth.
We ask this in the name of Jesus the Lord.
℟. **Amen.**   → No. 32, p. 75

Optional Solemn Blessings, p. 96, and Prayers Over the People, p. 104

"I came to bring fire to the earth. . . ."

AUGUST 19
20th SUNDAY IN ORDINARY TIME

ENTRANCE ANTIPHON Ps. 83 (84).9, 10

[God Our Strength]

God, our protector, keep us in mind; always give strength to your people. For if we can be with you even one day, it is better than a thousand without you. ➔ No. 2, p. 10

OPENING PRAYER [Joy Beyond Imagining]

God our Father,
may we love you in all things and above all
   things
and reach the joy you have prepared for us
beyond all our imagining.
We ask this through our Lord Jesus Christ,
   your Son,
who lives and reigns with you and the Holy
   Spirit,
one God, for ever and ever. ℟. **Amen.** ↓

FIRST READING Jer. 38.1-2ab, 4-6, 8-10   [Resurrection]

In a symbolic way the prophet's experience is a resurrection. He is buried in the cistern and later drawn up
from it.

A reading from the book of the prophet
Jeremiah

THE officials of King Zedekiah heard the
words that Jeremiah was saying to all the
people: "Thus says the Lord: 'Those who stay
in the city shall die; but those who go out to the
Chaldeans shall live.' "

Then the officials said to the king, "This man
ought to be put to death, because he is discour-
aging the soldiers who are left in this city, and
all the people, by speaking such words to them.
For this man is not seeking the welfare of this
people, but their harm."

King Zedekiah said, "Here he is; he is in your
hands; for the king is powerless against you."

So they took Jeremiah and threw him into
the cistern of Malchiah, the king's son, which
was in the court of the guard, letting Jeremiah
down by ropes. Now there was no water in the
cistern, but only mud, and Jeremiah sank in
the mud.

So Ebed-melech the Ethiopian, an officer in
the king's house, left the king's house and
spoke to the king, "My lord king, these men
have acted wickedly in all they did to the
prophet Jeremiah by throwing him into the cistern to die there of hunger, for there is no
bread left in the city." Then the king commanded Ebed-melech the Ethiopian, "Take

three men with you from here, and pull the prophet Jeremiah up from the cistern before he dies."—The word of the Lord. ℟. **Thanks be to God.** ↓

RESPONSORIAL PSALM Ps. 39 (40)

[The Lord Our Help]

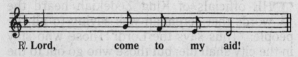

℟. **Lord,   come   to   my   aid!**

(NRSV Text)	(GRAIL Text)
I waited patiently for the Lord; he inclined to me and heard my cry.—℟.	I waited, I waited for the Lord and he stooped down to me; and heard my cry.—℟.
He drew me up from the desolate pit, out of the miry bog, and set my feet upon a rock, making my steps secure.—℟.	He drew me from the deadly pit, from the miry clay. He set my feet upon a rock and made my footsteps firm.—℟.
He put a new song in my mouth, a song of praise to our God. Many will see and fear, and put their trust in the Lord.—℟.	He put a new song into my mouth, praise of our God. Many shall see and fear and shall trust in the Lord.—℟.
As for me, I am poor and needy, but the Lord takes thought for me. You are my help and my deliverer; do not delay, O my God.—℟. ↓	As for me, wretched and poor, the Lord thinks of me. You are my rescuer, my help, O God, do not delay.—℟. ↓

SECOND READING Heb. 12.1-4   [Perseverance]

Take courage from the example of Christ. Do not lose sight of the eternal reward.

A reading from the letter to the Hebrews

SINCE we are surrounded by so great a cloud of witnesses, let us also lay aside every weight and the sin that clings so closely, and let us run with perseverance the race that is set before us, looking to Jesus the pioneer and perfecter of our faith, who for the sake of the joy that was set before him endured the cross, disregarding its shame, and has taken his seat at the right hand of the throne of God.

Consider Jesus who endured such hostility against himself from sinners, so that you may not grow weary or lose heart. In your struggle against sin you have not yet resisted to the point of shedding your blood.—The word of the Lord. ℟. **Thanks be to God.** ↓

GOSPEL ACCLAMATION Jn. 10.27   [Christ's Sheep]

(If the Alleluia is not sung, the acclamation is omitted.)

℣. Alleluia. ℟. **Alleluia.**

℣. My sheep listen to my voice, says the Lord; I know them, and they follow me.

℟. **Alleluia.** ↓

GOSPEL Lk. 12.49-53   [A Divided Household]

Many cannot find peace because they do not accept Christ. To them his coming is the cause of division.

℣. The Lord be with you. ℟. **And also with you.**
✠ A reading from the holy gospel according to Luke. ℟. **Glory to you, Lord.**

JESUS said to his disciples: "I came to bring fire to the earth, and how I wish it were already kindled! I have a baptism with which to be baptized, and what stress I am under until it is completed!

"Do you think that I have come to bring peace to the earth? No, I tell you, but rather division! From now on five in one household will be divided, three against two and two against three; they will be divided: father against son and son against father, mother against daughter and daughter against mother, mother-in-law against her daughter-in-law and daughter-in-law against mother-in-law."—The gospel of the Lord. ℟. **Praise to you, Lord Jesus Christ.**

→ No. 14, p. 18

PRAYER OVER THE GIFTS   [A Holy Exchange]

Lord,
accept our sacrifice
as a holy exchange of gifts.
By offering what you have given us
may we receive the gift of yourself.
We ask this in the name of Jesus the Lord.
℟. **Amen.**   → No. 21, p. 24 (Pref. 29-36)

COMMUNION ANTIPHON Ps. 129 (130).7

[Full Redemption]

With the Lord there is mercy, and fullness of redemption. ↓

PRAYER AFTER COMMUNION   [One with Christ]

God of mercy,
by this sacrament you make us one with
   Christ.
By becoming more like him on earth,
may we come to share his glory in heaven,
where he lives and reigns for ever and ever.
℟. **Amen.**   → No. 32, p. 75

Optional Solemn Blessings, p. 96, and Prayers Over the People, p. 104

"Strive to enter through the narrow door; for many . . .
will try to enter and will not be able."

AUGUST 26

21st SUNDAY IN ORDINARY TIME

ENTRANCE ANTIPHON Ps. 85 (86).1-3   [Save Us]

Listen, Lord, and answer me. Save your servant who trusts in you. I call to you all day long, have mercy on me, O Lord. ➜ No. 2, p. 10

OPENING PRAYER   [One in Mind and Heart]

Father,
help us to seek the values,
that will bring us enduring joy in this changing
   world.
In our desire for what you promise
make us one in mind and heart.
Grant this . . . for ever and ever. ℟. **Amen.** ↓

FIRST READING Isa. 66.18-21   [Salvation Offered to All]

Salvation is offered to all and will embrace all, even the alien, some of whom will receive the sacred duty to minister the Holy Mysteries.

A reading from the book of the prophet Isaiah

THUS says the Lord: "For I know their works and their thoughts, and I am coming to gather all nations and tongues; and they shall come and shall see my glory, and I will set a sign among them.

"From them I will send survivors to the nations, to Tarshish, Put, and Lud—which draw the bow—to Tubal and Javan, to the coastlands far away that have not heard of my fame or seen my glory; and they shall declare my glory among the nations.

"They shall bring all your kindred from all the nations as an offering to the Lord, on horses, and in chariots, and in litters, and on mules, and on dromedaries, to my holy mountain Jerusalem," says the Lord, "just as the Israelites bring a grain offering in a clean vessel to the house of the Lord.

"And I will also take some of them as priests and as Levites," says the Lord.—The word of the Lord. ℟. **Thanks be to God.** ↓

RESPONSORIAL PSALM Ps. 116 (117)   [God's Love]

℟. Go out   to   all   the   world and tell the Good News.

(℟. Go out to the whole world, and proclaim the Good News.)

(NRSV Text)	(Grail Text)
Praise the Lord, all you nations! Extol him, all you peoples!—℟.	O praise the Lord, all you nations, acclaim him all you peoples!—℟.
For great is his steadfast love toward us, and the faithfulness of the Lord endures forever.—℟. ↓	Strong is his love for us; he is faithful for ever.—℟. ↓

SECOND READING Heb. 12.5-7, 11-13 [Discipline]

Look beyond trials and tribulations, remain steadfast in faith, and rely on the goodness and love of God. For he disciplines those he loves.

A reading from the letter to the Hebrews

AND you have forgotten the exhortation that addresses you as children—
"My child, do not regard lightly the discipline of the Lord,
 or lose heart when you are punished by him;
for the Lord disciplines those whom he loves,
 and chastises every child whom he accepts."

Endure trials for the sake of discipline. God is treating you as children; for what child is there whom a parent does not discipline?

Now, discipline always seems painful rather than pleasant at the time, but later it yields the peaceful fruit of righteousness to those who have been trained by it.

Therefore lift your drooping hands and strengthen your weak knees, and make straight paths for your feet, so that what is lame may not be put out of joint, but rather be healed.—The word of the Lord. ℟. **Thanks be to God.** ↓

GOSPEL ACCLAMATION Jn. 14.6   [Through Christ]

(If the Alleluia is not sung, the acclamation is omitted.)

℣. Alleluia. ℟. **Alleluia.**

℣. I am the way, the truth, and the life, says the Lord;

no one comes to the Father except through me.

℟. **Alleluia.** ↓

GOSPEL Lk. 13.22-30   [Saved through Repentance]

The kingdom of God will extend to people from all over, but all who have rejected the Word will find themselves as outcasts.

℣. The Lord be with you. ℟. **And also with you.**

✤ A reading from the holy gospel according to Luke. ℟. **Glory to you, Lord.**

JESUS went through one town and village after another, teaching as he made his way to Jerusalem. Someone asked him, "Lord, will only a few be saved?"

Jesus said to them, "Strive to enter through the narrow door; for many, I tell you, will try to enter and will not be able.

"When once the owner of the house has got up and shut the door, and you begin to stand outside and to knock at the door, saying, 'Lord, open to us,' then in reply he will say to you, 'I do not know where you come from.'

"Then you will begin to say, 'We ate and drank with you, and you taught in our streets.' But the Lord will say, 'I do not know where you come from; go away from me, all you evildoers!'

"There will be weeping and gnashing of teeth when you see Abraham and Isaac and

Jacob and all the prophets in the kingdom of God, and you yourselves thrown out. Then people will come from east and west, from north and south, and will eat in the kingdom of God.

"Indeed, some are last who will be first, and some are first who will be last."—The gospel of the Lord. ℟. **Praise to you, Lord Jesus Christ.**

➙ No. 14, p. 18

PRAYER OVER THE GIFTS   [Peace and Unity]

Merciful God,
the perfect sacrifice of Jesus Christ
made us your people.
In your love,
grant peace and unity to your Church.
We ask this in the name of Jesus the Lord.
℟. **Amen.**   ➙ No. 21, p. 24 (Pref. 29-36)

COMMUNION ANTIPHON Ps. 103 (104).13-15

[God's Gift]

Lord, the earth is filled with your gift from heaven; man grows bread from earth, and wine to cheer his heart. ↓

PRAYER AFTER COMMUNION   [Pleasing God]

Lord,
may this eucharist increase within us
the healing power of your love.
May it guide and direct our efforts
to please you in all things.
We ask this in the name of Jesus the Lord.
℟. **Amen.**   ➙ No. 32, p. 75

Optional Solemn Blessings, p. 96, and Prayers Over the People, p. 104

"All who exalt themselves will be humbled. . . ."

SEPTEMBER 2

22nd SUNDAY IN ORDINARY TIME

ENTRANCE ANTIPHON Ps. 85 (86).3, 5   [Call to God]

I call to you all day long, have mercy on me, O Lord. You are good and forgiving, full of love for all who call to you.   → No. 2, p. 10

OPENING PRAYER   [Increasing Our Spiritual Gifts]

Almighty God,
every good thing comes from you.
Fill our hearts with love for you,
increase our faith,
and by your constant care
protect the good you have given us.
We ask this . . . for ever and ever. ℟. **Amen.** ↓

FIRST READING Sir. 3.17-20, 28-29   [Humility]

Know your own limitations. Live within your own capabilities.

A reading from the book of Sirach

514

MY child, perform your tasks with humility;
then you will be loved by those whom
God accepts.
The greater you are,
the more you must humble yourself;
so you will find favour in the sight of the Lord.
Many are lofty and renowned,
but to the humble the Lord reveals his secrets.
For great is the might of the Lord;
but by the humble he is glorified.
When calamity befalls the proud,
there is no healing,
for an evil plant has taken root in them.
The mind of the intelligent appreciates proverbs,
and an attentive ear is the desire of the wise.
The word of the Lord. ℟. **Thanks be to God.** ↓

RESPONSORIAL PSALM Ps. 67 (68)   [Home for Poor]

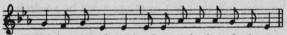

℟. **God, in your good-ness, you have made a home for the poor.**

(℟. **In your goodness, O God, you prepared a home for the poor.**)

(NRSV Text)	(GRAIL Text)
Let the righteous be joyful; let them exult before God; let them be jubilant with joy. Sing to God, sing praises to his name; his name is the Lord, be exultant before him.—℟.	The just shall rejoice at the presence of God, they shall exult and dance for joy. O sing to the Lord, make music to his name; rejoice in the Lord, exult at his presence.—℟.
Father of orphans and protector of widows is God in his holy habitation.	Father of the orphan, defender of the widow, such is God in his holy place.

God gives the desolate a home to live in;

he leads out the prisoners to prosperity.—℟.

Rain in abundance, O God, you showered abroad;

you restored your heritage when it languished;

your flock found a dwelling in it;

in your goodness, O God, you provided for the needy.—℟. ↓

God gives the lonely a home to live in;

he leads the prisoners forth into freedom.—℟.

You poured down, O God, a generous rain;

when your people were starved you gave them new life.

It was there that your people found a home,

prepared in your goodness, O God, for the poor.—℟. ↓

SECOND READING Heb. 12.18-19, 22-24a   **[Drawn to God]**

We are drawn to God who loves us and gives us faith. We are not driven to God out of fear.

A reading from the letter to the Hebrews

Y OU have not come to something that can be touched, a blazing fire, and darkness, and gloom, and a tempest, and the sound of a trumpet, and a voice whose words made the hearers beg that not another word be spoken to them.

But you have come to Mount Zion and to the city of the living God, the heavenly Jerusalem, and to innumerable angels in festal gathering, and to the assembly of the firstborn who are enroled in heaven, and to God the judge of all, and to the spirits of the righteous made perfect, and to Jesus, the mediator of a new covenant.—The word of the Lord. ℟. **Thanks be to God.** ↓

GOSPEL ACCLAMATION Mt. 11.29   **[Christ's Yoke]**

(If the Alleluia is not sung, the acclamation is omitted.)

℣. Alleluia. ℟. **Alleluia.**

℣. Take my yoke upon you;

learn from me, for I am gentle and lowly of heart.
℟. **Alleluia.** ↓

GOSPEL Lk. 14.1, 7-14   [The Reward of Humility]

> **Act in true humility. Do not be frustrated by trying to
> create an "image" for yourself.**

℣. The Lord be with you. ℟. **And also with you.**
✠ A reading from the holy gospel according to
Luke. ℟. **Glory to you, Lord.**

ON one occasion when Jesus was going to
the house of a leader of the Pharisees to
eat a meal on the sabbath, the lawyers and
Pharisees were watching him closely. When
Jesus noticed how the guests chose the places
of honour, he told them a parable.

"When you are invited by someone to a wedding banquet, do not sit down at the place of honour, in case someone more distinguished than
you has been invited by your host; and the host
who invited both of you may come and say to
you, 'Give this person your place,' and then in
disgrace you would start to take the lowest place.

"But when you are invited, go and sit down
at the lowest place, so that when your host
comes, he may say to you, 'Friend, move up
higher'; then you will be honoured in the presence of all who sit at the table with you. For all
who exalt themselves will be humbled, and
those who humble themselves will be exalted."

Jesus said also to the Pharisee who had invited him, "When you give a luncheon or a din-
ner, do not invite your friends or your brothers
or sisters or your relatives or rich neighbours,

in case they may invite you in return, and you would be repaid. But when you give a banquet, invite the poor, the crippled, the lame, and the blind. And you will be blessed, because they cannot repay you, for you will be repaid at the resurrection of the righteous."—The gospel of the Lord. ℟. **Praise to you, Lord Jesus Christ.**

→ No. 14, p. 18

PRAYER OVER THE GIFTS   [Promise of Salvation]

Lord,
may this holy offering
bring us your blessing
and accomplish within us
its promise of salvation.
Grant this through Christ our Lord.
℟. **Amen.**   → No. 21, p. 24 (Pref. 29-36)

COMMUNION ANTIPHON Ps. 30 (31).19

[God's Kindness]

O Lord, how great is the depth of the kindness which you have shown to those who love you. ↓

OR Mt. 5.9-10   [Blessed Are the Peacemakers]

Blessed are the peacemakers; they shall be called sons of God. Blessed are they who suffer persecution for the sake of justice; the kingdom of heaven is theirs. ↓

PRAYER AFTER COMMUNION   [Renewed in Love]

Lord,
you renew us at your table with the bread of life.
May this food strengthen us in love
and help us to serve you in each other.

We ask this in the name of Jesus the Lord.
℞. **Amen.**   → No. 32, p. 75

Optional Solemn Blessings, p. 96, and Prayers Over the People, p. 104

*"Whoever does not carry the cross and follow me
cannot be my disciple."*

SEPTEMBER 9

23rd SUNDAY IN ORDINARY TIME

ENTRANCE ANTIPHON Ps. 118 (119).137, 124 [Mercy]
**Lord, you are just, and the judgments you
make are right. Show mercy when you judge
me, your servant.**   → No. 2, p. 10

OPENING PRAYER   [Christian Freedom]
God our Father,
you redeem us
and make us your children in Christ.
Look upon us,
give us true freedom
and bring us to the inheritance you promised.
Grant this . . . for ever and ever. ℞. **Amen.** ↓

FIRST READING Wis. 9.13-18   [God's Counsel]

Our human knowledge (science) alone cannot reach the heights attained by faith.

A reading from the book of Wisdom

FOR who can learn the counsel of God?
Or who can discern what the Lord wills?
For the reasoning of mortals is worthless,
and our designs are likely to fail;
for a perishable body weighs down the soul,
and this earthy tent burdens the thoughtful mind.

We can hardly guess at what is on earth,
and what is at hand we find with labour;
but who has traced out what is in the heavens?
Who has learned your counsel,
unless you have given wisdom
and sent your holy spirit from on high?

And thus the paths of those on earth were set
    right,
and people were taught what pleases you,
and were saved by wisdom.
The word of the Lord. ℟. **Thanks be to God.** ↓

RESPONSORIAL PSALM Ps. 89 (90) [God Our Refuge]

℟. In ev-ery age, O Lord, you have been our refuge.

(℟. **O Lord, you have been our refuge from one generation to the next.**)

(NRSV Text)	(GRAIL Text)
You turn us back to dust, and say, "Turn back, you mortals."	You turn us back into dust and say: "Go back, children of the earth."
For a thousand years in your sight are like yesterday when it is past, or like a watch in the night.—℟.	To your eyes a thousand years are like yesterdays, come and gone,

You sweep them away; they are like a dream,

like grass that is renewed in the morning;

in the morning it flourishes and is renewed;

in the evening it fades and withers.—R̂.

So teach us to count our days
that we may gain a wise heart.
Turn, O Lord! How long?
Have compassion on your servants!—R̂.

Satisfy us in the morning with your steadfast love,

so that we may rejoice and be glad all our days.

Let the favour of the Lord our God be upon us,

and prosper for us the work of our hands.—R̂. ↓

no more than a watch in the night.—R̂.

You sweep us away like a dream,

like grass which springs up in the morning.

In the morning it springs up and flowers;

by evening it withers and fades.—R̂.

Make us know the shortness of our life

that we may gain wisdom of heart.

Lord, repent! Is your anger for ever?

Show pity to your servants.—R̂.

In the morning, fill us with your love;

we shall exult and rejoice all our days.

Let the favour of the Lord be upon us:

give success to the work of our hands.—R̂. ↓

SECOND READING Philem. 9b-10, 12-17

[Brothers in Christ]

Paul has converted a runaway slave, and he asks the slave's master to forgive the man.

A reading from the letter of Paul to Philemon

I, PAUL, do this as an old man, and now also as a prisoner of Christ Jesus. I am appealing to you for my child, Onesimus, whose father I have become during my imprisonment.

I am sending him, that is, my own heart, back to you. I wanted to keep him with me, so that he might be of service to me in your place during my imprisonment for the gospel; but I preferred to do nothing without your consent, in order that your good deed might be voluntary and not something forced.

Perhaps this is the reason he was separated from you for a while, so that you might have him back forever, no longer as a slave but more than a slave, a beloved brother—especially to me but how much more to you, both in the flesh and in the Lord.

So if you consider me your partner, welcome him as you would welcome me.—The word of the Lord. ℟. **Thanks be to God.** ↓

GOSPEL ACCLAMATION Ps. 118 (119).135 [Teach Us]
(If the Alleluia is not sung, the acclamation is omitted.)

℣. Alleluia. ℟. **Alleluia.**
℣. Let your face shine on your servant,
and teach me your laws.
℟. **Alleluia.** ↓

GOSPEL Lk. 14.25-33   [Following Christ]

We are all careful to estimate the cost of worldly ventures. We must also be willing to sacrifice whatever is necessary to preserve our faith.

℣. The Lord be with you. ℟. **And also with you.**
✝ A reading from the holy gospel according to Luke. ℟. **Glory to you, Lord.**

LARGE crowds were travelling with Jesus; and he turned and said to them, "Whoever comes to me and does not hate father and mother, spouse and children, brothers and sisters, yes, and even life itself, cannot be my disciple. Whoever does not carry the cross and follow me cannot be my disciple.

"For which of you, intending to build a tower, does not first sit down and estimate the cost, to see whether he has enough to complete it? Otherwise, when he has laid a foundation and is not able to finish, all who see it will begin to ridicule him, saying, 'This fellow began to build and was not able to finish.'

"Or what king, going out to wage war against another king, will not sit down first and consider whether he is able with ten thousand to oppose the one who comes against him with twenty thousand? If he cannot, then, while the other is still far away, he sends a delegation and asks for the terms of peace.

"So therefore, none of you can become my disciple if you do not give up all your possessions."—The gospel of the Lord. ℟. **Praise to you, Lord Jesus Christ.**   → No. 14, p. 18

PRAYER OVER THE GIFTS   [True Worship]

God of peace and love,
may our offering bring you true worship
and make us one with you.
We ask this in the name of Jesus the Lord.
℟. **Amen.**   → No. 21, p. 24 (Pref. 29-36)

COMMUNION ANTIPHON Ps. 41 (42).1-2   [Longing]

Like a deer that longs for running streams, my soul longs for you, my God. My soul is thirsting for the living God. ↓

OR Jn. 8.12   [The Light of Life]

I am the light of the world, says the Lord; the man who follows me will have the light of life. ↓

PRAYER AFTER COMMUNION   [Food and Life]

Lord,
your word and your sacrament
give us food and life.
May this gift of your Son
lead us to share his life for ever.
We ask this through Christ our Lord.
R̸. **Amen.**   → No. 32, p. 75

Optional Solemn Blessings, p. 96, and Prayers Over the People, p. 104

"Rejoice with me, for I have found my sheep. . . ."

SEPTEMBER 16

24th SUNDAY IN ORDINARY TIME

ENTRANCE ANTIPHON See Sir. 36.21-22 [God's Peace]

**Give peace, Lord, to those who wait for you
and your prophets will proclaim you as you deserve. Hear the prayers of your servant and of
your people Israel.**   → No. 2, p. 10

OPENING PRAYER   [Faithful in God's Service]

Almighty God,
our creator and guide,
may we serve you with all our heart
and know your forgiveness in our lives.
We ask this . . . for ever and ever. ℟. **Amen.** ↓

FIRST READING Ex. 32.7-11, 13-14 [The Plea of Moses]

Despite the unfaithfulness of his people, the Lord remains true to his covenant.

A reading from the book of Exodus

AT the top of Mount Sinai, the Lord said to
Moses, "Go down at once! Your people,
whom you brought up out of the land of Egypt,
have acted perversely; they have been quick to
turn aside from the way that I commanded
them; they have cast for themselves an image
of a calf, and have worshipped it and sacrificed
to it, and said, 'These are your gods, O Israel,
who brought you up out of the land of Egypt!' "

The Lord said to Moses, "I have seen this
people, how stiff-necked they are. Now let me
alone, so that my wrath may burn hot against
them and I may consume them; and of you I
will make a great nation."

But Moses implored the Lord his God, and
said, "O Lord, why does your wrath burn hot
against your people, whom you brought out of
the land of Egypt with great power and with a
mighty hand? Remember Abraham, Isaac, and
Israel, your servants, how you swore to them
by your own self, saying to them, 'I will multiply your descendants like the stars of heaven,

and all this land that I have promised I will give to your descendants, and they shall inherit it forever.' "

And the Lord changed his mind about the disaster that he planned to bring on his people.—The word of the Lord. ℟. **Thanks be to God.** ↓

RESPONSORIAL PSALM Ps. 50 (51) [A Contrite Heart]

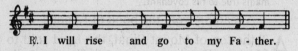

℟. I will rise and go to my Fa - ther.

(℟. I will leave this place and go to my Father.)

(NRSV Text)	(GRAIL Text)
Have mercy on me, O God, according to your steadfast love; according to your abundant mercy blot out my transgressions. Wash me thoroughly from my iniquity, and cleanse me from my sin.—℟.	Have mercy on me, God, in your kindness. In your compassion blot out my offense. O wash me more and more from my guilt and cleanse me from my sin.—℟.
Create in me a clean heart, O God, and put a new and right spirit within me. Do not cast me away from your presence, and do not take your holy spirit from me.—℟.	A pure heart create for me, O God, put a steadfast spirit within me. Do not cast me away from your presence, nor deprive me of your holy spirit.—℟.
O Lord, open my lips, and my mouth will declare your praise. The sacrifice acceptable to God is a broken spirit; a broken and contrite heart, O God, you will not despise.—℟. ↓	O Lord, open my lips and my mouth shall declare your praise. My sacrifice, a contrite spirit, a humbled, contrite heart you will not spurn.—℟. ↓

SECOND READING 1 Tim. 1.12-17   [God's Mercy]

Christ has come to bring salvation to sinners. We have but to turn to him and we will receive grace in over-flowing measure.

A reading from the first letter of Paul to Timothy

I AM grateful to Christ Jesus our Lord, who has strengthened me, because he judged me faithful and appointed me to his service, even though I was formerly a blasphemer, a persecutor, and a man of violence.

But I received mercy because I had acted ignorantly in unbelief, and the grace of our Lord overflowed for me with the faith and love that are in Christ Jesus.

The saying is sure and worthy of full acceptance, that Christ Jesus came into the world to save sinners—of whom I am the foremost.

But for that very reason I received mercy, so that in me, as the foremost, Jesus Christ might display the utmost patience, making me an example to those who would come to believe in him for eternal life.

To the King of the ages, immortal, invisible, the only God, be honour and glory forever and ever. Amen.—The word of the Lord. ℟. **Thanks be to God. ↓**

GOSPEL ACCLAMATION 2 Cor. 5.19   [Reconciliation]

(If the Alleluia is not sung, the acclamation is omitted.)

℣. Alleluia. ℟. **Alleluia.**

℣. God was in Christ, to reconcile the world to himself;

and the good news of reconciliation he has entrusted to us.

℟. **Alleluia.** ↓

GOSPEL Lk. 15.1-32 or 15.1-10   [The Prodigal Son]

Repentance, turning away from sin, brings joy to all.
Not only the one who repents, but all who love and
care.

*[If the "Short Form" is used, the indented text in
brackets is omitted.]*

℣. The Lord be with you. ℟. **And also with you.**
✠ A reading from the holy gospel according to
Luke. ℟. **Glory to you, Lord.**

ALL the tax collectors and sinners were
coming near to listen to Jesus. And the
Pharisees and the scribes were grumbling and
saying, "This fellow welcomes sinners and eats
with them."

So Jesus told them a parable: "Which one of
you, having a hundred sheep and losing one of
them, does not leave the ninety-nine in the
wilderness and go after the one that is lost until
he finds it? When he has found it, he lays it on
his shoulders and rejoices. And when he comes
home, he calls together his friends and neighbours, saying to them, 'Rejoice with me, for I
have found my sheep that was lost.' Just so, I tell
you, there will be more joy in heaven over one
sinner who repents than over ninety-nine righteous persons who need no repentance.

"Or what woman having ten silver coins, if she
loses one of them, does not light a lamp, sweep
the house, and search carefully until she finds it?

When she has found it, she calls together her friends and neighbours, saying, 'Rejoice with me, for I have found the coin that I had lost.' Just so, I tell you, there is joy in the presence of the angels of God over one sinner who repents."

[Then Jesus said, "There was a man who had two sons. The younger of them said to his father, 'Father, give me the share of the property that will belong to me.' So the father divided his property between them.

"A few days later the younger son gathered all he had and travelled to a distant country, and there he squandered his property in dissolute living. When he had spent everything, a severe famine took place throughout that country, and he began to be in need. So he went and hired himself out to one of the citizens of that country, who sent him to his fields to feed the pigs. The young man would gladly have filled himself with the pods that the pigs were eating; and no one gave him anything.

"But when he came to himself he said, 'How many of my father's hired hands have bread enough and to spare, but here I am dying of hunger! I will get up and go to my father, and I will say to him, "Father, I have sinned against heaven and before you; I am no longer worthy to be called your son; treat me like one of your hired hands."'

"So he set off and went to his father. But while he was still far off, his father saw him and was filled with compassion; he ran and put his arms around him and kissed him. Then the son said to him, 'Father, I have sinned against heaven and before you; I am no longer worthy to be called your son.'

"But the father said to his slaves, 'Quickly, bring out a robe—the best one—and put it on him; put a ring on his finger and sandals on his feet. And get the fatted calf and kill it, and let us eat and celebrate; for this son of mine was dead and is alive again; he was lost and is found!' And they began to celebrate.

"Now his elder son was in the field; and when he came and approached the house, he heard music and dancing. He called one of the slaves and asked what was going on. The slave replied, 'Your brother has come, and your father has killed the fatted calf, because he has got him back safe and sound.' Then the elder son became angry and refused to go in. His father came out and began to plead with him. But he answered his father, 'Listen! For all these years I have been working like a slave for you, and I have never disobeyed your command; yet you have never given me even a young goat so that I might celebrate with my friends. But when this son of yours came back, who has devoured your property with prostitutes, you killed the fatted calf for him!'

"Then the father said to him, 'Son, you are always with me, and all that is mine is yours. But we had to celebrate and rejoice, because this brother of yours was dead and has come to life; he was lost and has been found.' "]

The gospel of the Lord. ℟. **Praise to you, Lord Jesus Christ.**   ➙ No. 14, p. 18

PRAYER OVER THE GIFTS   [Hear Our Prayer]

Lord,
hear the prayers of your people
and receive our gifts.
May the worship of each one here
bring salvation to all.
Grant this through Christ our Lord.
℟. **Amen.**   ➙ No. 21, p. 24 (Pref. 29-36)

COMMUNION ANTIPHON Ps. 35 (36).7 [God's Mercy]

O God, how much we value your mercy! All mankind can gather under your protection. ↓

OR See 1 Cor. 10.16   [Share of Christ]

When we break the bread, we share in the body of the Lord; when we bless the cup, we share in the blood of Christ. ↓

PRAYER AFTER COMMUNION   [Eucharist and Spirit]

Lord,
may the eucharist you have given us
influence our thoughts and actions.
May your Spirit guide and direct us in your way.
We ask this in the name of Jesus the Lord.
℟. **Amen.**   ➙ No. 32, p. 75

Optional Solemn Blessings, p. 96, and Prayers Over the People, p. 104

"Give me an accounting of your management. . . ."

SEPTEMBER 23

25th SUNDAY IN ORDINARY TIME

ENTRANCE ANTIPHON   [Saviour of All]

I am the Saviour of all people, says the Lord.
Whatever their troubles, I will answer their cry,
and I will always be their Lord.   → No. 2, p. 10

OPENING PRAYER   [Growth in Love]

Father,
guide us, as you guide creation
according to your law of love.
May we love one another
and come to perfection
in the eternal life prepared for us.
Grant this . . . for ever and ever. R/. **Amen.** ↓

FIRST READING Am. 8.4-7   [The Just Are Persecuted]

The Lord will punish those who cheat and oppress the
poor. There is no place for the gouger, the con-artist,
the greedy.

A reading from the book of the prophet Amos

532

HEAR this, you that trample on the needy,
and bring to ruin the poor of the land,
saying, "When will the new moon be over so
that we may sell grain;
and the sabbath, so that we may offer wheat
for sale?
We will measure out less and charge more,
and tamper with the scales,
buying the poor for silver
and the needy for a pair of sandals,
and selling the sweepings of the wheat."

The Lord has sworn by the pride of Jacob:
"Surely I will never forget any of their deeds."
The word of the Lord. ℟. **Thanks be to God.** ↓

RESPONSORIAL PSALM Ps. 112 (113)   [Praise the Lord]

℟. **Praise the Lord who lifts up the poor.**

℟. Or: **Alleluia! Alleluia! Alleluia!**

(NRSV Text)

Praise, O servants of the Lord;
praise the name of the Lord.
Blessed be the name of the Lord
from this time on and forevermore.—
℟.

The Lord is high above all nations,
and his glory above the heavens.
Who is like the Lord our God, who is
seated on high,
who looks far down on the heavens
and the earth?—℟.

The Lord raises the poor from the dust,
and lifts the needy from the ash heap,

(GRAIL Text)

Praise, O servants of the Lord,
praise the name of the Lord!
May the name of the Lord be blessed
both now and for evermore.—℟.

High above all nations is the Lord,
above the heavens his glory.
Who is like the Lord, our God,
who has risen on high to his throne
yet stoops from the heights to look
down,
to look down upon heaven and
earth?—℟.

From the dust he lifts up the lowly,
from the dungheap he raises the poor

| to make them sit with princes, with the princes of his people.— ℟. ↓ | to set them in the company of rulers, yes, with the rulers of his people.— ℟. ↓ |

SECOND READING 1 Tim. 2.1-7   [Christ Our Mediator]

We should pray with a pure heart and blameless hands. Our prayers of the faithful in this Mass continue our prayer for all.

A reading from the first letter of Paul
to Timothy

MY dearly beloved, I urge that supplications, prayers, intercessions, and thanksgivings be made for everyone, for kings and all who are in high positions, so that we may lead a quiet and peaceable life in all godliness and dignity. This is right and is acceptable in the sight of God our Saviour, who desires everyone to be saved and to come to the knowledge of the truth.

For there is one God; there is also one mediator between God and the human race, Christ Jesus, himself human, who gave himself a ransom for all; this was attested at the right time.

For this I was appointed a herald and an apostle, a teacher of the Gentiles in faith and truth. I am telling the truth, I am not lying.— The word of the Lord. ℟. **Thanks be to God.** ↓

GOSPEL ACCLAMATION 2 Cor. 8.9   [Poor but Rich]

(If the Alleluia is not sung, the acclamation is omitted.)

℣. Alleluia. ℟. **Alleluia.**
℣. Jesus Christ was rich but he became poor, to make you rich out of his poverty.
℟. **Alleluia.** ↓

GOSPEL Lk. 16.1-13 or 16.10-13   [The Wily Manager]

If we are shrewd in an evil way, we may be admired by other evil people for our cleverness. But we cannot win in the long run. We cannot divide ourselves between God and worldly gain.

[If the "Short Form" is used, the indented text in brackets is omitted.]

℣. The Lord be with you. ℟. **And also with you.**
✛ A reading from the holy gospel according to Luke. ℟. **Glory to you, Lord.**

JESUS said to the disciples,
["There was a rich man who had a manager, and charges were brought to him that the manager was squandering his property. So the rich man summoned him and said to him, 'What is this that I hear about you? Give me an accounting of your management, because you cannot be my manager any longer.'

"Then the manager said to himself, 'What will I do, now that my master is taking the position away from me? I am not strong enough to dig, and I am ashamed to beg. I have decided what to do so that, when I am dismissed as manager, people may welcome me into their homes.'

"So, summoning his master's debtors one by one, he asked the first, 'How much do you owe my master?' He answered, 'A hundred jugs of olive oil.' He said to him, 'Take your bill, sit down quickly, and make it fifty.' Then he asked another, 'And how much do you owe?' He replied, 'A hundred containers of wheat.' He said to him, 'Take your bill and make it eighty.'

"And his master commended the dishonest manager because he had acted shrewdly; for the children of this age are more shrewd in dealing with their own generation than are the children of light.

"And I tell you, make friends for yourselves by means of dishonest wealth so that when it is gone, they may welcome you into the eternal homes.]

"Whoever is faithful in a very little is faithful also in much; and whoever is dishonest in a very little is dishonest also in much. If then you have not been faithful with the dishonest wealth, who will entrust to you the true riches? And if you have not been faithful with what belongs to another, who will give you what is your own?

"No slave can serve two masters; for a slave will either hate the one and love the other, or be devoted to the one and despise the other. You cannot serve God and wealth."—The gospel of the Lord. ℟. **Praise to you, Lord Jesus Christ.**

➜ No. 14, p. 18

PRAYER OVER THE GIFTS   [Gifts Become Eucharist]

Lord,
may these gifts which we now offer
to show our belief and our love
be pleasing to you.
May they become for us
the eucharist of Jesus Christ your Son,
who is Lord for ever and ever.
℟. **Amen.**   ➜ No. 21, p. 24 (Pref. 29-36)

COMMUNION ANTIPHON Ps. 118 (119).4-5 [God's Law]

You have laid down your precepts to be faithfully kept. May my footsteps be firm in keeping your commands. ↓

OR Jn. 10.14   [The Good Shepherd]

I am the Good Shepherd, says the Lord; I know my sheep, and mine know me. ↓

PRAYER AFTER COMMUNION [Eucharist in Action]

Lord,
help us with your kindness.
Make us strong through the eucharist.
May we put into action
the saving mystery we celebrate.
We ask this in the name of Jesus the Lord.
℟. **Amen.**   ➜ No. 32, p. 75

Optional Solemn Blessings, p. 96, and Prayers Over the People, p. 104

"He . . . saw Abraham far away with Lazarus by his side."

SEPTEMBER 30

26th SUNDAY IN ORDINARY TIME

ENTRANCE ANTIPHON Dan. 3.31, 29, 30, 43, 42

[God's Kindness]

O Lord, you had just cause to judge men as you did: because we sinned against you and disobeyed your will. But now show us your greatness of heart, and treat us with your unbounded kindness.

→ No. 2, p. 10

OPENING PRAYER [God's Forgiveness]

Father,
you show your almighty power
in your mercy and forgiveness.
Continue to fill us with your gifts of love.
Help us to hurry toward the eternal life you
 promise
and come to share in the joys of your kingdom.
Grant this . . . for ever and ever. ℟. **Amen.** ↓

FIRST READING Am. 6.1a, 4-7   [Lack of Compassion]

> The prophet Amos castigates those who sit in the lap of luxury and pay no attention to the needs of others.

A reading from the book of the prophet Amos

THUS says the Lord, the God of hosts:
"Alas for those who are at ease in Zion,
and for those who feel secure on Mount Samaria!

"Alas for those who lie on beds of ivory,
and lounge on their couches,
and eat lambs from the flock,
and calves from the stall;
who sing idle songs to the sound of the harp,
and like David improvise on instruments of music;
who drink wine from bowls,
and anoint themselves with the finest oils,
but are not grieved over the ruin of Joseph!

"Therefore they shall now be the first to go into exile,
and the revelry of those who lie in ease shall pass away."

The word of the Lord. ℟. **Thanks be to God.** ↓

RESPONSORIAL PSALM Ps. 145 (146)

[Praise the Lord]

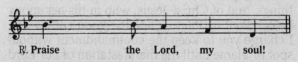

℟. **Praise   the Lord,   my   soul!**

(℟. **My soul give praise to the Lord.**)

℟. Or: **Alleluia! Alleluia! Alleluia!**

(NRSV Text)	(GRAIL Text)
It is the Lord who keeps faith forever, who executes justice for the oppressed; who gives food to the hungry. The Lord sets the prisoners free.—℞.	It is the Lord who keeps faith for ever, who is just to those who are oppressed. It is God who gives bread to the hungry, the Lord, who sets prisoners free.—℞.
The Lord opens the eyes of the blind and lifts up those who are bowed down; the Lord loves the righteous and watches over the strangers.—℞.	It is the Lord who gives sight to the blind, who raises up those who are bowed down, the Lord, who protects the stranger and upholds the widow and orphan.—℞.
The Lord upholds the orphan and the widow, but the way of the wicked he brings to ruin. The Lord will reign forever, your God, O Zion, for all generations.—℞. ↓	It is the Lord who loves the just but thwarts the path of the wicked. The Lord will reign for ever, Zion's God, from age to age. Alleluia.—℞. ↓

SECOND READING 1 Tim. 6.11-16   [A Virtuous Life]

In faith is salvation. Be positive and steadfast; hold firm for the Lord Jesus will come again.

A reading from the first letter of Paul to Timothy

AS for you, Timothy, man of God; pursue righteousness, godliness, faith, love, endurance, gentleness. Fight the good fight of the faith; take hold of the eternal life, to which you were called and for which you made the good confession in the presence of many witnesses.

In the presence of God, who gives life to all things, and of Christ Jesus, who in his testimony before Pontius Pilate made the good confession, I charge you to keep the commandment without spot or blame until the manifestation of our Lord Jesus Christ, which he will bring about at the right time. He is the blessed and only Sovereign, the King of kings and Lord of lords.

It is he alone who has immortality and dwells in unapproachable light, whom no one has ever seen or can see; to him be honour and eternal dominion. Amen.—The word of the Lord. ℟. **Thanks be to God.** ↓

GOSPEL ACCLAMATION 2 Cor. 8.9   [Rich in Christ]

(If the Alleluia is not sung, the acclamation is omitted.)

℣. Alleluia. ℟. **Alleluia.**
℣. Jesus Christ was rich but he became poor, to make you rich out of his poverty.
℟. **Alleluia.** ↓

GOSPEL Lk. 16.19-31   [Eternal Consolation]

Even the richest person cannot buy salvation. This comes from being faithful to the Word of God.

℣. The Lord be with you. ℟. **And also with you.**
✠ A reading from the holy gospel according to Luke. ℟. **Glory to you, Lord.**

JESUS told this parable to those among the Pharisees who loved money:

"There was a rich man who was dressed in purple and fine linen and who feasted sumptuously every day. And at his gate lay a poor man named Lazarus, covered with sores, who longed to satisfy his hunger with what fell from the rich man's table; even the dogs would come and lick his sores.

"The poor man died and was carried away by the angels to be with Abraham. The rich man also died and was buried. In Hades, where he was being tormented, he looked up and saw Abraham far away with Lazarus by his side. He called out, 'Father Abraham, have mercy on me, and send Lazarus to dip the tip of his finger in water and cool my tongue; for I am in agony in these flames.'

"But Abraham said, 'Child, remember that during your lifetime you received your good things, and Lazarus in like manner evil things; but now he is comforted here, and you are in agony. Besides all this, between you and us a great chasm has been fixed, so that those who might want to pass from here to you cannot do so, and no one can cross from there to us.'

"The man who had been rich said, 'Then, father, I beg you to send Lazarus to my father's house—for I have five brothers—that he may warn them, so that they will not also come into this place of torment.'

"Abraham replied, 'They have Moses and the prophets; they should listen to them.' He said, 'No, father Abraham; but if someone goes to them from the dead, they will repent.' Abraham said to him, 'If they do not listen to Moses and the prophets, neither will they be convinced even if someone rises from the dead.' "
—The gospel of the Lord. ℟. **Praise to you, Lord Jesus Christ.**   → No. 14, p. 18

PRAYER OVER THE GIFTS   [Offering as a Blessing]

God of mercy,
accept our offering
and make it a source of blessing for us.
We ask this in the name of Jesus the Lord.
℟. **Amen.**   → No. 21, p. 24 (Pref. 29-36)

COMMUNION ANTIPHON Ps. 118 (119).49-50 [Hope]

O Lord, remember the words you spoke to me, your servant, which made me live in hope and consoled me when I was downcast. ↓

OR 1 Jn. 3.16   [Offering of Self]

This is how we know what love is: Christ gave up his life for us; and we too must give up our lives for our brothers. ↓

PRAYER AFTER COMMUNION   [Union with Christ]

Lord,
may this eucharist
in which we proclaim the death of Christ
bring us salvation
and make us one with him in glory,
for he is Lord for ever and ever.
℟. **Amen.**   → No. 32, p. 75

Optional Solemn Blessings, p. 96, and Prayers Over the People, p. 104

"If you had faith the size of a mustard seed, you could
say to this mulberry tree, 'Be uprooted. . . .' "

OCTOBER 7

27th SUNDAY IN ORDINARY TIME

ENTRANCE ANTIPHON Esth. 13.9, 10-11 [Lord of All]

O Lord, you have given everything its place in the world, and no one can make it otherwise.

For it is your creation, the heavens and the earth and the stars: you are the Lord of all.
➜ No. 2, p. 10

OPENING PRAYER   [Peace and Salvation]

Father,
your love for us
surpasses all our hopes and desires.
Forgive our failings,
keep us in your peace
and lead us in the way of salvation.
We ask this . . . for ever and ever. ℟. **Amen.** ↓

FIRST READING Hab. 1.2-3; 2.2-4   [Reward of the Just]
We might become discouraged. But let us take heart; in God's own time the Lord will save us.

A reading from the book of the prophet
Habakkuk

HABAKKUK called out to the Lord:
"O Lord, how long shall I cry for help,
and you will not listen?
Or cry to you 'Violence!'
and you will not save?
Why do you make me see wrongdoing
and look at trouble?
Destruction and violence are before me;
strife and contention arise."

Then the Lord answered me and said:
"Write the vision;
make it plain on tablets,
so that a runner may read it.
For there is still a vision for the appointed time;
it speaks of the end, and does not lie.
If it seems to tarry, wait for it;

it will surely come, it will not delay.
Look at the proud!
Their spirit is not right in them,
but the righteous live by their faith."

The word of the Lord. ℟. **Thanks be to God.** ↓

RESPONSORIAL PSALM Ps. 94 (95)

[Worship the Lord]

℟. **If today you hear God's voice, harden not your hearts.**

(℟. **O that today you would listen to his voice! Harden not your hearts.**)

(NRSV Text)	(GRAIL Text)
O come, let us sing to the Lord; let us make a joyful noise to the rock of our salvation! Let us come into his presence with thanksgiving; let us make a joyful noise to him with songs of praise!—℟.	Come, ring out your joy to the Lord; hail the rock that saves us. Let us come before him, giving thanks, with songs let us hail the Lord.—℟.
O come, let us worship and bow down, let us kneel before the Lord, our Maker! For he is our God, and we are the people of his pasture, and the sheep of his hand.—℟.	Come in; let us bow and bend low; let us kneel before the God who made us for he is our God and we the people who belong to his pasture, the flock that is led by his hand.—℟.
O that today you would listen to his voice! Do not harden your hearts, as at Meribah, as on the day at Massah in the wilderness, when your ancestors tested me, and put me to the proof, though they had seen my work.—℟. ↓	O that today you would listen to his voice! "Harden not your hearts as at Meribah, as on that day at Massah in the desert when your forebears put me to the test; when they tried me though they saw my work."—℟. ↓

SECOND READING 2 Tim. 1.6-8, 13-14 [Gift of the Spirit]

Be firm in faith despite all adversity. The Holy Spirit, the spirit of strength, dwells in us.

A reading from the second letter of Paul
to Timothy

I REMIND you, Timothy, to rekindle the gift of God that is within you through the laying on of my hands; for God did not give us a spirit of cowardice, but rather a spirit of power and of love and of self-discipline. Do not be ashamed, then, of the testimony about our Lord or of me his prisoner, but join with me in suffering for the gospel, relying on the power of God.

Hold to the standard of sound teaching that you have heard from me, in the faith and love that are in Christ Jesus. Guard the good treasure entrusted to you, with the help of the Holy Spirit living in us.—The word of the Lord. ℟. **Thanks be to God.** ↓

GOSPEL ACCLAMATION 1 Pet. 1.25   [Eternal Word]

(If the Alleluia is not sung, the acclamation is omitted.)

℣. Alleluia. ℟. **Alleluia.**

℣. The word of the Lord stands for ever;
it is the word given to you, the good news.

℟. **Alleluia.** ↓

GOSPEL Lk. 17.5-10   [The Power of Faith]

Our faith is to be lived. We cannot be satisfied with merely doing no more than our duty. We must strive to excel.

℣. The Lord be with you. ℟. **And also with you.**
✙ A reading from the holy gospel according to Luke. ℟. **Glory to you, Lord.**

THE apostles said to the Lord, "Increase our faith!" The Lord replied, "If you had faith the size of a mustard seed, you could say to this mulberry tree, 'Be uprooted and planted in the sea,' and it would obey you.

"Who among you would say to your slave who has just come in from ploughing or tending sheep in the field, 'Come here at once and take your place at the table'? Would you not rather say to him, 'Prepare supper for me, put on your apron and serve me while I eat and drink; later you may eat and drink'? Do you thank the slave for doing what was commanded? So you also, when you have done all that you were ordered to do, say, 'We are worthless slaves; we have done only what we ought to have done!' "—The gospel of the Lord. ℟. **Praise to you, Lord Jesus Christ.**

➜ No. 14, p. 18

PRAYER OVER THE GIFTS   [Fullness of Redemption]

Father,
receive these gifts
which our Lord Jesus Christ
has asked us to offer in his memory.
May our obedient service   •
bring us to the fullness of your redemption.
We ask this in the name of Jesus the Lord.
℟. **Amen.**   ➜ No. 21, p. 24 (Pref. 29-36)

COMMUNION ANTIPHON Lam. 3.25   [Hope in God]

The Lord is good to those who hope in him, to those who are searching for his love. ↓

OR See 1 Cor. 10.17   [One Bread, One Body]

Because there is one bread, we, though many,

are one body, for we all share in the one loaf
and in the one cup. ↓

PRAYER AFTER COMMUNION   [Eucharistic Life]

Almighty God,
let the eucharist we share
fill us with your life.
May the love of Christ
which we celebrate here
touch our lives and lead us to you.
Grant this through Christ our Lord.
℟. **Amen.**   → No. 32, p. 75

Optional Solemn Blessings, p. 96, and Prayers Over the People, p. 104

"Get up . . .; your faith has made you well."

OCTOBER 14

28th SUNDAY IN ORDINARY TIME

ENTRANCE ANTIPHON Ps. 129 (130).3-4 **[Forgiving God]**
If you, O Lord, laid bare our guilt, who could
endure it? But you are forgiving, God of Israel.
     → No. 2, p. 10

OPENING PRAYER [Love in Action]

Lord,
our help and guide,
make your love the foundation of our lives.
May our love for you express itself
in our eagerness to do good for others.
Grant this through our Lord Jesus Christ, your
  Son,
who lives and reigns with you and the Holy
  Spirit,
one God, for ever and ever. ℟. **Amen.** ↓

FIRST READING 2 Kings 5.14-17   [Gratitude to God]

**The healing power of God comes to a man who does
not belong to the chosen people, and he proclaims his
faith in the Lord.**

A reading from the second book of Kings

NAAMAN, commander of the army of the
king of Aram and a mighty warrior,
obeyed Elisha: he went down and immersed
himself seven times in the Jordan, according to
the word of the man of God; his flesh was restored like the flesh of a young boy, and he was
clean.

Then he returned to the man of God, he and
all his company; Naaman came and stood before Elisha and said, "Now I know that there is
no God in all the earth except in Israel; please
accept a present from your servant."

But Elisha said, "As the Lord lives, whom I
serve, I will accept nothing!" Naaman urged Elisha to accept, but he refused.

Then Naaman said, "If not, please let two mule-loads of earth be given to your servant; for your servant will no longer offer burnt offering or sacrifice to any god except the Lord."—The word of the Lord. ℟. **Thanks be to God.** ↓

RESPONSORIAL PSALM Ps. 97 (98)   [Wondrous Deeds]

℟. **The Lord has revealed to the na-tions his sav-ing pow'r.**

(NRSV Text)

O sing to the Lord a new song,
for he has done marvellous things.
His right hand and his holy arm
have brought him victory.—℟.

The Lord has made known his victory;
he has revealed his vindication in the sight of the nations.
He has remembered his steadfast love and faithfulness to the house of Israel.—℟.

All the ends of the earth have seen the victory of our God.
Make a joyful noise to the Lord, all the earth;
break forth into joyous song and sing praises.—℟. ↓

(GRAIL Text)

Sing a new song to the Lord
for he has worked wonders.
His right hand and his holy arm
have brought him salvation.—℟.

The Lord has made known his salvation;
has shown his justice to the nations.
He has remembered his truth and love for the house of Israel.—℟.

All the ends of the earth have seen the salvation of our God.
Shout to the Lord, all the earth,
ring out your joy.—℟. ↓

SECOND READING 2 Tim. 2.8-13   [Life in Christ]

In Christ we have died. Through Christ we are to rise, and with him we shall reign.

A reading from the second letter of Paul to Timothy

REMEMBER Jesus Christ, raised from the dead, a descendant of David—that is my gospel, for which I suffer hardship, even to the point of being chained like a criminal. But the word of God is not chained.

Therefore I endure everything for the sake of the elect, so that they may also obtain the salvation that is in Christ Jesus, with eternal glory.

The saying is sure:
If we have died with him, we will also live with him;
if we endure, we will also reign with him;
if we deny him, he will also deny us;
if we are faithless, he remains faithful—
for he cannot deny himself.

The word of the Lord. ℟. **Thanks be to God.** ↓

GOSPEL ACCLAMATION 1 Thess. 5.18 [Give Thanks]

(If the Alleluia is not sung, the acclamation is omitted.)

℣. Alleluia. ℟. **Alleluia.**
℣. For all things give thanks to God,
because this is what he expects from you in Christ Jesus.
℟. **Alleluia.** ↓

GOSPEL Lk. 17.11-19   [Salvation through Faith]
The healing power of God comes through Christ, even to a man who does not belong to the chosen people. This man's faith prompts his thankfulness.

℣. The Lord be with you. ℟. **And also with you.**
✢ A reading from the holy gospel according to Luke. ℟. **Glory to you, Lord.**

ON the way to Jerusalem Jesus was going through the region between Samaria and Galilee.

As he entered a village, ten lepers approached him. Keeping their distance, they called out, saying, "Jesus, Master, have mercy on us!"

When Jesus saw them, he said to them, "Go and show yourselves to the priests." And as they went, they were made clean. Then one of them, when he saw that he was healed, turned back, praising God with a loud voice. He prostrated himself at Jesus' feet and thanked him. And he was a Samaritan.

Then Jesus asked, "Were not ten made clean? But the other nine, where are they? Was none of them found to return and give praise to God except this foreigner?"

Then Jesus said to the Samaritan, "Get up and go on your way; your faith has made you well."—The gospel of the Lord. ℞. **Praise to you, Lord Jesus Christ.**   → No. 14, p. 18

PRAYER OVER THE GIFTS   [Faith and Love]

Lord,
accept the prayers and gifts
we offer in faith and love.
May this eucharist bring us to your glory.
We ask this in the name of Jesus the Lord.
℞. **Amen.**   → No. 21, p. 24 (Pref. 29-36)

COMMUNION ANTIPHON Ps. 33 (34).10 [Providence]

The rich suffer want and go hungry, but nothing shall be lacking to those who fear the Lord. ↓

OR 1 Jn. 3.2   [Vision of God]

When the Lord is revealed we shall be like him, for we shall see him as he is. ↓

PRAYER AFTER COMMUNION   [Christ's Life]

Almighty Father,
may the body and blood of your Son
give us a share in his life,
for he is Lord for ever and ever.
℞. **Amen.**   ➙ No. 32, p. 75

Optional Solemn Blessings, p. 96, and Prayers Over the People, p. 104

"Will not God grant justice to his chosen ones
who cry to him day and night?"

OCTOBER 21

29th SUNDAY IN ORDINARY TIME

ENTRANCE ANTIPHON Ps. 16 (17).6, 8
                                      [Refuge in God]

I call upon you, God, for you will answer me;
bend your ear and hear my prayer. Guard me
as the pupil of your eye; hide me in the shade
of your wings.   ➙ No. 2, p. 10

OPENING PRAYER [Faithful Service]

Almighty and ever-living God,
our source of power and inspiration,
give us strength and joy
in serving you as followers of Christ,
who lives and reigns with you and the Holy
  Spirit,
one God, for ever and ever. ℟. **Amen.** ↓

FIRST READING Ex. 17.8-13 [God Our Warrior]

Moses prays without ceasing, not losing heart despite physical fatigue.

A reading from the book of Exodus

AMALEK came and fought with Israel at
Rephidim. Moses said to Joshua, "Choose
some men for us and go out, fight with
Amalek. Tomorrow I will stand on the top of
the hill with the staff of God in my hand."

So Joshua did as Moses told him, and fought
with Amalek, while Moses, Aaron, and Hur
went up to the top of the hill.

Whenever Moses held up his hands, Israel
prevailed; and whenever he lowered his hands,
Amalek prevailed. But Moses' hands grew
weary; so they took a stone and put it under
him, and he sat on it. Aaron and Hur held up
his hands, one on one side, and the other on
the other side; so his hands were steady until
the sun set.

And Joshua defeated Amalek and his people
with the sword.—The word of the Lord. ℟.
Thanks be to God. ↓

RESPONSORIAL PSALM Ps. 120 (121) [Our Guardian]

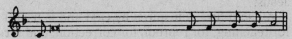

R̸. **Our help is from the Lord, who made heav'n and earth.**

(NRSV Text)	(GRAIL Text)
I lift up my eyes to the hills— from where will my help come? My help comes from the Lord, who made heaven and earth.—R̸.	I lift up my eyes to the mountains; from where shall come my help? My help shall come from the Lord who made heaven and earth.—R̸.
The Lord will not let your foot be moved; he who keeps you will not slumber. He who keeps Israel will neither slumber nor sleep.—R̸.	May he never allow you to stumble! Let him sleep not, your guard. No, he sleeps not nor slumbers, Israel's guard.—R̸.
The Lord is your keeper; the Lord is your shade at your right hand. The sun shall not strike you by day, nor the moon by night.—R̸.	The Lord is your guard and your shade; at your right side he stands. By day the sun shall not smite you nor the moon in the night.—R̸.
The Lord will keep you from all evil; he will keep your life. The Lord will keep your going out and your coming in from this time on and forever-more.—R̸. ↓	The Lord will guard you from evil, he will guard your soul. The Lord will guard your going and coming both now and for ever.—R̸. ↓

SECOND READING 2 Tim. 3.14—4.2 [Divine Inspiration]

The Bible is the source of teaching, the safe guide for the people of God in every good work.

A reading from the second letter of Paul to Timothy

CONTINUE in what you have learned and firmly believed, knowing from whom you learned it, and how from childhood you have known the sacred writings that are able to instruct you for salvation through faith in Christ Jesus.

All scripture is inspired by God and is useful for teaching, for reproof, for correction, and for training in righteousness, so that everyone who belongs to God may be proficient, equipped for every good work.

In the presence of God and of Christ Jesus, who is to judge the living and the dead, and in view of his appearing and his kingdom, I solemnly urge you: proclaim the message; be persistent whether the time is favourable or unfavourable; convince, rebuke, and encourage, with the utmost patience in teaching.— The word of the Lord. ℞. **Thanks be to God.** ↓

GOSPEL ACCLAMATION Heb. 4.12   [Living Word]

(If the Alleluia is not sung, the acclamation is omitted.)

℣. Alleluia. ℞. **Alleluia.**

℣. The word of God is living and active; it probes the thoughts and motives of our heart.

℞. **Alleluia.** ↓

GOSPEL Lk. 18.1-8   [The Need To Pray]

Jesus urges us to pray without ceasing and to have faith in the goodness of God.

℣. The Lord be with you. ℞. **And also with you.**
✛ A reading from the holy gospel according to Luke. ℞. **Glory to you, Lord.**

JESUS told the disciples a parable about their need to pray always and not to lose heart.

He said, "In a certain city there was a judge who neither feared God nor had respect for people. In that city there was a widow who kept coming to him and saying, 'Grant me justice against my opponent.'

"For a while the judge refused; but later he said to himself, 'Though I have no fear of God and no respect for anyone, yet because this widow keeps bothering me, I will grant her justice, so that she may not wear me out by continually coming.' "

And the Lord said, "Listen to what the unjust judge says. Will not God grant justice to his chosen ones who cry to him day and night? Will he delay long in helping them? I tell you, God will quickly grant justice to them.

"And yet, when the Son of Man comes, will he find faith on earth?"—The gospel of the Lord. ℟. **Praise to you, Lord Jesus Christ.**

➡ No. 14, p. 18

PRAYER OVER THE GIFTS   [Lives of Service]

Lord God,
may the gifts we offer
bring us your love and forgiveness
and give us freedom to serve you with our
  lives.
We ask this in the name of Jesus the Lord.
℟. **Amen.**   ➡ No. 21, p. 24 (Pref. 29-36)

COMMUNION ANTIPHON Ps. 32 (33).18-19
                                        [Divine Help]

See how the eyes of the Lord are on those who fear him, on those who hope in his love; that

he may rescue them from death and feed them in time of famine. ↓

PRAYER AFTER COMMUNION   [Fidelity]

Lord,
may this eucharist help us to remain faithful.
May it teach us the way to eternal life.
Grant this through Christ our Lord.
℟. **Amen.**   → No. 32, p. 75

Optional Solemn Blessings, p. 96, and Prayers Over the People, p. 104

"God, I thank you that I am not like other people."

OCTOBER 28
30th SUNDAY IN ORDINARY TIME

ENTRANCE ANTIPHON Ps. 104 (105).3-4

[Seek the Lord]

Let hearts rejoice who search for the Lord.
Seek the Lord and his strength, seek always
the face of the Lord.   → No. 2, p. 10

OPENING PRAYER   [Doing God's Will]

Almighty and ever-living God,
strengthen our faith, hope, and love.
May we do with loving hearts
what you ask of us
and come to share the life you promise.
We ask this . . . for ever and ever. ℞. **Amen.** ↓

FIRST READING Sir. 35.15-17, 20-22   [A God of Justice]

No one is unimportant in the sight of God. If we serve willingly God will receive our prayers.

A reading from the book of Sirach

THE Lord is the judge,
and with him there is no partiality.
He will not show partiality to the poor
but he will listen to the prayer of one who is
    wronged.
The Lord will not ignore the supplication of the
    orphan,
or the widow when she pours out her com-
    plaint.
The one whose service is pleasing to the Lord
    will be accepted,
and the prayer of such a person will reach to
    the clouds.

The prayer of the humble pierces the clouds,
and it will not rest until it reaches its goal;
it will not desist until the Most High responds
and does justice for the righteous,
and executes judgment.
Indeed, the Lord will not delay.
The word of the Lord. ℞. **Thanks be to God.** ↓

RESPONSORIAL PSALM Ps. 33 (34)

[Refuge in the Lord]

R̶. The   Lord   hears   the   cry of the poor.

(NRSV Text)	**(GRAIL Text)**
I will bless the Lord at all times; his praise shall continually be in my mouth. My soul makes its boast in the Lord; let the humble hear and be glad.— R̶.	I will bless the Lord at all times, his praise always on my lips; in the Lord my soul shall make its boast. The humble shall hear and be glad.— R̶.
The face of the Lord is against evildoers, to cut off the remembrance of them from the earth. When the righteous cry for help, the Lord hears, and rescues them from all their troubles.— R̶.	The Lord turns his face against the wicked to destroy their remembrance from the earth. They call and the Lord hears and rescues them in all their distress.— R̶.
The Lord is near to the brokenhearted, and saves the crushed in spirit. The Lord redeems the life of his servants; none of those who take refuge in him will be condemned. — R̶. ↓	The Lord is close to the brokenhearted; those whose spirit is crushed he will save. The Lord ransoms the souls of his servants. Those who hide in him shall not be condemned.— R̶. ↓

SECOND READING 2 Tim. 4.6-8, 16-18

[A Merited Crown]

Paul sees time running out and his life drawing to a close. He is comforted by faith in God's just judgment.

A reading from the second letter of Paul to Timothy

AS for me, I am already being poured out as a libation, and the time of my departure has come. I have fought the good fight, I have finished the race, I have kept the faith.

From now on there is reserved for me the crown of righteousness, which the Lord, the righteous judge, will give me on that day, and not only to me but also to all who have longed for his appearing.

At my first defense no one came to my support, but all deserted me. May it not be counted against them!

But the Lord stood by me and gave me strength, so that through me the message might be fully proclaimed and all the Gentiles might hear it. So I was rescued from the lion's mouth.

The Lord will rescue me from every evil attack and save me for his heavenly kingdom. To him be the glory forever and ever. Amen.—The word of the Lord. ℟. **Thanks be to God.** ↓

GOSPEL ACCLAMATION 2 Cor. 5.19 [Reconciliation]

(If the Alleluia is not sung, the acclamation is omitted.)

℣. Alleluia. ℟. **Alleluia.**
℣. God was in Christ, to reconcile the world to himself;
and the good news of reconciliation he has entrusted to us.
℟. **Alleluia.** ↓

GOSPEL Lk. 18.9-14   [The Value of Humility]

Pride brings no true reward but only projects an "image." In humility true values are seen.

℣. The Lord be with you. ℟. **And also with you.**
✚ A reading from the holy gospel according to Luke. ℟. **Glory to you, Lord.**

JESUS told this parable to some who trusted in themselves that they were righteous, and regarded others with contempt:

"Two men went up to the temple to pray, one a Pharisee and the other a tax collector. The Pharisee, standing by himself, was praying thus, 'God, I thank you that I am not like other people: thieves, rogues, adulterers, or even like this tax collector. I fast twice a week; I give a tenth of all my income.'

"But the tax collector, standing far off, would not even look up to heaven, but was beating his breast and saying, 'God, be merciful to me, a sinner!'

"I tell you, this man went down to his home justified rather than the other; for all who exalt themselves will be humbled, but all who humble themselves will be exalted."—The gospel of the Lord. ℟. **Praise to you, Lord Jesus Christ.**

→ No. 14, p. 18

PRAYER OVER THE GIFTS   [Glorifying God]

Lord God of power and might,
receive the gifts we offer
and let our service give you glory.
Grant this through Christ our Lord.
℟. **Amen.**   → No. 21, p. 24 (Pref. 29-36)

COMMUNION ANTIPHON Ps. 19 (20).5

[Victory of God]

We will rejoice at the victory of God and make our boast in his great name. ↓

OR Eph. 5.2   [Christ's Offering for Us]

Christ loved us and gave himself up for us as a fragrant offering to God. ↓

PRAYER AFTER COMMUNION [Good Communion]

Lord,
bring to perfection within us
the communion we share in this sacrament.
May our celebration have an effect in our lives.
We ask this in the name of Jesus the Lord.
℞. **Amen.**   → No. 32, p. 75

Optional Solemn Blessings, p. 96, and Prayers Over the People, p. 104

Zacchaeus "climbed a sycamore tree to see Jesus . . . ."

NOVEMBER 4

31st SUNDAY IN ORDINARY TIME

ENTRANCE ANTIPHON Ps. 37 (38).21-22 [Call for Help]

Do not abandon me, Lord. My God, do not go away from me! Hurry to help me, Lord, my Saviour.   → No. 2, p. 10

OPENING PRAYER   [Living the Faith]

God of power and mercy,
only with your help
can we offer you fitting service and praise.
May we live the faith we profess
and trust your promise of eternal life.
Grant this through our Lord Jesus Christ, your
    Son,
who lives and reigns with you and the Holy
    Spirit,
one God, for ever and ever. ℟. **Amen.** ↓

FIRST READING Wis. 11.22—12.2   [Imperishable Spirit]

> The Lord is the greatest. Everything else is insignificant;
> everything else depends on him.

A reading from the book of Wisdom

THE whole world before you, O Lord,
    is like a speck that tips the scales,
and like a drop of morning dew that falls on
    the ground.
But you are merciful to all,
for you can do all things,
and you overlook people's sins,
so that they may repent.

Lord, you love all things that exist,
and detest none of the things that you have
    made,
for you would not have made anything if you
    had hated it.
How would anything have endured
if you had not willed it?
Or how would anything not called forth by you
have been preserved?

You spare all things, for they are yours, O Lord,

you who love the living.

For your immortal spirit is in all things.

Therefore you correct little by little those who trespass,

and you remind and warn them of the things through which they sin,

so that they may be freed from wickedness

and put their trust in you, O Lord.

The word of the Lord. ℟. **Thanks be to God.** ↓

RESPONSORIAL PSALM Ps. 144 (145)

[Praise the Lord]

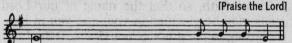

℟. **I will praise your name for ev - er   my king and my God.**

(℟. **I will bless your name for ever, O God my king.**)

(NRSV Text)	**(GRAIL Text)**
I will extol you, my God and King, and bless your name forever and ever. Every day I will bless you, and praise your name forever and ever.—℟.	I will give you glory, O God my king, I will bless your name for ever. I will bless you day after day and praise your name for ever.—℟.
The Lord is gracious and merciful, slow to anger and abounding in steadfast love. The Lord is good to all, and his compassion is over all that he has made.—℟.	You are kind and full of compassion, slow to anger, abounding in love. How good you are, Lord, to all, compassionate to all your creatures.—℟.
All your works shall give thanks to you, O Lord. and all your faithful shall bless you. They shall speak of the glory of your kingdom, and tell of your power.—℟.	All your creatures shall thank you, O Lord, and your friends shall repeat their blessing. They shall speak of the glory of your reign and declare your might, O God.—℟.

The Lord is faithful in all his words, and gracious in all his deeds.
The Lord upholds all who are falling. and raises up all who are bowed down.—R̸. ↓

You are faithful in all your words and loving in all your deeds.
You support all those who are falling and raise up all who are bowed down.—R̸. ↓

SECOND READING 2 Thess. 1.11—2.2 [Day of the Lord]

The Lord will come again. Do not be misled by false predictions; rather strive to be worthy of his call.

A reading from the second letter of Paul to the Thessalonians

WE always pray for you, asking that our God will make you worthy of his call and will fulfil by his power every good resolve and work of faith, so that the name of our Lord Jesus may be glorified in you, and you in him, according to the grace of our God and the Lord Jesus Christ.

As to the coming of our Lord Jesus Christ and our being gathered together to him, we beg you, brothers and sisters, not to be quickly shaken in mind or alarmed, either by spirit or by word or by letter, as though from us, to the effect that the day of the Lord is already here.—The word of the Lord. R̸. **Thanks be to God.** ↓

GOSPEL ACCLAMATION Jn. 3.16   [God's Love]

(If the Alleluia is not sung, the acclamation is omitted.)

V̸. Alleluia. R̸. **Alleluia.**

V̸. God loved the world so much, he gave us his only Son,
that all who believe in him might have eternal life.
R̸. **Alleluia.** ↓

GOSPEL Lk. 19.1-10   [Salvation]

No one is so evil, so bad, that he or she cannot be saved. God's love will bring his forgiveness and reunite all who repent.

℣. The Lord be with you. ℟. **And also with you.**
✚ A reading from the holy gospel according to Luke. ℟. **Glory to you, Lord.**

JESUS entered Jericho and was passing through it. A man was there named Zacchaeus; he was a chief tax collector and was rich. He was trying to see who Jesus was, but on account of the crowd he could not, because he was short in stature.

So he ran ahead and climbed a sycamore tree to see Jesus, because he was going to pass that way. When Jesus came to the place, he looked up and said to him, "Zacchaeus, hurry and come down; for I must stay at your house today."

So Zacchaeus hurried down and was happy to welcome Jesus. All who saw it began to grumble and said, "He has gone to be the guest of one who is a sinner."

Zacchaeus stood there and said to the Lord, "Look, half of my possessions, Lord, I will give to the poor; and if I have defrauded anyone of anything, I will pay back four times as much."

Then Jesus said of him, "Today salvation has come to this house, because Zacchaeus too is a son of Abraham. For the Son of Man came to seek out and to save the lost."—The gospel of the Lord. ℟. **Praise to you, Lord Jesus Christ.**

➥ No. 14, p. 18

PRAYER OVER THE GIFTS   [A Pure Sacrifice]

God of mercy,
may we offer a pure sacrifice
for the forgiveness of our sins.
We ask this through Christ our Lord.
℞. **Amen.**   → No. 21, p. 24 (Pref. 29-36)

COMMUNION ANTIPHON Ps. 15 (16).11   [Joy]

**Lord, you will show me the path of life and fill
me with joy in your presence.** ↓

OR Jn. 6.58   [Life]

**As the living Father sent me, and I live be-
cause of the Father, so he who eats my flesh
and drinks my blood will live because of me.** ↓

PRAYER AFTER COMMUNION   [Hope]

Lord,
you give us new hope in this eucharist.
May the power of your love
continue its saving work among us
and bring us to the joy you promise.
We ask this in the name of Jesus the Lord.
℞. **Amen.**   → No. 32, p. 75

Optional Solemn Blessings, p. 96, and Prayers Over the People, p. 104

"He is God not of the dead, but of the living."

NOVEMBER 11

32nd SUNDAY IN ORDINARY TIME

ENTRANCE ANTIPHON Ps. 87 (88).2 [Answer to Prayer]

Let my prayer come before you, Lord; listen
and answer me. ➜ No. 2, p. 10

OPENING PRAYER [Health of Mind and Body]

God of power and mercy,
protect us from all harm.
Give us freedom of spirit
and health in mind and body
to do your work on earth.
We ask this . . . for ever and ever. ℟. **Amen.** ↓

FIRST READING 2 Macc. 7.1-2, 9-14 [Martyrdom]

Faith in the resurrection, a belief held even before the
coming of Christ, gives strength to endure all trials.

A reading from the second book of Maccabees

IT happened that seven brothers and their
mother were arrested and were being com-

pelled by King Antiochus, under torture with whips and thongs, to partake of unlawful swine's flesh. One of the brothers, speaking for all, said, "What do you intend to ask and learn from us? For we are ready to die rather than transgress the laws of our ancestors."

After the first brother had died, they brought forward the second for their sport. And when he was at his last breath, he said to King, "You accursed wretch, you dismiss us from this present life, but the King of the universe will raise us up to an everlasting renewal of life, because we have died for his laws."

After him, the third was the victim of their sport. When it was demanded, he quickly put out his tongue and courageously stretched forth his hands, and said nobly, "I got these from Heaven, and because of God's laws I disdain them, and from God I hope to get them back again."

As a result the king himself and those with him were astonished at the young man's spirit, for he regarded his sufferings as nothing.

After the third brother too had died, they maltreated and tortured the fourth in the same way.

When he was near death, he said to his torturers, "One cannot but choose to die at the hands of mortals and to cherish the hope God gives of being raised again by him. But for you, there will be no resurrection to life!"—The word of the Lord. ℟. **Thanks be to God.** ↓

RESPONSORIAL PSALM Ps. 16 (17)   [Joy in the Lord]

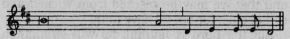

℟. **Lord, when your glory ap-pears, my joy will be full.**

(NRSV Text)	**(GRAIL Text)**
Hear a just cause, O Lord; attend to my cry; give ear to my prayer from lips free of deceit.—℟.	Lord, hear a cause that is just, pay heed to my cry. Turn your ear to my prayer, no deceit is on my lips.—℟.
My steps have held fast to your paths; my feet have not slipped. I call upon you, for you will answer me, O God; incline your ear to me, hear my words.—℟.	I kept my feet firmly in your paths; there was no faltering in my steps. I am here and I call, you will hear me, O God. Turn your ear to me; hear my words.—℟.
Guard me as the apple of the eye; hide me in the shadow of your wings. As for me, I shall behold your face in righteousness; when I awake I shall be satisfied, beholding your likeness.—℟. ↓	Guard me as the apple of your eye. Hide me in the shadow of your wings. As for me, in my justice I shall see your face and be filled, when I awake, with the sight of your glory.—℟. ↓

SECOND READING 2 Thess. 2.16—3.5   [Fear No Evil]

Have faith, fear no evil, the Lord is constant. He is our strength.

A reading from the second letter of Paul
to the Thessalonians

MAY our Lord Jesus Christ himself and God our Father, who loved us and through grace gave us eternal comfort and good hope, comfort your hearts and strengthen them in every good work and word.

Brothers and sisters, pray for us, so that the word of the Lord may spread rapidly and be glorified everywhere, just as it is among you, and that we may be rescued from wicked and evil people; for not all have faith.

But the Lord is faithful; he will strengthen you and guard you from the evil one. And we have confidence in the Lord concerning you, that you are doing and will go on doing the things that we command. May the Lord direct your hearts to the love of God and to the steadfastness of Christ.—The word of the Lord. ℞. **Thanks be to God.** ↓

GOSPEL ACCLAMATION Rev. 1.5, 6   [Firstborn]

(If the Alleluia is not sung, the acclamation is omitted.)

℣. Alleluia. ℞. **Alleluia.**
℣. Jesus Christ is the firstborn of the dead;
glory and kingship be his for ever and ever.
℞. **Alleluia.** ↓

GOSPEL Lk. 20.27-38 or 20.27, 34-38   [Alive for God]

Our God is God of the living who reveals the mystery of resurrection.

[If the "Short Form" is used, the indented text in brackets is omitted.]

℣. The Lord be with you. ℞. **And also with you.**
✣ A reading from the holy gospel according to Luke. ℞. **Glory to you, Lord.**

SOME Sadducees, those who say there is no resurrection, came to Jesus
[and asked him a question, "Teacher, Moses wrote for us that if a man's brother dies, leaving a wife but no children, the man shall marry the widow and raise up

children for his brother. Now there were seven brothers; the first married, and died childless; then the second and the third married her, and so in the same way all seven died childless.

"Finally the woman also died. In the resurrection, therefore, whose wife will the woman be?—for the seven had married her."]

Jesus said to them, "Those who belong to this age marry and are given in marriage; but those who are considered worthy of a place in that age and in the resurrection from the dead neither marry nor are given in marriage. Indeed they cannot die any more, because they are like angels and are children of God, being children of the resurrection.

"And the fact that the dead are raised Moses himself showed in the story about the bush, where he speaks of the Lord as the God of Abraham, the God of Isaac, and the God of Jacob. Now he is God not of the dead, but of the living; for to him all of them are alive."—The gospel of the Lord. ℟. **Praise to you, Lord Jesus Christ.**   → No. 14, p. 18

PRAYER OVER THE GIFTS   [Following Christ]

God of mercy,
in this eucharist we proclaim the death of the
    Lord.
Accept the gifts we present
and help us follow him with love,
for he is Lord for ever and ever.
℟. **Amen.**   → No. 21, p. 24 (Pref. 29-36)

COMMUNION ANTIPHON Ps. 22 (23).1-2

[Our Shepherd]

The Lord is my shepherd; there is nothing I shall want. In green pastures he gives me rest, he leads me beside the waters of peace. ↓

OR Lk. 24.35   [Jesus in the Eucharist]

The disciples recognized the Lord Jesus in the breaking of bread. ↓

PRAYER AFTER COMMUNION   [Serving God]

Lord,
we thank you for the nourishment you give us
through your holy gift.
Pour out your Spirit upon us
and in the strength of this food from heaven
keep us single-minded in your service.
We ask this in the name of Jesus the Lord.
℟. **Amen.**   → No. 32, p. 75

Optional Solemn Blessings, p. 96, and Prayers Over the People, p. 104

"The days will come when not one stone will be left
upon another; all will be thrown down."

NOVEMBER 18

33rd SUNDAY IN ORDINARY TIME

ENTRANCE ANTIPHON Jer. 29.11, 12, 14 [God Hears]
The Lord says: my plans for you are peace and
not disaster; when you call to me, I will listen
to you, and I will bring you back to the place
from which I exiled you. → No. 2, p. 10

OPENING PRAYER [Faithful Service]
Father of all that is good,
keep us faithful in serving you,
for to serve you is lasting joy.
We ask this . . . for ever and ever. ℟. **Amen.** ↓

FIRST READING Mal. 4.1-2 [Judgment Day]
The time of judgment is coming. For the faithful it will
be a day of glory.

A reading from the book of the prophet
Malachi

THE Lord says this:
"See, the day is coming, burning like an oven,

575

when all the arrogant and all evildoers will be
    stubble;
the day that comes shall burn them up," says
    the Lord of hosts,
"so that it will leave them neither root nor
    branch.
"But for you who revere my name
the sun of righteousness shall rise,
with healing in its wings."
The word of the Lord. ℟. **Thanks be to God.** ↓

RESPONSORIAL PSALM Ps. 97 (98) **[Rule with Justice]**

℟. **The Lord comes to rule the earth with jus - tice.**

(℟. **The Lord comes to rule the world with justice. Alleluia.**)

(NRSV Text)	(GRAIL Text)
Sing praises to the Lord with the lyre, with the lyre and the sound of melody.	Sing psalms to the Lord with the harp with the sound of music.
With trumpets and the sound of the horn	With trumpets and the sound of the horn
make a joyful noise before the King, the Lord.—℟.	acclaim the King, the Lord.—℟.
Let the sea roar, and all that fills it; the world and those who live in it.	Let the sea and all within it, thunder; the world, and all its peoples.
Let the floods clap their hands; let the hills sing together for joy at the presence of the Lord.—℟.	Let the rivers clap their hands and the hills ring out their joy at the presence of the Lord.—℟.
For the Lord is coming, coming to judge the earth.	For the Lord comes, comes to rule the earth.
He will judge the world with righteousness, and the peoples with equity.—℟. ↓	He will rule the world with justice and the peoples with fairness.—℟. ↓

SECOND READING 2 Thess. 3.7-12 [Models for Imitation]

We must all work together and cooperate with one another. No one can sit back and enjoy the fruits of another's labour.

A reading from the second letter of Paul
to the Thessalonians

Brothers and sisters, you yourselves know how you ought to imitate us; we were not idle when we were with you, and we did not eat anyone's bread without paying for it; but with toil and labour we worked night and day, so that we might not burden any of you.

This was not because we do not have that right, but in order to give you an example to imitate. For even when we were with you, we gave you this command: "Anyone unwilling to work should not eat."

For we hear that some of you are living in idleness, mere busybodies, not doing any work. Now such persons we command and exhort in the Lord Jesus Christ to do their work quietly and to earn their own living.—The word of the Lord. R̠. **Thanks be to God.** ↓

GOSPEL ACCLAMATION Lk. 21.28   [Redemption]

(If the Alleluia is not sung, the acclamation is omitted.)

V̠. Alleluia. R̠. **Alleluia.**
V̠. Lift up your heads and see;
your redemption is near at hand.
R̠. **Alleluia.** ↓

GOSPEL Lk. 21.5-19   [Salvation in Christ]

Nothing in this world will last for ever and we can be sure of trials and tribulations. But if we put our trust and hope in Christ, we will find life.

℣. The Lord be with you. ℟. **And also with you.**
✠ A reading from the holy gospel according to
Luke. ℟. **Glory to you, Lord.**

WHEN some were speaking about the temple,
how it was adorned with beautiful stones
and gifts dedicated to God, Jesus said, "As for
these things that you see, the days will
come when not one stone will be left upon another; all will be thrown down."

They asked him, "Teacher, when will this be,
and what will be the sign that this is about to take
place?"

And Jesus said, "Beware that you are not led
astray; for many will come in my name and say, 'I
am he!' and, 'The time is near!' Do not go after
them.

"When you hear of wars and insurrections, do
not be terrified; for these things must take place
first, but the end will not follow immediately."

Then Jesus said to them, "Nation will rise
against nation, and kingdom against kingdom;
there will be great earthquakes, and in various
places famines and plagues; and there will be
dreadful portents and great signs from heaven.

"But before all this occurs, they will arrest you
and persecute you; they will hand you over to
synagogues and prisons, and you will be brought
before kings and governors because of my name.

"This will give you an opportunity to testify. So
make up your minds not to prepare your defense
in advance; for I will give you words and a wisdom that none of your opponents will be able to
withstand or contradict.

"You will be betrayed even by parents, by brothers and sisters, and by relatives and friends; and they will put some of you to death. You will be hated by all because of my name. But not a hair of your head will perish. By your endurance you will gain your souls."—The gospel of the Lord. ℞. **Praise to you, Lord Jesus Christ.**

→ No. 14, p. 18

PRAYER OVER THE GIFTS   [Eternal Life]

Lord God,
may the gifts we offer
increase our love for you
and bring us to eternal life.
We ask this in the name of Jesus the Lord.
℞. **Amen.**   → No. 21, p. 24 (Pref. 29-36)

COMMUNION ANTIPHON Ps. 72 (73).28

[Hope in God]

It is good for me to be with the Lord and to put my hope in him. ↓

OR Mk. 11.23, 24   [Believing Prayer]

I tell you solemnly, whatever you ask for in prayer, believe that you have received it, and it will be yours, says the Lord. ↓

PRAYER AFTER COMMUNION   [Growth in Love]

Father,
may we grow in love
by the eucharist we have celebrated
in memory of the Lord Jesus,
who is Lord for ever and ever.
℞. **Amen.**   → No. 32, p. 75

Optional Solemn Blessings, p. 96, and Prayers Over the People, p. 104

"The Lord will reign for ever."

NOVEMBER 25

CHRIST THE KING

(34th SUNDAY IN ORDINARY TIME)

ENTRANCE ANTIPHON Rev. 5.12; 1.6 [Christ's Glory]

The Lamb who was slain is worthy to receive strength and divinity, wisdom and power and honour: to him be glory and power for ever.

➜ No. 2, p. 10

OPENING PRAYER [King of the Universe]

Almighty and merciful God,
you break the power of evil
and make all things new
in your Son Jesus Christ, the King of the universe.
May all in heaven and earth acclaim your glory
and never cease to praise you.
We ask this . . . for ever and ever. ℞. **Amen.** ↓

FIRST READING 2 Sam. 5.1-3   [Shepherd My People]

> David is anointed to be king in fulfillment of the promise of the Lord.

A reading from the second book of Samuel

ALL the tribes of Israel came to David at Hebron, and said, "Look, we are your bone
and flesh. For some time, while Saul was king
over us, it was you who led out Israel and
brought it in. The Lord said to you: 'It is you
who shall be shepherd of my people Israel, you
who shall be ruler over Israel.' "

So all the elders of Israel came to the king at
Hebron; and King David made a covenant with
them at Hebron before the Lord, and they
anointed David king over Israel.—The word of
the Lord. ℟. **Thanks be to God.** ↓

RESPONSORIAL PSALM Ps. 121 (122) [House of God]

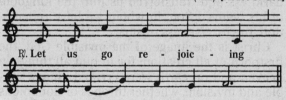

℟. Let   us   go   re - joic - ing

to   the   house —   of   the   Lord.

(℟. **I rejoiced when I heard them say: let us go rejoicing to the house of the Lord.**)

(NRSV Text)	(GRAIL Text)
I was glad when they said to me,	I rejoiced when I heard them say:
"Let us go to the house of the Lord!"	"Let us go to God's house."
Our feet are standing	And now our feet are standing
within your gates, O Jerusalem.—℟.	within your gates, O Jerusalem.—℟.
Jerusalem—built as a city	Jerusalem is built as a city
that is bound firmly together.	strongly compact.

To it the tribes go up,
the tribes of the Lord.—℟.

As it was decreed for Israel,
to give thanks to the name of the Lord.
For there the thrones for judgement were set up,
the thrones of the house of David.—℟. ↓

It is there that the tribes go up,
the tribes of the Lord.—℟.

For Israel's law it is,
there to praise the Lord's name.
There were set the thrones of judgment
of the house of David.—℟. ↓

SECOND READING Col. 1.12-20　　[Primacy of Christ]

We belong to the kingdom of God through his Son who has dominion over all creation.

A reading from the letter of Paul to the Colossians

GIVE thanks to the Father, who has enabled you to share in the inheritance of the saints in the light.

The Father has rescued us from the power of darkness and transferred us into the kingdom of his beloved Son, in whom we have redemption, the forgiveness of sins.

Christ is the image of the invisible God, the firstborn of all creation; for in him all things in heaven and on earth were created, things visible and invisible, whether thrones or dominions or rulers or powers—all things have been created through him and for him. Christ is before all things, and in him all things hold together.

Christ is the head of the body, the church; he is the beginning, the firstborn from the dead, so that he might come to have first place in everything. For in Christ all the fullness of God was pleased to dwell, and through him God was pleased to reconcile to himself all things, whether on earth or in heaven, by making peace through the blood of his cross.—The word of the Lord. ℟. **Thanks be to God.** ↓

GOSPEL ACCLAMATION Mk. 11.9, 10 [Hail Our King]
(If the Alleluia is not sung, the acclamation is omitted.)

℣. Alleluia. ℟. **Alleluia.**

℣. Blessed is the one who inherits the kingdom of David our father;

blessed is the one who comes in the name of the Lord.

℟. **Alleluia.** ↓

GOSPEL Lk. 23.35-43   [Jesus the King]

The Son of David, King of the Jews, the crucified Saviour, reigns—he is King of paradise.

℣. The Lord be with you. ℟. **And also with you.**
✠ A reading from the holy gospel according to Luke. ℟. **Glory to you, Lord.**

WHEN Jesus had been crucified, the people stood by watching; the leaders scoffed at him, saying, "He saved others; let him save himself if he is the Messiah of God, his chosen one!" The soldiers also mocked Jesus, coming up and offering him sour wine, and saying, "If you are the King of the Jews, save yourself!" There was also an inscription over Jesus, "This is the King of the Jews."

One of the criminals who were hanged there kept deriding Jesus and saying, "Are you not the Messiah? Save yourself and us!"

But the other rebuked him, saying, "Do you not fear God, since you are under the same sentence of condemnation? And we indeed have been condemned justly, for we are getting what we deserve for our deeds, but this man has done nothing wrong." Then he said, "Jesus, remember me when you come into your kingdom."

Jesus replied, "Truly I tell you, today you will be with me in Paradise."—The gospel of the Lord. ℟. **Praise to you, Lord Jesus Christ.**

→ No. 14, p. 18

PRAYER OVER THE GIFTS   [Unity and Peace]

Lord,
we offer you the sacrifice
by which your Son reconciles mankind.
May it bring unity and peace to the world.
We ask this through Christ our Lord. ℟. **Amen.** ↓

PREFACE (51)   [Marks of Christ's Kingdom]

FATHER, all-powerful and ever-living God,
we do well always and everywhere to give you
    thanks.
You anointed Jesus Christ, your only Son, with
    the oil of gladness,
as the eternal priest and universal king.
As priest he offered his life on the altar of the
    cross
and redeemed the human race
by this one perfect sacrifice of peace.
As king he claims dominion over all creation,
that he may present to you, his almighty
    Father,
an eternal and universal kingdom:
a kingdom of truth and life,
a kingdom of holiness and grace,

a kingdom of justice, love, and peace.
And so, with all the choirs of angels in heaven
we proclaim your glory
and join in their unending hymn of praise:

→ No. 23, p. 25

COMMUNION ANTIPHON Ps. 28 (29).10-11

[Eternal Reign]

**The Lord will reign for ever and will give his
people the gift of peace.** ↓

PRAYER AFTER COMMUNION   [Kingdom of Joy]

Lord,
you give us Christ, the King of all creation,
as food for everlasting life.
Help us to live by his gospel
and bring us to the joy of his kingdom,
where he lives and reigns for ever and ever.
℟. **Amen.**   → No. 32, p. 75

Optional Solemn Blessings, p. 96, and Prayers Over the People, p. 104

HYMNAL

1

O Come, O Come, Emmanuel

Tr. J. M. Neale, 1816-66
and others

Veni Emmanuel
Melody adapted by
T. Helmore, 1811-90

1. O come, O come, Em - man - u - el, And ran -
2. O come, thou rod of Jes - se, free Thine own
3. O come, thou day-spring, come and cheer Our spir -
4. O come, thou key of Da - vid, come, And o -
5. O come, O come, thou Lord of might, Who to

1. som cap - tive Is - ra - el, That mourns in
2. from Sa - tan's tyr - an - ny; From depths of
3. its by thine ad - vent here; Dis - perse the
4. pen wide our heav'n - ly home; Make safe the
5. thy tribes, from Si - nai's height, In an - cient

1. low - ly ex - ile here, Un - til the Son of
2. hell thy peo - ple save, And give them vic - t'ry
3. gloom - y clouds of night, And death's dark shad-ows
4. way that leads on high, And close the path to
5. times didst give the law In cloud, in ma - jes -

Refrain:

1. God ap-pear.
2. o'er the grave.
3. put to flight. Re - joice! Re-joice! O Is -
4. mis - er - y.
5. ty, and awe.

ra - el. To thee shall come Em - man - u - el.

586

Hark, a Mystic Voice Is Sounding

Tr. E. Caswall, 1849

En Clara Vox
R.L. de Pearsall, 1795-1856

1.

Hark, a mystic voice is sounding;
"Christ is nigh," It seems to
say;
"Cast away the dreams of
darkness,
O ye children of the day."

2.

Startled at the solemn warning,
Let the earthbound soul arise;

Christ her sun, all sloth dispel-
ling,
Shines upon the morning
skies.

3.

Lo, the Lamb so long ex-
pected
Comes with pardon down
from heav'n;
Let us haste, with tears of sorrow,
One and all, to be forgiv'n.

The Coming of Our God

1.

The coming of our Lord
Our thought must now employ;
Then let us meet him on the
road.
With song of holy joy.

2.

The co-eternal Son
A maiden's offspring see;

A servant's form Christ put-
teth on;
To set his people free.

3.

Daughter of Sion, rise
To greet thine Infant King;
Not let thy thankless heart de-
spise
The pardon he doth bring

O Come, Divine Messiah

Anne Pellegrin, 1663-1745
Sr. St. Mary of St. Philip

Venez Divin Messie
16th Century French
Harm. G. Ridout, 1971

O come, divine Messiah!
The world in silence waits the
day
When hope shall sing its tri-
umph,
And sadness flee away.

Chorus: Sweet Saviour, haste,
Come, come to earth:
Dispel the night, and show
thy face,
And bid us hail the dawn of
grace.
O come, divine Messiah,
The world in silence waits
the day
When hope shall sing its tri-
umph,
And sadness flee away.

5

Hark! The Herald Angels Sing

1. Hark! The herald angels sing,
"Glory to the new-born King.
Peace on earth, and mercy mild,
God and sinners reconciled."
Joyful, all ye nations, rise,
Join the triumph of the skies.
With th'angelic host proclaim,
"Christ is born in Bethlehem."

—*Refrain*. Hark! The herald angels sing,
"Glory to the newborn King."

2. Christ, by highest heav'n adored,
Christ, the everlasting Lord.
Late in time behold him come,
Off-spring of a virgin's womb.
Veiled in flesh, the Godhead see;
Hail th'incarnate Deity!
Pleased as Man with men to appear,
Jesus, our Emmanuel. —*Refrain*

6

Silent Night

Silent night, holy night!
  All is calm, all is bright.
'Round yon Virgin Mother and
  Child.
Holy Infant so tender and
  mild:
Sleep in heavenly peace,
  Sleep in heavenly peace!

Silent night, holy night!
  Shepherds quake at the
    sight!
Glories stream from heaven
  afar.
Heav'nly hosts sing Alleluia:
Christ, the Saviour is born,
  Christ, the Saviour is born!

7

We Three Kings

1. We three kings of Orient are
Bearing gifts we traverse afar,
Field and fountain, moor and mountain,
Following yonder Star.

Refrain: O Star of wonder, Star of night,
Star with royal beauty bright,
Westward leading, still proceeding,
Guide us to thy perfect light.

2. Born a king on Bethlehem's plain,
Gold I bring to crown Him again,
King forever, ceasing never,
Over us all to reign. —*Refrain*

O Come, All Ye Faithful

8

1. O come, all ye faithful, joyful and triumphant,
   O come ye, O come ye to Bethlehem;
   Come and behold him born the King of angels.

   —*Refrain:* O come, let us adore him,
   O come, let us adore him,
   O come, let us adore him, Christ the Lord.

2. Sing choirs of angels, Sing in exultation,
   Sing all ye citizens of Heav'n above;
   Glory to God in the highest. —*Refrain*

3. See how the shepherd summoned to his cradle,
   Leaving their flocks draw nigh with lowly fear;
   We too will thither bend our joyful footsteps. —*Refrain*

The First Noel

9

1. The first Noel the angel did say,
   Was to certain poor shepherds in fields as they lay;
   In fields where they lay keeping their sheep
   On a cold winter's night that was so deep.

   —*Refrain:* Noel, Noel, Noel, Noel,
   Born is the King of Israel.

2. They looked up and saw a star,
   Shining in the east, beyond them far,
   And to the earth it gave great light,
   And so it continued both day and night. —*Refrain*

3. This star drew nigh to the northwest,
   O'er Bethlehem it took its rest,
   And there it did both stop and stay,
   Right over the place where Jesus lay. —*Refrain*

4. Then entered in those wise men three,
   Full reverently upon their knee,
   And offered there in his presence,
   Their gold and myrrh and frankincense. —*Refrain*

589

10

Angels We Have Heard on High

1. Angels we have heard on high,
   Sweetly singing o'er the plain,
   And the mountains in reply
   Echoing their joyous strain.

   Refrain: **Gloria in excelsis Deo.** (Repeat)

2. Shepherds, why this jubilee,
   Why your joyous strains prolong?
   Say, what may the tidings be
   Which inspire your heav'nly song? —*Refrain*

3. Come to Bethlehem and see
   Him whose birth the angels sing;
   Come, adore on bended knee
   Christ the Lord, the newborn King. —*Refrain*

11

Joy to the World

1.
Joy to the world! The Lord is
   come;
   Let earth receive her King;
Let every heart prepare him
   room,
   And heav'n and nature sing,
And heav'n and nature sing,
   And heaven, and heaven
   and nature sing.

2.
Joy to the world! the Saviour
   reigns;
   Let men their songs employ,
While fields and floods,
   Rocks, hills, and plains,
Repeat the sounding joy,
   Repeat the sounding joy,
Repeat, repeat the sounding
   joy.

12

O Sing a Joyous Carol

1. O sing a joyous carol
   Unto the Holy Child,
   And praise with gladsome
   voices
   His mother undefiled.
   Our gladsome voices greet-
   ing
   Shall hail our Infant King;
   And our sweet Lady listens
   When joyful voices sing.

2. Who is there meekly lying
   In yonder stable poor?
   Dear children, it is Jesus;
   He bids you now adore.
   Who is there kneeling by
   him?
   In Virgin beauty fair?
   It is our Mother Mary,
   She bids you all draw
   near.

Lord, Who throughout These 40 Days

1. Lord, Who throughout these forty days
   For us did fast and pray,
   Teach us to overcome our sins
   And close by you to stay.

2. As you with Satan did contend
   And did the vic'try win,
   O give us strength in you to fight,
   In you to conquer sin.

3. As you did hunger and did thirst,
   So teach us, gracious Lord,
   To die to self and so to live
   By your most holy word.

O Faithful Cross

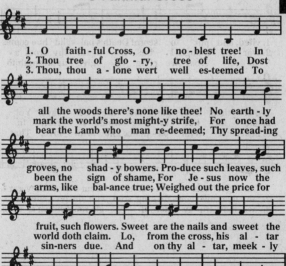

1. O faith - ful Cross, O no - blest tree! In
2. Thou tree of glo - ry, tree of life, Dost
3. Thou, thou a - lone wert well es-teemed To

all the woods there's none like thee! No earth - ly
mark the world's most might-y strife, For once had
bear the Lamb who man re-deemed; Thy spread-ing

groves, no shad - y bowers. Pro-duce such leaves, such
been the sign of shame, For Je - sus now the
arms, like bal-ance true; Weighed out the price for

fruit, such flowers. Sweet are the nails and sweet the
world doth claim. Lo, from the cross, his al - tar
sin-ners due. And on thy al - tar, meek - ly

wood That bears a load so sweet, so good!
throne, He gent - ly draws and rules his own.
laid, The lamb of God a - tone - ment made.

15 O Sacred Head, Surrounded

H.W. Baker, 1861
A.T. Russell, 1851, alt.

Passion Chorale
H. L. Hassler, 1601
Adapted, J.S. Bach, 1685-1750

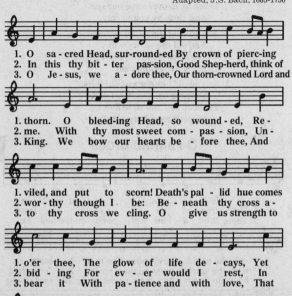

1. O sa - cred Head, sur-round-ed By crown of pierc-ing
2. In this thy bit - ter pas-sion, Good Shep-herd, think of
3. O Je - sus, we a - dore thee, Our thorn-crowned Lord and

1. thorn. O bleed-ing Head, so wound - ed, Re -
2. me. With thy most sweet com - pas - sion, Un -
3. King. We bow our hearts be - fore thee, And

1. viled, and put to scorn! Death's pal - lid hue comes
2. wor - thy though I be: Be - neath thy cross a -
3. to thy cross we cling. O give us strength to

1. o'er thee, The glow of life de - cays, Yet
2. bid - ing For ev - er would I rest, In
3. bear it With pa - tience and with love, That

1. an - gel hosts a - dore thee, And trem-ble as they gaze.
2. thy dear love con - fid - ing, And with thy pre-sence blest.
3. we may tru - ly mer - it A glo-rious crown a - bove.

All Glory, Laud and Honour

St. Theodulph of Orleans, c. 820
Tr. J.M. Neale, 1854, alt.

St. Theodulph
M. Teachner, 1615

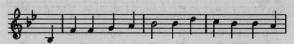

1. All glo - ry, laud, and hon - our To thee, Re-deem-er,

1. King, To whom the lips of chil - dren Made

Fine

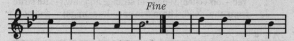

1. sweet ho - san - nas ring. 2. Thou art the King of
3. The com - pa - ny of
4. The peo - ple of the
5. To thee be - fore thy
6. Thou didst ac - cept their

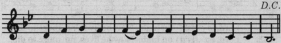

2. Is - rael, Thou Da - vid's roy - al Son. Who
3. an - gels Are prais - ing thee on high, And
4. He - brews With palms be - fore thee went; Our
5. pas - sion They sang their hymns of praise; To
6. prais - es, Ac - cept the pray'rs we bring, Who

D.C.

2. in the Lord's name com-est, The King and bles-sed One.
3. mor-tal men and all things Cre - a - ted make re - ply.
4. praise and pray'r and an - thems Be - fore thee we pre-sent.
5. thee now high ex - alt - ed Our mel - o - dy we raise.
6. in all good de - light-est, Thou good and gra-cious King.

Christ the Lord Is Ris'n Today

Jane E. Leeson, c. 1851,
based on Victimae Paschali

Victimae Paschali
Traditional

1. Christ, the Lord is   ris'n to - day, Chris-tians, haste your
2. Christ, the vic-tim   un - de-filed, Man to God has
3. Christ, who once for   sin - ers bled, Now the first - born

1. vows to pay;   Of - fer ye your prais - es meet
2. rec - on - ciled; When in strange and aw - ful strife
3. from the dead, Thron'd in end - less might   and pow'r

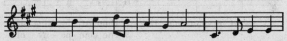

1. At the pas - chal   vic-tim's feet.   For the sheep the
2. Met to - geth - er   death and life;   Chris-tians, on this
3. Lives and reigns for   ev - er more.   Hail, e - ter - nal

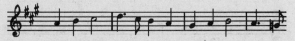

1. Lamb has bled, Sin-less in the sinners' stead; Christ, the
2. hap - py day Haste with joy your vows to pay. Christ, the
3. hope on high! Hail, thou King of vic - to - ry! Hail, thou

1. Lord, is   ris'n on high, Now he lives, no more to die!
2. Lord, is   ris'n on high, Now he lives, no more to die!
3. Prince of life a-dored! Help and save us, gra-cious Lord.

The Strife is O'er

Tr. F. Pott, 1861, alt.

Victory
Palestrina, 1591
Adapted W.H. Monk, 1861

1. The strife is o'er, the bat - tle done;
2. Death's might-iest pow'rs have done their worst,
3. On the third morn he rose a - gain,
4. Lord, by the stripes which wound - ed thee,

1. Now is the Vic - tor's tri - umph won;
2. But Je - sus has his foes dis - persed;
3. Glo - rious in maj - es - ty to reign;
4. From death's dread sting thy ser - vants free,

1. O let the song of praise be sung!
2. Let shouts of joy and praise out - burst!
3. O let us swell the joy - ful strain!
4. That we may live, and sing to thee:

Al - le - lu - ia!

O God, Our Help in Ages Past

1.

O God, our help in ages past,
　Our hope for years to come,
Our shelter from the stormy
　　blast,
　And our eternal home.

2.

Beneath the shadow of Thy
　　throne,
　Thy saints have dwelt se-
　　cure,
Sufficient is Thine arm alone,
　And our defence is sure.

3.

Before the hills in order stood,
　Or earth received her frame,
From everlasting Thou art
　　God,
　To endless years the same.

4.

A thousand ages in Thy sight,
　Are like an evening gone.
Short as the watch that ends
　　the night,
Before the rising sun.

Jesus Christ Is Ris'n Today

1. Je - sus Christ is ris'n to - day,
2. Hymns of praise then let us sing,
3. But the pains which he en - dured,
4. Sing we to our God a - bove,

Al - -

- le - lu - ia!

1. Our tri - um - phant
2. Un - to Christ our
3. Our sal - va - tion
4. Praise e - ter - nal

1. ho - ly day,
2. heav'n - ly King,
3. have pro - cured;
4. as his love.

Al - - le -

lu - ia!

1. Who did once up - on the cross,
2. Who en - dured the cross and grave,
3. Now a - bove the sky he's King,
4. Praise him, all ye heav'nly host,

Al - - le - lu - ia!

1. Suf - fer to re - deem our loss.
2. Sin - ners to re - deem and save.
3. Where the an - gels ev - er sing.
4. Fa - ther, Son and Ho - ly Ghost.

Al - - le - lu - ia!

That Eastertide with Joy was Bright

Verses 1, 2: tr. J.M. Neale, 1851 Lasst   Uns Erfreuen
Verse 3: tr. J. Chambers, 1857, alt.   Geistliches Kirchengesang, 1623

21

1. That East - er - tide with joy was bright, The
2. He showed to them his hands, his side, Where
3. To God the Fa - ther let us sing, To

1. sun shone out with fair - er light, Al - le -
2. yet those glo - rious wounds a - bide, Al - le -
3. God the Son, our ris - en King, Al - le -

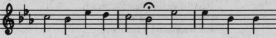

1. lu - ia, al - le - lu - ia, When, to their long -
2. lu - ia, al - le - lu - ia, The to - kens true
3. lu - ia, al - le - lu - ia, And e - qual - ly

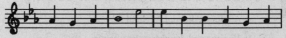

1. ing eyes re - stored, The glad a - pos - tles saw their
2. which made it plain. Their Lord in - deed was ris'n a -
3. let us a - dore The Ho - ly Spir - it ev - er -

1. Lord, Al - le - lu - ia, al - le - lu - ia, Al - le -
2. gain, Al - le - lu - ia, al - le - lu - ia, Al - le -
3. more, Al - le - lu - ia, al - le - lu - ia, Al - le -

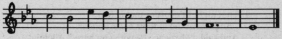

1. lu - ia, al - le - lu - ia, al - le - lu - ia!
2. lu - ia, al - le - lu - ia, al - le - lu - ia!
3. lu - ia, al - le - lu - ia, al - le - lu - ia!

22 ## At the Lamb's High Feast We Sing

1. At the Lamb's high feast we sing
     Praise to our victor'ous King.
   He has washed us in the tide
     Flowing from his opened side;
   Praise we him whose love divine
     Gives his sacred Blood for wine,
   Gives his Body for the feast,
     Christ the Victim, Christ the Priest.

2. When the Paschal blood is poured,
     Death's dark Angel sheathes his sword;
   Israel's hosts triumphant go
     Through the wave that drowns the foe.
   Christ the Lamb, whose Blood was shed,
     Paschal victim, Paschal bread;
   With sincerity and love
     Eat we Manna from above.

23 ## Ye Sons and Daughters, Let Us Sing

Alleluia! Alleluia! Alleluia!

1. Ye sons and daughters, let us sing!
     The King of heav'n, our glorious King,
   From death today rose triumphing. Alleluia!

2. That Easter morn, at break of day,
     The faithful women went their way
   To seek the tomb where Jesus lay. Alleluia!

3. An angel clothed in white they see,
     Who sat and spoke unto the three,
   "Your Lord has gone to Galilee." Alleluia!

4. That night th'apostles met in fear,
     And Christ did in their midst appear.
   And said, "My peace be with you here." Alleluia!

5. How blest are they who have not seen
     And yet whose faith has constant been,
   For they eternal life shall win. Alleluia!

All Hail, Adored Trinity

24

Verses 1, 2, 3: Anglo Saxon, 11th cent.
Praise God: Thomas Ken, 1709

Louis Bourgeois, 1551

1. All hail, a-dor-ed Trin-i-
2. Three Per-sons praise we ev-er-
3. O Trin-i-ty, O U-ni-

1. ty; All praise, e-ter-nal U-ni-ty:
2. more, And thee th'E-ter-nal One a-dore:
3. ty, Be pres-ent as we wor-ship thee;

1. O God the Fa-ther, God the
2. In thy sure mer-cy ev-er
3. And to the an-gel's songs in

1. Son, And God the Spir-it, ev-er One.
2. kind, May we our true pro-tec-tion find.
3. light Our prayers and prais-es now u-nite.

Sing We Triumphant Hymns of Praise

25

1. Sing we triumphant hymns of praise
   To greet our Lord these festive days.
   Alleluia, alleluia!
   Who by a road before untrod
   Ascended to the throne of God.
   Alleluia, alleluia.
   Alleluia, alleluia, alleluia!

2. In wond'ring awe His faithful band
   Upon the Mount of Olives stand.
   Alleluia, alleluia!
   And with the Virgin Mother see
   Their Lord ascend in majesty.
   Alleluia, alleluia.
   Alleluia, alleluia, alleluia!

599

26 Praise God from Whom All Blessings Flow

1. Praise God, from whom all blessings flow;
   Praise him, all creatures here below;
   Praise him above, ye heav'nly host;
   Praise Father, Son, and Holy Ghost.

2. All people that on earth do dwell,
   Sing to the Lord with cheerful voice;
   Him serve with mirth, his praise forth tell,
   Come ye before him and rejoice.

3. Know that the Lord is God indeed:
   Without our aid he did us make;
   We are his folk, he doth us feed,
   And for his sheep he doth us take.

4. O enter then his gates with praise,
   Approach with joy his courts unto;
   Praise, laud, and bless his name always,
   For it is seemly so to do.

27 Come, Holy Ghost

1. Come, Holy Ghost, Creator blest,
   And in our hearts take up your rest;
   Come with your grace and heav'nly aid
   To fill the hearts which you have made,
   To fill the hearts which you have made.

2. O Comforter, to you we cry,
   The heav'nly gift of God most high;
   The fount of life and fire of love,
   And sweet anointing from above,
   And sweet anointing from above.

3. To every sense your light impart,
   And shed your love in ev'ry heart.
   To our weak flesh, your strength supply:
   Unfailing courage from on high,
   Unfailing courage from on high.

4. O grant that we through you may come
   To know the Father and the Son,
   And hold with firm, unchanging faith,
   That you are Spirit of them both,
   That you are Spirit of them both.

O Holy Spirit, Lord of Peace

Tr. J. Chandler, 1806-76, alt.

Jeremiah Clark, 1709

28

1. O Ho-ly Spir-it, Lord of grace, E-ter-nal fount of love, In-flame, we pray, our in-most hearts With fire from heav'n a-bove.

2. As thou in bond of love dost join The Fa-ther and the Son, So fill us all with mu-tual love, U-nite our hearts as one.

3. All glo-ry to the Fa-ther be, All glo-ry to the Son, And Ho-ly Spir-it ev-er more While end-less a-ges run.

Creator Spirit, Lord of Grace

29

1. Creator Spirit, Lord of grace
   Make thou our hearts thy dwelling place
   And with thy might celestial, aid
   The souls of those whom thou hast made.

2. O to our souls thy light impart;
   And give thy love to every heart;
   Turn all our weakness into might,
   O thou the source of life and light.

3. To God the Father let us sing
   To God the Son, our risen king;
   And equally with thee adore
   The Spirit, God forevermore.

30 Now Thank We All Our God

M. Rinkart, 1586-1649
Tr. Catherine Winkworth, 1858

Nun Danket
J. Crüger, 1647

1. Now thank we all our God, With heart, and hand, and voic-es, Who won-drous things hath done, In whom his world re-joic-es; Who from our moth-er's arms Hath blessed us on our way With count-less gifts of love, And still is ours to-day.

2. O may this boun-teous God Through all our life be near us! With ev-er joy-ful hearts And bless-ed peace to cheer us; And keep us in his grace, And guide us when per-plex'd And free us from all ills In this world and the next.

3. All praise and thanks to God The Fa-ther now be giv-en, The Son, and him who reigns With them in high-est heav-en, The one e-ter-nal God, Whom heav'n and earth a-dore; For thus it was, is now, And shall be, ev-er-more.

31 We Gather Together

1. We gather together to ask the Lord's blessing;
   He chastens and hastens his will to make known;
   The wicked oppressing now cease from distressing:
   Sing praises to his name; he forgets not his own.

2. Beside us to guide us, our God with us joining,
   Ordaining, maintaining his kingdom divine;
   So from the beginning the fight we were winning:
   Thou, Lord, wast at our side; all glory be thine.

Holy, Holy, Holy

R. Heber, 1826, alt.

Nicaea
J. B. Dykes, 1861

1. Ho - ly, ho - ly, ho - ly! Lord God Al -
2. Ho - ly, ho - ly, ho - ly! an - gel hosts a -
3. Ho - ly, ho - ly, ho - ly! though the dark - ness
4. Ho - ly, ho - ly, ho - ly! Lord God Al -

1. might - y! Ear - ly in the morn - ing our
2. dore thee, Cast - ing down their gol - den crowns a -
3. hide thee, Though the eye of sin - ful man thy
4. might - y All thy works shall praise thy name, in

1. song shall rise to thee; Ho - ly, ho - ly
2. round the glas - sy sea. Che - ru - bim and
3. glo - ry may not see, On - ly thou art
4. earth, and sky, and sea; Ho - ly, ho - ly

1. ho - ly! mer - ci - ful and might - y:
2. sera - phim fall - ing down be - fore thee:
3. ho - ly! there is none be - side thee:
4. ho - ly! mer - ci - ful and might - y:

1. God in three Per - sons, bless-ed Trin - i - ty:
2. Which wert, and art, and ev - er more shall be.
3. Per - fect in pow'r, in love, and pur - i - ty:
4. God in three Per - sons, bless-ed Trin - i - ty:

33 Faith of Our Fathers

1. Faith of our fathers, living still,
   In spite of dungeon, fire and sword;
   O how our hearts beat high with joy
   When'ver we hear that glorious word!

   Refrain: Faith of our fathers, holy faith,
   We will be true to thee til death.

2. Faith of our fathers! We will love
   Both friends and foe in all our strife.
   And preach thee too, as love knows how,
   By kindly word and virtuous life. —*Refrain*

3. Faith of our fathers! Mary's pray'r
   Shall keep our country close to thee;
   And through the truth that comes from God
   Mankind shall prosper and be free. —*Refrain*

34 Holy God, We Praise Thy Name

1. Holy God, we praise thy name!
   Lord of all, we bow before thee!
   All on earth thy sceptre claim,
   All in heaven above adore thee.
   Infinite thy vast domain,
   Everlasting is thy reign. *Repeat last two lines*

2. Hark! the loud celestial hymn
   Angel choirs above are raising;
   Cherubim and seraphim,
   In unceasing chorus praising,
   Fill the heavens with sweet accord;
   Holy, holy, holy Lord! *Repeat last two lines*

35 Redeemer, King and Saviour

1.

Redeemer, King and Saviour
Your death we celebrate
So good, yet born our brother,
You live in human state.
O Saviour, in your dying
You do your Father's will,
Give us the strength to suffer
To live for others still.

2.

Your dying and your rising
Give hope and life to all.
Your faithful way of giving
Embraces great and small.
Help us to make our journey,
to walk your glorious way,
And from the night of dying
To find a joy-filled day.

To Jesus Christ, Our Sovereign King

36

M.B. Hellriegel

Ich Glaub An Gott
Mainz, 1900

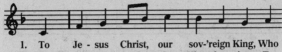

1. To Je - sus Christ, our sov-'reign King, Who
2. Your reign ex - tend, O King be - nign, To
3. To you and to your Church, great King, We

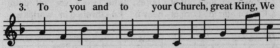

1. is the word's sal - va - tion, All praise and hom - age
2. ev - 'ry land and na - tion; For in your king-dom,
3. pledge our hearts' ob - la - tion; Un - til be - fore your

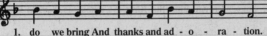

1. do we bring And thanks and ad - o - ra - tion.
2. Lord di - vine, A - lone we find sal - va - tion.
3. throne we sing In end - less ju - bi - la - tion:

Refrain:

Christ, Je - sus, Vic - tor! Christ, Je-sus, Rul - er!

Christ, Je - sus, Lord and Re - deem - er!

O Lord, I Am Not Worthy

37

1. O Lord, I am not worthy,
   That thou shouldst come to me,
   But speak the word of comfort:
   My spirit healed shall be.

2. And humbly I'll receive thee,
   The bridegroom of my soul,
   No more by sin to grieve thee
   Or fly thy sweet control.

3. O Sacrament most holy,
   O Sacrament divine,
   All praise and all thanksgiving
   Be every moment thine.

38 Crown Him with Many Crowns

M. Bridges, 1851
and others

Diademata
G.J. Elvey, 1868

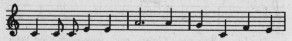

1. Crown him with man-y crowns. The Lamb up-on his
2. Crown him the Lord of Lords, Who o-ver all doth
3. Crown him the Lord of heav'n En-throned in worlds a-

1. throne: Hark, how the heav'n-ly an-them drowns All
2. reign, Who once on earth th'in-car-nate Word, For
3. bove; Crown him the King, to whom is giv'n The

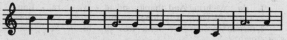

1. mu-sic but its own! A-wake my soul, and sing Of
2. ran-somed sin-ners slain, Now lives in realms of light, Where
3. won-drous name of Love. Crown him with man-y crowns. As

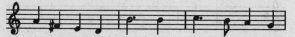

1. him who died for thee. And hail him as thy
2. saints with an-gels sing Their songs be-fore him
3. thrones be-fore him fall. Crown him, ye kings, with

1. match-less King Through all e-ter-ni-ty.
2. day and night, Their God, Re-deem-er, King.
3. man-y crowns, For he is King of all.

606

Let All Mortal Flesh Keep Silence

Liturgy of St. James
Tr. G. Moultrie, 1864

Traditional French Carol

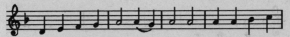

1. Let all mor-tal flesh keep si-lence, And with fear and
2. King of kings, yet born of Ma-ry, As of old on
3. Rank on rank the host of heav-en Spreads its van-guard
4. At his feet the six-winged ser-aph; Cher-u-bim with

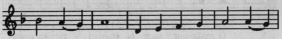

1. trem-bling stand; Pon-der noth-ing earth-ly-
2. earth he stood, Lord of lords in hu-man
3. on the way, As the Light of light de-
4. sleep-less eye, Veil their fac-es to the

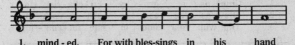

1. mind-ed, For with bles-sings in his hand
2. ves-ture, In the bod-y and the blood
3. scen-deth From the realms of end-less day
4. Pre-sence, As with cease-less voice they cry.

1. Christ our God to earth de-secend - -
2. He will give to all the faith - -
3. That the pow'rs of hell may van - -
4. "Al-le-lu-ia, Al-le-lu - -

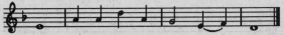

1. eth, Our full hom-age to de-mand.
2. ful His own self for heav'n-ly food.
3. ish As the dark-ness clears a-way.
4. ia, Al-le-lu-ia, Lord most high!"

40 Lord, Who at Your First Eucharist Did Pray

W.H. Turton, 1881, alt.

Song I
O. Gibbons, 1623

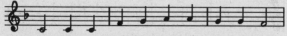

1. Lord, who at your first Eu - cha - rist did pray
2. For all your Church, O Lord, we in - ter - cede;
3. So, Lord, at length when sa - cra - ments shall cease,

1. That all your Church might be for ev - er one,
2. O make our lack of char - i - ty to cease;
3. May we be one with all your Church a - bove,

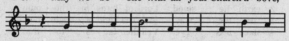

1. Grant us at ev - 'ry Eu - cha - rist to
2. Draw us the near - er each to each, we
3. One with your saints in one un - end - ing

1. say With long - ing heart and soul, "Your will be
2. plead, By draw - ing all to you, O prince of
3. peace, One with your saints in one un - bound - ed

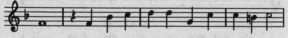

1. done." O may we all one bread, one bod - y be
2. peace; Thus may we all one bread, one bod - y be
3. love: More bless-ed still in peace and love to be

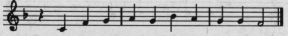

1. Through this blest Sa - cra - ment of u - ni - ty.
2. Through this blest Sa - cra - ment of u - ni - ty.
3. One with the Trin - i - ty in u - ni - ty.

608

Sing of Mary, Pure and Lowly

Roland F. Palmer

Pleading Saviour
Plymouth Collection, 1855

1. Sing of Mary, pure and low - ly,
2. Sing of Je - sus, son of Ma - ry,
3. Glo - ry be to God the Fa - ther;

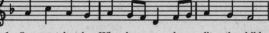

1. Vir - gin - moth-er un - de - filed, Sing of God's own
2. In the home at Na - za - reth. Toil and la - bour
3. Glo - ry be to God the Son; Glo - ry be to

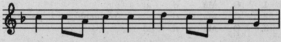

1. Son most ho - ly, Who be - came her lit - tle child.
2. can - not wea - ry Love en - dur - ing un - to death.
3. God the Spir - it; Glo - ry to the Three in One.

1. Fair - est child of fair - est moth - er,
2. Con - stant was the love he gave her,
3. From the heart of bless - ed Ma - ry,

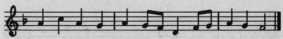

1. God the Lord who came to earth, Word made flesh, our
2. Though he went forth from her side, Forth to preach, and
3. From all saints the song as - cends, And the Church the

1. ver - y broth - er, Takes our na - ture by his birth.
2. heal, and suf - fer, Till on Cal - va - ry he died.
3. strain re - ech - oes Un - to earth's re - mo-test ends.

42 # Hail, Holy Queen, Enthroned Above

Traditional

Salve Regina Caelitum
Traditional

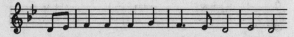

1. Hail, ho - ly Queen en - throned a - bove, O Ma-
2. Our life, our sweet-ness here be - low, O Ma-
3. We hon - our you for Christ, your son, O Ma-

1. ri - a! Hail, moth-er of mer - cy and of love,
2. ri - a! Our hope in sor - row and in woe,
3. ri - a! Who has for us re - demp-tion won,

Refrain:

1. O Ma - ri - a!
2. O Ma - ri - a! Tri - umph all ye
3. O Ma - ri - a!

che - ru - bim, Sing with us, ye se - ra - phim,

Heav'n and earth re - sound the hymn: Sal - ve,

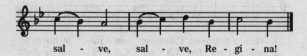

sal - ve, sal - ve, Re - gi - na!

610

Immaculate Mary

Anon.

Lourdes
Traditional Lourdes Melody

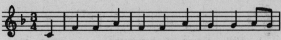

1. Im - mac - u - late Ma - ry, your prais - es we
2. In heav - en, the bless - ed your glo - ry pro -
3. Your name is our pow - er, your vir - tues our
4. We pray for our moth - er, the Church up - on

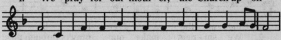

1. sing, You reign now in heav - en with Je - sus our King.
2. claim; On earth, we your chil - dren in - voke your fair name.
3. light, Your love is our com - fort, your plead - ing our might.
4. earth, And bless, dear - est la - dy, the land of our birth.

Refrain:

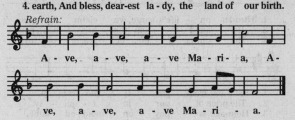

A - ve, a - ve, a - ve Ma - ri - a, A -

ve, a - ve, a - ve Ma - ri - a.

Hail, O Star of Ocean

1. Hail, O Star of Ocean,
   Portal of the sky!
   Ever Virgin Mother
   Of the Lord most high.

2. O by Gabriel's Ave
   Uttered long ago,
   Eva's name reversing
   Brought us peace below.

Hail, Queen of Heav'n the Ocean Star

J. Lingrad, c. 1084

Stella
English Traditional

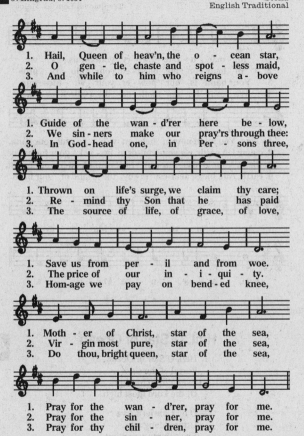

1. Hail, Queen of heav'n, the o-cean star,
2. O gen-tle, chaste and spot-less maid,
3. And while to him who reigns a-bove

1. Guide of the wan-d'rer here be-low,
2. We sin-ners make our pray'rs through thee:
3. In God-head one, in Per-sons three,

1. Thrown on life's surge, we claim thy care;
2. Re-mind thy Son that he has paid
3. The source of life, of grace, of love,

1. Save us from per-il and from woe.
2. The price of our in-i-qui-ty.
3. Hom-age we pay on bend-ed knee,

1. Moth-er of Christ, star of the sea,
2. Vir-gin most pure, star of the sea,
3. Do thou, bright queen, star of the sea,

1. Pray for the wan-d'rer, pray for me.
2. Pray for the sin-ner, pray for me.
3. Pray for thy chil-dren, pray for me.

For All the Saints

W.W. How, 1864

Sine Nomine
R. Vaughan Williams, 1906

1. For all the saints, who from their la-bours rest, who thee by faith be-fore the world con-fess'd, Thy name, O Je-sus, be for ev-er blest. Al-
2. Thou wast their rock, their for-tress and their might: Thou, Lord, their Cap-tain in the well-fought fight; Thou in the dark-ness drear, their one true light. Al-
3. O may thy sol-diers, faith-ful, true and bold, Fight as the saints who no-bly fought of old, And win, with them, the vic-tor's crown of gold. Al-
4. O blest com-mun-ion, fel-low-ship di-vine, We fee-bly strug-gle, they in glo-ry shine: Yet all are one in thee, for all are thine. Al-

1-4 le-lu-ia, al-le-lu-ia!

Music from the English Hymnal,
used by permission of Oxford University Press

Joseph, Be Our Guide and Pattern

Muriel Newton-White, 1971

Oriel
C. Ett, Cantica Sacra, 1840

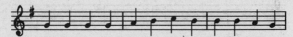

1. Jo - seph, be our guide and pat - tern, Faith - ful to your
2. Faith - ful to the guid - ing vis - ion, List'-ning to the
3. Lead - ing them through man - y dan - gers To the home in
4. Work - man skilled with saw and ham - mer, Strong to earn the
5. Train - ing Christ, the grow - ing Mas - ter, In the skill - ful
6. Jo - seph, cho - sen as our pa - tron In this dear and

1. sa - cred trust, Strong pro - tec - tor of the Vir - gin
2. an - gel's word; Shield - ing Ma - ry from all slan - der,
3. Na - za - reth, Hum - bly for their needs pro - vid - ing
4. dai - ly bread, From the gifts of God cre - a - ting
5. use of tools; Teach - ing him, the world's Re - deem - er,
6. love - ly land, Hear us as we sing your prais - es:

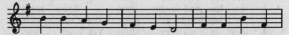

1. And the in - fant, Je - sus Christ. Jo - seph, firm and
2. Guard - ing Christ, the lit - tle Lord. Jo - seph, true and
3. In your wise and stead - fast faith. Jo - seph, brave, ob -
4. Use - ful things to meet man's need. Jo - seph, strong and
5. Craft - man's love of wood and nails. Jo - seph, hum - ble,
6. Pray for us to God, our Lord. Jo - seph, just and

1. faith - ful, guide us, Jo - seph, walk the way with us.
2. trust - ing, guide us, Jo - seph, walk the way with us.
3. e - dient, guide us, Jo - seph, walk the way with us.
4. stead-fast, guide us, Jo - seph, walk the way with us.
5. help - ful, guide us, Jo - seph, walk the way with us.
6. ho - ly, guide us, Jo - seph, walk the way with us.

We Praise Thee, O God, Our Redeemer

Julia C. Cory, 1882-1963. alt.

Kremser
Netherlands Melody, 1626

48

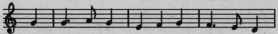

1. We praise thee, O God, our Re - deem - er, Cre -
2. We wor - ship thee, God of our fa - thers, we
3. With voic - es u - nit - ed our prais - es we

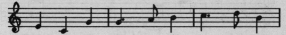

1. a - tor, In grate - ful de - vo - tion our
2. bless thee; Through trou - ble and tem - pest our
3. of - fer, And glad - ly our songs of true

1. trib - ute we bring. We lay it be - fore thee, we
2. guide hast thou been. When per - ils o'er - take us, thou
3. wor - ship we raise. Our sins now con - fess - ing, we

1. kneel and a - dore thee, We bless thy ho - ly
2. wilt not for - sake us, And with thy help, O
3. pray for thy bless - ing; To thee, our great Re-

1. name, glad prais - es we sing.
2. Lord, life's bat - tles we win.
3. deem - er, for ev - er be praise.

A Mighty Fortress Is Our God

Verses 1, 2: anon.
Verse 3: R. Nachtwey, 1964
based on Psalm 45 and M. Luther

Ein' Feste Burg
M. Luther, 1483-1546

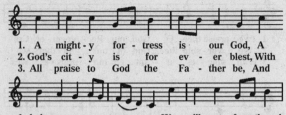

1. A might-y for-tress is our God, A
2. God's cit-y is for ev-er blest, With
3. All praise to God the Fa-ther be, And

1. help-er ev-er near us. We will not fear, though
2. liv-ing wa-ters well-ing; Since God is there, she
3. thanks for our cre-a-tion; All praise to Christ, the

1. earth be moved, For God is here to cheer us. Al-
2. stands un-moved 'Mid tu-mults round her swell-ing; God
3. Fa-ther's Son, And thanks for our sal-va-tion; And

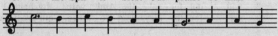

1. though the moun-tains quake And earth's foun-da-tions
2. speaks and all is peace, From war the na-tions
3. to the Spir-it blest Our praise be man-i-

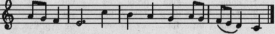

1. shake, Though an-gry bil-lows roar And break a-
2. cease; The Lord of hosts is nigh, Our fa-thers'
3. fest; To God the One in Three All glo-ry

1. gainst the shore, Our might-y God will hear us.
2. God most high Is our e-ter-nal dwell-ing.
3. ev-er be, All praise and ad-o-ra-tion.

Praise to the Lord, the Almighty

J. Neander, 1950-80
Tr. Catherine Winkworth, 1863, alt.

Lobe Den Herren
Stralsund Gesangbuch, 1665

50

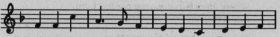

1. Praise to the Lord, the Al - might - y, the King of cre -
2. Praise to the Lord, let us of - fer our gifts at the
3. Praise to the Lord, who does pros-per our work and de -
4. Praise to the Lord, O let all that is in us a -

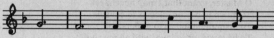

1. a - tion! O my soul, praise him for
2. al - tar. Let not our sins and of -
3. fend us; Sure - ly his good - ness and
4. dore him. All that has life and breath

1. he is your health and sal - va - tion.
2. fen - ces now cause us to fal - ter.
3. mer - cy here dai - ly at - tend us;
4. come now re - joi - cing be - fore him.

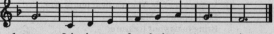

1. All you who hear, now to the al - tar draw
2. Christ the high priest, bids us all join in the
3. Pon - der a - new what the Al - might - y can
4. Let the A - men sound from his peo - ple a -

1. near; Join in pro - found ad - o - ra - tion.
2. feast, Vic - tims with him on the al - tar.
3. do, If with his love he be - friends us.
4. gain, As we here wor-ship be - fore him.

51 Peace Prayer of St. Francis

Make me a channel of your peace.
Where there is hatred, let me bring your love.
Where there is injury, your pardon, Lord.
And where there's doubt, true faith in you.

Make me a channel of your peace.
Where there's despair in life, let me bring hope.
Where there is darkness only light.
And where there's sadness ever joy.

O Master, grant that I may never seek
So much to be consoled as to console.
To be understood as to understand.
To be loved, as to love, with all my soul.

Make me a channel of your peace.
It is in pardoning that we are pardoned.
In giving to all men that we receive.
And in dying that we're born to eternal life.

52 O Most Holy One

1. O most holy one, O most lowly one,
   Loving virgin, Maria!
   Mother, maid of fairest love,
   Lady, queen of all above,
   Ora, ora pro nobis.

2. Virgin ever fair, Mother, hear our prayer,
   Look upon us, Maria!
   Bring to us your treasure,
   Grace beyond all measure,
   Ora, ora pro nobis.

Amazing Grace

53

1. A - maz - ing grace! how
2. 'Twas grace that taught my
3. The Lord has prom - ised
4. Through man - y dan - gers,
5. When we've been there ten

1. sweet the sound That saved a
2. heart to fear, And grace my
3. good to me, His word my
4. toils, and snares, I have al -
5. thou - sand years, Bright shin - ing

1. wretch like me! I once — was
2. fears re - leaved; How pre - cious
3. hope se - cures; He will — my
4. read - y come; 'Tis grace — has
5. as the sun, We've no less

1. lost, but now — am found, Was
2. did that grace — ap - pear The
3. shield and por - tion be, As
4. brought me safe — thus far, And
5. days to sing — God's praise Than

1. blind, but now I see.
2. hour I first be - lieved!
3. long as life en - dures.
4. grace will lead me home.
5. when we'd first be - gun.

54

Gift of Finest Wheat

Official Hymn of the Eucharistic Congress, 1976

Omer Westendorf   Robert E. Kreutz

Refrain: **You satisfy the hungry heart**
With gift of finest wheat;
Come give to us, O Saving Lord,
The bread of life to eat.

1.

As when the shepherd calls his
  sheep,
They know and heed his voice;
So when you call your fam'ly,
  Lord,
We follow and rejoice.

2.

With joyful lips we sing to you
Our praise and gratitude,
That you should count us wor-
  thy, Lord,
To share this heav'nly food.

3.

Is not the cup we bless and
  share
The blood of Christ outpoured?
Do not one cup, one loaf de-
  clare
Our oneness in the Lord?

4.

The myst'ry of your presence,
  Lord,
No mortal tongue can tell:
Who all the world cannot con-
  tain
Comes in our hearts to dwell.

5.

You give yourself to us, O
  Lord;
Then selfless let us be,
To serve each other in your
  name,
In truth and charity.

55

Sing, My Tongue, the Saviour's Glory

1.

Sing, my tongue, the Saviour's
  glory,
Of his flesh the myst'ry sing;
Of the Blood, all price exceed-
  ing,
Shed by our immortal King,
Destined for the world's re-
  demption,
From a noble womb to spring.

2.

Of a pure and spotless Virgin
Born for us on earth below,
He, as Man, with man convers-
  ing,
Stayed, the seeds of truth to
  sow;
Then he closed in solemn order
Wondrously his life of woe.

3.

On the night of that Last Sup-
per,
Seated with his chosen band,
He the Paschal victim eating,
First fulfils the Law's com-
mand;
Then as food to his Apostles
Gives himself with his own
Hand.

4.

Word made flesh the bread of
nature
By his word to Flesh he turns;
Wine into his blood he changes
What though sense no change
discerns?
Only be the heart in earnest,
Faith its lesson quickly learns.

(Tantum ergo)

5.

Down in adoration falling
Lo! the sacred Host we hail;
Lo! o'er ancient forms depart-
ing,
Newer rites of grace prevail;
Faith for all defects supplying,
Where the feeble senses fail.

6.

To the Everlasting Father,
And the Son who reigns on
high,
With the Holy Ghost proceed-
ing
Forth from each eternally
Be salvation, honour, blessing,
Might and endless majesty.
Amen.

Lord, Dismiss Us with Thy Blessing 56

1.

Lord, dismiss us with thy
blessing;
Fill our hearts with joy and
peace;
May we all, thy love possess-
ing,
Triumph in redeeming grace:
O refresh us, O refresh us,
And the world its turmoil
cease.

2.

Thanks to thee and adoration
For the scriptures' joyful
sound,
May the fruit of thy redemp-
tion
In our hearts and lives abound;
Ever faithful, ever faithful
To the ways of truth be found.

The King of Glory 57

W. F. Jabusch   Israeli Folksong

Refrain: The King of Glory comes,
the people rejoices;
Open the gates before him,
lift up your voices.

1. Who is the King of Glory;
how shall we call him?
He is Emmanuel,
the promised of ages.

2. In all of Galilee,
In city or village,
He goes among his people
Curing their illness.

58   Praise the Lord of Heaven

T.B. Browne, 1844, alt.

Une Vaine Crainte
French Carol Melody

1.

Praise the Lord of heaven; / Praise him in the height!
Praise him, all ye angels, / Praise him stars and light;
Praise him, earth and waters, / Praise him, all ye skies;
When his word commanded, / All things did arise.

2.

Praise the Lord, ye fountains / Of the depths and seas,
Rocks and hills and mountains, / Cedars and all trees;
Praise him, clouds and vapours, / Snow and hail and fire,
Nature all fulfilling / Only his desire.

3.

Praise him, all ye nations, / Rulers and all kings;
Praise him, men and maidens, / All created things;
Glorious and mighty / Is his name alone;
All the earth his footstool, / Heaven is his throne.

59   To Christ the Prince of Peace

1. To Christ the prince of Peace
   And the Son of God most high,
   The Father of the world to come,
   Sing we with holy joy.
   Deep in his heart for us
   The wound of love he bore;
   That love wherewith he
   Still inflames the hearts that him adore.

2. O Jesus, Victim blest,
   What else but love divine
   Could thou constrain to open thus
   That sacred Heart of thine.
   O fount of endless Life,
   O Spring of Waters Clear,
   O Flame Celestial,
   Cleansing all who unto thee draw near.

622

Praise, My Soul, The King of Heaven

60

F. Lyte

John Goss

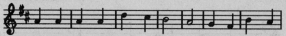

1. Praise, my soul, the King of hea - ven; To his feet thy
2. Praise him for his grace and fa - vour To our fa - thers
3. Fa - ther - like he tends and spares us; Well our fee - ble

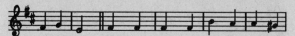

1. tri - bute bring; Ran-somed, healed, re-stored, for-giv - en,
2. in dis - tress; Praise him, still the same for ev - er,
3. frame he knows; In his hands he gen - tly bears us,

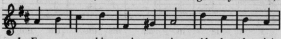

1. Ev - er-more his prais - es sing: Al - le - lu - ia!
2. Slow to chide, and swift to bless: Al - le - lu - ia!
3. Res - cues us from all our foes; Al - le - lu - ia!

1. Al - le - lu - ia! Praise the ev - er - last - ing King.
2. Al - le - lu - ia! Glo - rious in his faith - ful - ness.
3. Al - le - lu - ia! Wide - ly as his mer - cy flows.

Praise the Lord, Ye Heav'ns, Adore Him

61

1. Praise the Lord, ye heav'ns, adore him
Praise him, angels in the height.
Sun and moon, rejoice before him.
Praise him, all you stars of light.
Praise the Lord, for he has spoken:
Worlds his mighty voice obeyed.
Laws which never shall be broken
For their guidance he has made.

2. Praise the Lord, for he is glorious,
Never shall his promise fail.
God has made his saints victorious.
Sin and death shall not prevail.
Praise the God of our salvation.
Hosts on high, his pow'r proclaim:
Heav'n and earth and all creation,
Praise and magnify his name.

Alleluia! Sing to Jesus

Melody: Hymnal 1940, no. 347-b

W.C. Dix   Rowland H. Prichard

1. Al - le - lu - ia! Sing to
2. Al - le - lu - ia! Not as

1. Je - sus! His the scep-ter, his the throne;
2. or - phans Are we left in sor - row now;

1. Al - le - lu - ia! his the tri - umph;
2. Al - le - lu - ia! he is near us,

1. His the vic - to - ry— a - lone,
2. Faith be - lieves nor ques - tions how:

1. Hark! the songs of peace-ful Si - on
2. Though the cloud from sight re - ceived him,

1. Thun - der like a migh - ty flood;
2. When the for - ty days were o'er.

1. Je - sus out of ev'ry na - tion
2. Shall our hearts for - get his prom - ise.

1. Has re - deemed us by his blood.
2. "I am with you ev - er - more"?

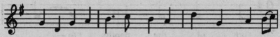

1. Al - le - lu - ia! Al - le - lu - ia! Hearts and voic - es
2. Now the i - ron bars are bro - ken, Christ from death to _
3. Al - le - lu - ia! Al - le - lu - ia! Glo - ry be to _

1. heav'n-ward raise; Sing to God a hymn of glad-ness,
2. life is born, Glo - rious life, and life im - mor - tal,
3. God on high; Al - le - lu - ia to the Sav - iour,

1. Sing to God a hymn of praise. He who on the
2. On this ho-ly East-er morn. Christ has tri - umphed,
3. Who has won the vic-to - ry. Al - le - lu - ia,

1. cross a vic - tim, For the world's sal - va - tion bled,
2. and we con-quer, By his might - y en - ter - prise,
3. to the Spir - it, Fount of love_ and sanc - ti - ty;

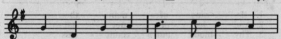

1. Je - sus Christ, the King of glo - ry,
2. We with him to life e - ter - nal
3 Al - le - lu - ia! Al - le - lu - ia!

1. Now is ris - en from the dead.
2. By his re - sur - rec - tion rise.
3. To the Tri - une Ma - jes - ty.

Out of the Depths

Anon.   V. Novello

1. Out of the depths to —
2. Oh, hear our pray'rs and —
3. To be ap - peased in

1. thee, O Lord, I cry, —
2. sighs, Re - deem - er blest, —
3. wraths, dear Lord, is thine;

1. Lord gra - cious, turn thine ear to
2. And grant thy ho - ly souls e -
3. Thou mer - cy with thy jus - tice

1. sup - pliant — sign;
2. ter - nal — rest.
3. canst com — bine;

1. If sins of man thou —
2. And let per - pet - ual —
3. Thy blood our count - less

1. scan - nest, who may stand —
2. light up - on them shine; —
3. stains can wash a — way:

1. That search - ing eye of thine and
2. For though not spot - less, still these
3. This is thy law, our hope and

1. chast' — ning — hand!
2. souls — are — thine.
3. stead — fast stay.

Were You There

1. Were you there when they crucified my Lord?
   Were you there when they crucified my Lord?
   Oh! sometimes it causes me
   To tremble, tremble, tremble.
   Were you there when they crucified my Lord?

2. Were you there when they nailed him to the tree?
   Were you there when they nailed him to the tree?
   Oh! sometimes it causes me
   To tremble, tremble, tremble.
   Were you there when they nailed him to the tree?

3. Were you there when they laid him in the tomb?
   Were you there when they laid him in the tomb?
   Oh! sometimes it causes me
   To tremble, tremble, tremble.
   Were you there when they laid him in the tomb?

4. Were you there when the stone was rolled away?

O Canada

R. S. Weir, 1908

O Canada! Our home and native land!
True patriot love in all thy sons command.
With glowing hearts we see thee rise.
The True North strong and free;
From far and wide, O Canada,
We stand on guard for thee.
God keep our land glorious and free!
O Canada! we stand on guard for thee.

O Canada

A.B. Routhier

O Canada! Terre de nos aieux,
Ton front est ceint de fleurons glorieux!
Car ton bras sait porter l'epee,
Il sait porter la croix!
Ton histoíre est une epopee
Des plus briliants exploits.
Et ta valeur, de foi trempee,
Protegera nos foyers et nos droits.
Protegera nos foyers et nos droits.

TREASURY OF PRAYERS

These prayers reflect the traditions of the Catholic Church. Individuals and families may find them helpful as they pray.

PRAISE AND THANKS

Blessed are you, Lord God:
blessed are you for ever.
Holy is your name:
blessed are you for ever.
Great is your mercy for your people:
blessed are you for ever. Amen!

Father, Son, and Holy Spirit,
we praise you and give you glory:
we bless you for calling us to be your holy people.

Remain in our hearts,
and guide us in our love and service.
Help us to let our light shine before others
and lead them to the way of faith.

Holy Trinity of love,
we praise you now and for ever. Amen!

We praise you, Father of all:
we thank you for calling us to be your people,
and for choosing us to give you glory.
In a special way we thank you for . . .

Cleanse our hearts and our lives
with your holy word
and make our prayer pleasing to you.
Guide us by your Spirit
as we follow in the paths of Jesus our brother.

All glory and praise are yours, Father,
for ever and ever. Amen!

Let us give glory to the Father
through the Son
in the Holy Spirit,
for God has made us his people, his Church,
and calls us to sing his praises.

All honor and glory and thanks are his,
and praise and worship belong to him.
To God be glory in his Church
for ever and ever! Amen!

Thanks for a beautiful day: _On a beautiful day we
may thank God and praise him for his many gifts:_

Father of Jesus,
we praise you and give you glory
for the wonderful things you do for us:
for life and health,
for friends and family,
for this splendid day.

For these reasons, we pray as Jesus taught us:
Our Father . . .

MORNING PRAYERS

_With our risen Lord. we praise our Father and offer our
day and our work._

**In the ✠ name of the Father, and of the Son,
and of the Holy Spirit. Amen!**

Father, help your people.
Be with us as we pray.

MORNING PSALM:

_We may pray one of these psalms, or last Sunday's respon-
sorial psalm, adding the_ Glory (be) to the Father _at the
end._

_Ps. 22 (23)—from Mass for Second Scrutiny (4th Sun. of
Lent)_

_Ps. 94 (95)—from Mass for First Scrutiny (3rd Sun. of
Lent)_

Ps. 96 (97)—from Christmas Mass (at Dawn)
Ps. 115 (116)—from Mass for Holy Thursday
*On Sunday, it is appropriate to use Ps. 118 (119) from
    Easter Sunday Mass.*
*On Friday, it is appropriate to use Ps. 50 (51) from Ash
    Wednesday Mass.*

PSALM OF PRAISE:

One of these Psalms may be prayed, adding the Glory (be)
to the Father *at the end.*

Ps. 46 (47)—from Mass for Passion Sunday
Ps. 66 (67)—from Mass of January 1
Ps. 95 (96)—from Christmas Mass (at Midnight)
Ps. 97 (98)—from Christmas Mass (During the Day)

READING:

*One of the first two readings from last Sunday, or another
appropriate text from God's word.*

A moment of silent prayer follows the reading.

Canticle of Zechariah   Lk. 1.68-79

Blessed ✠ be the Lord, the God of Israel;
he has come to his people and set them free.

He has raised up for us a mighty saviour,
born of the house of his servant David.

Through his holy prophets he promised of old
    that he would save us from our enemies,
    from the hands of all who hate us.

He promised to show mercy to our fathers
and to remember his holy covenant.

This was the oath he swore to our father Abraham:
to set us free from the hands of our enemies,
free to worship him without fear,
holy and righteous in his sight
    all the days of our life.

You, my child, shall be called
the prophet of the Most High,
for you will go before the Lord to prepare his way,
to give his people knowledge of salvation
by the forgiveness of their sins.

In the tender compassion of our Lord
the dawn from on high shall break upon us,
to shine on those who dwell in darkness
and the shadow of death,
and to guide our feet into the way of peace.

Glory to the Father . . . .

Or Glory to God in the highest *(see page 14) may be prayed or sung.*

Prayers for All People

Lord Jesus, we come to you for help:
Lord, have mercy.

Help us to love you more this day. R/.
Teach us to see you in other people. R/.
Help us to be ready to serve others. R/.
Give us strength to carry our cross with you. R/.
In moments of sorrow, be with us today. R/.
Help us to do everything for the glory of your
     Father. R/.
Help us to build the kingdom by our life today. R/.

Other petitions may be added.

Lord Jesus, our brother,
hear our prayers for your people.
Help us to work with you today
to honour your Father and save the world.

Lord Jesus,
we praise you for ever and ever. Amen!

THE LORD'S PRAYER: *With Jesus and all his people on earth and in heaven, we sing or say:* Our Father . . . *(page 71).*

BLESSING: *The parents, one of the family, or all may say:*

May our loving God bless us,
Father, Son, and Holy Spirit. Amen!

All may share in a sign of peace and love.

EVENING PRAYERS

At the end of the day, we join Jesus and his Church in offering thanks to our loving God. A candle may be lighted.

In the ✠ name of the Father, and of the Son, and of the Holy Spirit. Amen!

Father, help your people.
Be with us as we pray.

PSALMS:

We may pray one or two of these psalms, or last Sunday's responsorial psalm, adding the Glory (be) to the Father *after each psalm:*

Ps. 29 (30)—from Easter Vigil Service after Second Reading

Ps. 50 (51)—from Mass for Ash Wednesday

Ps. 103 (104)—from Mass for Pentecost Sunday

Ps. 129 (130)—from Mass for Third Scrutiny (5th Sun. of Lent)

READING:

One of the first two readings from last Sunday, or another appropriate text from God's word.

A moment of silent prayer follows the reading.

Canticle of Mary   Lk. 1.46-55

My soul ✠ proclaims the greatness of the Lord,
my spirit rejoices in God my Saviour
for he has looked with favour on his lowly servant.

From this day all generations will call me blessed:
the Almighty has done great things for me,
and holy is his Name.

He has mercy on those who fear him
in every generation.

He has shown the strength of his arm,
he has scattered the proud in their conceit.

He has cast down the mighty from their thrones,
and has lifted up the lowly.

He has filled the hungry with good things,
and the rich he has sent away empty.

He has come to the help of his servant Israel
for he has remembered his promise of mercy,
the promise he made to our fathers,
to Abraham and his children for ever.

Glory to the Father.

Or we may sing the Holy, holy, holy Lord, *from page 25.*

Prayers for all people:

Let us pray to God our Father:
Lord, hear our prayer.
For the people of God everywhere. ℟.
For peace in the world. ℟.
For the people who are suffering. ℟.
For the sick and the dying. ℟.
For our family, friends, and neighbours. ℟.
For . . .

Other petitions may be added.

Prayer:

Blessed are you, Father of light,
Lord of all the universe:
in the name of Jesus our Lord we pray for your
    world.
Grant peace to your people,
strength to the weak,
courage to the downhearted,
and guidance to all in despair.
Send your Spirit to conquer evil,
and make your kingdom come among us.

Father, we ask this grace
through Jesus Christ our Lord. Amen!

THE LORD'S PRAYER: *With Jesus and all his people
on earth and in heaven, we sing or say:* Our Father . . .
(page 71).

BLESSING: *The parents, one of the family, or all may say:*

May our loving God bless us,
Father, Son, ✠ and Holy Spirit. Amen!

All may share a sign of peace and love.

BEFORE AND AFTER SCRIPTURE

Before:

Lord, open our hearts:
let your Spirit speak to us
as we read your word.

After:

Father, we thank you
for speaking to us today
through your holy word.

Or another prayer of thanks may be said (pages 628-629).

MEAL PRAYERS

When we are eating or drinking, or doing anything else, we can do it for the glory of God (1 Cor. 10:31). We may use these prayers or other familiar ones, or make up our own.

Before our meal:

Lord Jesus, our brother,
we praise you for saving us.
Bless ✠ us in your love
as we gather in your name,
and bless ✠ this meal that we share.

Jesus, we praise you for ever. Amen!

or:

Father of us all,
this meal is a sign of your love for us:
bless ✠ us and bless ✠ our food,
and help us to give you glory each day
through Jesus Christ our Lord. Amen!

After our meal:

Loving Father, we praise you
for all the gifts you give us:
for life and health,
for faith and love,
and for this meal we have shared together.

Father, we thank you
through Christ our Lord. Amen!

or:

Thank you, Father, for your gifts:
help us to love you more. Amen!

or:

Father, we thank you for your love
and for giving us food and drink.
Help us to praise you today
in the name of Jesus our Lord. Amen!

A PRAYER FOR OUR FAMILY

Blessed are you, loving Father,
ruler of the universe:

You have given us your Son as your leader,
and have made us temples of your Holy Spirit.

Fill our family with your light and peace.
Have mercy on all who suffer,
and bring us to everlasting joy with you.

Father,
we bless your name for ever and ever. Amen!

PARENT'S PRAYER

All praise to you, Lord Jesus, lover of children:
bless our family,
and help us to lead our children to you.

Give us light and strength,
and courage when our task is difficult.
Let your Spirit fill us with love and peace,
so that we may help our children to love you.

All glory and praise are yours, Lord Jesus,
for ever and ever. Amen!

PRAYER OF SORROW

Psalm 50 (51): *from the Mass for Ash Wednesday.*

A prayer for mercy:

Lord Jesus, you have called us
to be children of light:

Lord, have mercy.   **Lord, have mercy.**

Christ, you have suffered on the cross for us:
Christ, have mercy.   **Christ, have mercy.**

Lord Jesus, you are the saviour of the world:
Lord, have mercy.   **Lord, have mercy.**

Other prayers. We may sing or say Lamb of God *(see page 73), or* I confess to almighty God *(see page 12).*

JESUS PRAYER

We may use this simple prayer at any time,

Lord Jesus Christ, Son of God,
have mercy on me.

or:

Lord Jesus Christ, Son of God,
have mercy on us.

or:

Jesus, our Lord and our brother,
save us in your love.

MARIAN ANTHEM

Blessed are you, mother of my Lord,
for you have believed the word of God.

In faith and love,
you have pondered the words and actions of God
in your life and the life of God's people.

With Jesus we call you mother.
Pray for us,
and ask your Son to lead us to the Father. Amen!

PRAYER FOR PEACE

Lord Jesus Christ, we praise you:
bring peace into the world
by bringing your peace into the hearts of all.
Help us to turn away from sin
and to follow you in love and service.

Glory be yours, and honour,
for ever and ever. Amen!

A PRAYER FOR VOCATIONS

Heavenly Father, Lord of the harvest,
call many members of our community
to be generous workers for your people
and to gather in your harvest.
Send them to share the Good News of Jesus
with all the people of the earth.

Father,
we ask this prayer
through Christ our Lord. Amen!

THANKS FOR FAMILY AND FRIENDS

Blessed are you, loving Father,
for all your gifts to us.
Blessed are you for giving us family and friends
to be with us in times of joy and sorrow,
to help us in days of need,
and to rejoice with us in moments of celebration.

Father,
we praise you for your Son Jesus,
who knew the happiness of family and friends,
and in the love of your Holy Spirit.
Blessed are you for ever and ever. Amen!

FAMILY BLESSINGS

Family gathering: *When the family is gathered for a special occasion, a feast, a holiday, a reunion, or any other special time:*

Father in heaven,
we praise you for giving us your Son
to be our saviour and Lord.
Bless us all as we gather here today, [tonight,]
and let us live happily in your love.

Hear our prayer, loving Father,
for we ask this in Jesus' name. Amen!

Children: *Parents may bless their children each day, or on special occasions. These or similar words may be used:*

Simple form:

May God bless ✝ you, N.,
and keep you in love.

The child answers: **Amen!**

At bedtime:

Heavenly Father,
bless N., and keep him/her in your love.
Grant him/her a good rest tonight,
and send your angels to protect him/her.
In the name of the Father, and of the ✝ Son,
and of the Holy Spirit.

The child answers: **Amen!**

PRAYER FOR A BIRTHDAY
OF A FAMILY MEMBER

This prayer may be offered at a meal or birthday party:

Heavenly Father,
we praise you for all your gifts to us.
In a special way, we thank you for N.
Bless him/her on this birthday,
and keep him/her always in your love.

Bless us too, holy Father,
and this food with which we celebrate.
Help us all to praise you and give you glory
through Jesus Christ our Lord.

All answer: Amen!

PRAYER FOR
A WEDDING ANNIVERSARY

N. and N.,
may God bless you and grant you joy.
May he deepen your love for each other.
May he bless ✢ you in your family and friends,
and lead you to unending happiness in heaven.

May almighty God,
Father, Son, ✢ and Holy Spirit,
bless us all, and keep us in his love for ever.

All answer: Amen!

WHEN VISITING A SICK PERSON:

Heavenly Father,
look with mercy on N.,
and help him/her in this time of sickness.
Restore him/her to health, we pray,
through Christ our Lord.

All answer: Amen!

or:

Lord Jesus,
lover of the sick,
be with *N.* in his /her sickness.
Help him /her to accept this illness
as a sharer in your cross,
and bring him /her back to full health.

Lord Jesus,
we praise you,
for you are Lord for ever and ever.

All answer: Amen!

PRAYER FOR THE POPE

All praise and glory are yours, Lord Jesus:
you have made us your body, your Church,
and help us to bear fruit for our heavenly Father.

You chose St. Peter as the rock,
and sent him to feed your flock
and to strengthen his brothers and sisters.
Continue to help your Church
through the guidance of our pope,
and keep us faithful in your service.

Jesus, our brother,
you are Lord for ever and ever. Amen!

PRAYERS BEFORE MASS

Act of Faith

Lord Jesus Christ, I firmly believe that you are present in this Blessed Sacrament as true God and true Man, with your Body and Blood, Soul and Divinity. My Redeemer and my Judge, I adore your Divine Majesty together with the angels and saints. I believe, O Lord; increase my faith.

Act of Hope

Good Jesus, in you alone I place all my hope. You are my salvation and my strength, the Source of all good. Through your mercy, through your Passion and Death, I hope to obtain the pardon of my sins, the grace of final perseverance and a happy eternity.

Act of Love

Jesus, my God, I love you with my whole heart and above all things, because you are the one supreme Good and an infinitely perfect Being. You have given your life for me, a poor sinner, and in your mercy you have even offered yourself as food for my soul. My God, I love you. Inflame my heart so that I may love you more.

Act of Contrition

O my Saviour, I am truly sorry for having offended you because you are infinitely good and sin displeases you. I detest all the sins of my life and I desire to atone for them. Through the merits of your Precious Blood, wash from my soul all stain of sin, so that, cleansed in body and soul, I may worthily approach the Most Holy Sacrament of the Altar.

PRAYERS AFTER MASS

Act of Faith

Jesus, I firmly believe that you are present within me as God and Man, to enrich my soul with graces and to fill my heart with the happiness of the blessed. I believe that you are Christ, the Son of the living God!

Act of Adoration

With deepest humility, I adore you, my Lord and God; you have made my soul your dwelling place. I adore you as my Creator from whose hands I came and with whom I am to be happy forever.

Act of Love

Dear Jesus, I love you with my whole heart, my whole soul, and with all my strength. May the love of your own Sacred Heart fill my soul and purify it so that I may die to the world for love of you, as you died on the Cross for love of me. My God, you are all mine; grant that I may be all yours in time and in eternity.

Act of Thanksgiving

From the depths of my heart I thank you, dear Lord, for your infinite kindness in coming to me. How good you are to me! With your most holy Mother and all the angels, I praise your mercy and generosity toward me, a poor sinner. I thank you for nourishing my soul with your Sacred Body and Precious Blood. I will try to show my gratitude to you in the Sacrament of your love, by obedience to your holy commandments, by fidelity to my duties, by kindness to my neighbour and by an earnest endeavor to become like you in my daily conduct.

Act of Offering

Jesus, you have given yourself to me, now let me give myself to you; I give you my body, that it may be chaste and pure. I give you my soul, that it may be free from sin. I give you my heart, that it may always love you. I give you every thought, word, and deed of my life, and I offer all for your honour and glory.

Prayer to Christ the King

O Christ Jesus, I acknowledge you as King of the universe. All that has been created has been made for you. Exercise over me all your rights. I renew my baptismal promises, renouncing Satan and all his works and pomps. I promise to live a good Christian life and to do all in my power to procure the triumph of the rights of God and your Church.

Divine Heart of Jesus, I offer you my poor actions in order to obtain that all hearts may acknowledge your sacred Royalty, and that thus the reign of your peace may be established throughout the universe. Amen.

Indulgenced Prayer before a Crucifix

Look down upon me, good and gentle Jesus, while before your face I humbly kneel, and with a burning soul pray and beseech you to fix deep in my heart lively sentiments of faith, hope and charity, true contrition for my sins, and a firm purpose of amendment, while I contemplate with great love and tender pity your five wounds, pondering over them within me, calling to mind the words which David, your prophet, said of you, my good Jesus: "They have pierced my hands and my feet; they have numbered all my bones" (Ps 21, 17-18).

A *plenary indulgence* is granted on each Friday of Lent and Passiontide to the faithful, who after Communion piously recite the above prayer before an image of Christ crucified; on other days of the year the indulgence is *partial (No. 22).*

STATIONS OF THE CROSS

The Way of the Cross is a devotion in which we medi-tate on Christ's Passion and Death in order to put their meaning into our lives.

Prayer before the Stations

Heavenly Father, grant that I who meditate on the Passion and Death of Your Son, Jesus Christ, may imitate in my life His love and self-giving to You and to others. Grant this through Christ our Lord. Amen.

STATIONS
of the
CROSS

1. Jesus Is Condemned to Death

O Jesus, help me to appreciate Your sanctifying grace more and more.

2. Jesus Bears His Cross

O Jesus, You chose to die for me. Help me to love You always with all my heart.

3. Jesus Falls the First Time

O Jesus, make me strong to conquer my wicked passions, and to rise quickly from sin.

4. Jesus Meets His Mother

O Jesus, grant me a tender love for Your Mother, who offered You for love of me.

STATIONS
of the
CROSS

5. Jesus is Helped by Simon

O Jesus, like Simon lead me ever closer to You through my daily crosses and trials.

6. Jesus and Veronica

O Jesus, imprint Your image on my heart that I may be faithful to You all my life.

7. Jesus Falls a Second Time

O Jesus, I repent for having offended You. Grant me forgiveness of all my sins.

8. Jesus Speaks to the Women

O Jesus, grant me tears of compassion for Your sufferings and of sorrow for my sins.

STATEONS
of the
CROSS

9. Jesus Falls a Third Time

O Jesus, let me never yield to despair. Let me come to You in hardship and spiritual distress.

10. He is Stripped of His Garments

O Jesus, let me sacrifice all my attachments rather than imperil the divine life of my soul.

11. Jesus is Nailed to the Cross

O Jesus, strengthen my faith and increase my love for You. Help me to accept my crosses.

12. Jesus Dies on the Cross

O Jesus, I thank You for making me a child of God. Help me to forgive others.

STATIONS
of the
CROSS

13. Jesus is Taken down from the Cross

O Jesus, through the intercession of Your holy Mother, let me be pleasing to You.

14. Jesus is Laid in the Tomb

O Jesus, strengthen my will to live for You on earth and bring me to eternal bliss in heaven.

Prayer after the Stations

JESUS, You became an example of humility, obedience and patience, and preceded me on the way of life bearing Your Cross. Grant that, inflamed with Your love, I may cheerfully take upon myself the sweet yoke of Your Gospel together with the mortification of the Cross and follow You as a true disciple so that I may be united with You in heaven. Amen.

THE HOLY ROSARY

Prayer before the Rosary

QUEEN of the Holy Rosary, you have deigned to come to Fatima to reveal to the three shepherd children the treasures of grace hidden in the Rosary. Inspire my heart with a sincere love of this devotion, in order that by meditating on the Mysteries of our Redemption which are recalled in it, I may be enriched with its fruits and obtain peace for the world, the conversion of sinners and of Russia, and the favor which I ask of you in this Rosary. *(Here mention your request.)* I ask it for the greater glory of God, for your own honor, and for the good of souls, especially for my own. Amen.

The Five Joyful Mysteries

1. The Annunciation
For the love of humility.

Said on Mondays and Saturdays [except during Lent], and the Sundays from Advent to Lent.

2. The Visitation
For charity toward my neighbor.

4. The Presentation
For the virtue of obedience.

3. The Nativity
For the spirit of poverty.

5. Finding in the Temple
For the virtue of piety.

651

The Five Luminous Mysteries*

Said on Thursdays [except during Lent].

*Added to the Mysteries of the Rosary by Pope John Paul II in his Apostolic Letter of October 16, 2002, entitled *The Rosary of the Virgin Mary*.

3. Proclamation of the Kingdom
For seeking God's forgiveness.

1. The Baptism of Jesus
For living my Baptismal Promises.

4. The Transfiguration
Becoming a New Person in Christ.

2. The Wedding at Cana
For doing whatever Jesus says. 652

5. Institution of the Eucharist
For active participation at Mass.

The Five Sorrowful Mysteries

1. Agony in the Garden
For true contrition.

Said on Tuesdays and Fridays throughout the year, and every day from Ash Wednesday until Easter.

2. Scourging at the Pillar
For the virtue of purity.

4. Carrying of the Cross
For the virtue of patience.

3. Crowning with Thorns
For moral courage.

5. The Crucifixion
For final perseverance.

The Five

Glorious

Mysteries

Said on Wednesdays [except during Lent], and the Sundays from Easter to Advent.

3. Descent of the Holy Spirit
For love of God.

1. The Resurrection
For the virtue of faith.

4. Assumption of the B.V.M.
For devotion to Mary.

2. The Ascension
For the virtue of hope.

5. Crowning of the B.V.M.
For eternal happiness.

VARIOUS PRAYERS

Prayer to St. Joseph

O Blessed St. Joseph, loving father and faithful guardian of Jesus, and devoted spouse of the Mother of God, I beg you to offer God the Father his divine Son, bathed in blood on the Cross. Through the holy Name of Jesus obtain for us from the Father the favor we implore.

For the Sick

Father, your Son accepted our sufferings to teach us the virtue of patience in human illness. Hear the prayers we offer for our sick brothers and sisters. May all who suffer pain, illness or disease realize that they are chosen to be saints, and know that they are joined to Christ in his suffering for the salvation of the world, who lives and reigns with you and the Holy Spirit, one God, for ever and ever.

For Religious Vocations

Father, you call all who believe in you to grow perfect in love by following in the footsteps of Christ your Son. May those whom you have chosen to serve you as religious provide by their way of life a convincing sign of your kingdom for the Church and the whole world.

For the Parliament

Father, you guide and govern everything with order and love. Look upon the assembly of our national leaders and fill them with the spirit of your wisdom. May they always act in accordance with your will, and may their decisions be for the peace and well-being of all.

PRAYERS IN ACCORD WITH
THE LITURGICAL YEAR

ADVENT SEASON

Prayer to Help Others Find Christ

O Lord Jesus, I thank you for the gift of faith and for the continual grace you give me to nourish and strengthen it. Enable me to cultivate the genuine desire for you that lies beneath the zealous search for justice, truth, love, and peace found in our contemporaries. Encourage these searchings, O Lord, and grant that all true seekers may look beyond the present moment and catch sight of your countenance in the world.

Prayer for Christ's Triple Coming

Lamb of God, you once came to rid the world of sin; cleanse me now of every stain of sin. Lord, you came to save what was lost; come once again with your salvific power so that those you redeemed will not be punished. I have come to know you in faith; may I have unending joy when you come again in glory.

Prayer for Christ's Coming in Grace

O Lord Jesus, during this Advent come to us in your grace. Come to prepare our hearts, minds, and bodies to welcome you on Christmas Day. Come to comfort us in sadness, to cheer us in loneliness, to refresh us in weariness, to strengthen us in temptations, to lead us in time of doubt, and to exult with us in joy.

CHRISTMAS SEASON

Prayer to Jesus, God's Greatest Gift

O Jesus, I believe that the greatest proof of God's love is His gift to us of you, His only Son. All love tends to become like that which it loves. You love human beings; therefore you became man. Infinite love and mercy caused you, the Second Person of the Blessed Trinity, to leave the Kingdom of eternal bliss, to descend from the throne of your majesty, and to become a helpless babe. Eventually you even suffered and died and rose that we might live.

You wished to enter the world as a child in order to show that you were true Man. But you become man also that we may become like God. In exchange for the humanity which you take from us you wish to make us share in your Divinity by sanctifying grace, so that you may take sole possession of us. Grant me the grace to love you in return with a deep, personal, and productive love.

Prayer for Christ's Rebirth in the Church

O Lord Jesus Christ, we ask you to incarnate in us your invisible Divinity. What you accomplished corporally in Mary accomplish now spiritually in your Church. May the Church's sure faith conceive you, its unstained intelligence give birth to you, and its soul united with the power of the Most High preserve you forever.

SEASON OF LENT

Prayer to be Freed of the Seven Deadly Sins

O meek Saviour and Prince of Peace, implant in me the virtues of gentleness and patience. Let me curb the fury of *anger* and restrain all resentment and impatience so as to overcome evil with good, attain your peace, and rejoice in your love.

O Model of humility, divest me of all *pride and arrogance.* Let me acknowledge my weakness and sinfulness, so that I may bear mockery and contempt for your sake and esteem myself as lowly in your sight.

O Teacher of abstinence, help me to serve you rather than my appetites. Keep me from *gluttony*—the inordinate love of food and drink— and let me hunger and thirst for your justice.

O Lover of purity, remove all *lust* from my heart, so that I may serve you with a pure mind and a chaste body.

O Father of the poor, help me to avoid all *covetousness* for earthly goods and give me a love for heavenly things. Inspire me to give to the needy, just as you gave your life that I might inherit eternal treasures.

O Exemplar of love, keep me from all *envy* and ill-will. Let the grace of your love dwell in me that I may rejoice in the happiness of others and bewail their adversities.

O zealous Lover of souls, keep me from all *sloth* of mind or body. Inspire me with zeal for your glory, so that I may do all things for you and in you.

Prayer of Contrition

Merciful Father, I am guilty of sin. I confess my sins before you and I am sorry for them. Your promises are just; therefore I trust that you will forgive me my sins and cleanse me from every stain of sin. Jesus himself is the propitiation for my sins and those of the whole world. I put my hope in his atonement. May my sins be forgiven through his name, and in his blood may my soul be made clean.

Prayer to Know Jesus Christ

O Lord Jesus, like St. Paul, may I count everything as loss in comparison with the supreme advantage of knowing you. I want to know you and what your Passion and Resurrection can do. I also want to share in your sufferings in the hope that if I resemble you in death I may somehow attain to the resurrection from the dead.

Give me grace to make every effort to supplement faith with moral courage, moral courage with knowledge, knowledge with self-control, self-control with patience, patience with piety, piety with affection, and affection with love for all my brothers and sisters in Christ. May these virtues keep me both active and fruitful and bring me to the deep knowledge of you, Lord Jesus Christ.

EASTER SEASON

Prayer in Praise of Christ's Humanity

O risen Lord, your body was part of your power, rather than you a part of its weakness.

For this reason you could not but rise again, if you were to die—because your body, once taken by you, never was or could be separated from you even in the grave.

I keep your most holy body before me as the pledge of my own resurrection. Though I die, it only means that my life is changed, for I shall rise again.

Teach me to live as one who believes in the great dignity and sanctity of the material frame which you have given to me.

Prayer to the Holy Spirit

Holy Spirit of light and love, you are the substantial love of the Father and the Son; hear my prayer.

Bounteous bestower of most precious gifts, grant me a strong and living faith, which makes me accept all revealed truths and shape my conduct in accord with them. Give me a most confident hope in all divine promises which prompts me to abandon myself unreservedly to you and your guidance.

Infuse into me a love of perfect goodwill, which makes me accomplish God's will in all things and act according to God's least desires. Make me love not only my friends but my enemies as well in imitation of Jesus Christ who through you offered himself on the Cross for all people. Holy Spirit, animate, inspire, and guide me, and help me to be always a true follower of Jesus.

ORDINARY TIME

Prayer for a Productive Faith

O Lord, increase my faith and let it bear fruit in my life. Let it bind me fast to other Christians in the common certitude that our Master is the God-Man who gave his life for all. Let me listen in faith to the Divine word that challenges me.

Help me to strive wholeheartedly under the promptings of my faith in the building of a world ruled by love. Enable me to walk in faith toward the indescribable future that you have promised to all who possess a productive faith in you.

Prayer to Christ in the World

Lord Jesus, let us realize that every action of ours no matter how small or how secular enables us to be in touch with you. Let our interest lie in created things—but only in absolute dependence upon your presence in them. Let us pursue you and you alone through the reality of created things. Let this be our prayer—to become closer to you by becoming more human.

Let us become a true branch on the vine that is you, a branch that bears much fruit. Let us accept you in our lives in the way it pleases you to come into them: as Truth, to be spoken; as Life, to be lived; as Light, to be shared; as Love, to be followed; as Joy, to be given; as Peace, to be spread about; as Sacrifice, to be offered among our relatives and friends, among our neighbours and all people.

Prayer to be Generous in Giving

Lord Jesus, you came to tell us that the meaning of life consists in giving. You told us that those who cling too tightly to what they have—without thought for others—end up by losing everything. You gave us new values by which to measure the worth of a person's life.

Help me to realize it is not temporal success or riches or fame that necessarily gives life meaning. Rather it is the service rendered to others in your Name that brings fulfillment and makes my life worthwhile. May all my activity help build God's kingdom: my suffering bear genuine fruit, my obedience bring true freedom, and my death lead to eternal life.

Prayer to Discern God's Call

Heavenly Father, your call never comes to us in a vacuum; it comes to us in the circumstances of our ordinary lives.

Therefore, our response cannot be given only in the privacy of our own minds; it must overflow into our daily lives. You call us through our family, through our community or Church, and through the world.

Help me to see that when I say No to the legitimate requests of my family, my community, or my world, I say No to you. You have ordained that whatever advances the true progress of self, of the Church, and of the world is my way of saying Yes to your call. May I take advantage of the daily opportunities which you place at my disposal to answer your call affirmatively.

NEW RITE OF PENANCE

(Extracted from the Rite of Penance)

Texts for the Penitent

The penitent should prepare for the celebration of the sacrament by prayer, reading of Scripture, and silent reflection. The penitent should think over and should regret all sins since the last celebration of the sacrament.

RECEPTION OF THE PENITENT

The penitent enters the confessional or other place set aside for the celebration of the sacrament of penance. After the welcoming of the priest, the penitent makes the sign of the cross saying:

In the ✚ name of the Father, and of the Son, and of the Holy Spirit. Amen.

The penitent is invited to have trust in God and replies:

Amen.

READING OF THE WORD OF GOD

The penitent then listens to a text of Scripture which tells about God's mercy and calls us to conversion.

CONFESSION OF SINS AND ACCEPTANCE OF SATISFACTION

The penitent speaks to the priest in a normal, conversational fashion. The penitent tells when he or she last celebrated the sacrament and then confesses his or her sins. The penitent then listens to any advice the priest may give and accepts the satisfaction from the priest. The penitent should ask any appropriate questions.

PRAYER OF THE PENITENT AND ABSOLUTION
Prayer

Before the absolution is given, the penitent expresses sorrow for sins in these or similar words:

My God,
I am sorry for my sins with all my heart.
In choosing to do wrong
and failing to do good,
I have sinned against you
whom I should love above all things.
I firmly intend, with your help,
to do penance,
to sin no more,
and to avoid whatever leads me to sin.
Our Saviour Jesus Christ
suffered and died for us.
In his name, my God, have mercy.

OR: Remember, Lord, your compassion and mercy
which you showed long ago.
Do not recall the sins and failings of my youth.
In your mercy remember me, Lord, because of
your goodness.

OR: Wash me from my guilt
and cleanse me of my sin.
I acknowledge my offence;
my sin is before me always.

OR: Father, I have sinned against you
and am not worthy to be called your son/daughter.
Be merciful to me, a sinner.

OR: Father of mercy,
like the prodigal son
I return to you and say:
"I have sinned against you
and am no longer worthy to be called your son."
Christ Jesus, Saviour of the world,
I pray with the repentant thief
to whom you promised Paradise:
"Lord, remember me in your kingdom."
Holy Spirit, fountain of love,
I call on you with trust:
"Purify my heart,
and help me to walk as a child of light."

OR: Lord Jesus,
you opened the eyes of the blind,
healed the sick,
forgave the sinful woman,
and after Peter's denial confirmed him in your
love.
Listen to my prayer,
forgive all my sins,
renew your love in my heart,
help me to live in perfect unity with my fellow
Christians
that I may proclaim your saving power to all the
world.

OR: Lord Jesus,
you chose to be called the friend of sinners.
By your saving death and resurrection
free me from my sins.
May your peace take root in my heart
and bring forth a harvest
of love, holiness, and truth.

OR: Lord Jesus Christ,
you are the Lamb of God;
you take away the sins of the world.
Through the grace of the Holy Spirit
restore me to friendship with your Father,
cleanse me from every stain of sin
and raise me to new life
for the glory of your name.

OR: Lord God,
in your goodness have mercy on me:
do not look on my sins,
but take away all my guilt.
Create in me a clean heart
and renew within me an upright spirit.

OR: Lord Jesus, Son of God,
have mercy on me, a sinner.

ABSOLUTION

If the penitent is not kneeling, he or she bows his or her head as the priest extends his hands (or at least extends his right hand).

God, the Father of mercies,
through the death and resurrection of his Son
has reconciled the world to himself
and sent the Holy Spirit among us
for the forgiveness of sins;
through the ministry of the Church
may God give you pardon and peace,
and I absolve you from your sins
in the name of the Father, and of the Son,
and of the Holy Spirit. Amen.

PROCLAMATION OF PRAISE OF GOD AND DISMISSAL

Penitent and priest give praise to God.

Priest: Give thanks to the Lord, for he is good.
Penitent: His mercy endures for ever.

Then the penitent is dismissed by the priest.

Form of Examination of Conscience

This suggested form for an examination of conscience should be completed and adapted to meet the needs of different individuals and to follow local usages.

In an examination of conscience, before the sacrament of penance, each individual should ask himself these questions in particular:

1. What is my attitude to the sacrament of penance? Do I sincerely want to be set free from sin, to turn again to God, to begin a new life, and to enter into a deeper friendship with God? Or do I look on it as a burden, to be undertaken as seldom as possible?

2. Did I forget to mention, or deliberately conceal, any grave sins in past confessions?

3. Did I perform the penance I was given? Did I make reparation for any injury to others? Have I tried to put into practice my resolution to lead a better life in keeping with the Gospel?

Each individual should examine his or her life in the light of God's word.

I. The Lord says: "You shall love the Lord your God with your whole heart."

1. Is my heart set on God, so that I really love him above all things and am faithful to his commandments, as a son loves his father? Or am I more concerned about the things of this world? Have I a right intention in what I do?

2. God spoke to us in his Son. Is my faith in God firm and secure? Am I wholehearted in accepting the Church's teaching? Have I been careful to grow in my understanding of the faith, to hear God's word, to listen to instructions on the faith, to avoid dangers to faith? Have I been always strong and fearless in professing my faith in God and the Church? Have I been willing to be known as a Christian in private and public life?

3. Have I prayed morning and evening? When I pray, do I really raise my mind and heart to God or is it a matter of words only? Do I offer God my difficulties, my joys, and my sorrows? Do I turn to God in time of temptation?

4. Have I love and reverence for God's name? Have I offended him in blasphemy, swearing falsely, or taking his name in vain? Have I shown disrespect for the Blessed Virgin Mary and the saints?

5. Do I keep Sundays and feast days holy by taking a full part, with attention and devotion, in the liturgy, and especially in the Mass? Have I fulfilled the precept of annual confession and of communion during the Easter season?

6. Are there false gods that I worship by giving them greater attention and deeper trust than I give to God: money, superstition, spiritism, or other occult practices?

II. The Lord says: "Love one another as I have loved you."

1.   Have I a genuine love for my neighbours? Or do I use them for my own ends, or do to them what I would not want done to myself? Have I given grave scandal by my words or actions?

2.   In my family life, have I contributed to the well-being and happiness of the rest of the family by patience and genuine love? Have I been obedient to parents, showing them proper respect and giving them help in their spiritual and material needs? Have I been careful to give a Christian upbringing to my children, and to help them by good example and by exercising authority as a parent? Have I been faithful to my husband/wife in my heart and in my relations with others?

3.   Do I share my possessions with the less fortunate? Do I do my best to help the victims of oppression, misfortune, and poverty? Or do I look down on my neighbour, especially the poor, the sick, the elderly, strangers, and people of other races?

4.   Does my life reflect the mission I received in confirmation? Do I share in the apostolic and charitable works of the Church and in the life of my parish? Have I helped to meet the needs of the Church and of the world and prayed for them: for unity in the Church, for the spread of the Gospel among the nations, for peace and justice, etc.?

5.   Am I concerned for the good and prosperity of the human community in which I live, or do I spend my life caring only for myself? Do I share to the best of my ability in the work of promoting justice, morality, harmony, and love in human relations? Have I done my duty as a citizen? Have I paid my taxes?

6.   In my work or profession am I just, hard-working, honest, serving society out of love for others? Have I paid a fair wage to my employees? Have I been faithful to my promises and contracts?

7.   Have I obeyed legitimate authority and given it due respect?

8. If I am in a position of responsibility or authority, do I use this for my own advantage or for the good of others, in a spirit of service?

9. Have I been truthful and fair, or have I injured others by deceit, calumny, detraction, rash judgment, or violation of a secret?

10. Have I done violence to others by damage to life or limb, reputation, honor, or material possessions? Have I involved them in loss? Have I been responsible for advising an abortion or procuring one? Have I kept up hatred for others? Am I estranged from others through quarrels, enmity, insults, anger? Have I been guilty of refusing to testify to the innocence of another because of selfishness?

11. Have I stolen the property of others? Have I desired it unjustly and inordinately? Have I damaged it? Have I made restitution of other people's property and made good their loss?

12. If I have been injured, have I been ready to make peace for the love of Christ and to forgive, or do I harbour hatred and the desire for revenge?

III. Christ our Lord says: "Be perfect as your Father is perfect."

1. Where is my life really leading me? Is the hope of eternal life my inspiration? Have I tried to grow in the life of the Spirit through prayer, reading the word of God and meditating on it, receiving the sacraments, self-denial? Have I been anxious to control my vices, my bad inclinations and passions, e.g., envy, love of food and drink? Have I been proud and boastful, thinking myself better in the sight of God and despising others as less important than myself? Have I imposed my own will on others, without respecting their freedom and rights?

2. What use have I made of time, of health and strength, of the gifts God has given to me to be used like the talents in the Gospel? Do I use them to become more perfect every day? Or have I been lazy and too much given to leisure?

3. Have I been patient in accepting the sorrows and disappointments of life? How have I performed mortification so as

to "fill up what is wanting to the sufferings of Christ"? Have I kept the precept of fasting and abstinence?

4.   Have I kept my senses and my whole body pure and chaste as a temple of the Holy Spirit consecrated for resurrection and glory, and as a sign of God's faithful love for men and women, a sign that is seen most perfectly in the sacrament of matrimony? Have I dishonoured my body by fornication, impurity, unworthy conversation or thoughts, evil desires or actions? Have I given in to sensuality? Have I indulged in reading, conversation, shows, and entertainments that offend against Christian and human decency? Have I encouraged others to sin by my own failure to maintain these standards? Have I been faithful to the moral law in my married life?

5.   Have I gone against my conscience out of fear or hypocrisy?

6.   Have I always tried to act in the true freedom of the sons of God according to the law of the Spirit, or am I the slave of forces within me?

A Prayer for Forgiveness

Lord Jesus, our brother and our king,
we thank you for loving us,
for suffering and dying to save us from sin,
for rising to new life in glory,
and for calling us to share
in your life and joy.

Have mercy on us in our weakness.
Give us your Spirit to lead us to sorrow,
to turn us away from our sins
and to bring us back to your love.

Lord Jesus, hear our prayer. Amen!

HYMN INDEX

WHY . . . You should have a
MISSAL . . . of Your OWN!

AT MASS . . . for complete participation and understanding

- ✔ TO RECITE or SING . . . your parts with understanding and devotion.
- ✔ TO LISTEN . . . attentively to the Word of God.
- ✔ TO UNITE . . . with the prayers of the priest.
- ✔ TO HOLD . . . attention and increase your devotion.
- ✔ TO HELP . . . during short periods recommended for personal prayer.

AT HOME . . . to guide your Christian Life and personal spiritual reading

- ✔ TO PREPARE . . . yourself for Mass by reading over the texts and helpful commentary.
- ✔ TO SEE . . . the liturgical year as a whole.
- ✔ TO GUIDE . . . your life in the spirit of the liturgy.
- ✔ TO MODEL . . . your prayers on liturgical sources.
- ✔ TO MEDITATE . . . often on the Word of God.

IDEAL GIFT   New American Bible